Contents

20050801open（ふとい）

http://www.minariendou.com

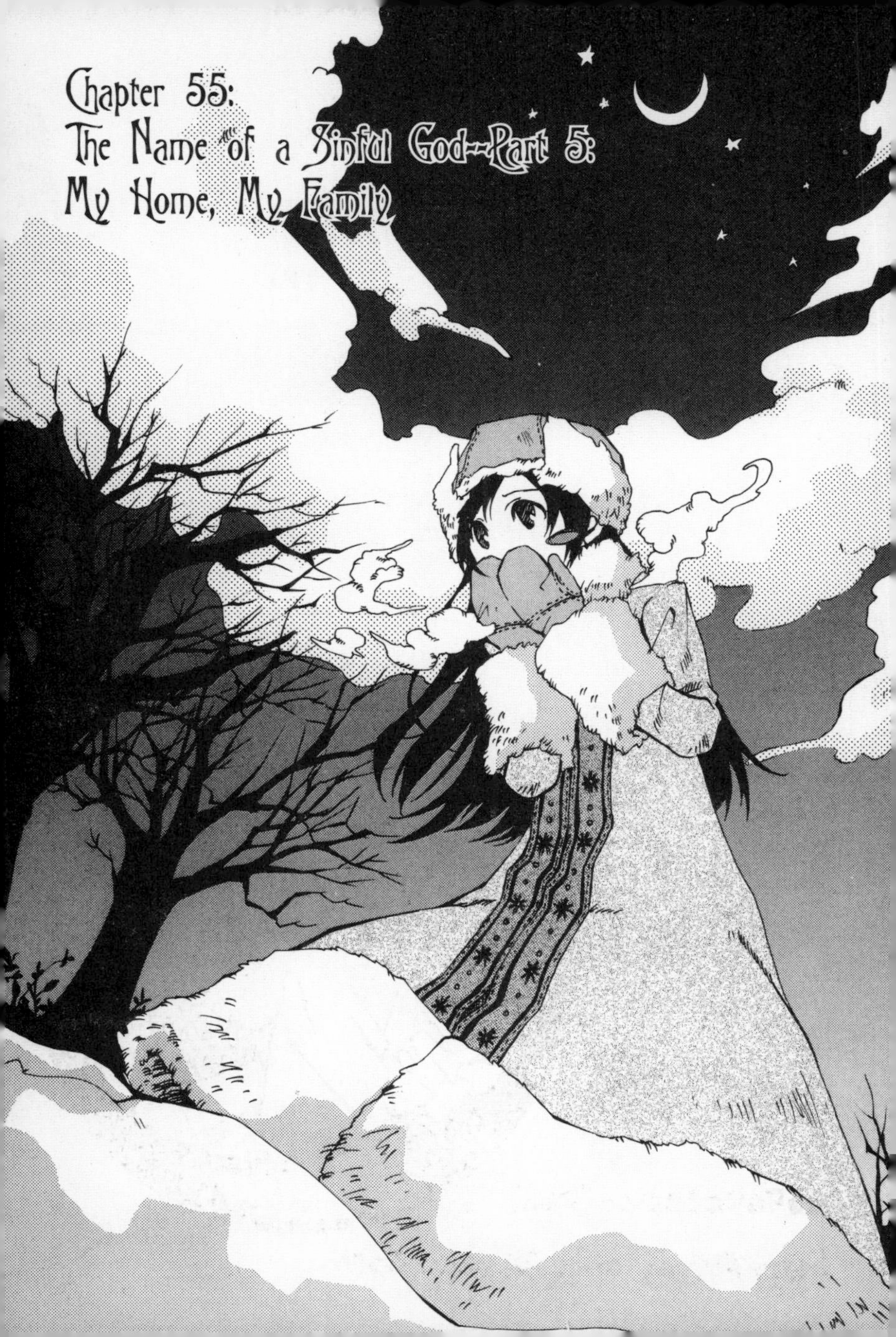
Chapter 55:
The Name of a Sinful God--Part 5:
My Home, My Family

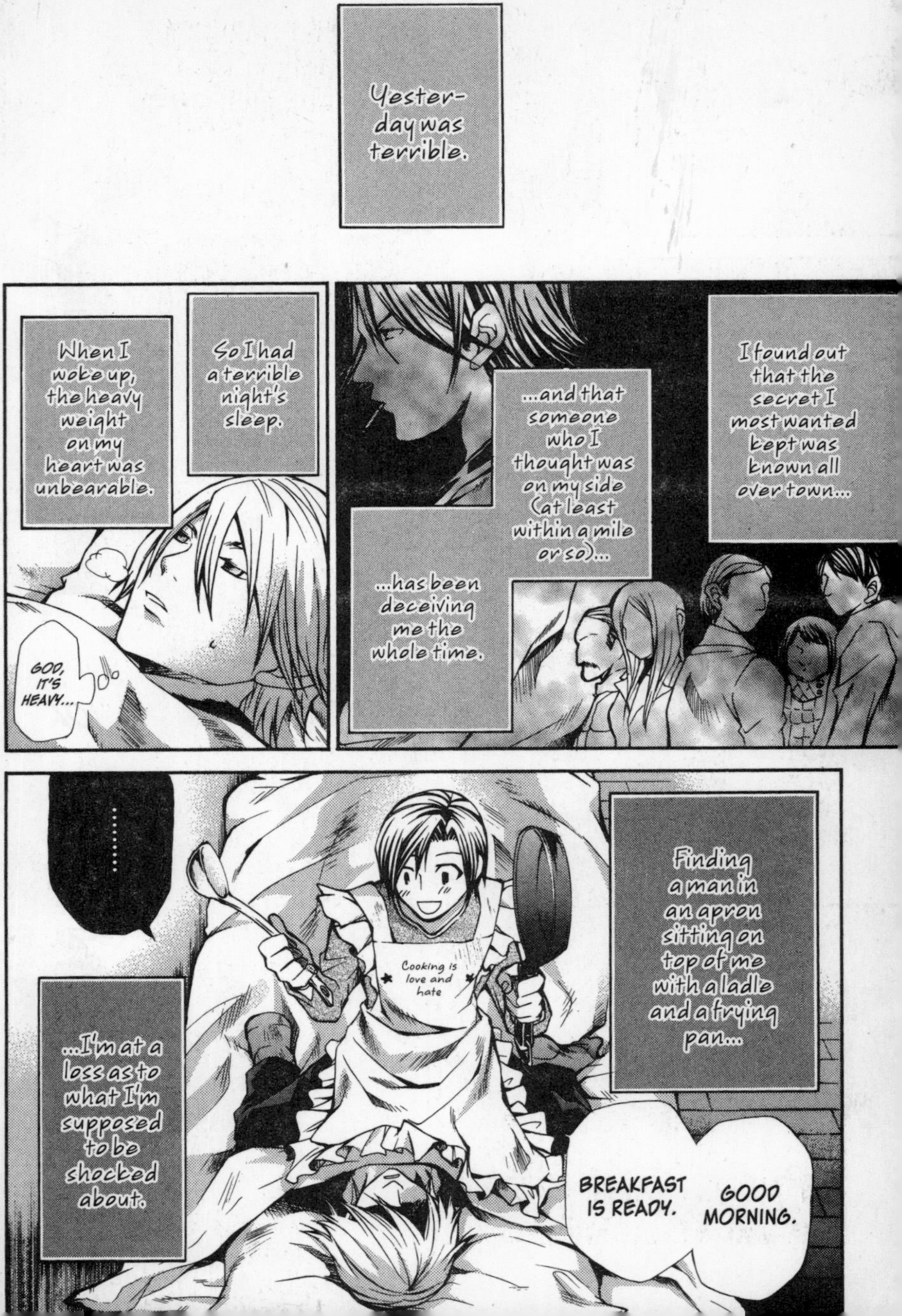
Yester-day was terrible.
I found out that the secret I most wanted kept was known all over town...
...and that someone who I thought was on my side (at least within a mile or so)...
...has been deceiving me the whole time.
So I had a terrible night's sleep.
When I woke up, the heavy weight on my heart was unbearable.
GOD, IT'S HEAVY...
Finding a man in an apron sitting on top of me with a ladle and a frying pan...
Cooking is love and hate
GOOD MORNING.
BREAKFAST IS READY.
......
...I'm at a loss as to what I'm supposed to be shocked about.

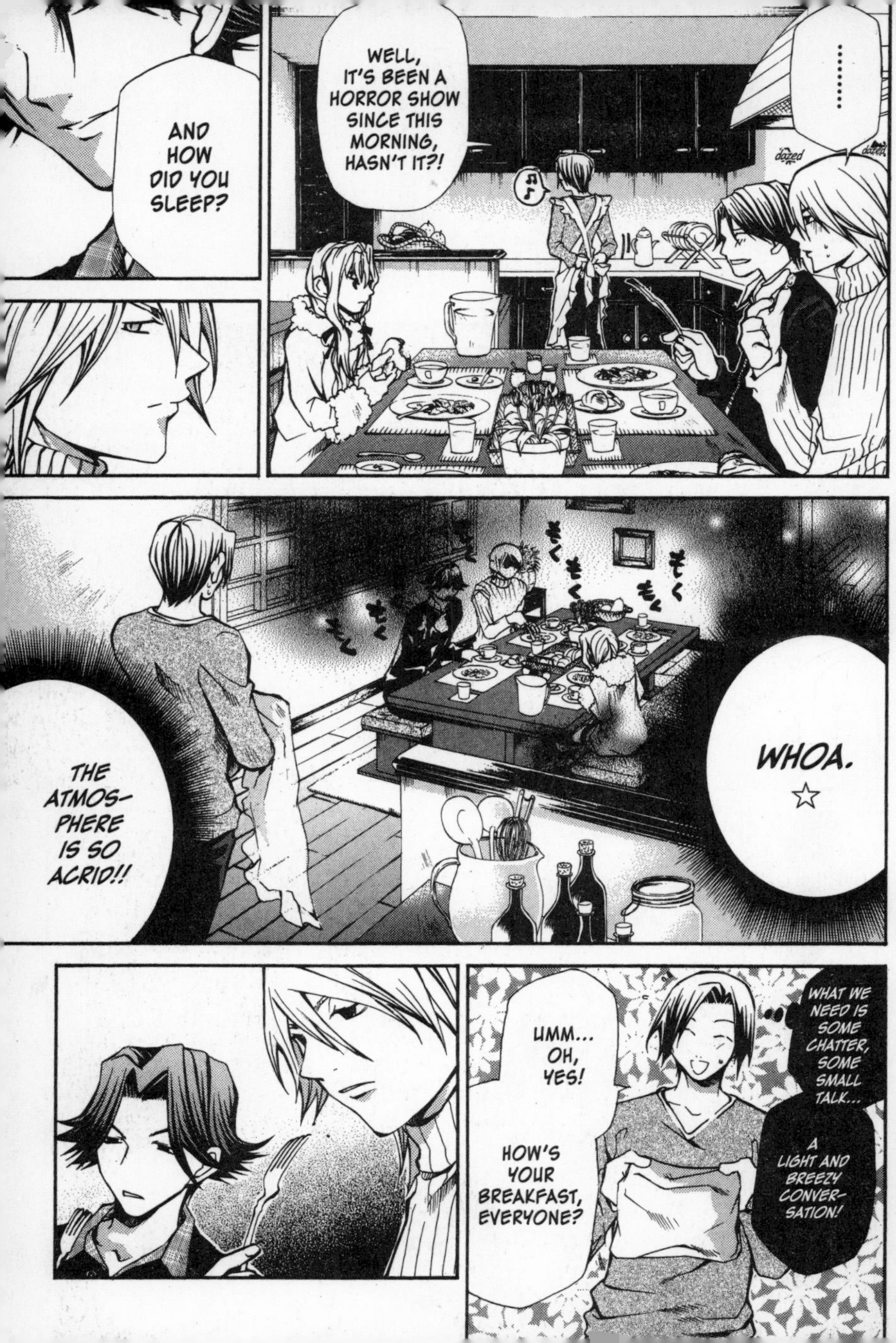
......
dazed
dazed
WELL, IT'S BEEN A HORROR SHOW SINCE THIS MORNING, HASN'T IT?!
AND HOW DID YOU SLEEP?
もく もく
もく もく
もく もく
WHOA. ☆
THE ATMOS-PHERE IS SO ACRID!!
WHAT WE NEED IS SOME CHATTER, SOME SMALL TALK...
A LIGHT AND BREEZY CONVER-SATION!
UMM... OH, YES!
HOW'S YOUR BREAKFAST, EVERYONE?

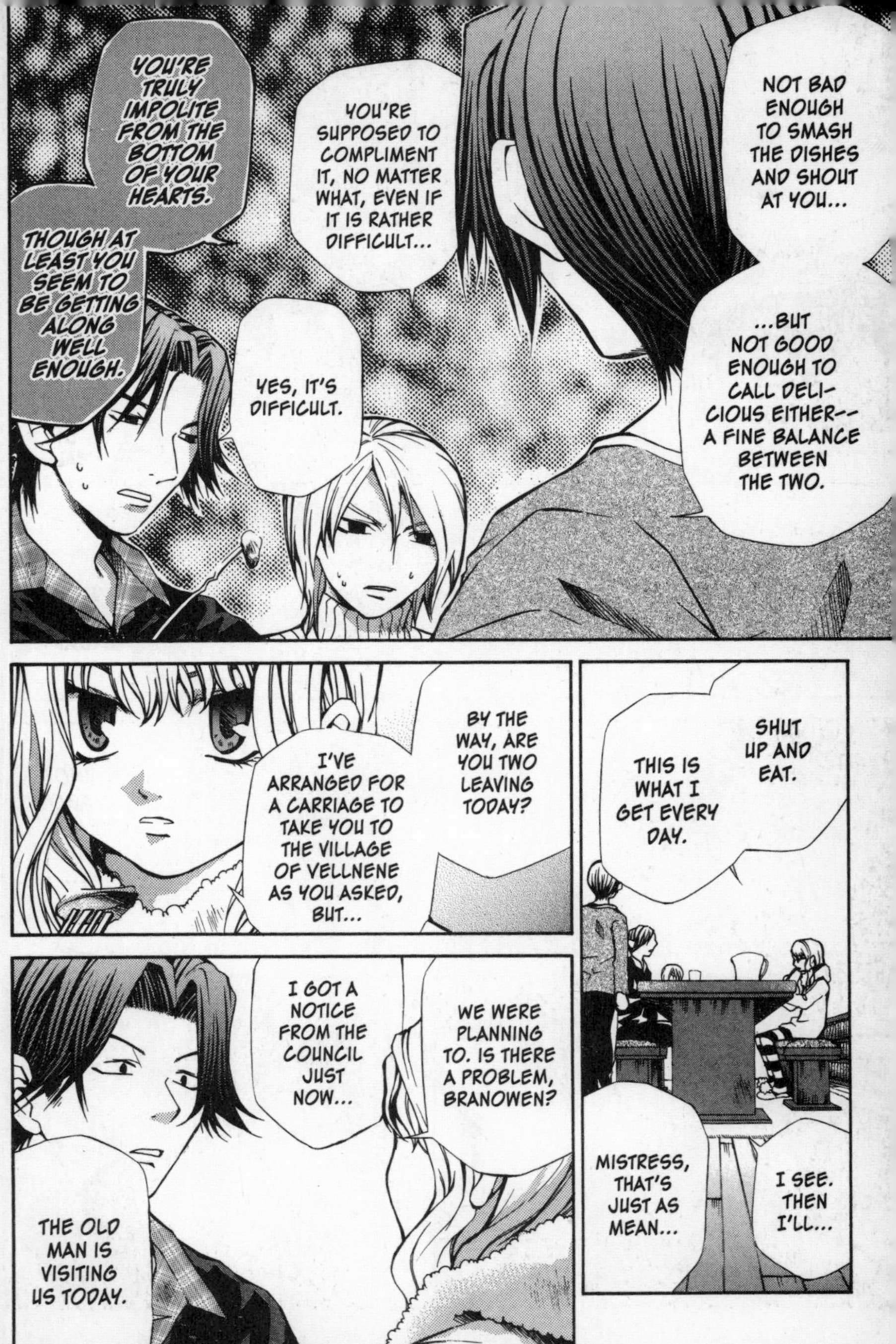
NOT BAD ENOUGH TO SMASH THE DISHES AND SHOUT AT YOU...
...BUT NOT GOOD ENOUGH TO CALL DELI-CIOUS EITHER--A FINE BALANCE BETWEEN THE TWO.
YOU'RE SUPPOSED TO COMPLIMENT IT, NO MATTER WHAT, EVEN IF IT IS RATHER DIFFICULT...
YES, IT'S DIFFICULT.
YOU'RE TRULY IMPOLITE FROM THE BOTTOM OF YOUR HEARTS.
THOUGH AT LEAST YOU SEEM TO BE GETTING ALONG WELL ENOUGH.
SHUT UP AND EAT.
THIS IS WHAT I GET EVERY DAY.
I SEE. THEN I'LL...
MISTRESS, THAT'S JUST AS MEAN...
BY THE WAY, ARE YOU TWO LEAVING TODAY?
I'VE ARRANGED FOR A CARRIAGE TO TAKE YOU TO THE VILLAGE OF VELLNENE AS YOU ASKED, BUT...
WE WERE PLANNING TO. IS THERE A PROBLEM, BRANOWEN?
I GOT A NOTICE FROM THE COUNCIL JUST NOW...
THE OLD MAN IS VISITING US TODAY.

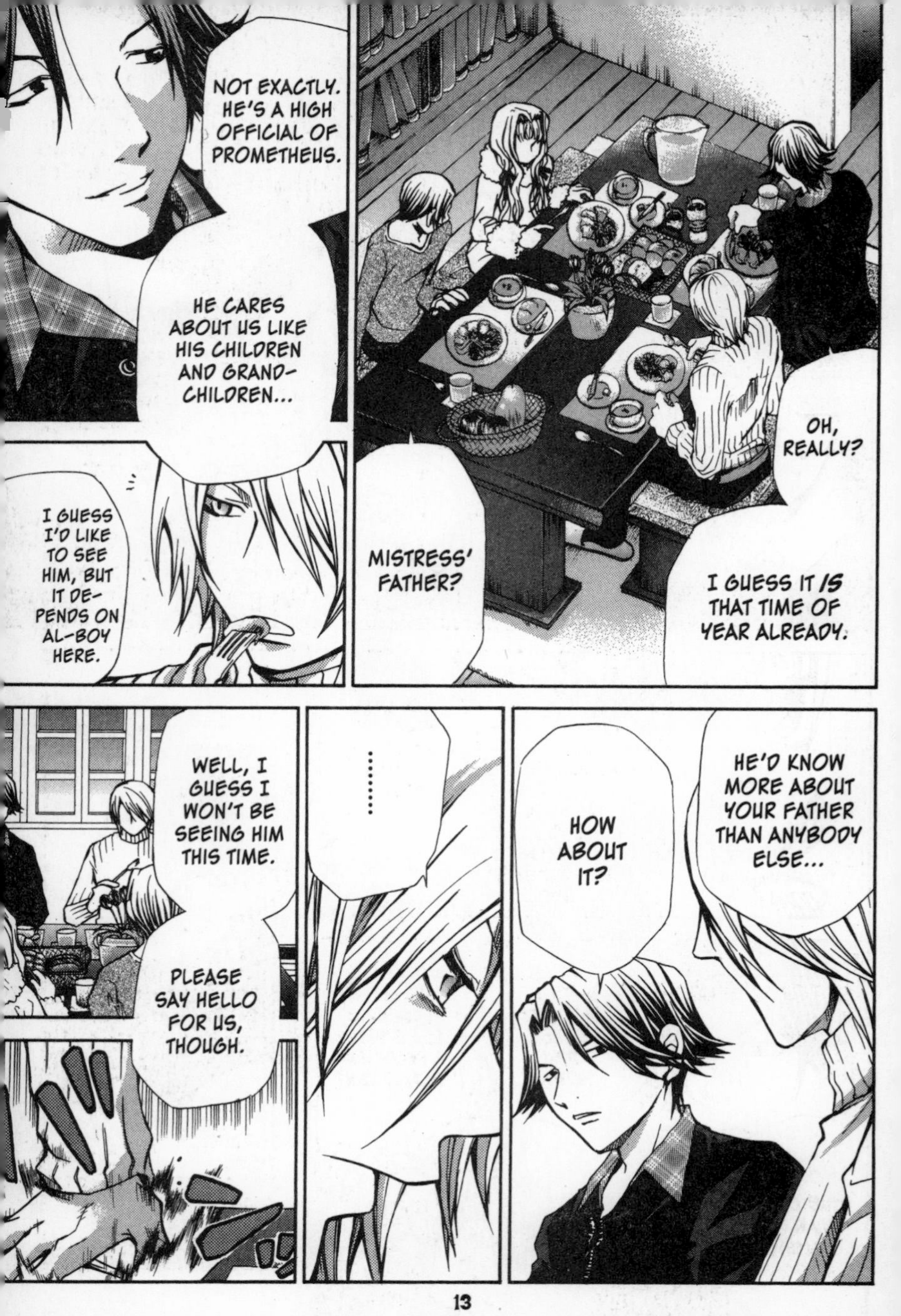
OH, REALLY?
I GUESS IT *IS* THAT TIME OF YEAR ALREADY.
MISTRESS' FATHER?
NOT EXACTLY. HE'S A HIGH OFFICIAL OF PROMETHEUS.
HE CARES ABOUT US LIKE HIS CHILDREN AND GRAND-CHILDREN...
I GUESS I'D LIKE TO SEE HIM, BUT IT DE-PENDS ON AL-BOY HERE.
HE'D KNOW MORE ABOUT YOUR FATHER THAN ANYBODY ELSE...
HOW ABOUT IT?
......
WELL, I GUESS I WON'T BE SEEING HIM THIS TIME.
PLEASE SAY HELLO FOR US, THOUGH.

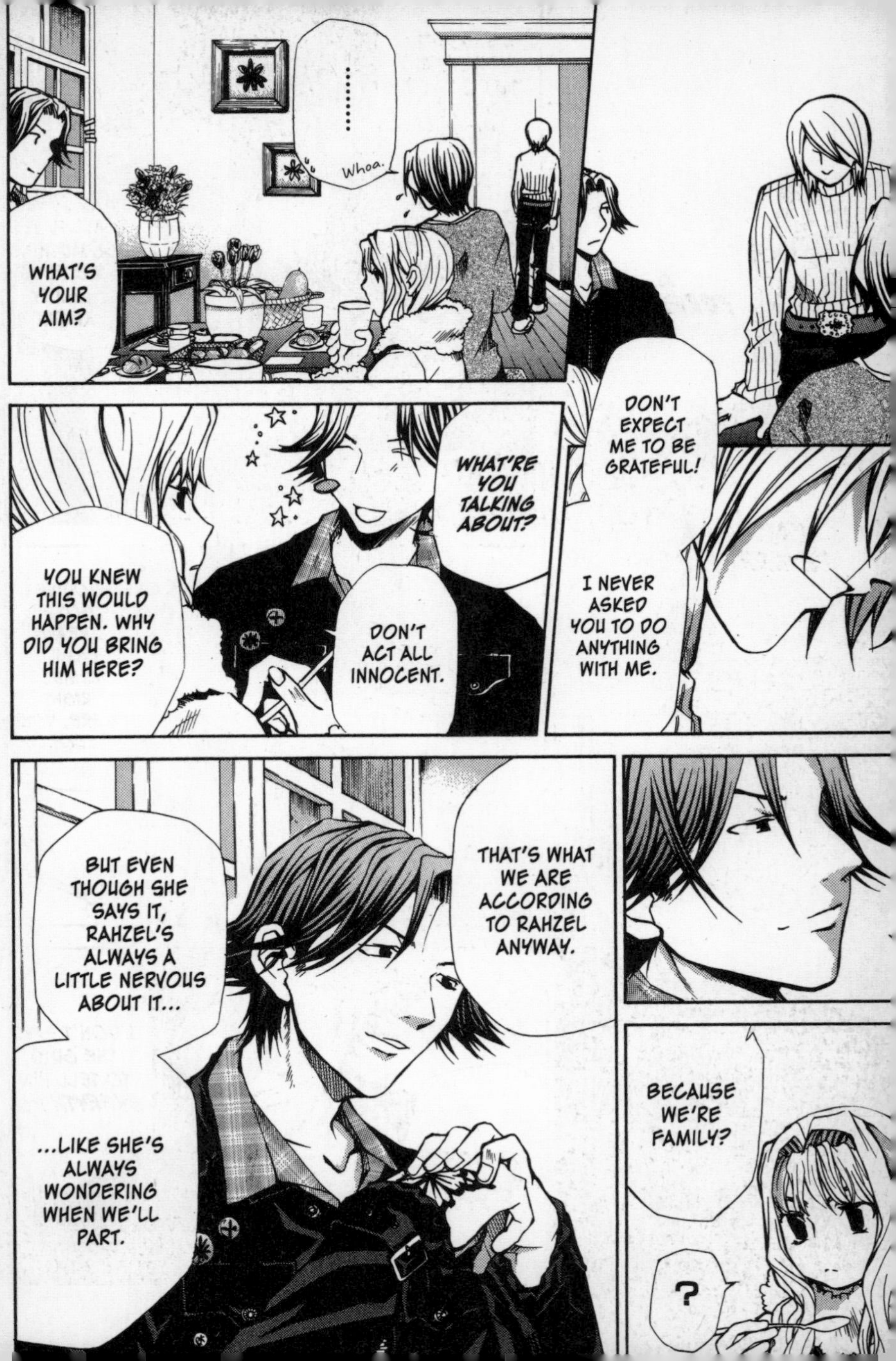
DON'T EXPECT ME TO BE GRATEFUL!
......
Whoa.
WHAT'S YOUR AIM?
I NEVER ASKED YOU TO DO ANYTHING WITH ME.
WHAT'RE YOU TALKING ABOUT?
DON'T ACT ALL INNOCENT.
YOU KNEW THIS WOULD HAPPEN. WHY DID YOU BRING HIM HERE?
BECAUSE WE'RE FAMILY?
?
THAT'S WHAT WE ARE ACCORDING TO RAHZEL ANYWAY.
BUT EVEN THOUGH SHE SAYS IT, RAHZEL'S ALWAYS A LITTLE NERVOUS ABOUT IT...
...LIKE SHE'S ALWAYS WONDERING WHEN WE'LL PART.

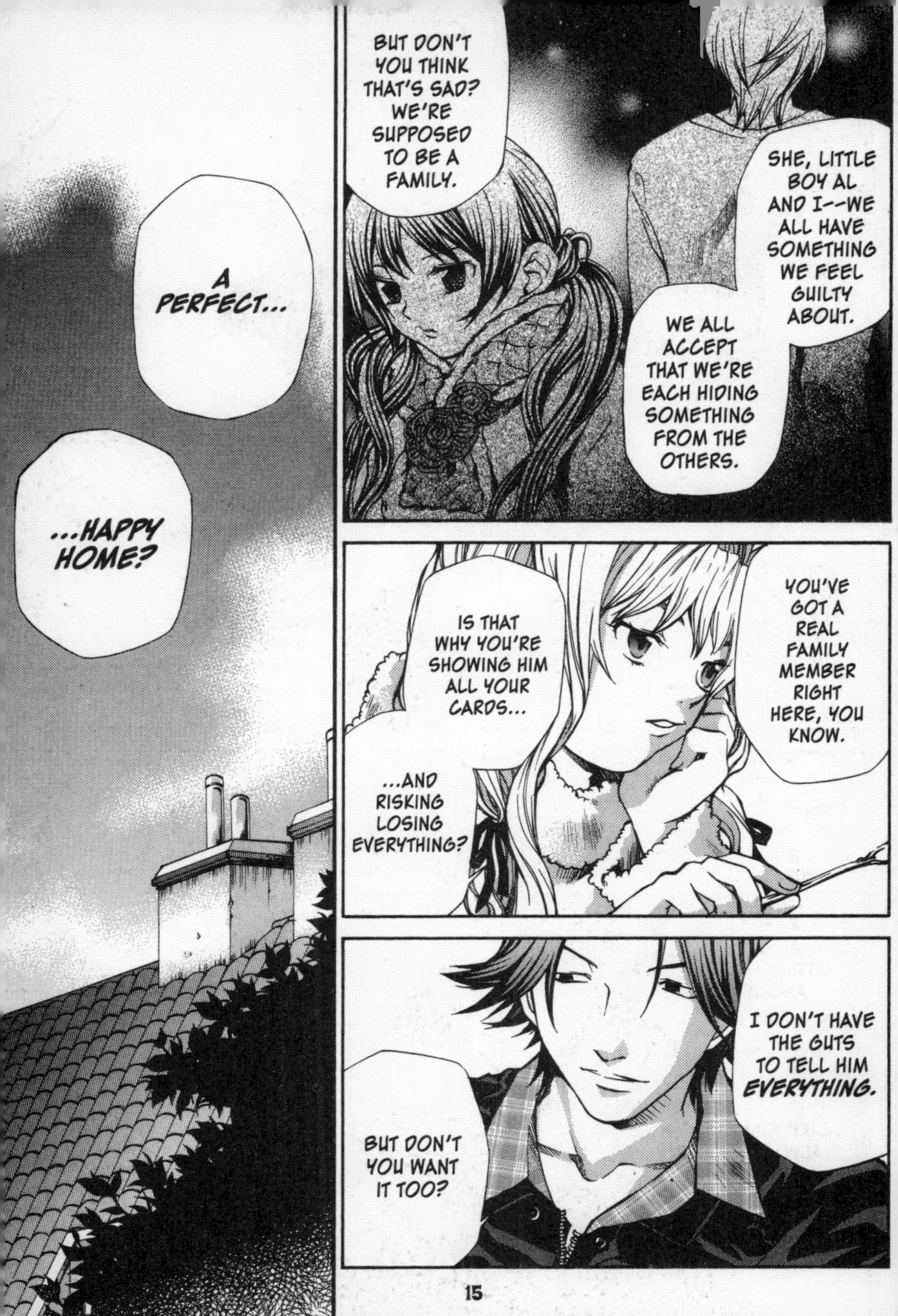
SHE, LITTLE BOY AL AND I--WE ALL HAVE SOMETHING WE FEEL GUILTY ABOUT.
WE ALL ACCEPT THAT WE'RE EACH HIDING SOMETHING FROM THE OTHERS.
BUT DON'T YOU THINK THAT'S SAD? WE'RE SUPPOSED TO BE A FAMILY.
YOU'VE GOT A REAL FAMILY MEMBER RIGHT HERE, YOU KNOW.
IS THAT WHY YOU'RE SHOWING HIM ALL YOUR CARDS...
...AND RISKING LOSING EVERYTHING?
I DON'T HAVE THE GUTS TO TELL HIM *EVERYTHING.*
BUT DON'T YOU WANT IT TOO?
A PERFECT...
...HAPPY HOME?

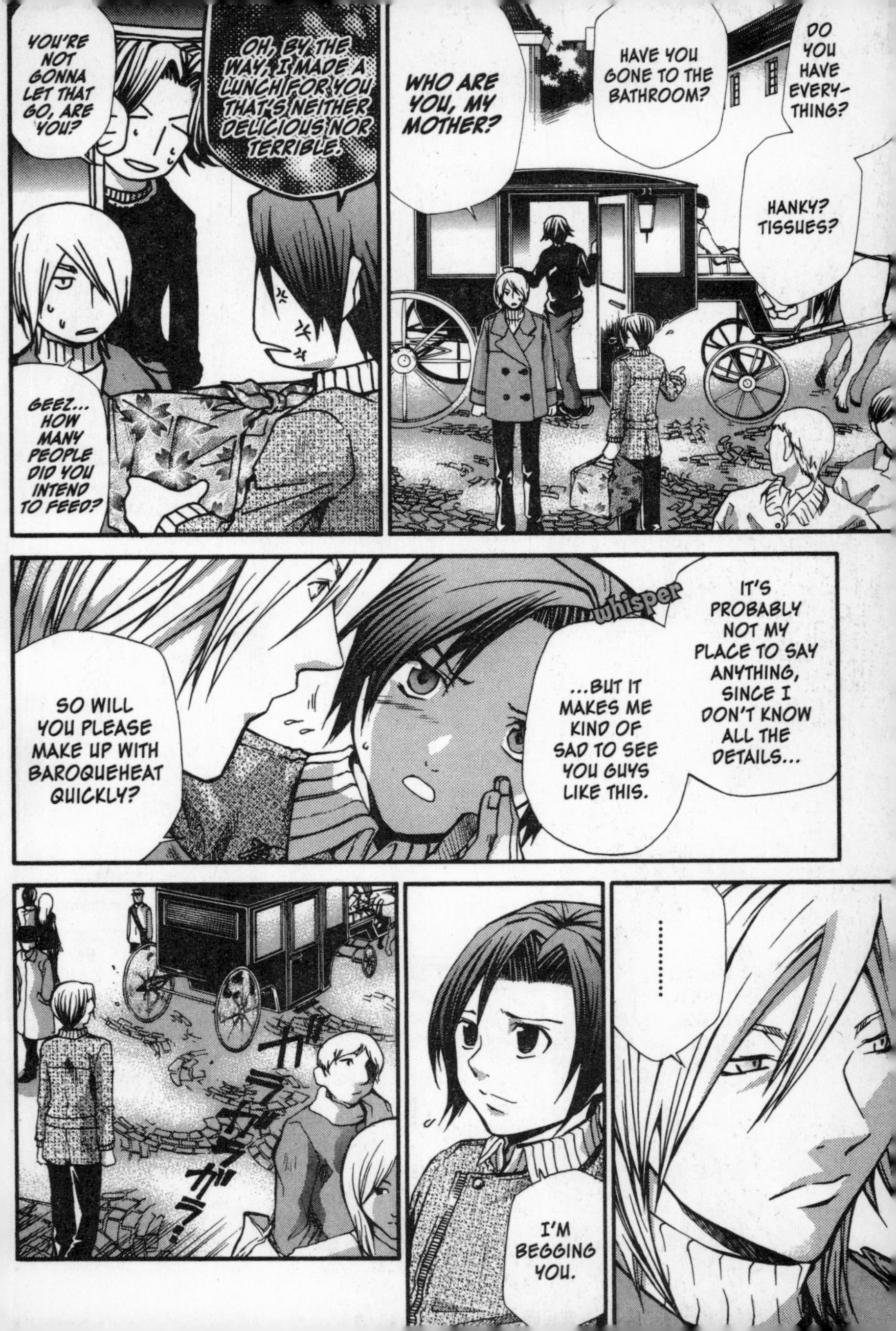
DO YOU HAVE EVERY-THING?
HAVE YOU GONE TO THE BATHROOM?
HANKY? TISSUES?
WHO ARE YOU, MY MOTHER?
OH, BY THE WAY, I MADE A LUNCH FOR YOU THAT'S NEITHER DELICIOUS NOR TERRIBLE.
YOU'RE NOT GONNA LET THAT GO, ARE YOU?
GEEZ... HOW MANY PEOPLE DID YOU INTEND TO FEED?
whisper
IT'S PROBABLY NOT MY PLACE TO SAY ANYTHING, SINCE I DON'T KNOW ALL THE DETAILS...
...BUT IT MAKES ME KIND OF SAD TO SEE YOU GUYS LIKE THIS.
SO WILL YOU PLEASE MAKE UP WITH BAROQUEHEAT QUICKLY?
......
I'M BEGGING YOU.

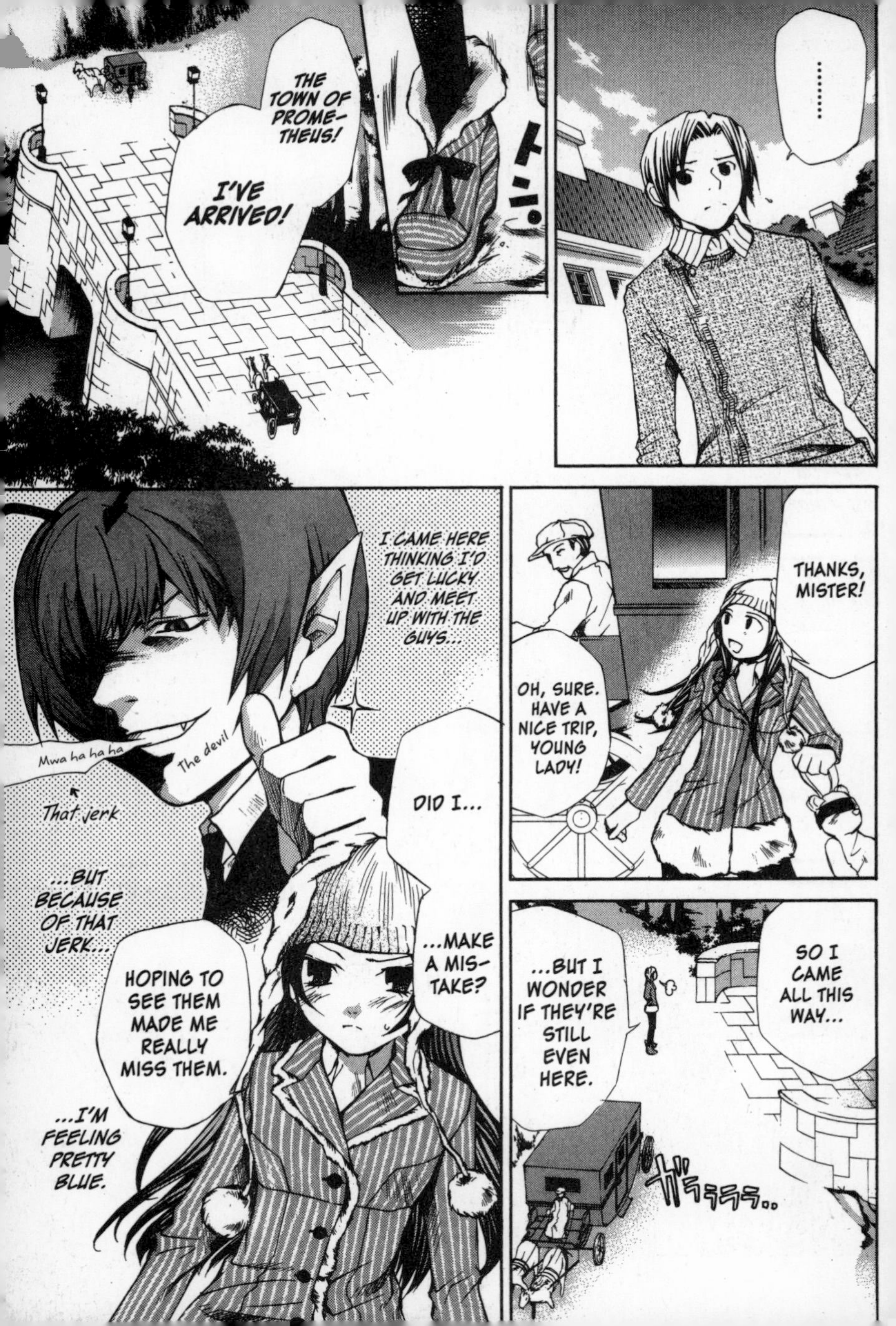

……
トン!
THE TOWN OF PROMETHEUS!
I'VE ARRIVED!
THANKS, MISTER!
OH, SURE. HAVE A NICE TRIP, YOUNG LADY!
SO I CAME ALL THIS WAY...
...BUT I WONDER IF THEY'RE STILL EVEN HERE.
ガラララララ..
I CAME HERE THINKING I'D GET LUCKY AND MEET UP WITH THE GUYS...
The devil
Mwa ha ha ha
That jerk
...BUT BECAUSE OF THAT JERK...
DID I...
...MAKE A MISTAKE?
HOPING TO SEE THEM MADE ME REALLY MISS THEM.
...I'M FEELING PRETTY BLUE.

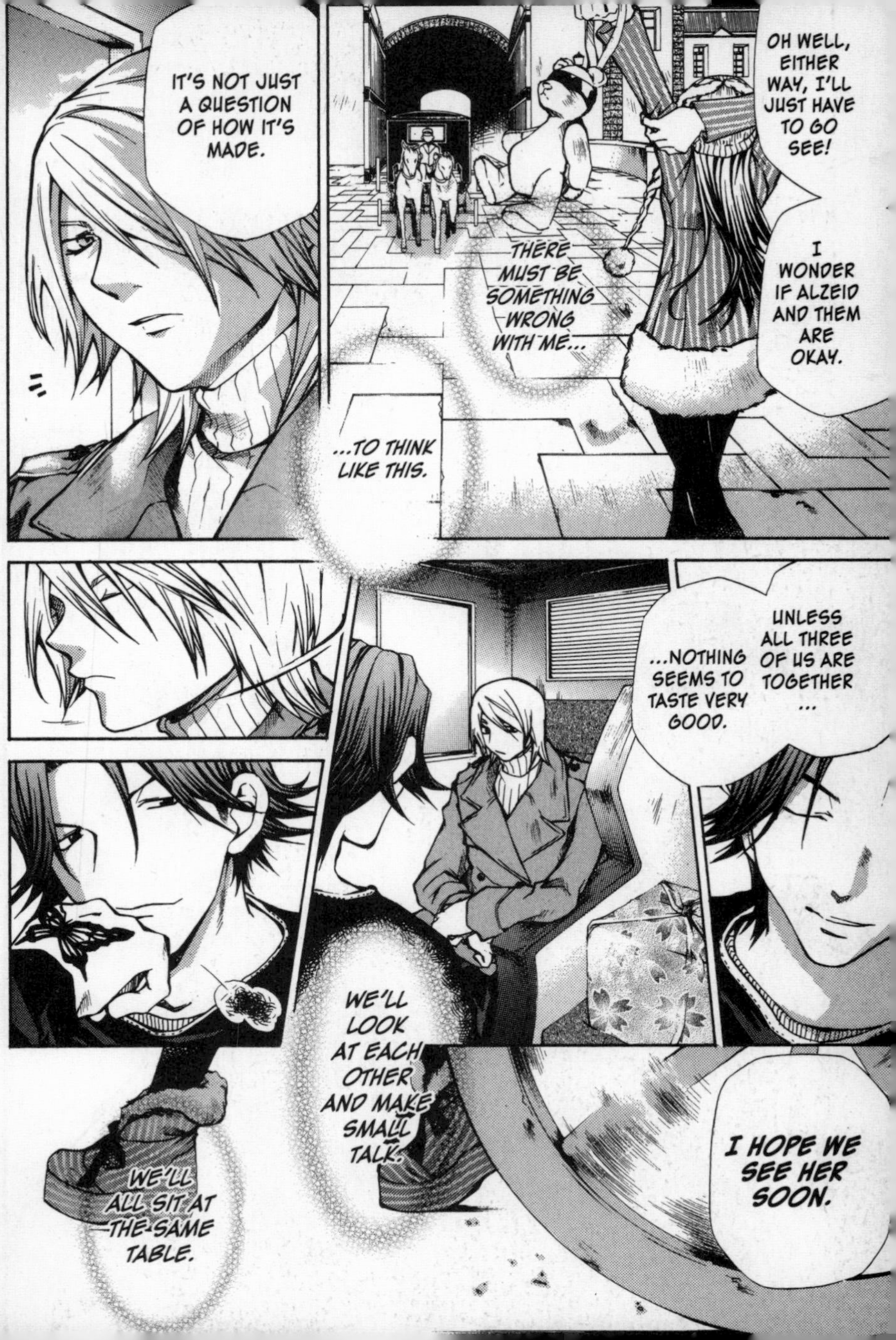
OH WELL, EITHER WAY, I'LL JUST HAVE TO GO SEE!
I WONDER IF ALZEID AND THEM ARE OKAY.
THERE MUST BE SOMETHING WRONG WITH ME...
...TO THINK LIKE THIS.
IT'S NOT JUST A QUESTION OF HOW IT'S MADE.
UNLESS ALL THREE OF US ARE TOGETHER...
...NOTHING SEEMS TO TASTE VERY GOOD.
I HOPE WE SEE HER SOON.
WE'LL LOOK AT EACH OTHER AND MAKE SMALL TALK.
WE'LL ALL SIT AT THE SAME TABLE.

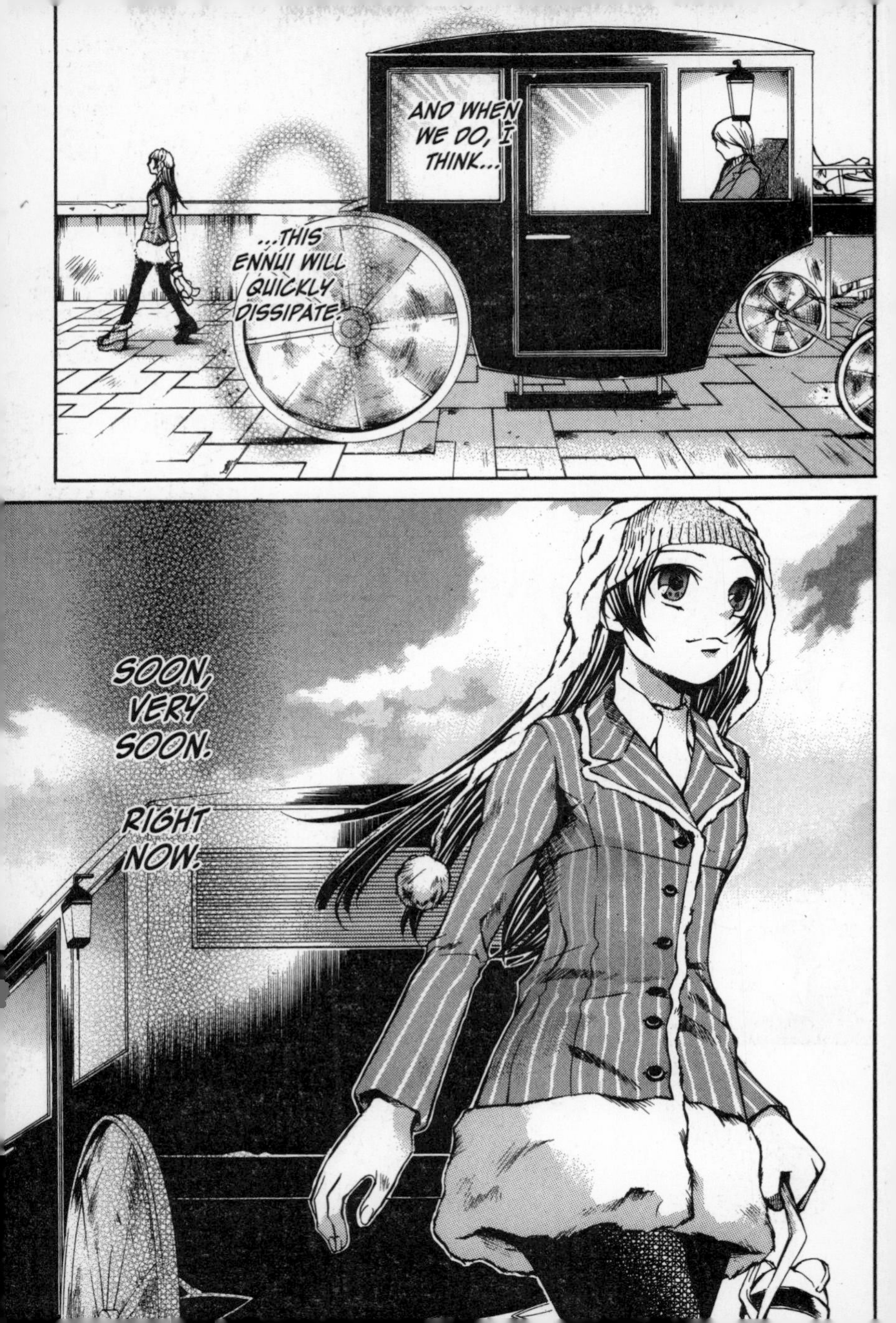
AND WHEN WE DO, I THINK...
...THIS ENNUI WILL QUICKLY DISSIPATE.
SOON, VERY SOON.
RIGHT NOW.

Editor
Yo→suke Sugino

Assistant works
Kaori Komori
Alice Tsukada
Shu→ko Yonemoto
Ayako Masaki

Author: Minari Endoh

I've started
cat ears.

Because it's
summer(?)

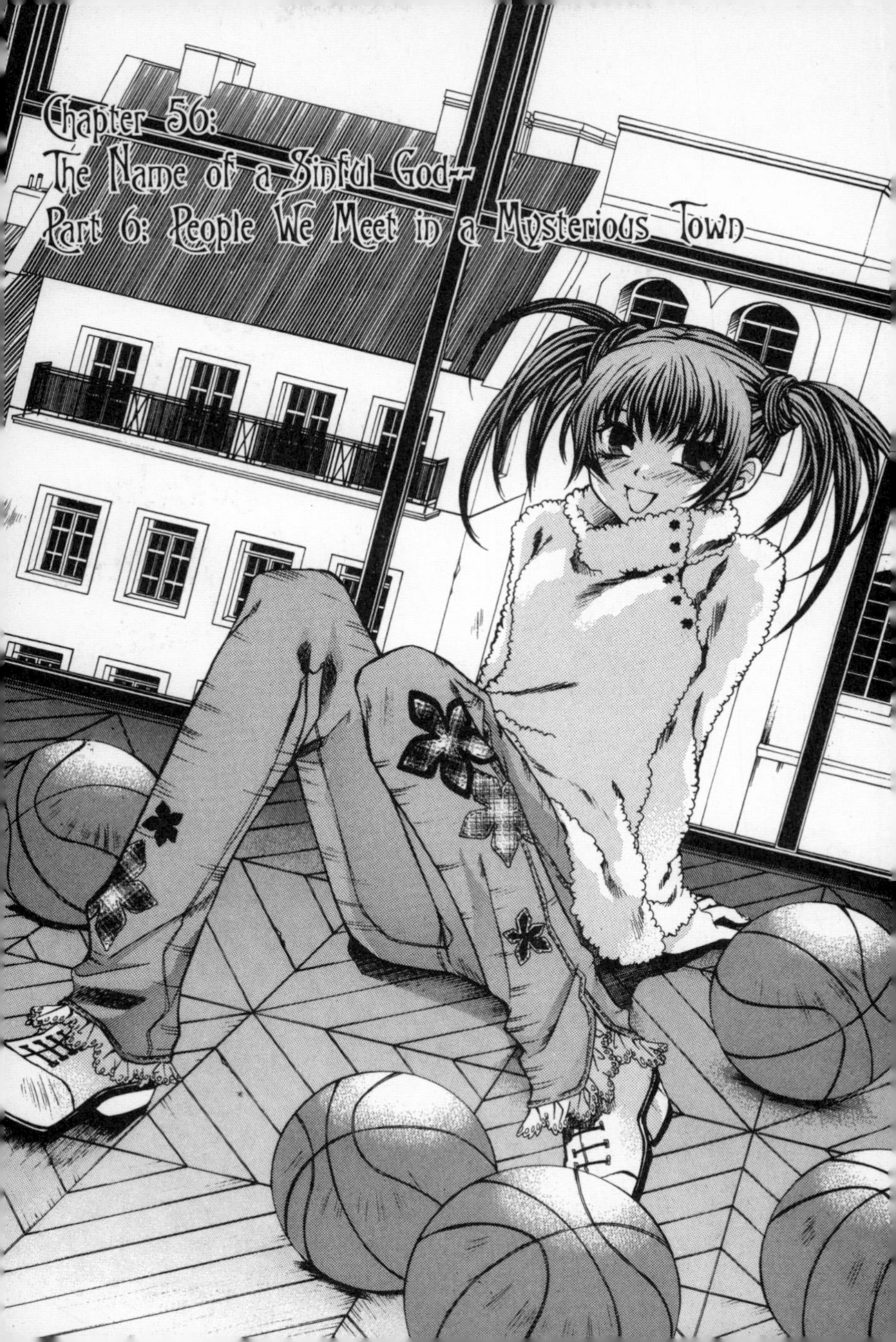
Chapter 56:
"The Name of a Sinful God"
Part 6: People We Meet in a Mysterious Town

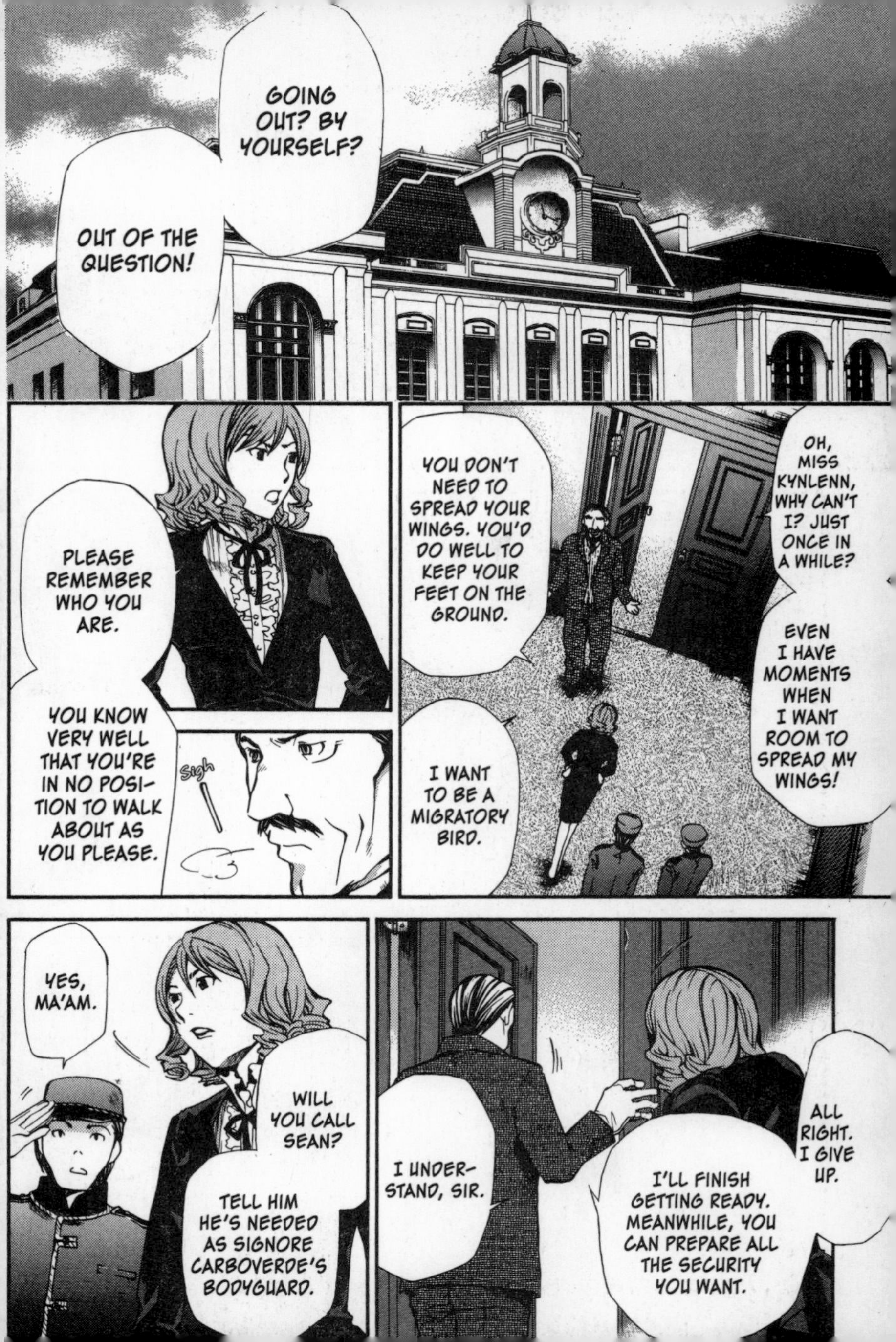
GOING OUT? BY YOURSELF?
OUT OF THE QUESTION!
OH, MISS KYNLENN, WHY CAN'T I? JUST ONCE IN A WHILE?
EVEN I HAVE MOMENTS WHEN I WANT ROOM TO SPREAD MY WINGS!
I WANT TO BE A MIGRATORY BIRD.
YOU DON'T NEED TO SPREAD YOUR WINGS. YOU'D DO WELL TO KEEP YOUR FEET ON THE GROUND.
PLEASE REMEMBER WHO YOU ARE.
YOU KNOW VERY WELL THAT YOU'RE IN NO POSITION TO WALK ABOUT AS YOU PLEASE.
Sigh
ALL RIGHT. I GIVE UP.
I'LL FINISH GETTING READY. MEANWHILE, YOU CAN PREPARE ALL THE SECURITY YOU WANT.
I UNDERSTAND, SIR.
WILL YOU CALL SEAN?
TELL HIM HE'S NEEDED AS SIGNORE CARBOVERDE'S BODYGUARD.
YES, MA'AM.

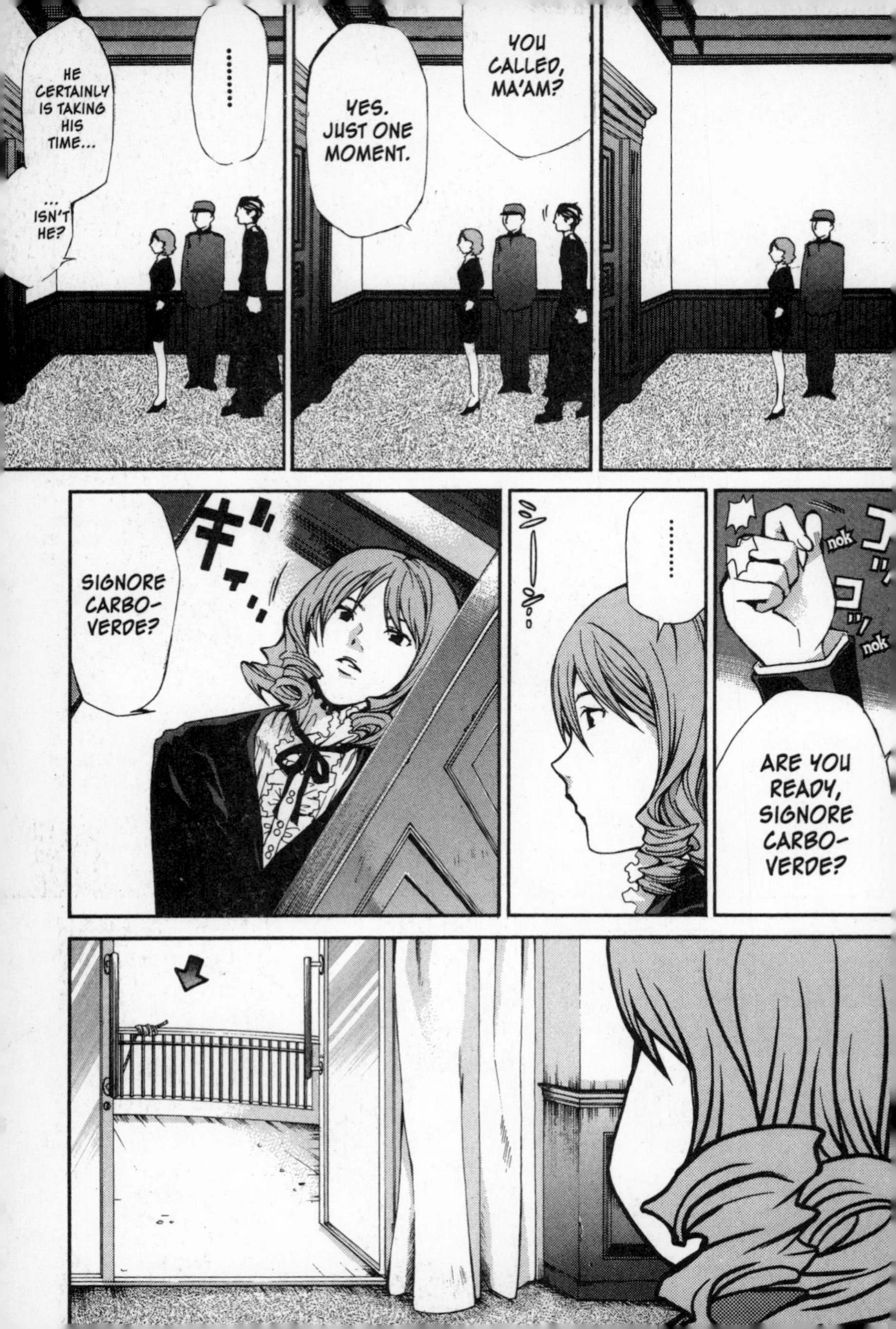
YOU CALLED, MA'AM?
YES. JUST ONE MOMENT.
....
HE CERTAINLY IS TAKING HIS TIME...
...ISN'T HE?
nok
nok
ARE YOU READY, SIGNORE CARBO-VERDE?
....
SIGNORE CARBO-VERDE?

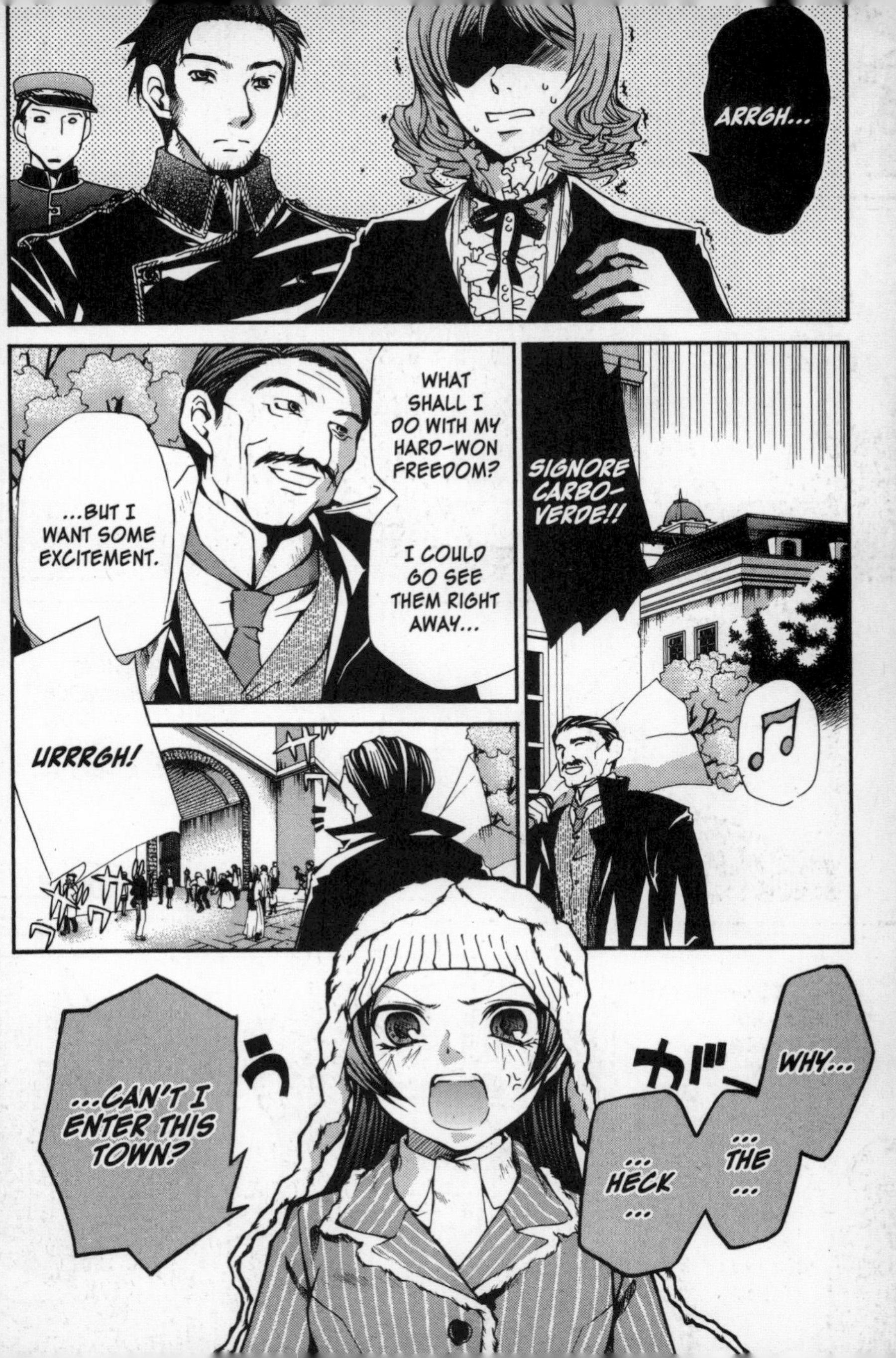
ARRGH...
SIGNORE CARBO-VERDE!!
WHAT SHALL I DO WITH MY HARD-WON FREEDOM?
I COULD GO SEE THEM RIGHT AWAY...
...BUT I WANT SOME EXCITEMENT.
URRRGH!
WHY...
...THE...
...HECK...
...CAN'T I ENTER THIS TOWN?

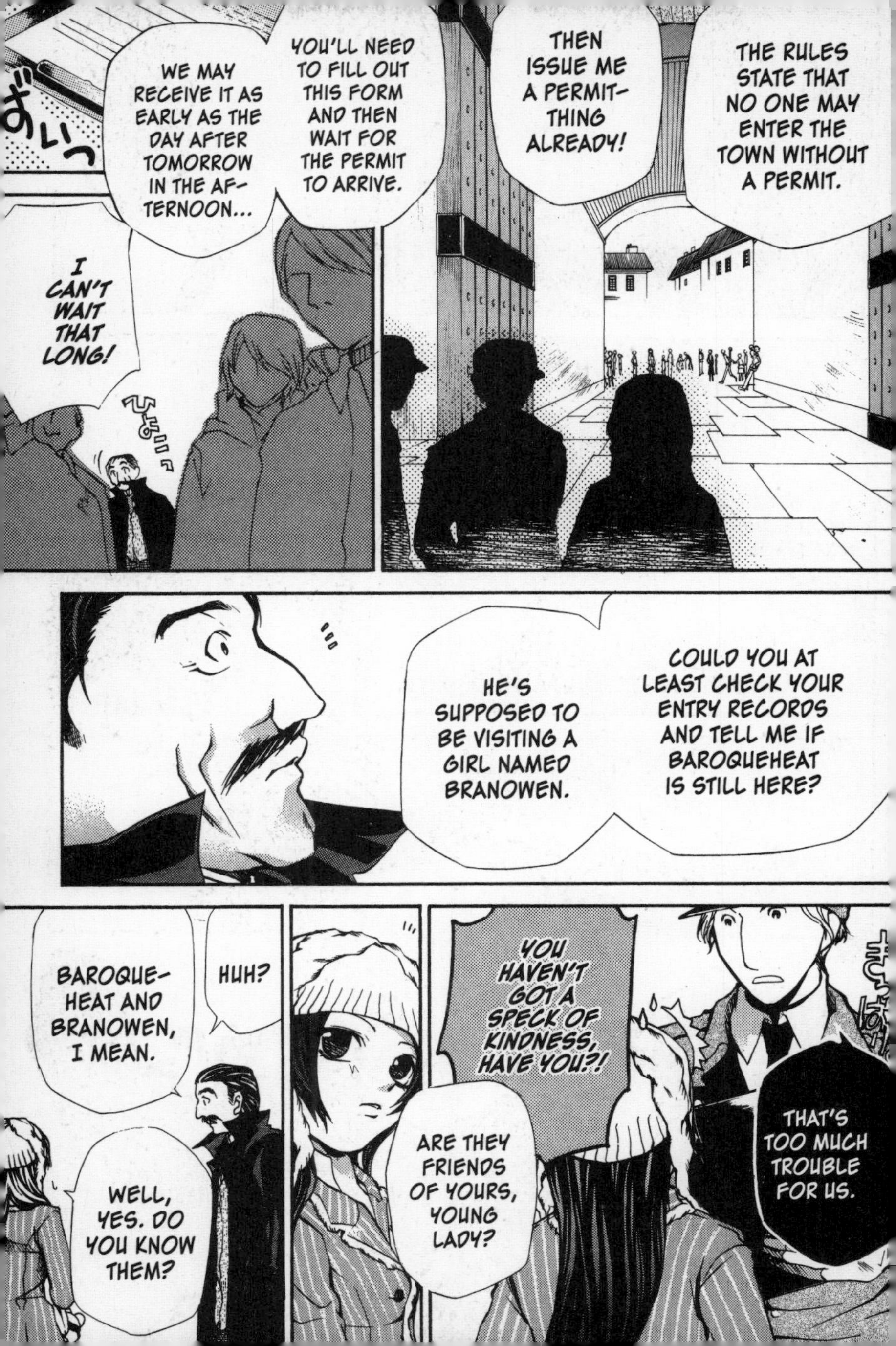
THE RULES STATE THAT NO ONE MAY ENTER THE TOWN WITHOUT A PERMIT.
THEN ISSUE ME A PERMIT-THING ALREADY!
YOU'LL NEED TO FILL OUT THIS FORM AND THEN WAIT FOR THE PERMIT TO ARRIVE.
WE MAY RECEIVE IT AS EARLY AS THE DAY AFTER TOMORROW IN THE AFTERNOON...
I CAN'T WAIT THAT LONG!
COULD YOU AT LEAST CHECK YOUR ENTRY RECORDS AND TELL ME IF BAROQUEHEAT IS STILL HERE?
HE'S SUPPOSED TO BE VISITING A GIRL NAMED BRANOWEN.
THAT'S TOO MUCH TROUBLE FOR US.
YOU HAVEN'T GOT A SPECK OF KINDNESS, HAVE YOU?!
ARE THEY FRIENDS OF YOURS, YOUNG LADY?
HUH?
BAROQUEHEAT AND BRANOWEN, I MEAN.
WELL, YES. DO YOU KNOW THEM?

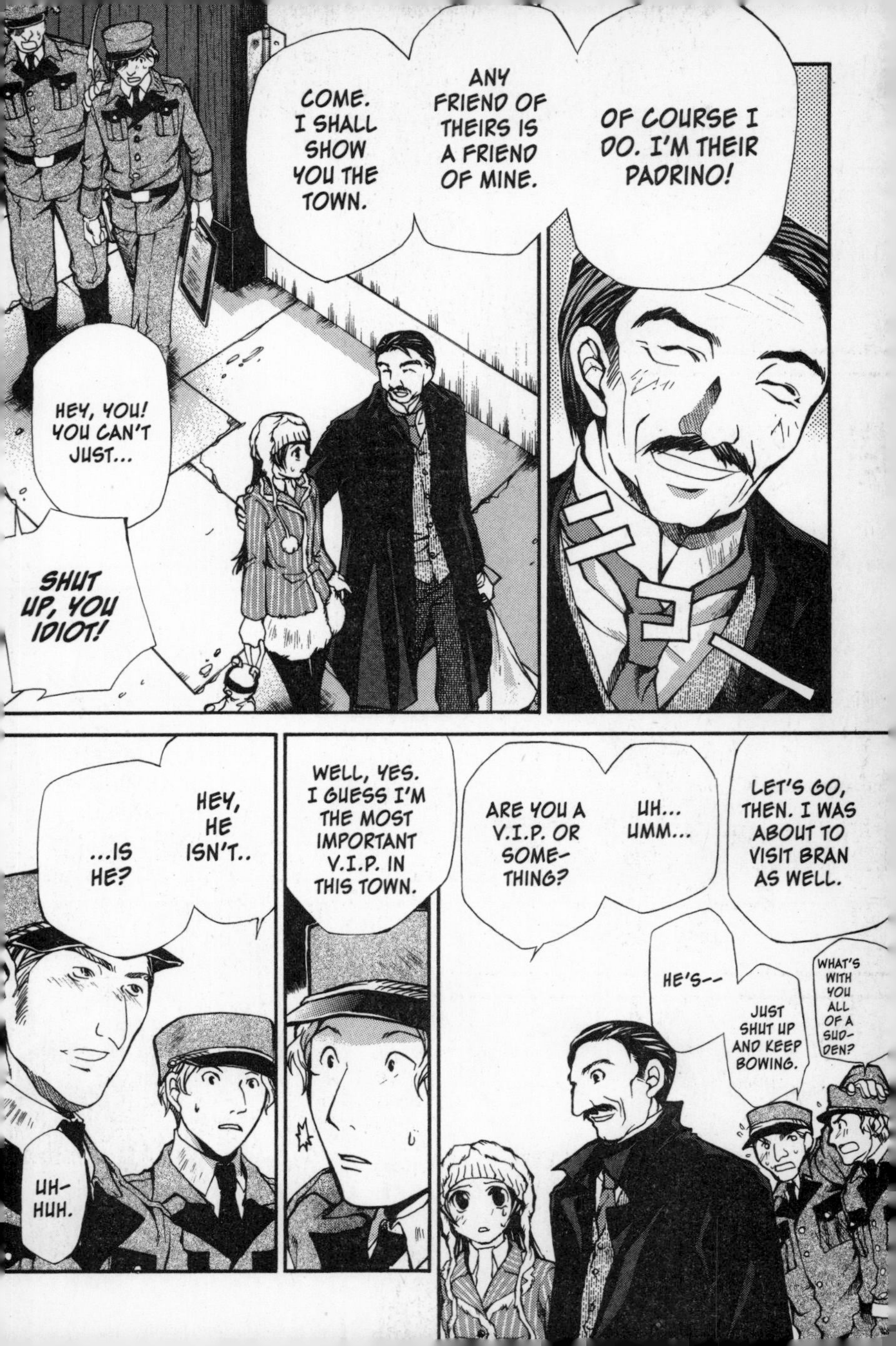
OF COURSE I DO. I'M THEIR PADRINO!
ANY FRIEND OF THEIRS IS A FRIEND OF MINE.
COME. I SHALL SHOW YOU THE TOWN.
HEY, YOU! YOU CAN'T JUST...
SHUT UP, YOU IDIOT!
LET'S GO, THEN. I WAS ABOUT TO VISIT BRAN AS WELL.
UH... UMM...
ARE YOU A V.I.P. OR SOME-THING?
WHAT'S WITH YOU ALL OF A SUD-DEN?
HE'S--
JUST SHUT UP AND KEEP BOWING.
WELL, YES. I GUESS I'M THE MOST IMPORTANT V.I.P. IN THIS TOWN.
HEY, HE ISN'T..
...IS HE?
UH-HUH.

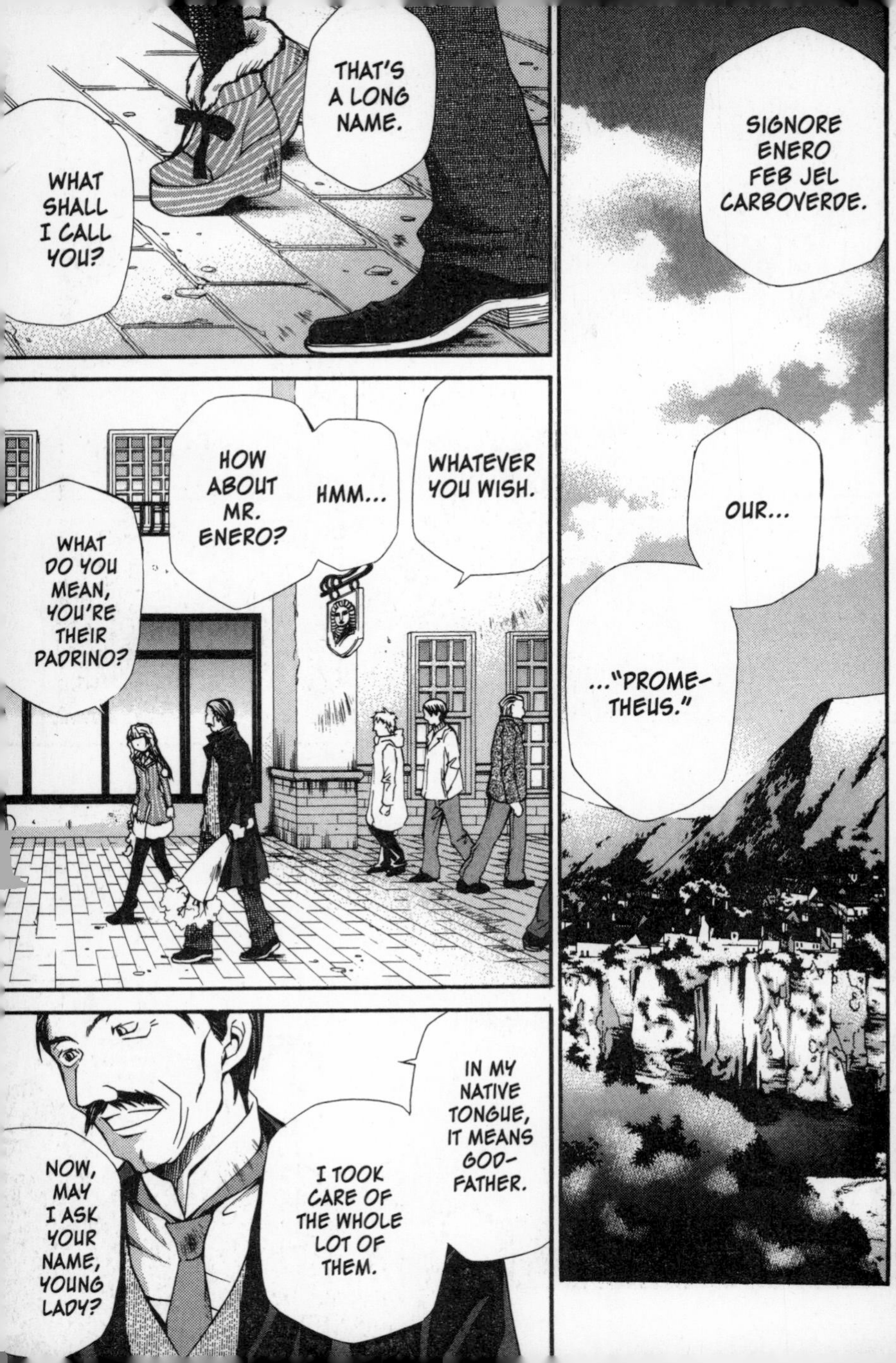
SIGNORE ENERO FEB JEL CARBOVERDE.
OUR...
..."PROME-THEUS."
THAT'S A LONG NAME.
WHAT SHALL I CALL YOU?
WHATEVER YOU WISH.
HMM...
HOW ABOUT MR. ENERO?
WHAT DO YOU MEAN, YOU'RE THEIR PADRINO?
IN MY NATIVE TONGUE, IT MEANS GOD-FATHER.
I TOOK CARE OF THE WHOLE LOT OF THEM.
NOW, MAY I ASK YOUR NAME, YOUNG LADY?

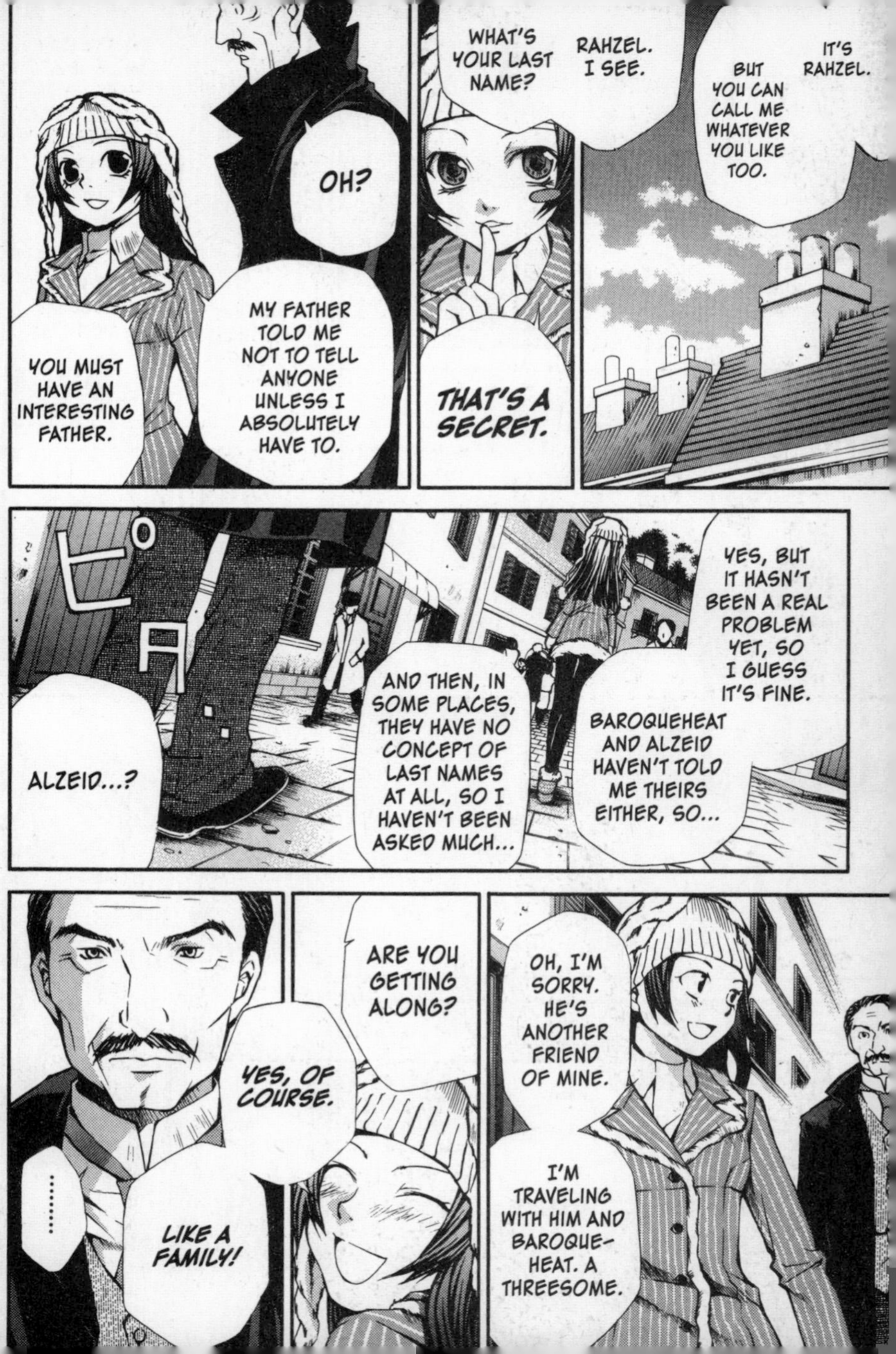
IT'S RAHZEL.
BUT YOU CAN CALL ME WHATEVER YOU LIKE TOO.
RAHZEL. I SEE.
WHAT'S YOUR LAST NAME?
THAT'S A SECRET.
OH?
MY FATHER TOLD ME NOT TO TELL ANYONE UNLESS I ABSOLUTELY HAVE TO.
YOU MUST HAVE AN INTERESTING FATHER.
YES, BUT IT HASN'T BEEN A REAL PROBLEM YET, SO I GUESS IT'S FINE.
AND THEN, IN SOME PLACES, THEY HAVE NO CONCEPT OF LAST NAMES AT ALL, SO I HAVEN'T BEEN ASKED MUCH...
BAROQUEHEAT AND ALZEID HAVEN'T TOLD ME THEIRS EITHER, SO...
ピタ
ALZEID...?
OH, I'M SORRY. HE'S ANOTHER FRIEND OF MINE.
I'M TRAVELING WITH HIM AND BAROQUE-HEAT. A THREESOME.
ARE YOU GETTING ALONG?
YES, OF COURSE.
LIKE A FAMILY!
......

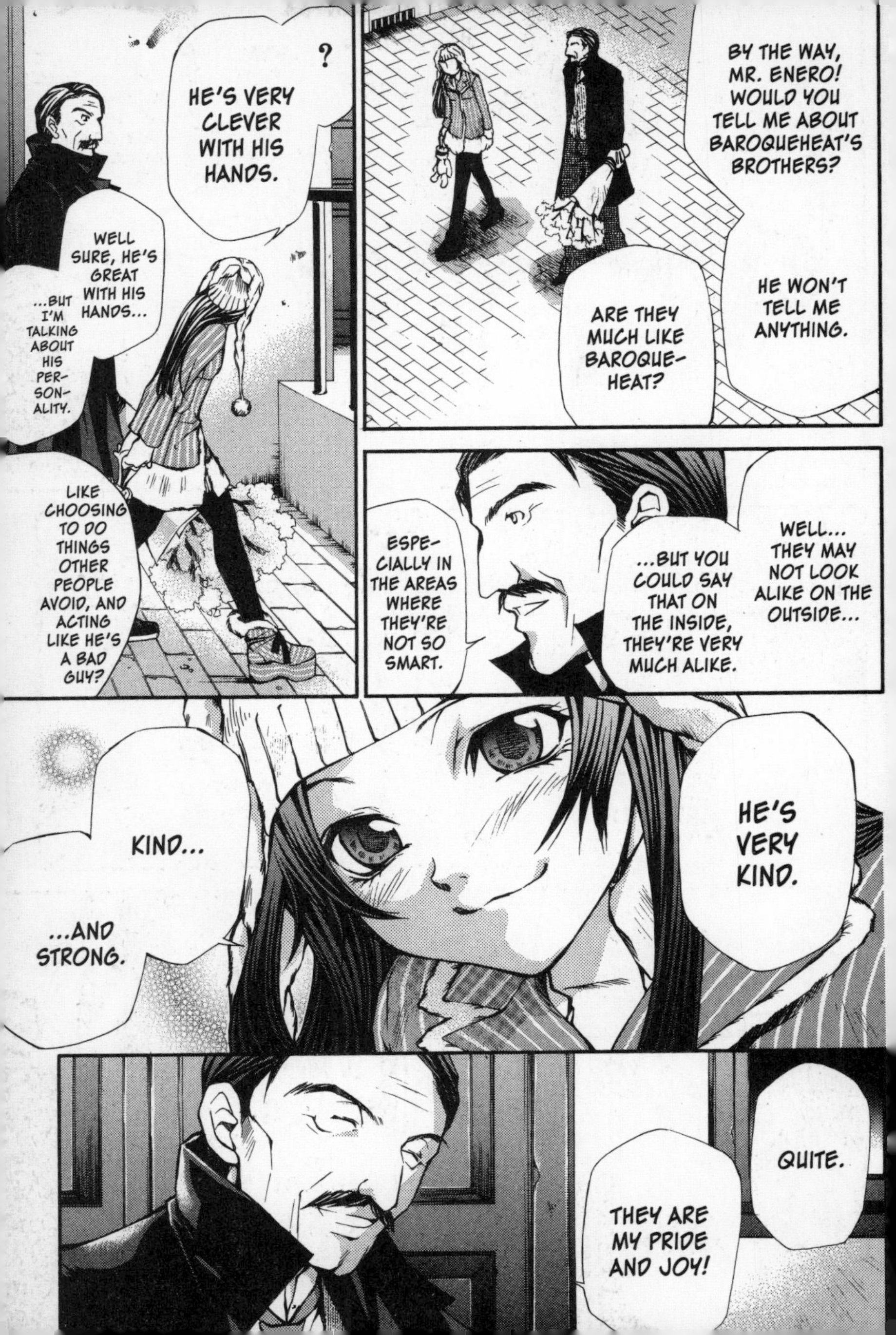
BY THE WAY, MR. ENERO! WOULD YOU TELL ME ABOUT BAROQUEHEAT'S BROTHERS?
HE WON'T TELL ME ANYTHING.
ARE THEY MUCH LIKE BAROQUE-HEAT?
WELL... THEY MAY NOT LOOK ALIKE ON THE OUTSIDE...
...BUT YOU COULD SAY THAT ON THE INSIDE, THEY'RE VERY MUCH ALIKE.
ESPE-CIALLY IN THE AREAS WHERE THEY'RE NOT SO SMART.
?
HE'S VERY CLEVER WITH HIS HANDS.
WELL SURE, HE'S GREAT WITH HIS HANDS...
...BUT I'M TALKING ABOUT HIS PER-SON-ALITY.
LIKE CHOOSING TO DO THINGS OTHER PEOPLE AVOID, AND ACTING LIKE HE'S A BAD GUY?
HE'S VERY KIND.
KIND...
...AND STRONG.
QUITE.
THEY ARE MY PRIDE AND JOY!

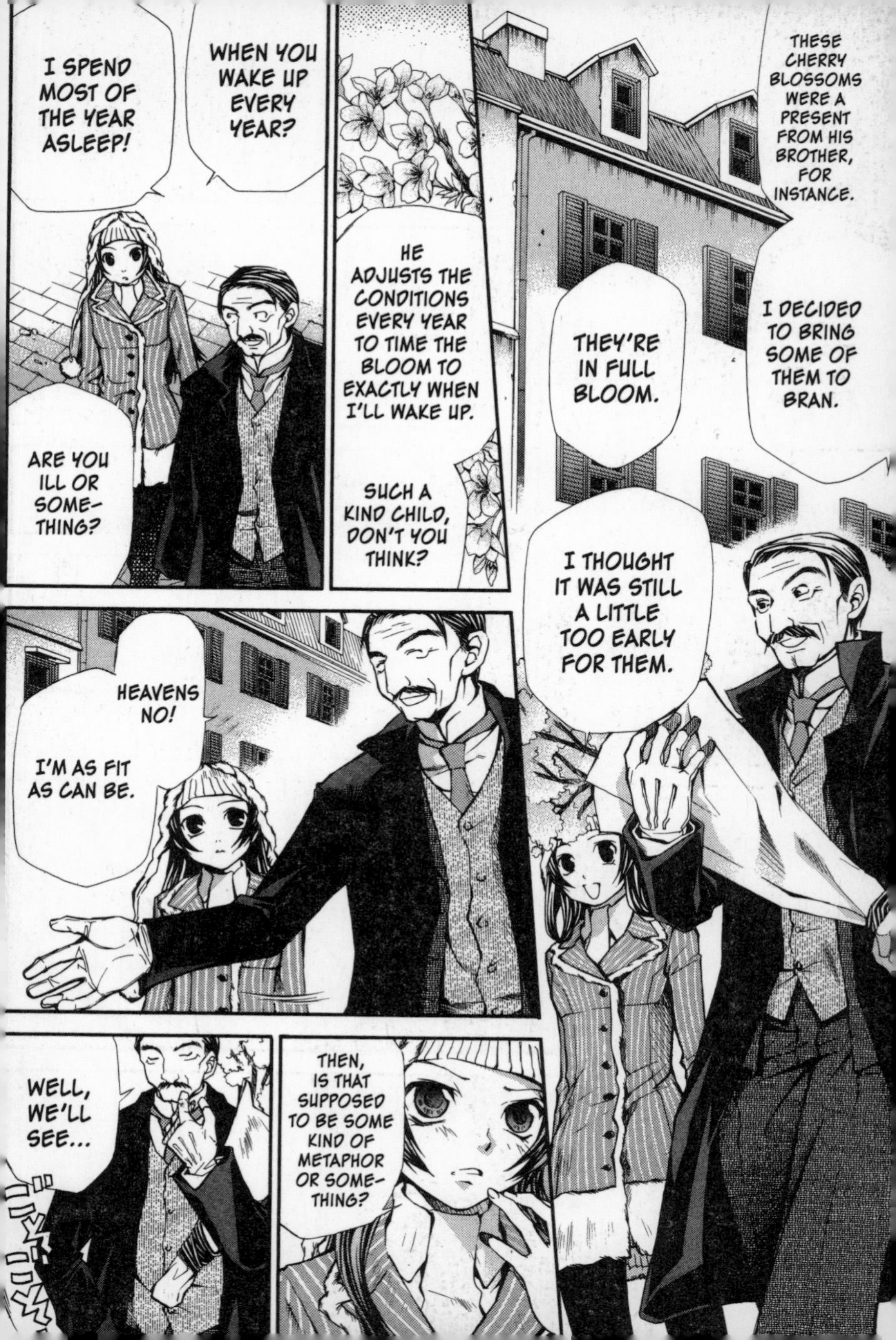
THESE CHERRY BLOSSOMS WERE A PRESENT FROM HIS BROTHER, FOR INSTANCE.
I DECIDED TO BRING SOME OF THEM TO BRAN.
THEY'RE IN FULL BLOOM.
I THOUGHT IT WAS STILL A LITTLE TOO EARLY FOR THEM.
HE ADJUSTS THE CONDITIONS EVERY YEAR TO TIME THE BLOOM TO EXACTLY WHEN I'LL WAKE UP.
SUCH A KIND CHILD, DON'T YOU THINK?
WHEN YOU WAKE UP EVERY YEAR?
I SPEND MOST OF THE YEAR ASLEEP!
ARE YOU ILL OR SOME-THING?
HEAVENS NO!
I'M AS FIT AS CAN BE.
THEN, IS THAT SUPPOSED TO BE SOME KIND OF METAPHOR OR SOME-THING?
WELL, WE'LL SEE...

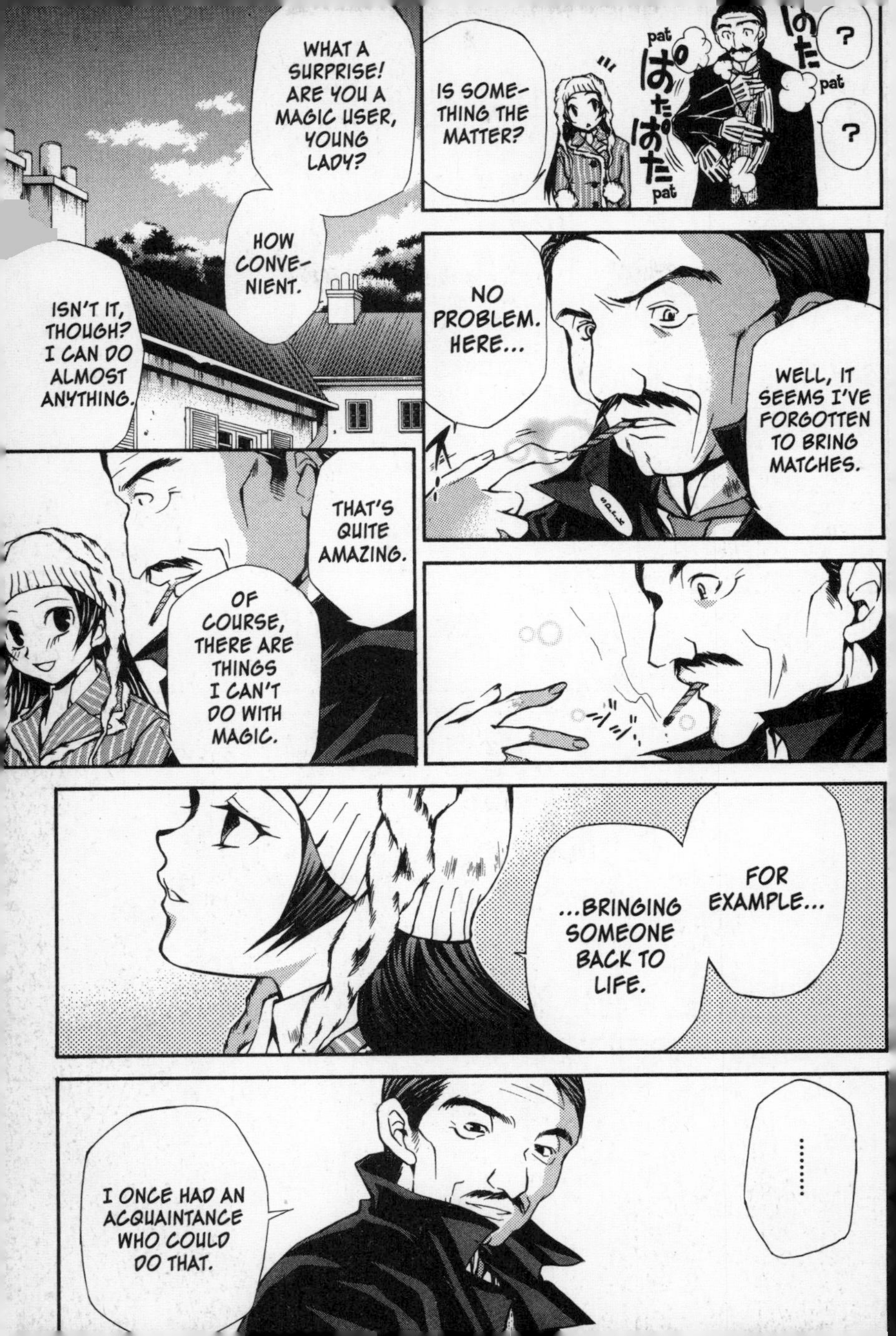

ぱた
pat
?
pat
?
ぱたぱた
pat
IS SOME-THING THE MATTER?
WELL, IT SEEMS I'VE FORGOTTEN TO BRING MATCHES.
NO PROBLEM. HERE...
WHAT A SURPRISE! ARE YOU A MAGIC USER, YOUNG LADY?
HOW CONVE-NIENT.
ISN'T IT, THOUGH? I CAN DO ALMOST ANYTHING.
THAT'S QUITE AMAZING.
OF COURSE, THERE ARE THINGS I CAN'T DO WITH MAGIC.
FOR EXAMPLE...
...BRINGING SOMEONE BACK TO LIFE.
....
I ONCE HAD AN ACQUAINTANCE WHO COULD DO THAT.

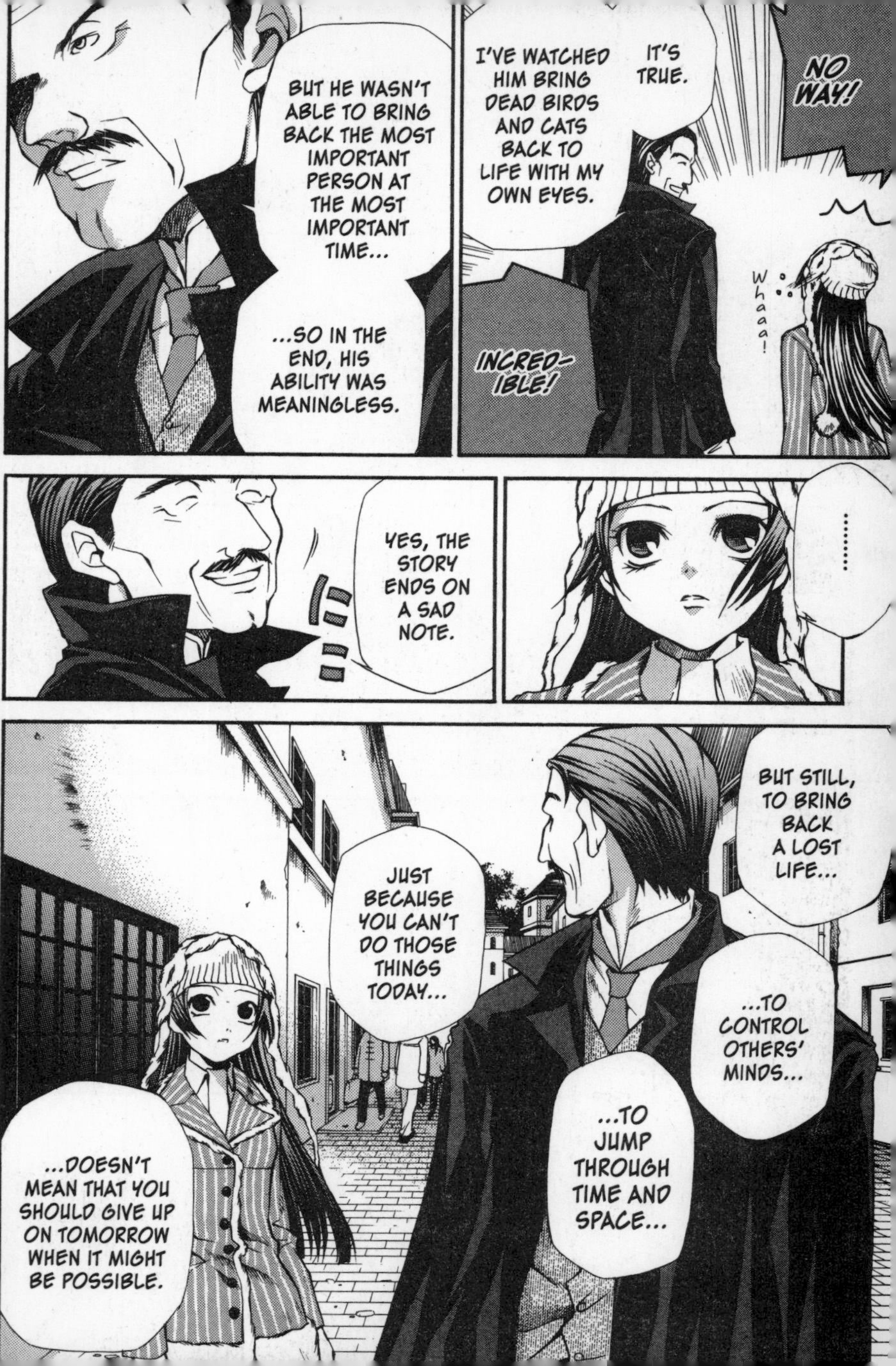
NO WAY!
IT'S TRUE.
I'VE WATCHED HIM BRING DEAD BIRDS AND CATS BACK TO LIFE WITH MY OWN EYES.
Whaaa!
INCREDIBLE!
BUT HE WASN'T ABLE TO BRING BACK THE MOST IMPORTANT PERSON AT THE MOST IMPORTANT TIME...
...SO IN THE END, HIS ABILITY WAS MEANINGLESS.
......
YES, THE STORY ENDS ON A SAD NOTE.
BUT STILL, TO BRING BACK A LOST LIFE...
...TO CONTROL OTHERS' MINDS...
...TO JUMP THROUGH TIME AND SPACE...
JUST BECAUSE YOU CAN'T DO THOSE THINGS TODAY...
...DOESN'T MEAN THAT YOU SHOULD GIVE UP ON TOMORROW WHEN IT MIGHT BE POSSIBLE.

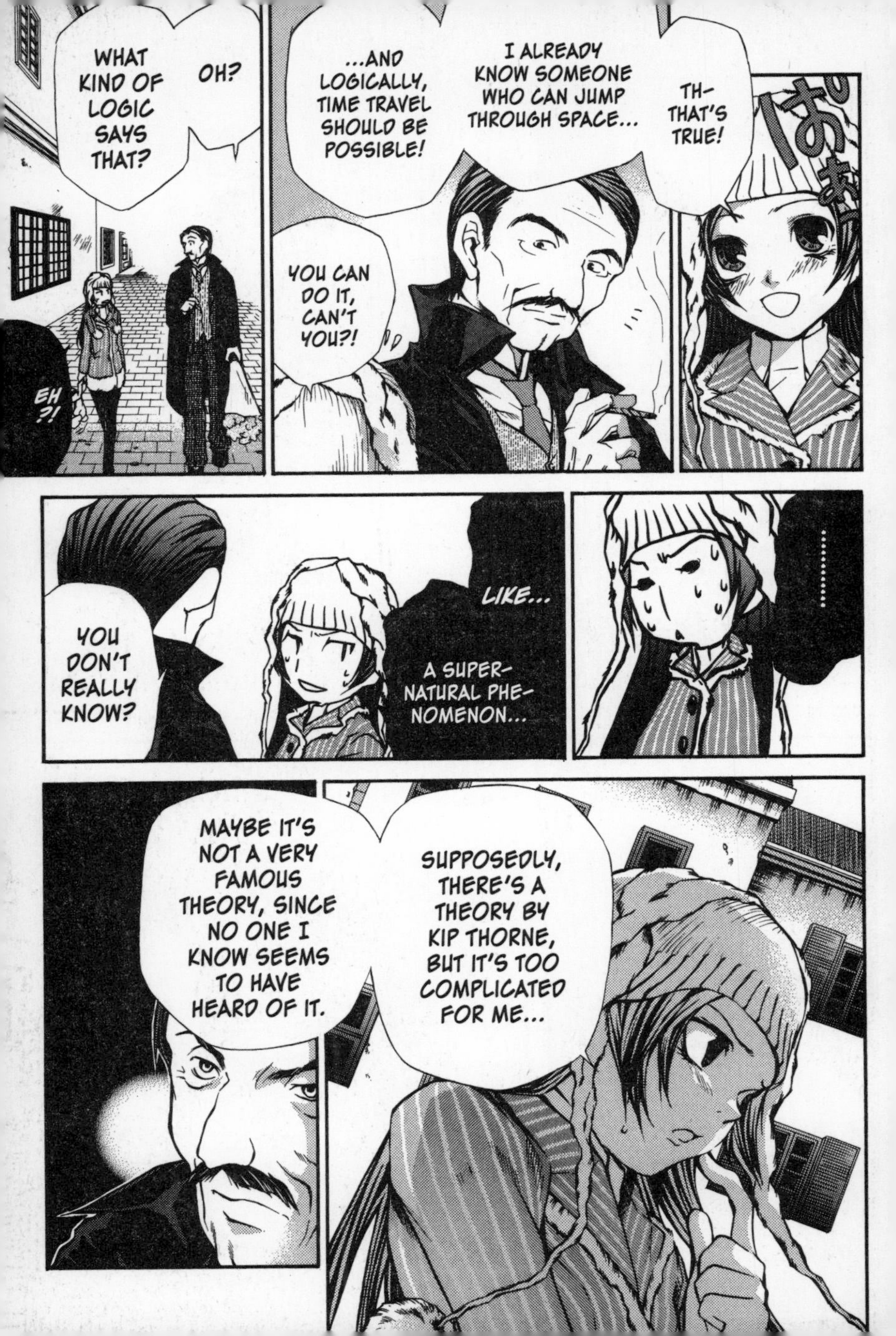
TH- THAT'S TRUE!
I ALREADY KNOW SOMEONE WHO CAN JUMP THROUGH SPACE...
...AND LOGICALLY, TIME TRAVEL SHOULD BE POSSIBLE!
YOU CAN DO IT, CAN'T YOU?!
OH?
WHAT KIND OF LOGIC SAYS THAT?
EH?!
......
LIKE...
A SUPER-NATURAL PHE-NOMENON...
YOU DON'T REALLY KNOW?
SUPPOSEDLY, THERE'S A THEORY BY KIP THORNE, BUT IT'S TOO COMPLICATED FOR ME...
MAYBE IT'S NOT A VERY FAMOUS THEORY, SINCE NO ONE I KNOW SEEMS TO HAVE HEARD OF IT.

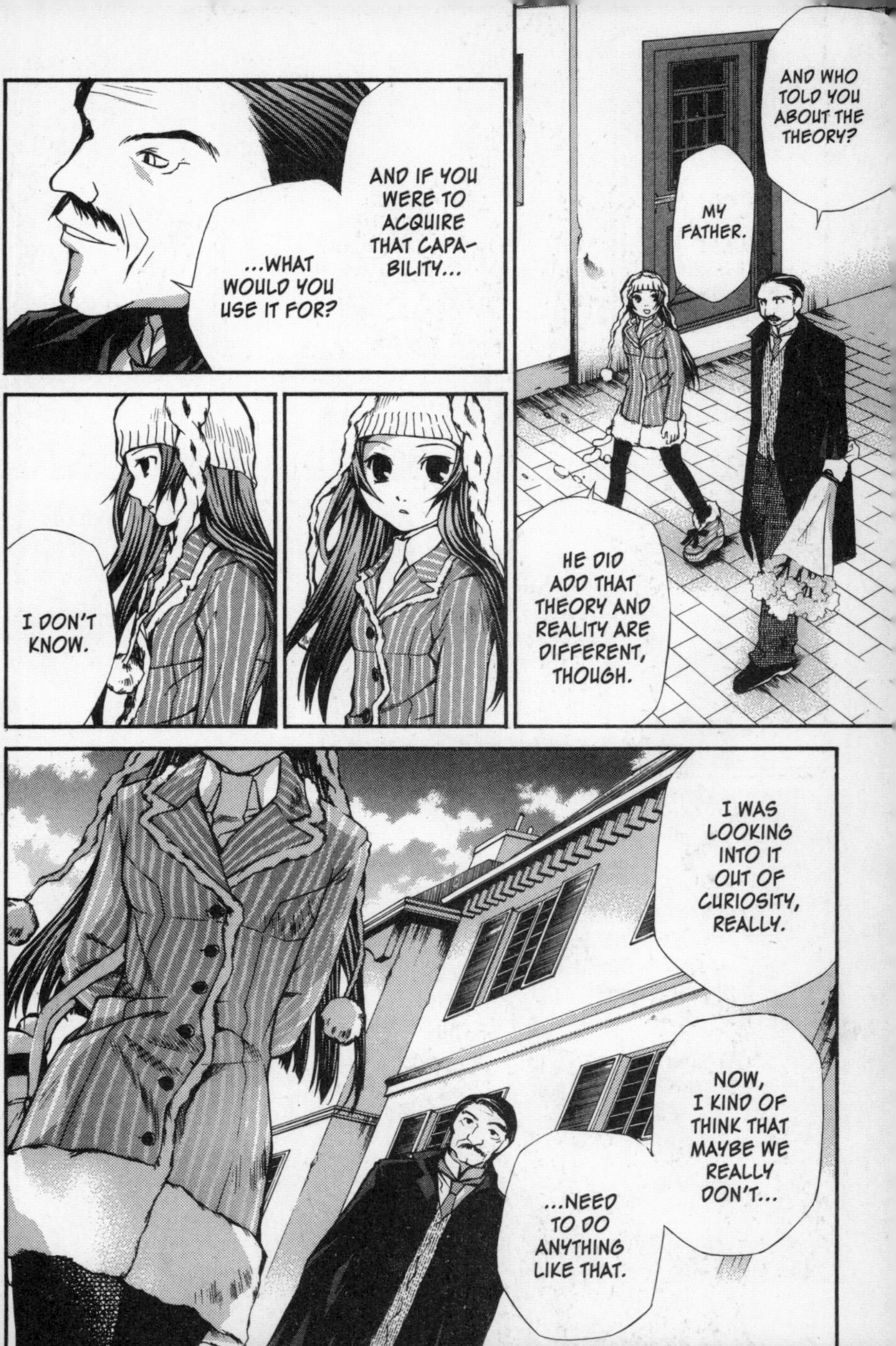
AND WHO TOLD YOU ABOUT THE THEORY?
MY FATHER.
HE DID ADD THAT THEORY AND REALITY ARE DIFFERENT, THOUGH.
AND IF YOU WERE TO ACQUIRE THAT CAPA-BILITY...
...WHAT WOULD YOU USE IT FOR?
I DON'T KNOW.
I WAS LOOKING INTO IT OUT OF CURIOSITY, REALLY.
NOW, I KIND OF THINK THAT MAYBE WE REALLY DON'T...
...NEED TO DO ANYTHING LIKE THAT.

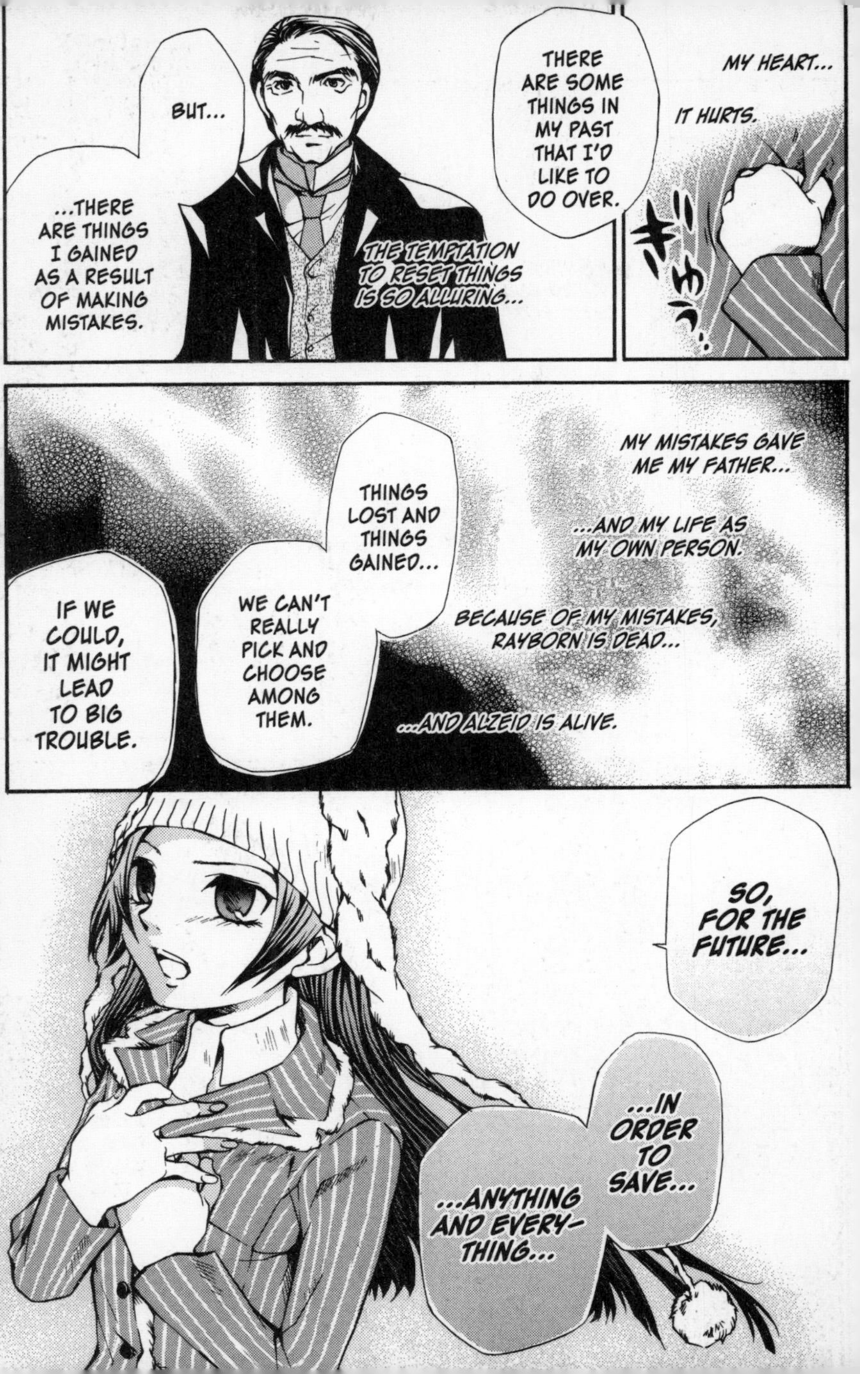
MY HEART...
IT HURTS.
ぎゅっ
THERE ARE SOME THINGS IN MY PAST THAT I'D LIKE TO DO OVER.
BUT...
...THERE ARE THINGS I GAINED AS A RESULT OF MAKING MISTAKES.
THE TEMPTATION TO RESET THINGS IS SO ALLURING...
MY MISTAKES GAVE ME MY FATHER...
...AND MY LIFE AS MY OWN PERSON.
THINGS LOST AND THINGS GAINED...
BECAUSE OF MY MISTAKES, RAYBORN IS DEAD...
...AND ALZEID IS ALIVE.
WE CAN'T REALLY PICK AND CHOOSE AMONG THEM.
IF WE COULD, IT MIGHT LEAD TO BIG TROUBLE.
SO, FOR THE FUTURE...
...IN ORDER TO SAVE...
...ANYTHING AND EVERY-THING...

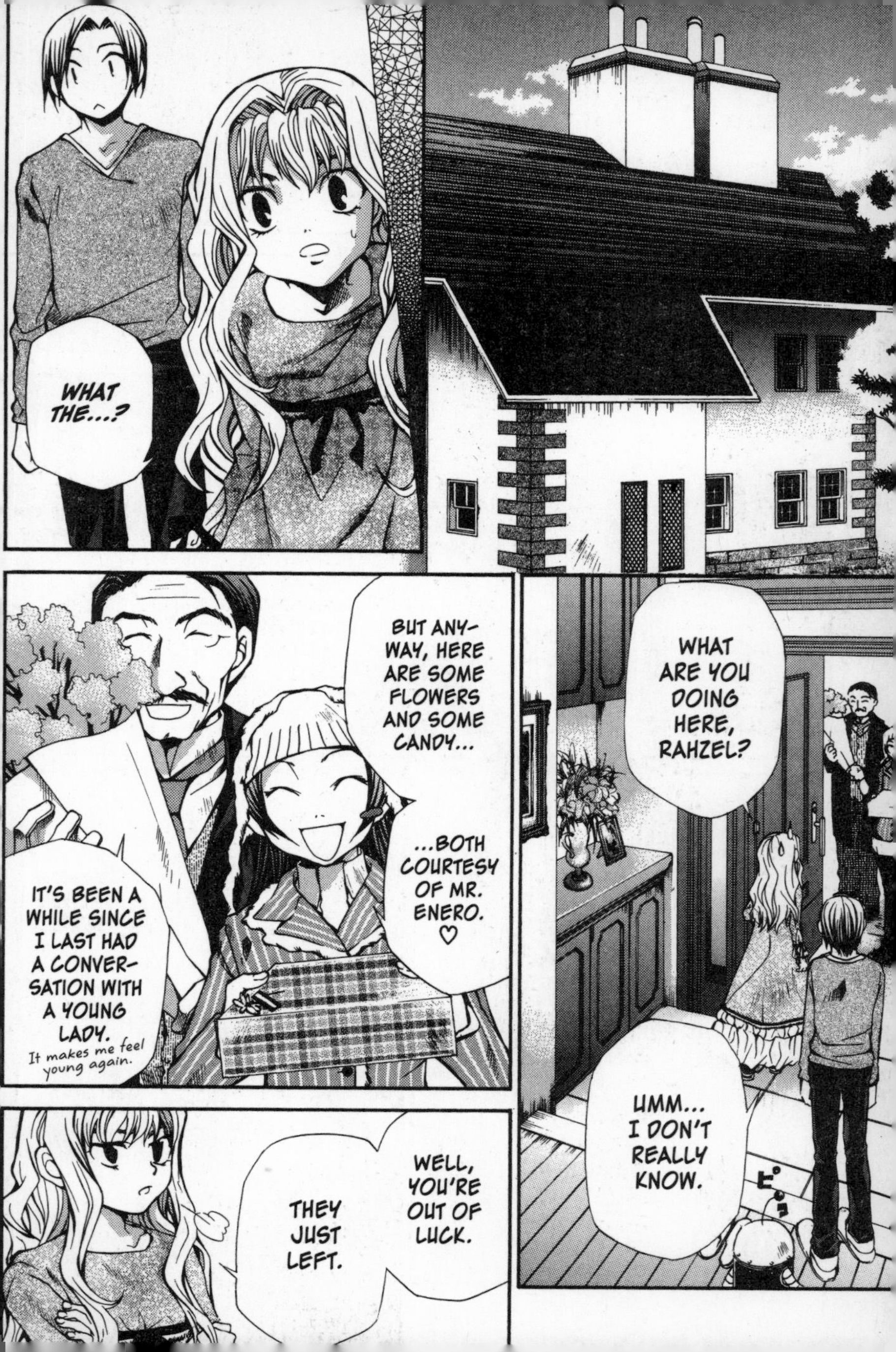
WHAT THE...?
WHAT ARE YOU DOING HERE, RAHZEL?
UMM... I DON'T REALLY KNOW.
BUT ANY-WAY, HERE ARE SOME FLOWERS AND SOME CANDY...
...BOTH COURTESY OF MR. ENERO. ♡
IT'S BEEN A WHILE SINCE I LAST HAD A CONVERSATION WITH A YOUNG LADY.
It makes me feel young again.
WELL, YOU'RE OUT OF LUCK.
THEY JUST LEFT.

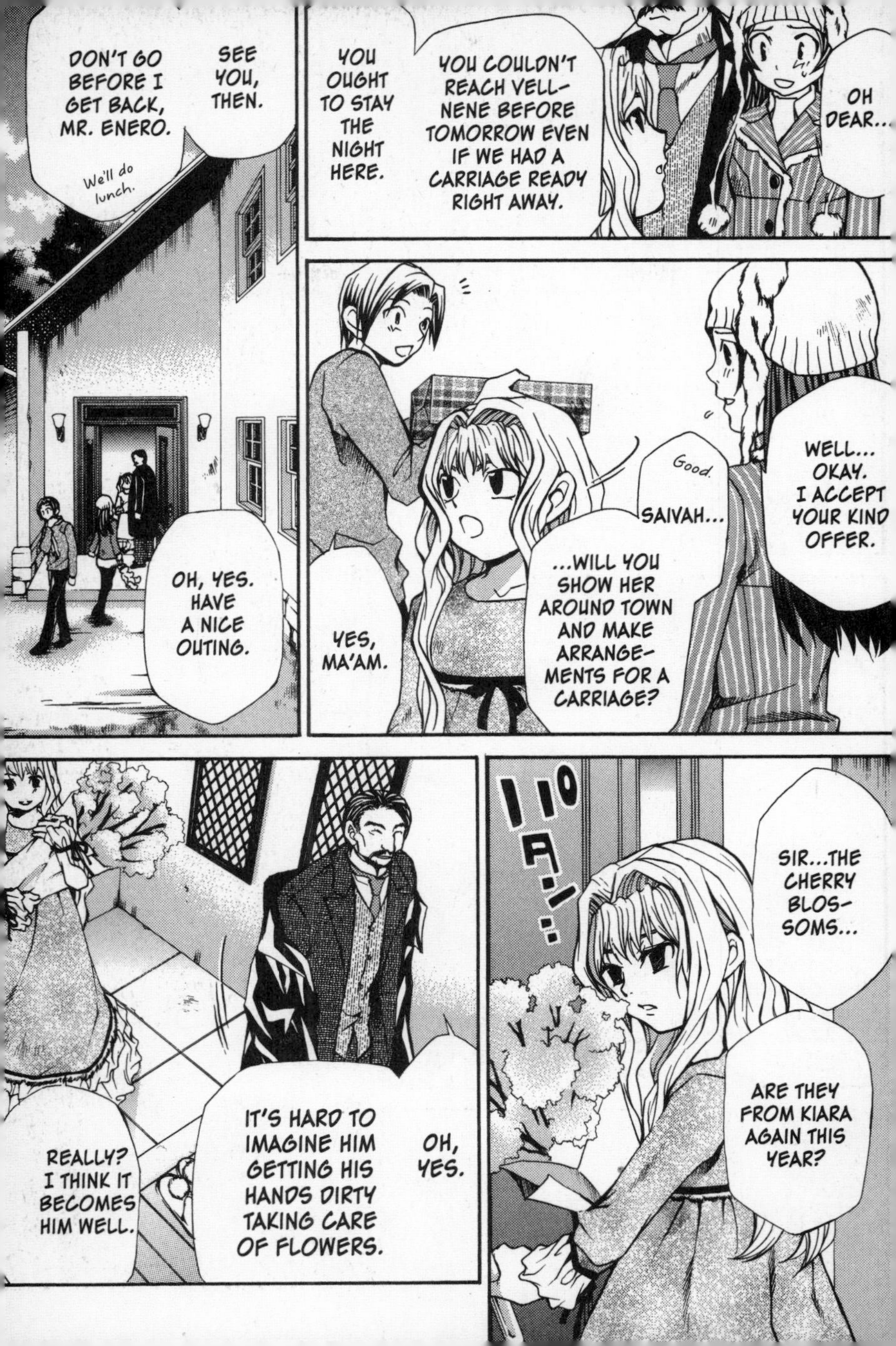
OH DEAR...
YOU COULDN'T REACH VELL-NENE BEFORE TOMORROW EVEN IF WE HAD A CARRIAGE READY RIGHT AWAY.
YOU OUGHT TO STAY THE NIGHT HERE.
WELL... OKAY. I ACCEPT YOUR KIND OFFER.
Good.
SAIVAH...
...WILL YOU SHOW HER AROUND TOWN AND MAKE ARRANGE-MENTS FOR A CARRIAGE?
YES, MA'AM.
SEE YOU, THEN.
DON'T GO BEFORE I GET BACK, MR. ENERO.
We'll do lunch.
OH, YES. HAVE A NICE OUTING.
SIR...THE CHERRY BLOS-SOMS...
ARE THEY FROM KIARA AGAIN THIS YEAR?
OH, YES.
IT'S HARD TO IMAGINE HIM GETTING HIS HANDS DIRTY TAKING CARE OF FLOWERS.
REALLY? I THINK IT BECOMES HIM WELL.

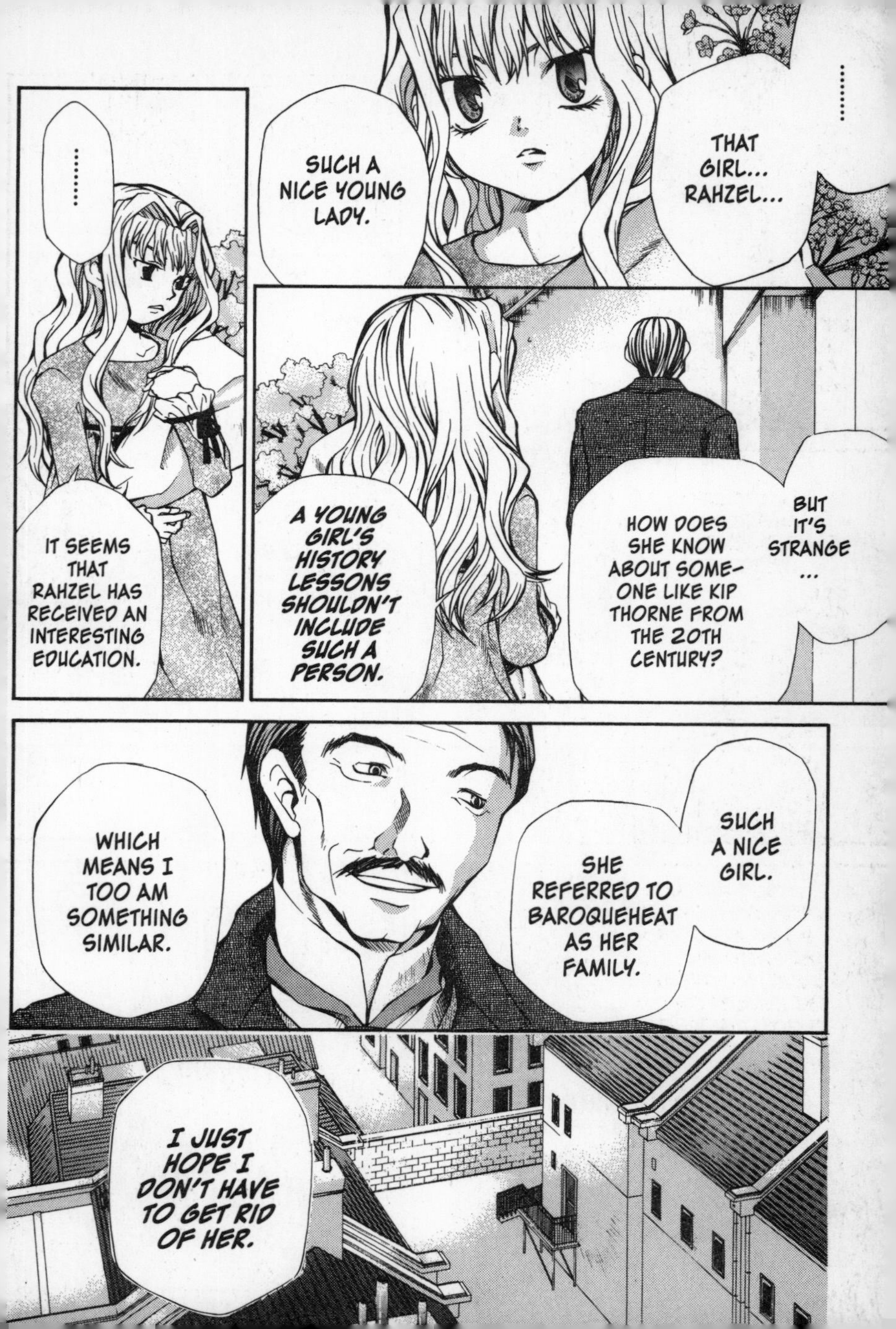
......
THAT GIRL... RAHZEL...
SUCH A NICE YOUNG LADY.
BUT IT'S STRANGE...
HOW DOES SHE KNOW ABOUT SOME-ONE LIKE KIP THORNE FROM THE 20TH CENTURY?
A YOUNG GIRL'S HISTORY LESSONS SHOULDN'T INCLUDE SUCH A PERSON.
......
IT SEEMS THAT RAHZEL HAS RECEIVED AN INTERESTING EDUCATION.
SUCH A NICE GIRL.
SHE REFERRED TO BAROQUEHEAT AS HER FAMILY.
WHICH MEANS I TOO AM SOMETHING SIMILAR.
I JUST HOPE I DON'T HAVE TO GET RID OF HER.

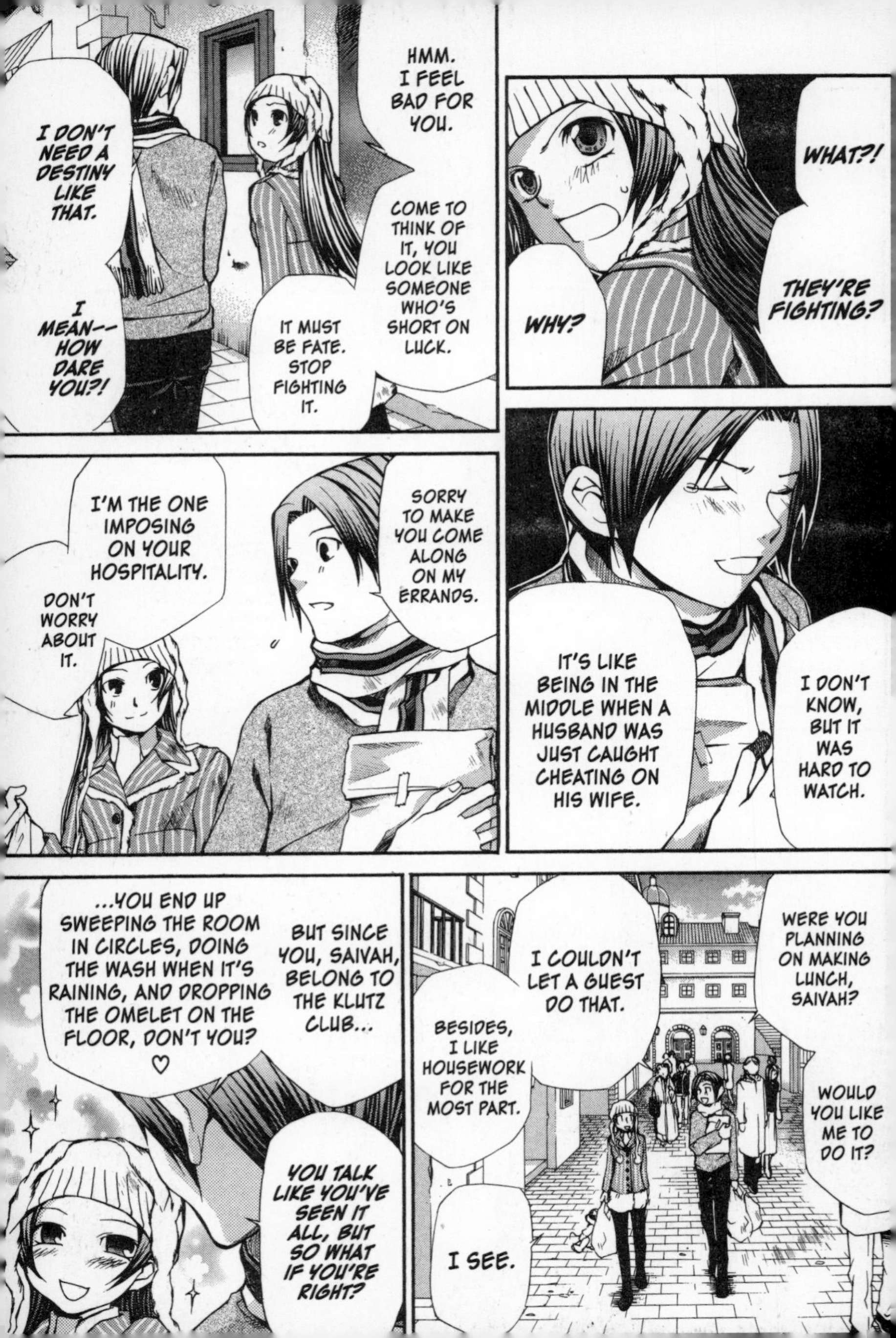
WHAT?!
THEY'RE FIGHTING?
WHY?
HMM. I FEEL BAD FOR YOU.
COME TO THINK OF IT, YOU LOOK LIKE SOMEONE WHO'S SHORT ON LUCK.
IT MUST BE FATE. STOP FIGHTING IT.
I DON'T NEED A DESTINY LIKE THAT.
I MEAN-- HOW DARE YOU?!
I DON'T KNOW, BUT IT WAS HARD TO WATCH.
IT'S LIKE BEING IN THE MIDDLE WHEN A HUSBAND WAS JUST CAUGHT CHEATING ON HIS WIFE.
SORRY TO MAKE YOU COME ALONG ON MY ERRANDS.
I'M THE ONE IMPOSING ON YOUR HOSPITALITY.
DON'T WORRY ABOUT IT.
WERE YOU PLANNING ON MAKING LUNCH, SAIVAH?
WOULD YOU LIKE ME TO DO IT?
I COULDN'T LET A GUEST DO THAT.
BESIDES, I LIKE HOUSEWORK FOR THE MOST PART.
I SEE.
BUT SINCE YOU, SAIVAH, BELONG TO THE KLUTZ CLUB...
...YOU END UP SWEEPING THE ROOM IN CIRCLES, DOING THE WASH WHEN IT'S RAINING, AND DROPPING THE OMELET ON THE FLOOR, DON'T YOU? ♡
YOU TALK LIKE YOU'VE SEEN IT ALL, BUT SO WHAT IF YOU'RE RIGHT?

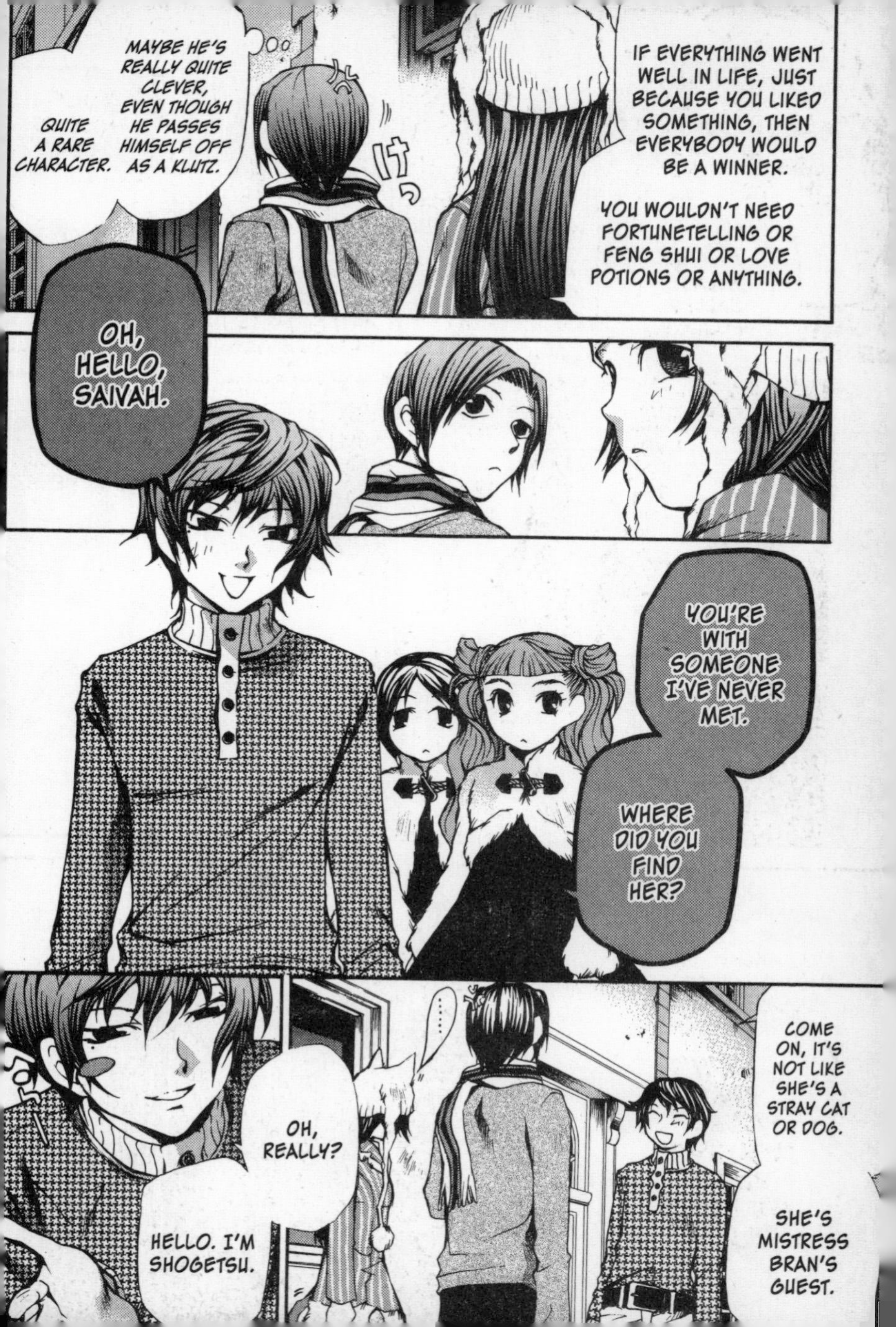
IF EVERYTHING WENT WELL IN LIFE, JUST BECAUSE YOU LIKED SOMETHING, THEN EVERYBODY WOULD BE A WINNER.
YOU WOULDN'T NEED FORTUNETELLING OR FENG SHUI OR LOVE POTIONS OR ANYTHING.
けっ
MAYBE HE'S REALLY QUITE CLEVER, EVEN THOUGH HE PASSES HIMSELF OFF AS A KLUTZ.
QUITE A RARE CHARACTER.
OH, HELLO, SAIVAH.
YOU'RE WITH SOMEONE I'VE NEVER MET.
WHERE DID YOU FIND HER?
COME ON, IT'S NOT LIKE SHE'S A STRAY CAT OR DOG.
SHE'S MISTRESS BRAN'S GUEST.
......
OH, REALLY?
HELLO. I'M SHOGETSU.

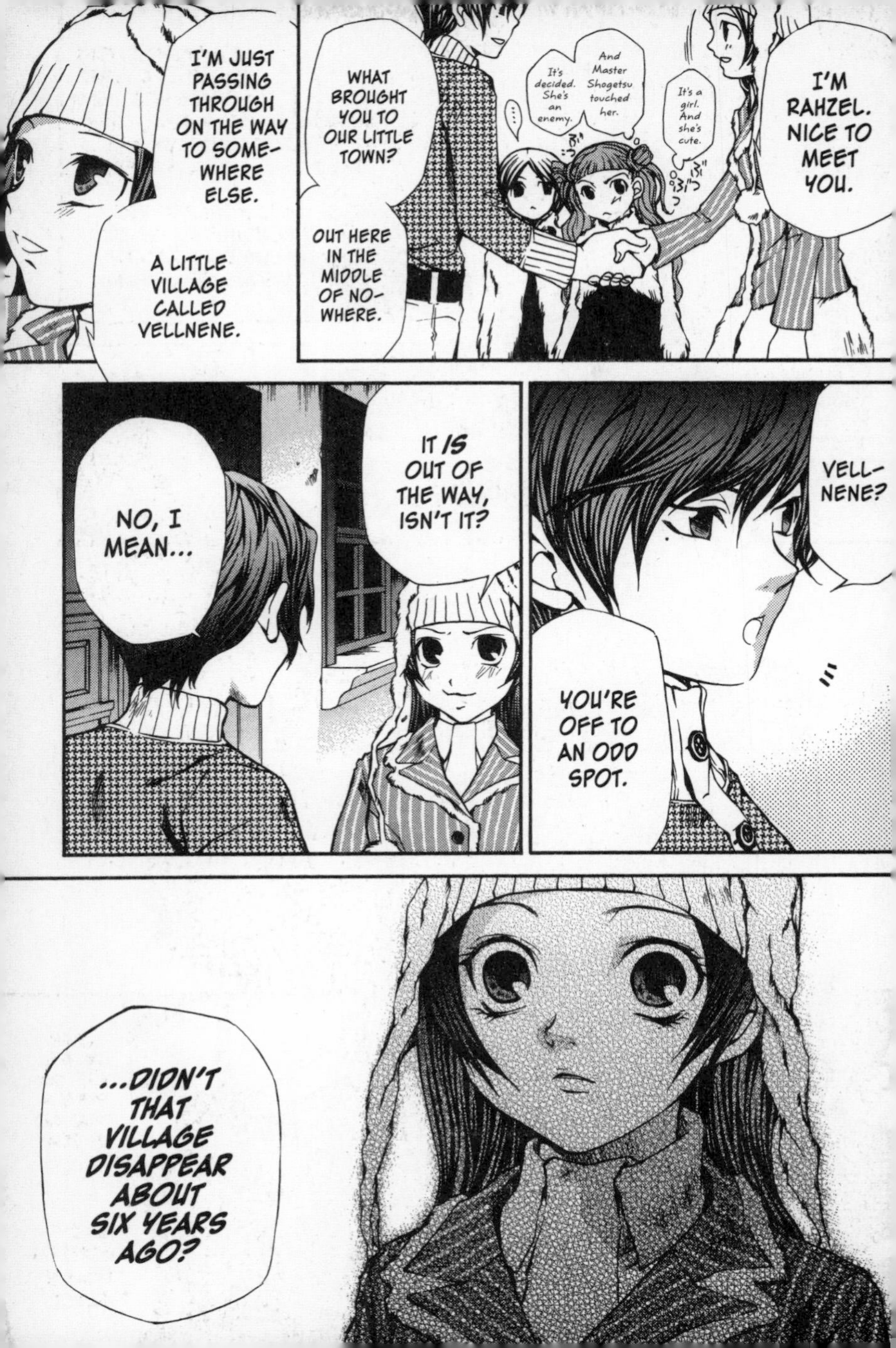
I'M RAHZEL. NICE TO MEET YOU.
It's a girl. And she's cute.
And Master Shogetsu touched her.
It's decided. She's an enemy.
...
WHAT BROUGHT YOU TO OUR LITTLE TOWN?
OUT HERE IN THE MIDDLE OF NO-WHERE.
I'M JUST PASSING THROUGH ON THE WAY TO SOME-WHERE ELSE.
A LITTLE VILLAGE CALLED VELLNENE.
VELL-NENE?
YOU'RE OFF TO AN ODD SPOT.
IT *IS* OUT OF THE WAY, ISN'T IT?
NO, I MEAN...
...DIDN'T THAT VILLAGE DISAPPEAR ABOUT SIX YEARS AGO?

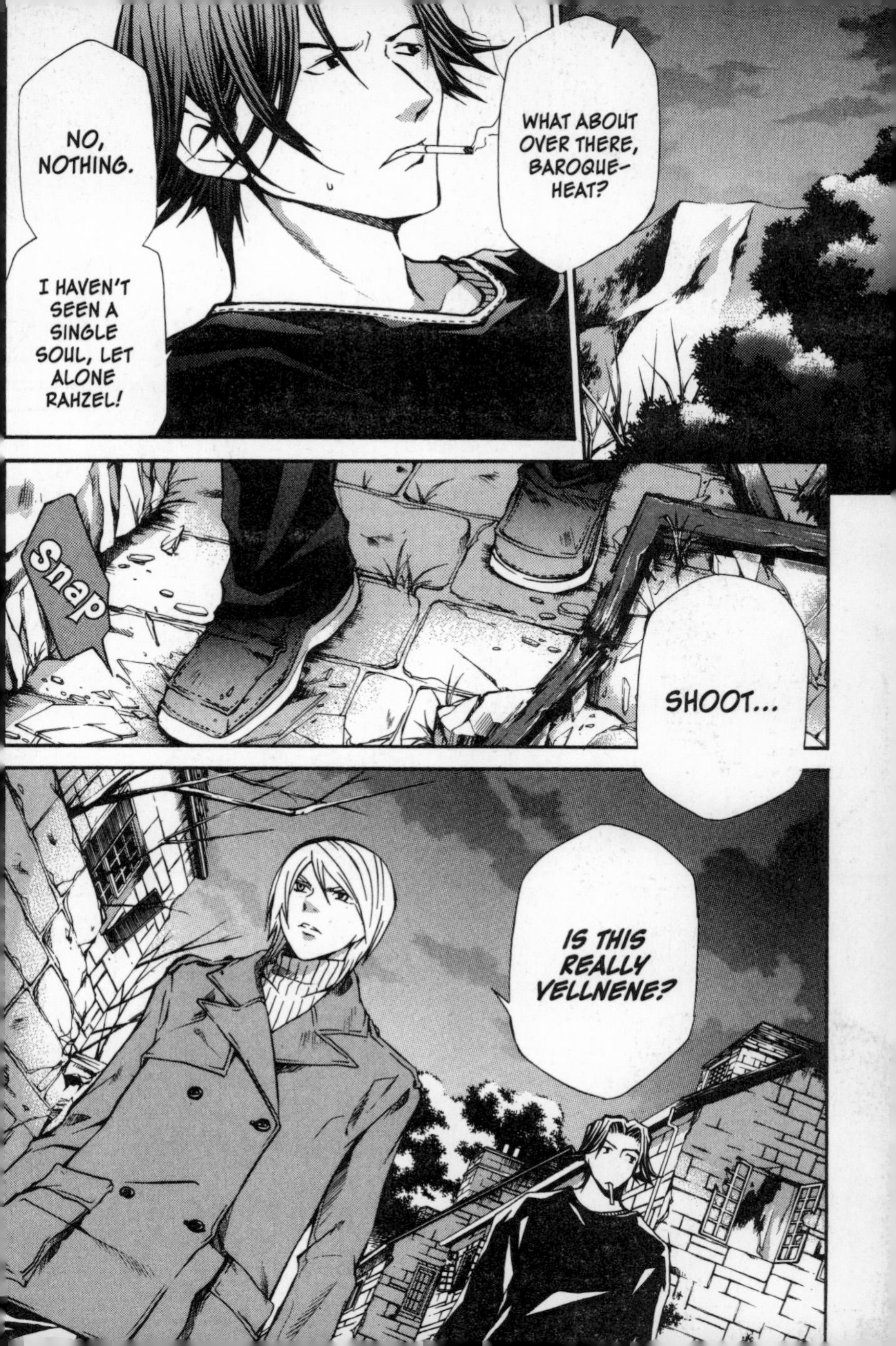
WHAT ABOUT OVER THERE, BAROQUE-HEAT?
NO, NOTHING.
I HAVEN'T SEEN A SINGLE SOUL, LET ALONE RAHZEL!
SHOOT...
Snap
IS THIS REALLY VELLNENE?

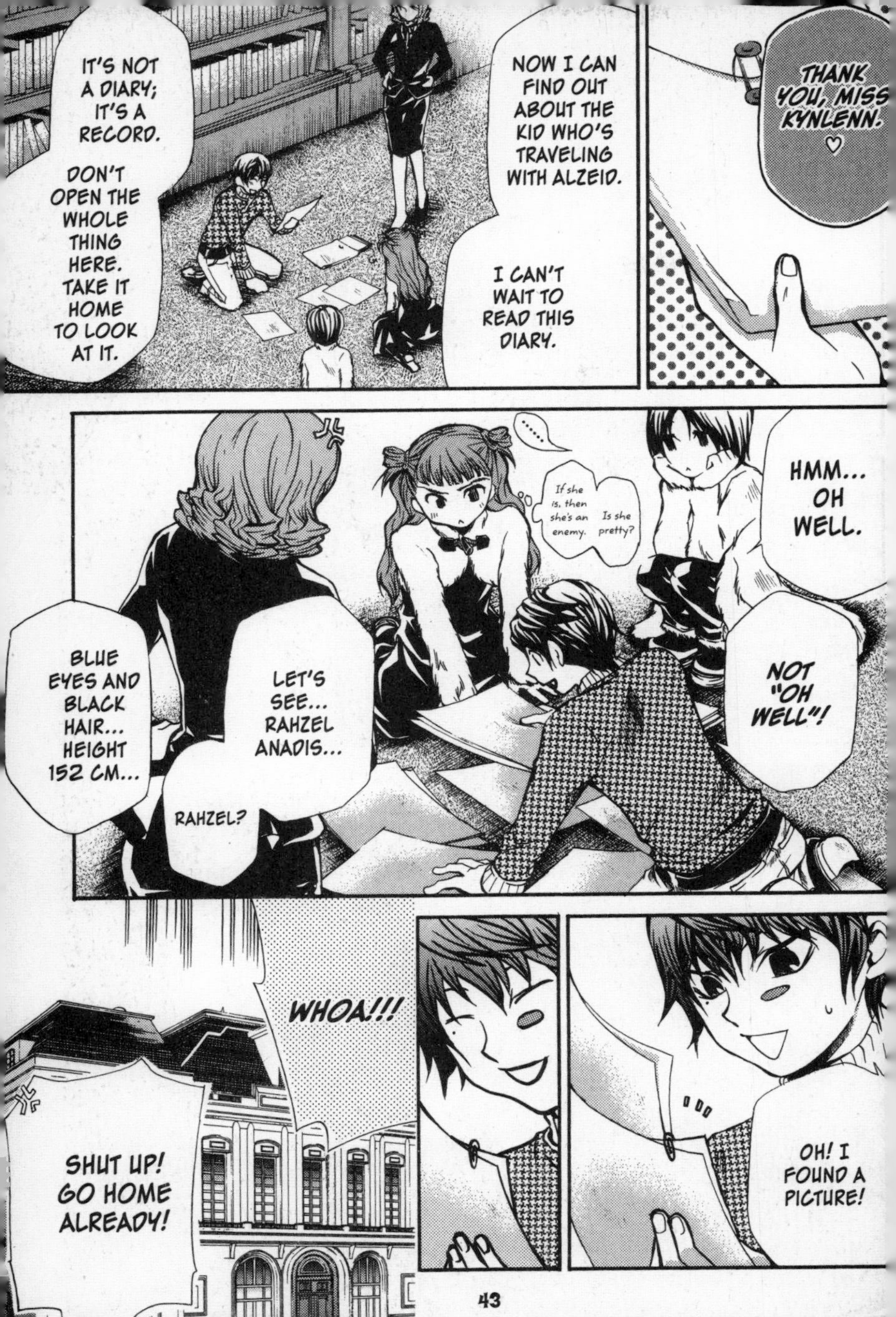
THANK YOU, MISS KYNLENN. ♡
NOW I CAN FIND OUT ABOUT THE KID WHO'S TRAVELING WITH ALZEID.
I CAN'T WAIT TO READ THIS DIARY.
IT'S NOT A DIARY; IT'S A RECORD.
DON'T OPEN THE WHOLE THING HERE. TAKE IT HOME TO LOOK AT IT.
HMM... OH WELL.
......
Is she pretty?
If she is, then she's an enemy.
NOT "OH WELL"!
LET'S SEE... RAHZEL ANADIS...
BLUE EYES AND BLACK HAIR... HEIGHT 152 CM...
RAHZEL?
OH! I FOUND A PICTURE!
WHOA!!!
SHUT UP! GO HOME ALREADY!

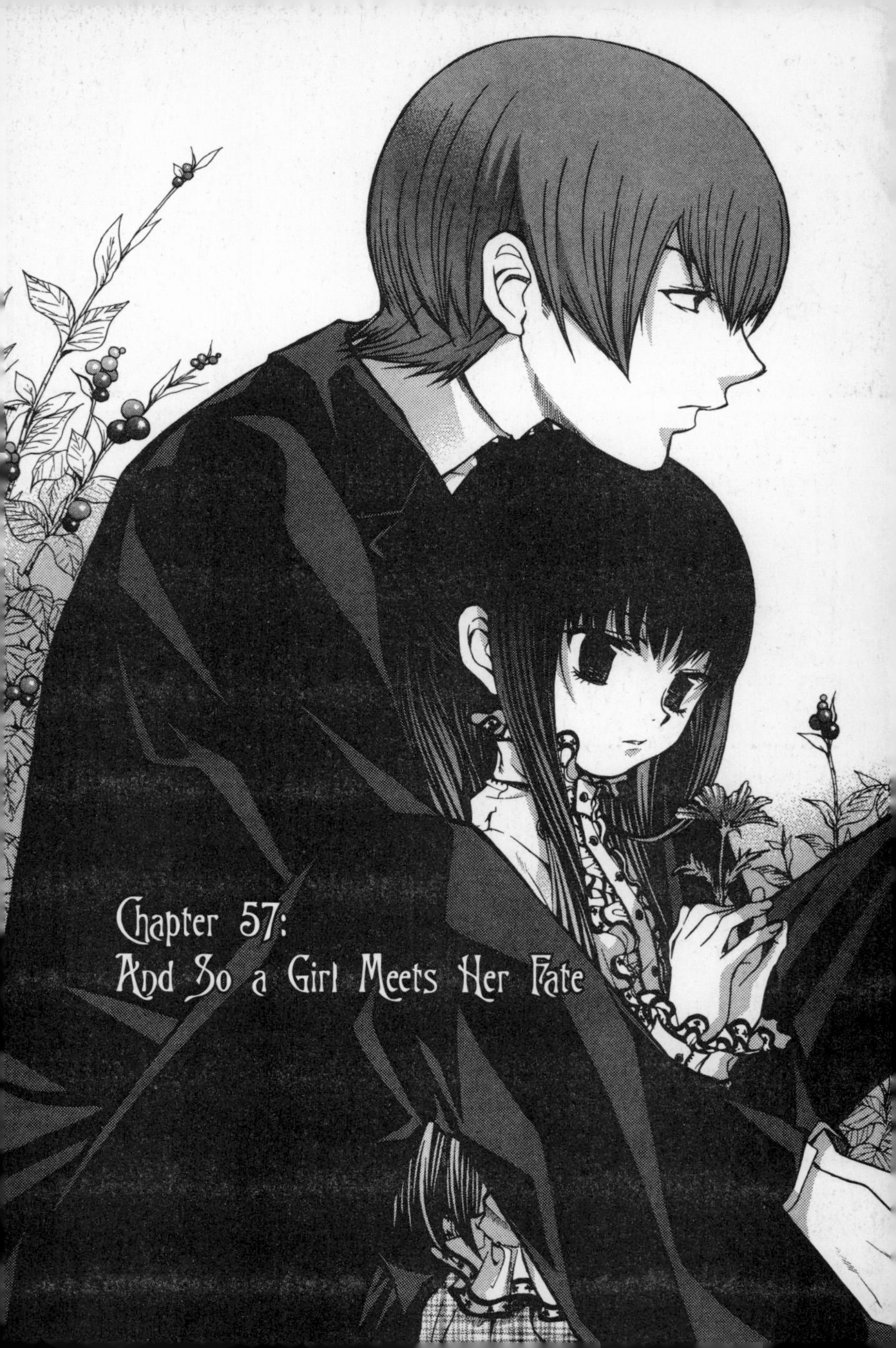
Chapter 57:
And So a Girl Meets Her Fate

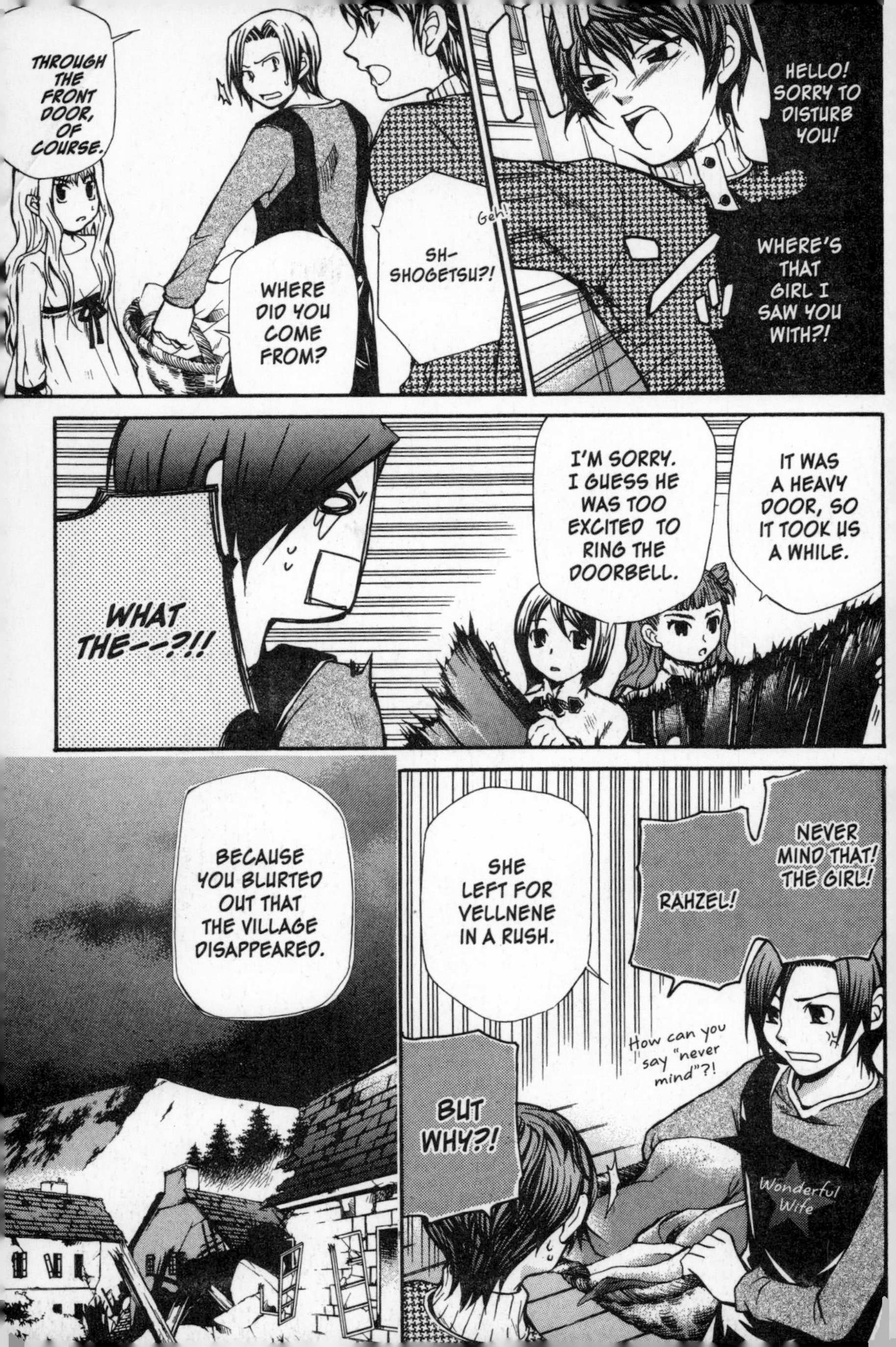
HELLO! SORRY TO DISTURB YOU!
WHERE'S THAT GIRL I SAW YOU WITH?!
Geh!
SH-SHOGETSU?!
WHERE DID YOU COME FROM?
THROUGH THE FRONT DOOR, OF COURSE.
IT WAS A HEAVY DOOR, SO IT TOOK US A WHILE.
I'M SORRY. I GUESS HE WAS TOO EXCITED TO RING THE DOORBELL.
WHAT THE--?!!
NEVER MIND THAT! THE GIRL!
RAHZEL!
SHE LEFT FOR VELLNENE IN A RUSH.
How can you say "never mind"?!
BUT WHY?!
Wonderful Wife
BECAUSE YOU BLURTED OUT THAT THE VILLAGE DISAPPEARED.

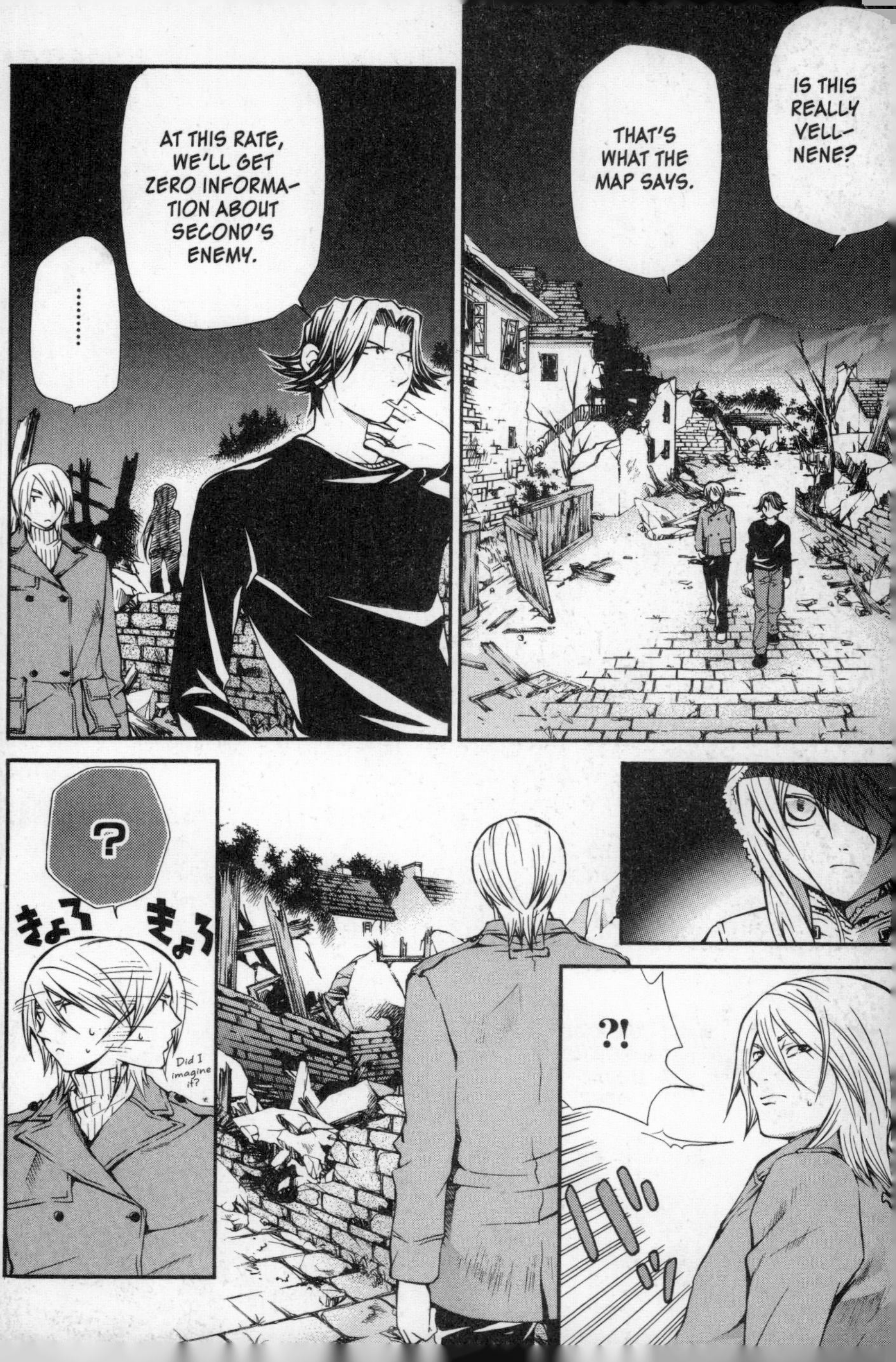
IS THIS REALLY VELL-NENE?
THAT'S WHAT THE MAP SAYS.
AT THIS RATE, WE'LL GET ZERO INFORMA-TION ABOUT SECOND'S ENEMY.
......
?!
?
きょろ きょろ
Did I imagine it?

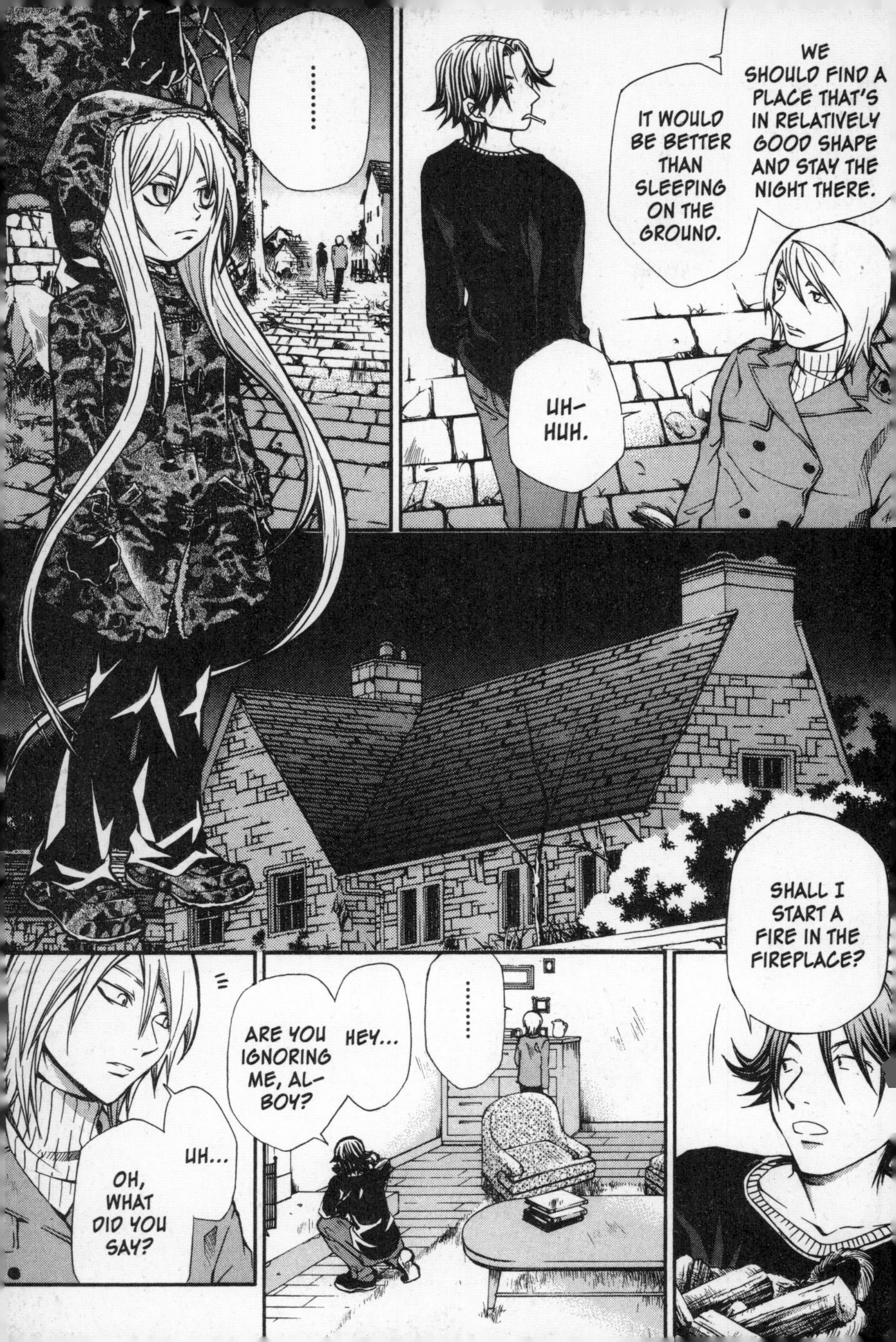
WE SHOULD FIND A PLACE THAT'S IN RELATIVELY GOOD SHAPE AND STAY THE NIGHT THERE.
IT WOULD BE BETTER THAN SLEEPING ON THE GROUND.
UH-HUH.
......
SHALL I START A FIRE IN THE FIREPLACE?
......
HEY...
ARE YOU IGNORING ME, AL-BOY?
UH...
OH, WHAT DID YOU SAY?

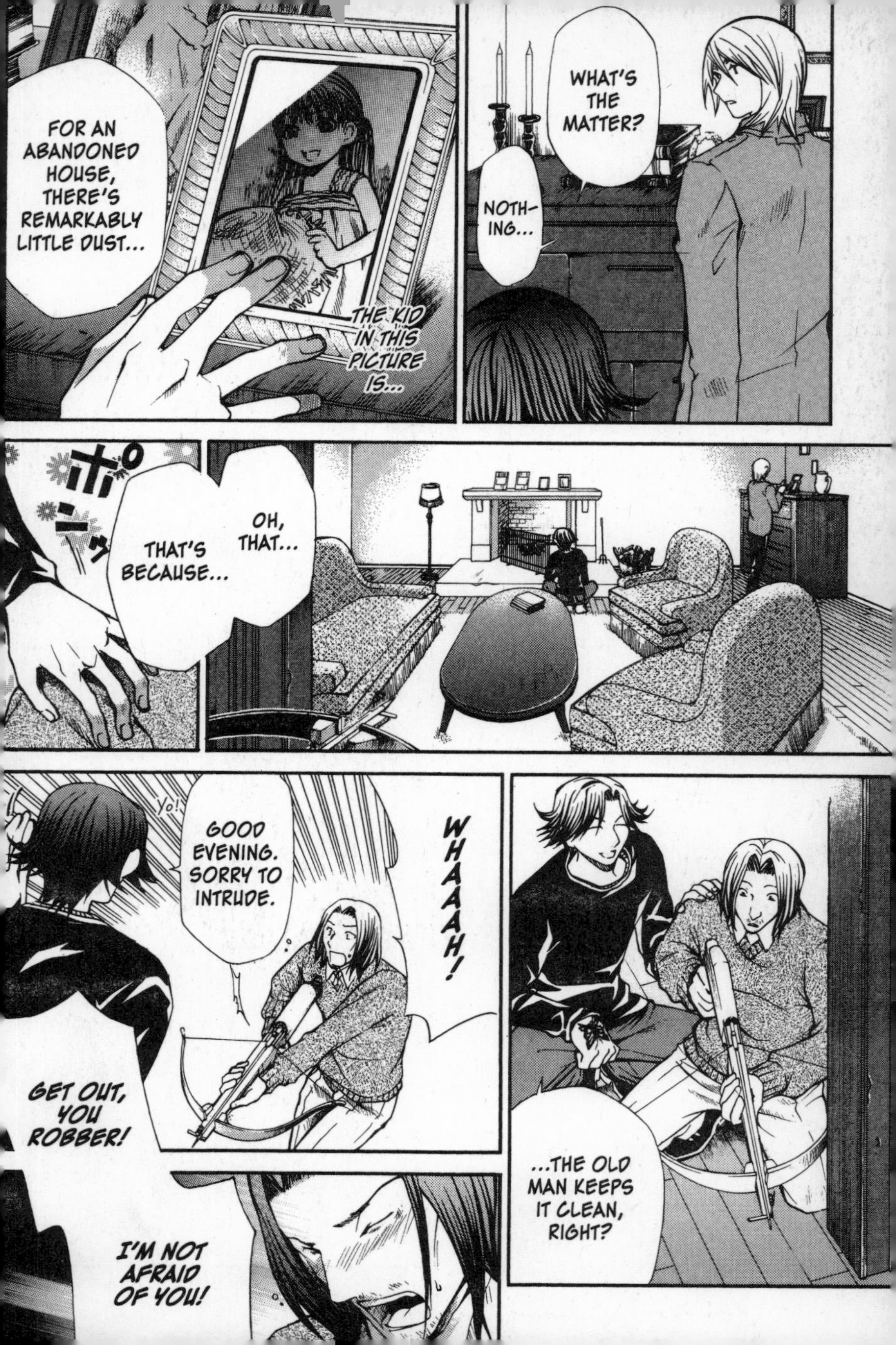
WHAT'S THE MATTER?
NOTHING...
FOR AN ABANDONED HOUSE, THERE'S REMARKABLY LITTLE DUST...
THE KID IN THIS PICTURE IS...
OH, THAT...
THAT'S BECAUSE...
ポーッ
...THE OLD MAN KEEPS IT CLEAN, RIGHT?
Yo!
GOOD EVENING. SORRY TO INTRUDE.
WHAAAAH!
GET OUT, YOU ROBBER!
I'M NOT AFRAID OF YOU!

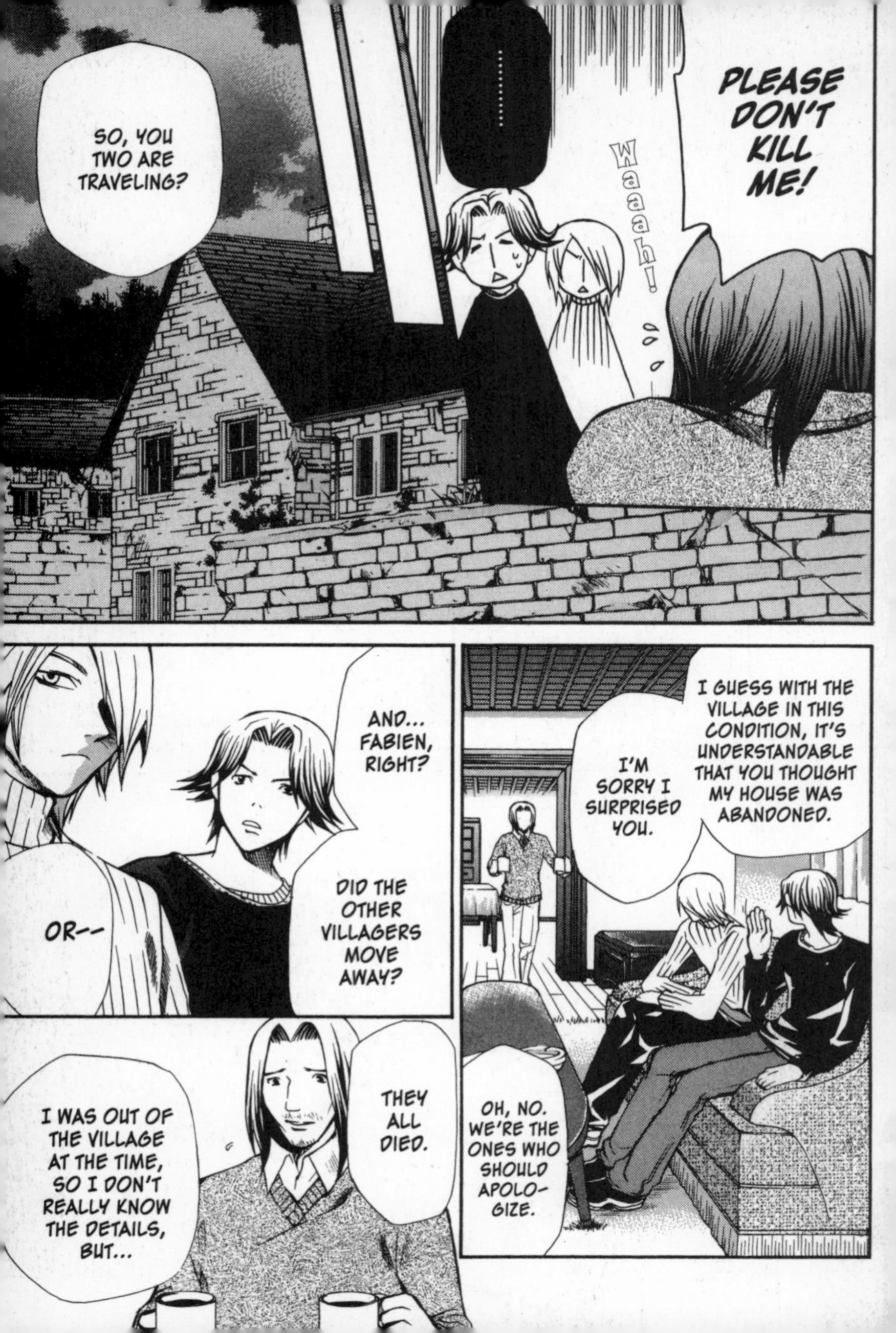
PLEASE DON'T KILL ME!
Waaah!
SO, YOU TWO ARE TRAVELING?
I GUESS WITH THE VILLAGE IN THIS CONDITION, IT'S UNDERSTANDABLE THAT YOU THOUGHT MY HOUSE WAS ABANDONED.
I'M SORRY I SURPRISED YOU.
OH, NO. WE'RE THE ONES WHO SHOULD APOLO-GIZE.
AND... FABIEN, RIGHT?
DID THE OTHER VILLAGERS MOVE AWAY?
OR--
THEY ALL DIED.
I WAS OUT OF THE VILLAGE AT THE TIME, SO I DON'T REALLY KNOW THE DETAILS, BUT...

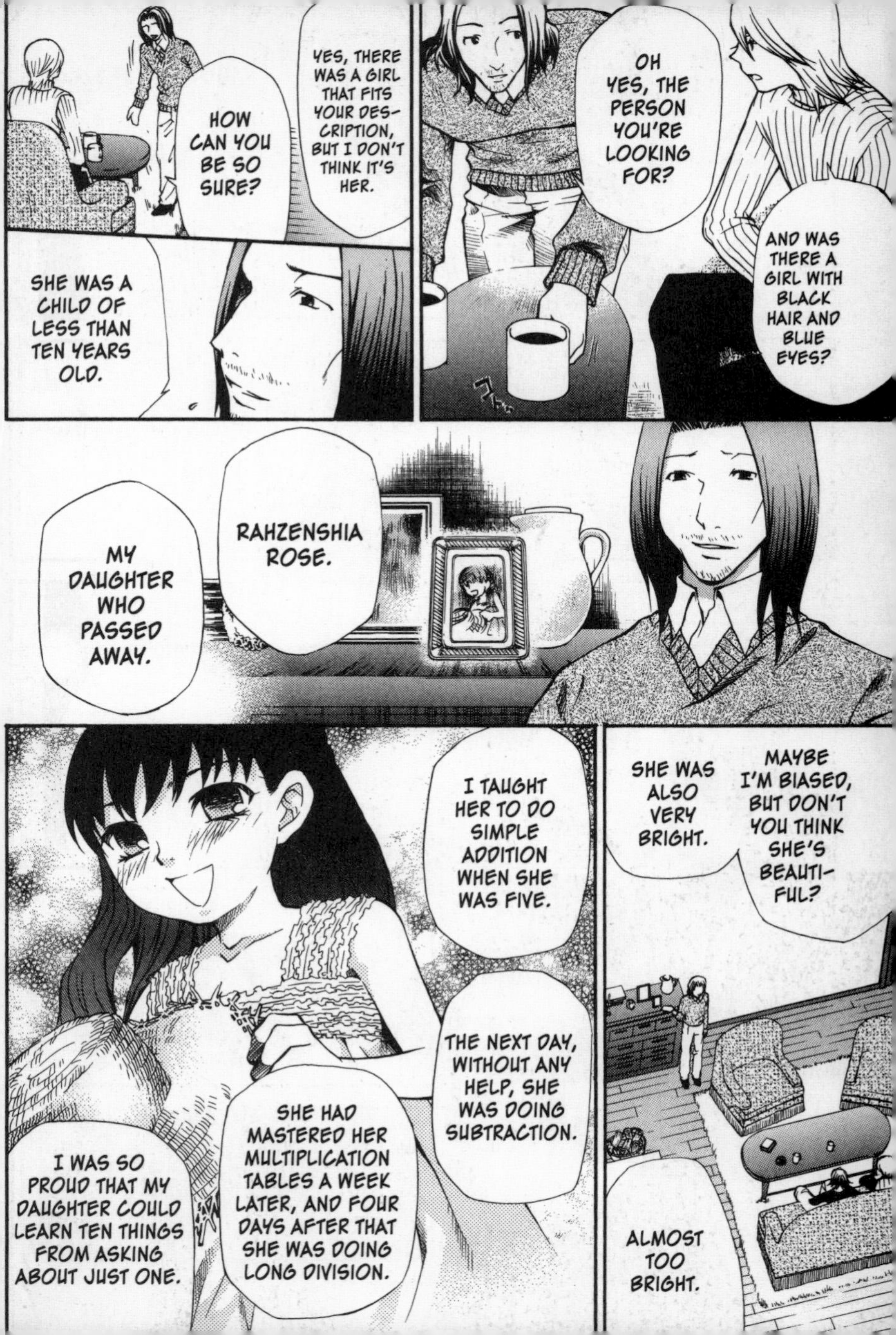
AND WAS THERE A GIRL WITH BLACK HAIR AND BLUE EYES?
OH YES, THE PERSON YOU'RE LOOKING FOR?
YES, THERE WAS A GIRL THAT FITS YOUR DES-CRIPTION, BUT I DON'T THINK IT'S HER.
HOW CAN YOU BE SO SURE?
SHE WAS A CHILD OF LESS THAN TEN YEARS OLD.
RAHZENSHIA ROSE.
MY DAUGHTER WHO PASSED AWAY.
MAYBE I'M BIASED, BUT DON'T YOU THINK SHE'S BEAUTI-FUL?
SHE WAS ALSO VERY BRIGHT.
ALMOST TOO BRIGHT.
I TAUGHT HER TO DO SIMPLE ADDITION WHEN SHE WAS FIVE.
THE NEXT DAY, WITHOUT ANY HELP, SHE WAS DOING SUBTRACTION.
SHE HAD MASTERED HER MULTIPLICATION TABLES A WEEK LATER, AND FOUR DAYS AFTER THAT SHE WAS DOING LONG DIVISION.
I WAS SO PROUD THAT MY DAUGHTER COULD LEARN TEN THINGS FROM ASKING ABOUT JUST ONE.

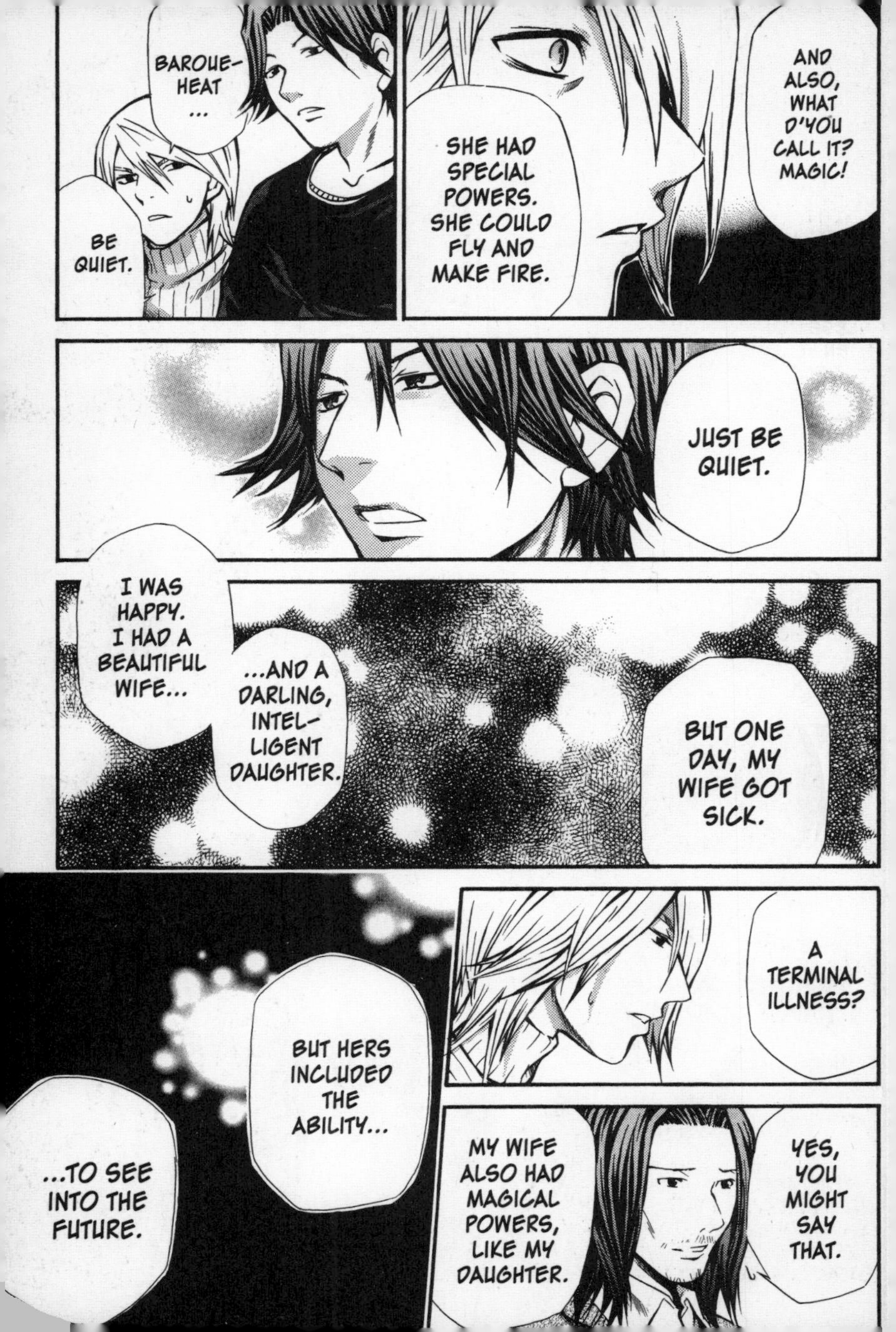
AND ALSO, WHAT D'YOU CALL IT? MAGIC!
SHE HAD SPECIAL POWERS. SHE COULD FLY AND MAKE FIRE.
BAROUE-HEAT ...
BE QUIET.
JUST BE QUIET.
I WAS HAPPY. I HAD A BEAUTIFUL WIFE...
...AND A DARLING, INTEL-LIGENT DAUGHTER.
BUT ONE DAY, MY WIFE GOT SICK.
A TERMINAL ILLNESS?
YES, YOU MIGHT SAY THAT.
MY WIFE ALSO HAD MAGICAL POWERS, LIKE MY DAUGHTER.
BUT HERS INCLUDED THE ABILITY...
...TO SEE INTO THE FUTURE.

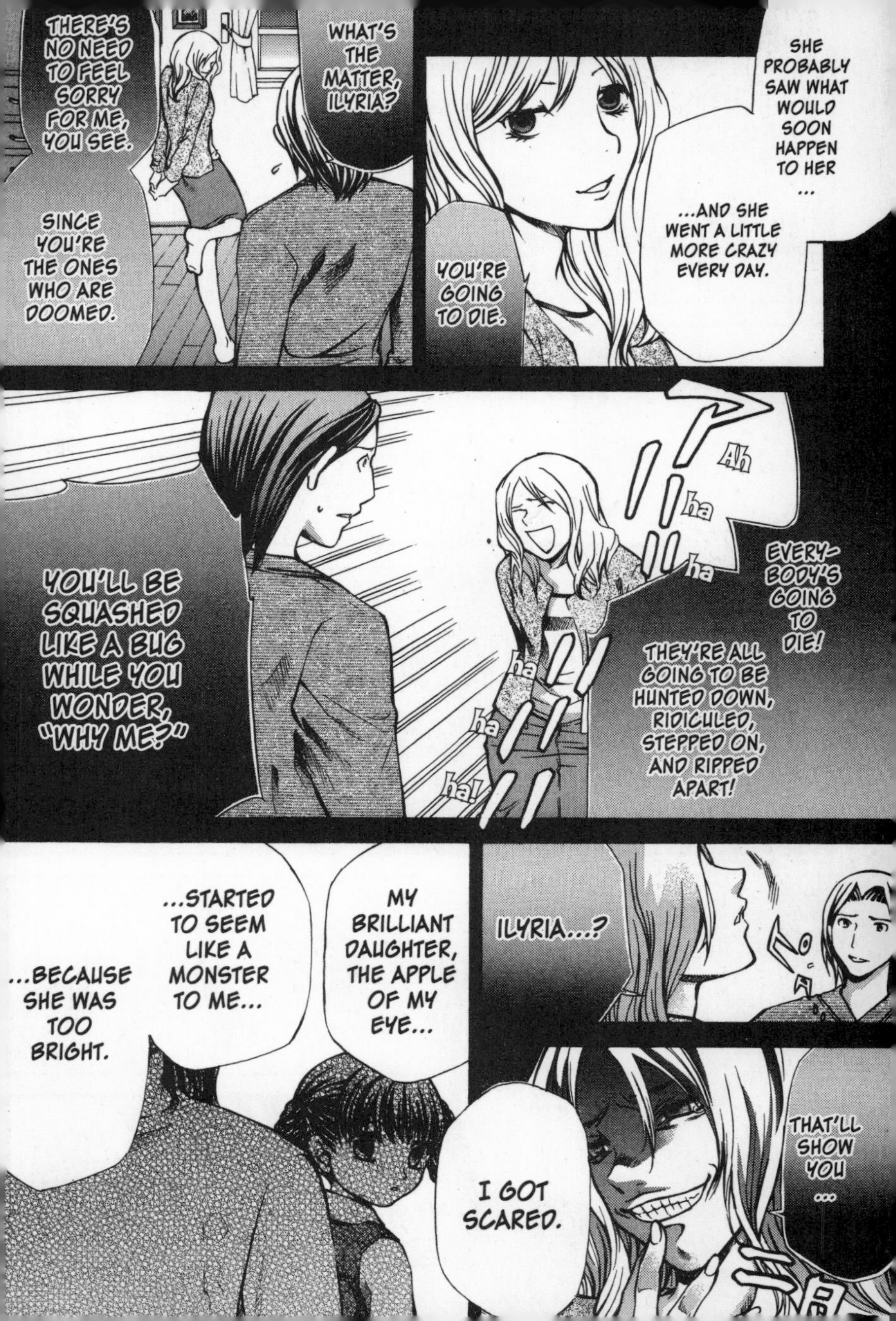
SHE PROBABLY SAW WHAT WOULD SOON HAPPEN TO HER ...
...AND SHE WENT A LITTLE MORE CRAZY EVERY DAY.
YOU'RE GOING TO DIE.
WHAT'S THE MATTER, ILYRIA?
THERE'S NO NEED TO FEEL SORRY FOR ME, YOU SEE.
SINCE YOU'RE THE ONES WHO ARE DOOMED.
Ah ha ha
EVERY-BODY'S GOING TO DIE!
THEY'RE ALL GOING TO BE HUNTED DOWN, RIDICULED, STEPPED ON, AND RIPPED APART!
ha ha ha!
YOU'LL BE SQUASHED LIKE A BUG WHILE YOU WONDER, "WHY ME?"
ILYRIA...?
THAT'LL SHOW YOU ...
I GOT SCARED.
MY BRILLIANT DAUGHTER, THE APPLE OF MY EYE...
...STARTED TO SEEM LIKE A MONSTER TO ME...
...BECAUSE SHE WAS TOO BRIGHT.

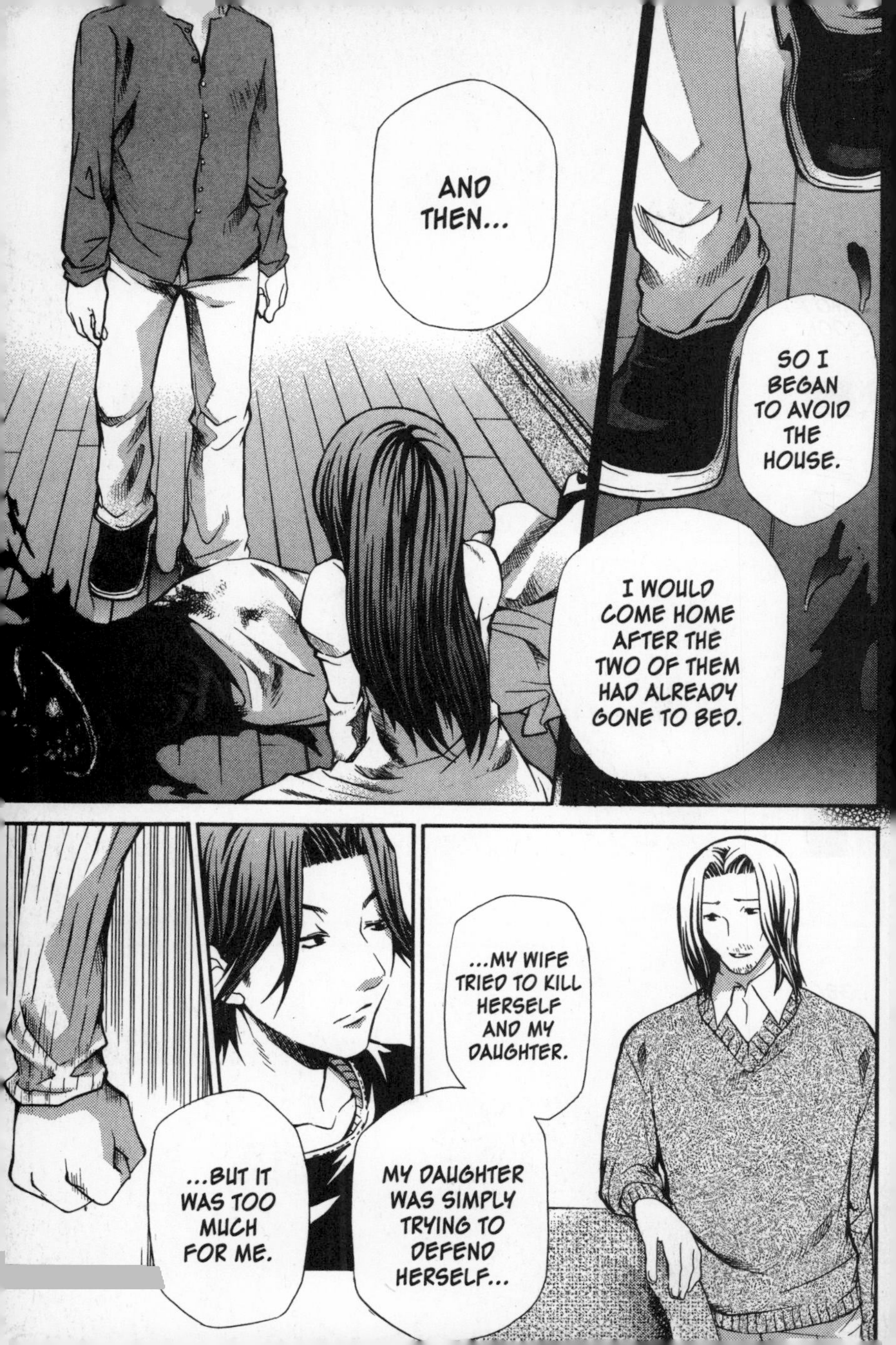
SO I BEGAN TO AVOID THE HOUSE.
I WOULD COME HOME AFTER THE TWO OF THEM HAD ALREADY GONE TO BED.
AND THEN...
...MY WIFE TRIED TO KILL HERSELF AND MY DAUGHTER.
MY DAUGHTER WAS SIMPLY TRYING TO DEFEND HERSELF...
...BUT IT WAS TOO MUCH FOR ME.

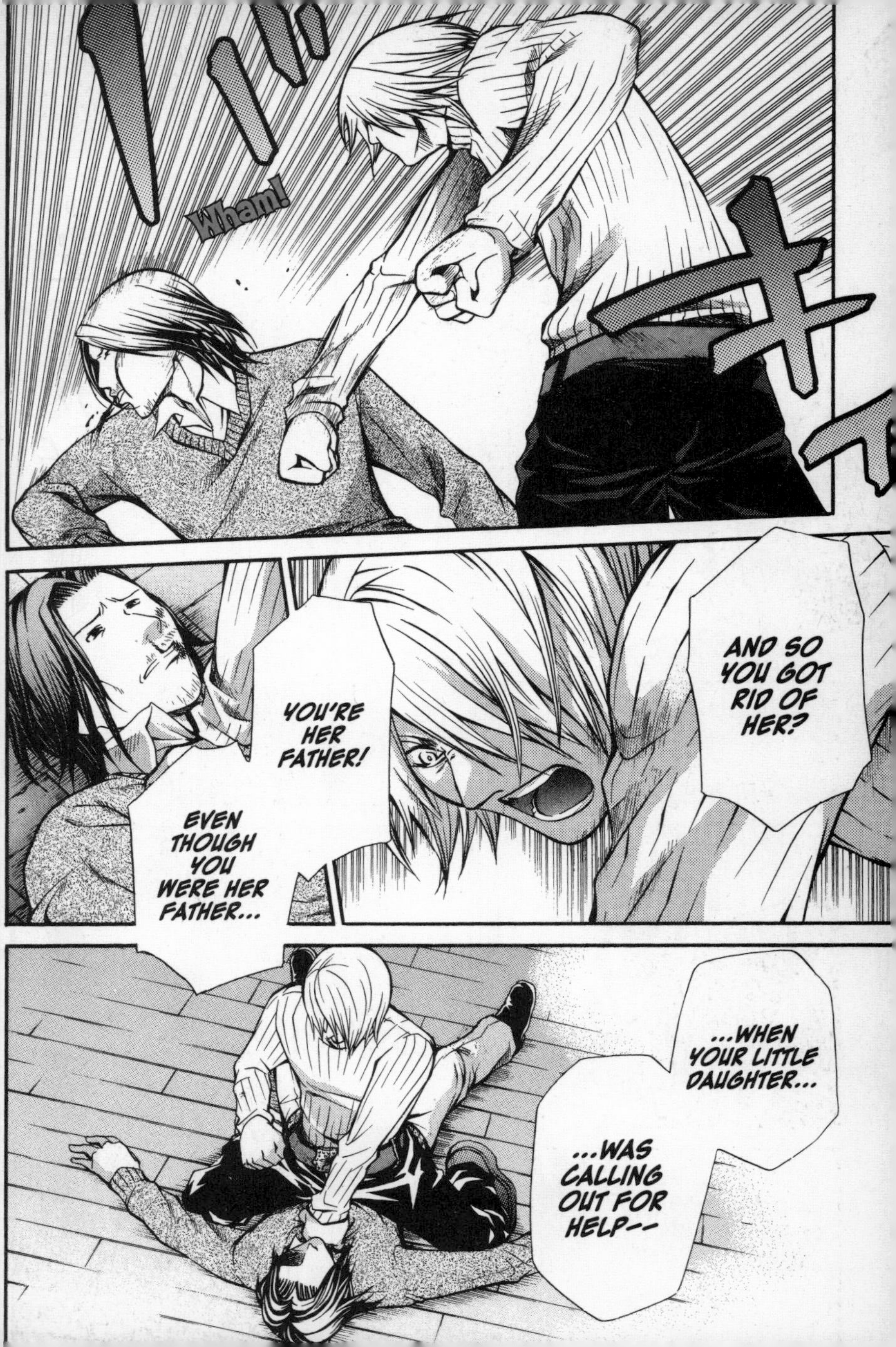
Wham!
AND SO YOU GOT RID OF HER?
YOU'RE HER FATHER!
EVEN THOUGH YOU WERE HER FATHER...
...WHEN YOUR LITTLE DAUGHTER...
...WAS CALLING OUT FOR HELP--

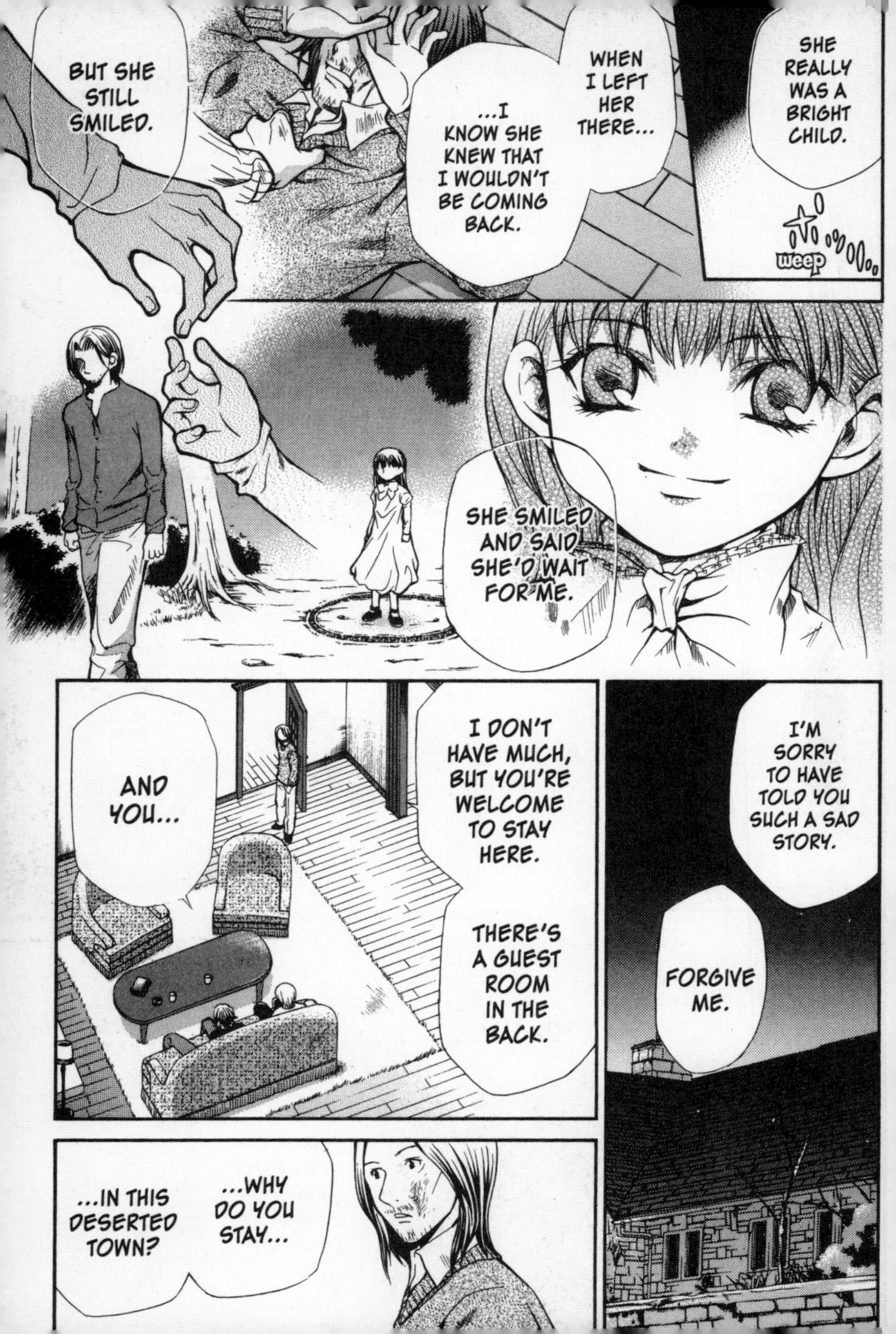
SHE REALLY WAS A BRIGHT CHILD.
weep
WHEN I LEFT HER THERE...
...I KNOW SHE KNEW THAT I WOULDN'T BE COMING BACK.
BUT SHE STILL SMILED.
SHE SMILED AND SAID SHE'D WAIT FOR ME.
I'M SORRY TO HAVE TOLD YOU SUCH A SAD STORY.
FORGIVE ME.
I DON'T HAVE MUCH, BUT YOU'RE WELCOME TO STAY HERE.
THERE'S A GUEST ROOM IN THE BACK.
AND YOU...
...WHY DO YOU STAY...
...IN THIS DESERTED TOWN?

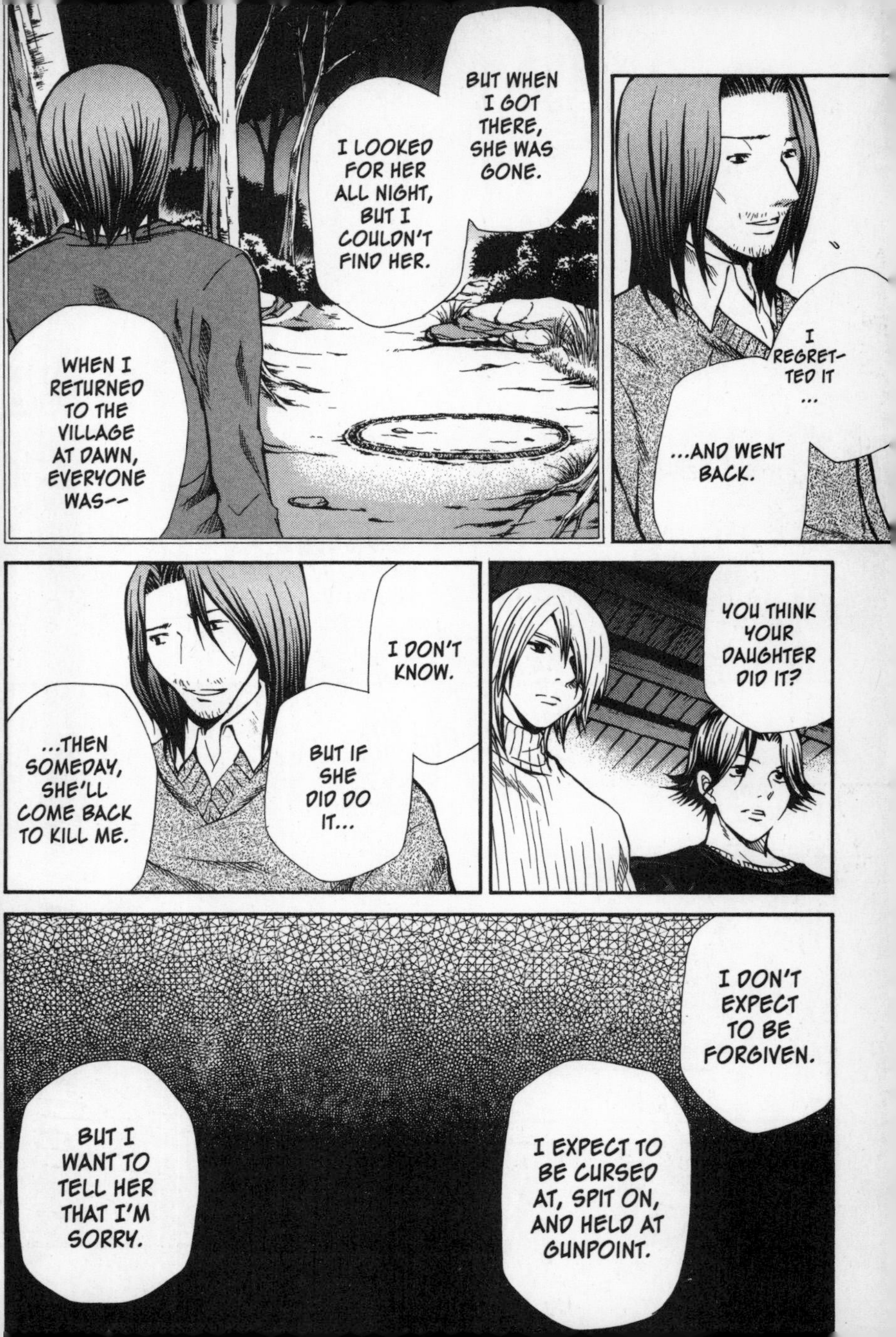
I REGRETTED IT ...
...AND WENT BACK.
BUT WHEN I GOT THERE, SHE WAS GONE.
I LOOKED FOR HER ALL NIGHT, BUT I COULDN'T FIND HER.
WHEN I RETURNED TO THE VILLAGE AT DAWN, EVERYONE WAS--
YOU THINK YOUR DAUGHTER DID IT?
I DON'T KNOW.
BUT IF SHE DID DO IT...
...THEN SOMEDAY, SHE'LL COME BACK TO KILL ME.
I DON'T EXPECT TO BE FORGIVEN.
I EXPECT TO BE CURSED AT, SPIT ON, AND HELD AT GUNPOINT.
BUT I WANT TO TELL HER THAT I'M SORRY.

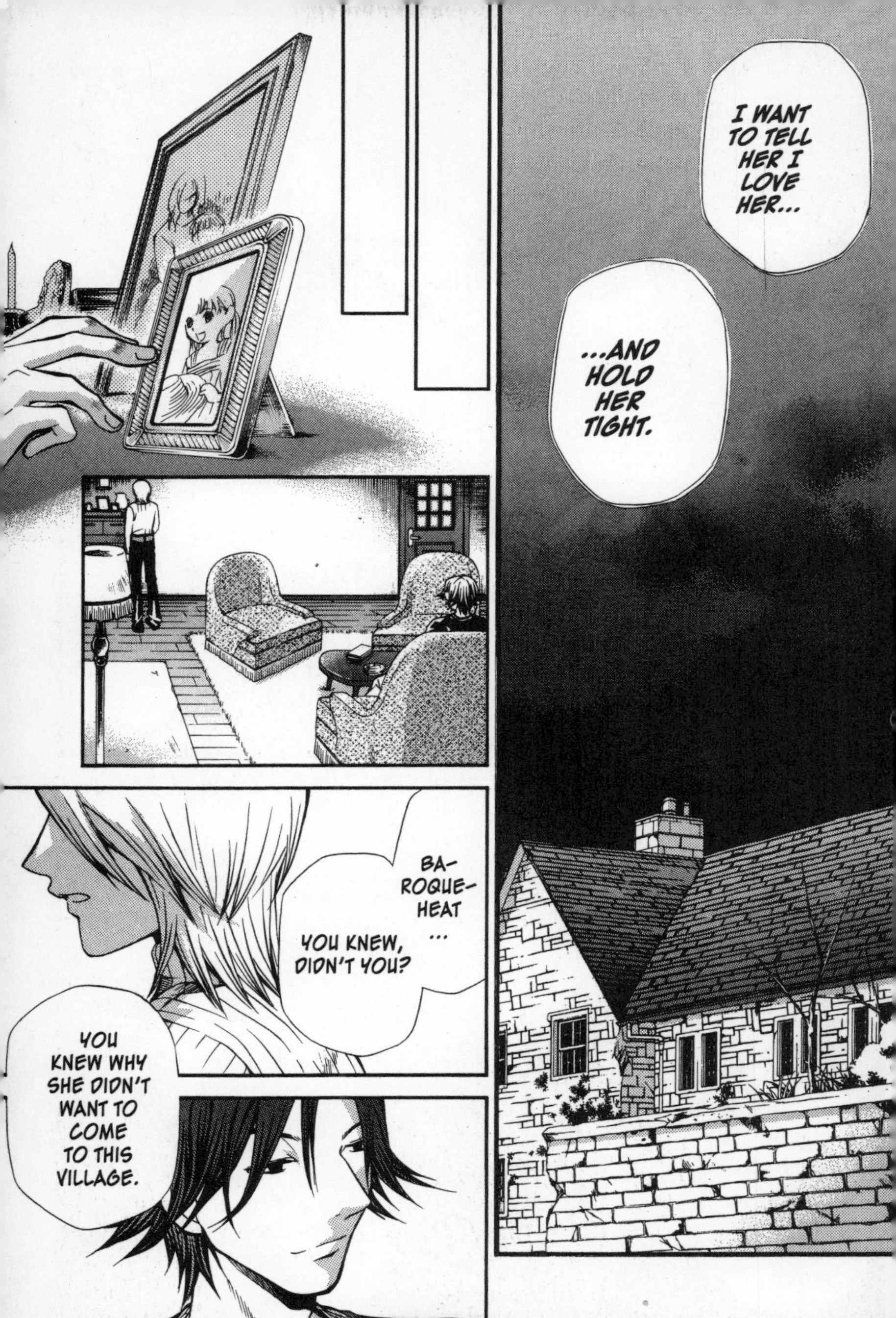
I WANT TO TELL HER I LOVE HER...
...AND HOLD HER TIGHT.
BAROQUE-HEAT...
YOU KNEW, DIDN'T YOU?
YOU KNEW WHY SHE DIDN'T WANT TO COME TO THIS VILLAGE.

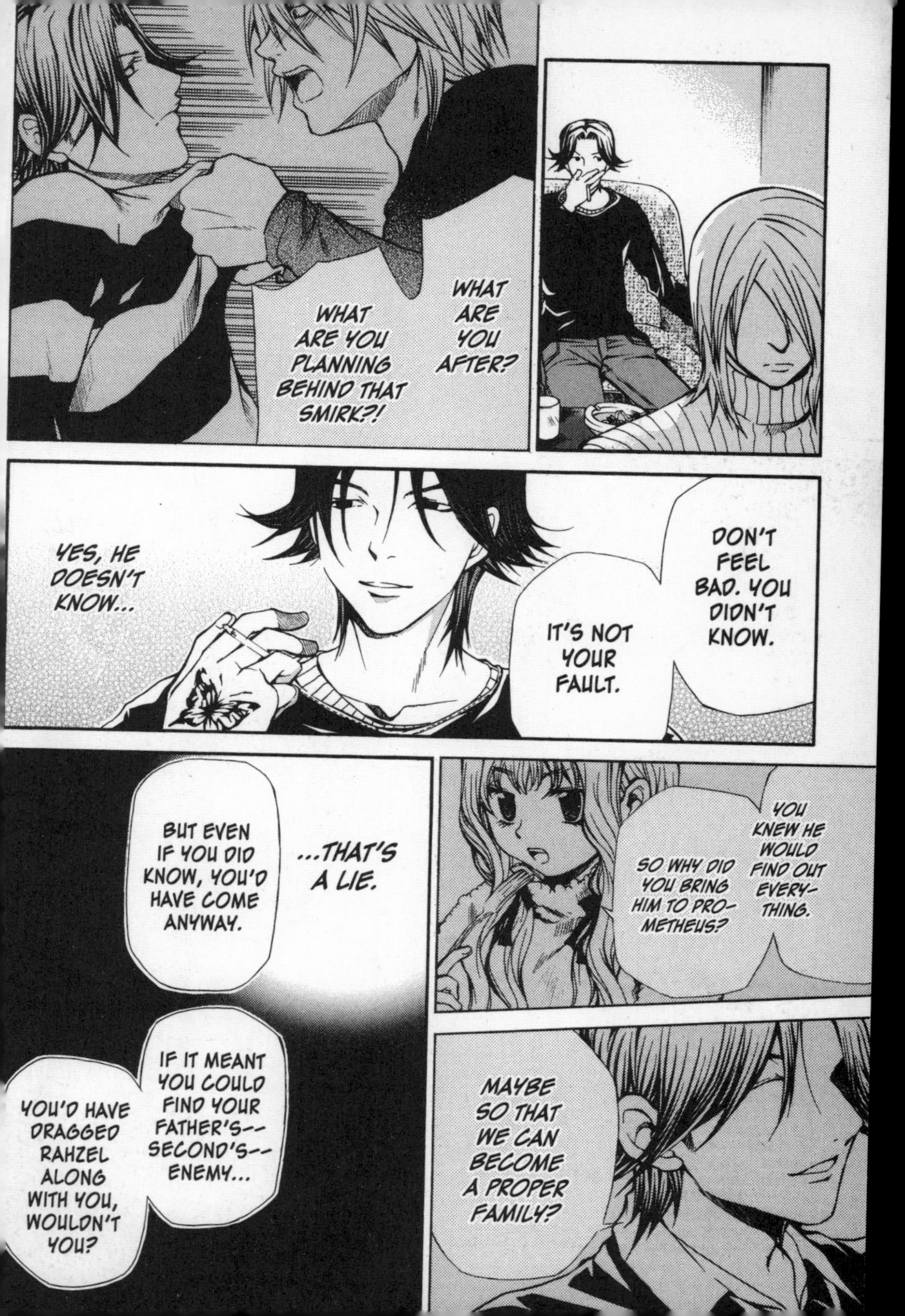
WHAT ARE YOU AFTER?
WHAT ARE YOU PLANNING BEHIND THAT SMIRK?!
DON'T FEEL BAD. YOU DIDN'T KNOW.
IT'S NOT YOUR FAULT.
YES, HE DOESN'T KNOW...
YOU KNEW HE WOULD FIND OUT EVERY-THING.
SO WHY DID YOU BRING HIM TO PRO-METHEUS?
MAYBE SO THAT WE CAN BECOME A PROPER FAMILY?
...THAT'S A LIE.
BUT EVEN IF YOU DID KNOW, YOU'D HAVE COME ANYWAY.
IF IT MEANT YOU COULD FIND YOUR FATHER'S--SECOND'S--ENEMY...
YOU'D HAVE DRAGGED RAHZEL ALONG WITH YOU, WOULDN'T YOU?

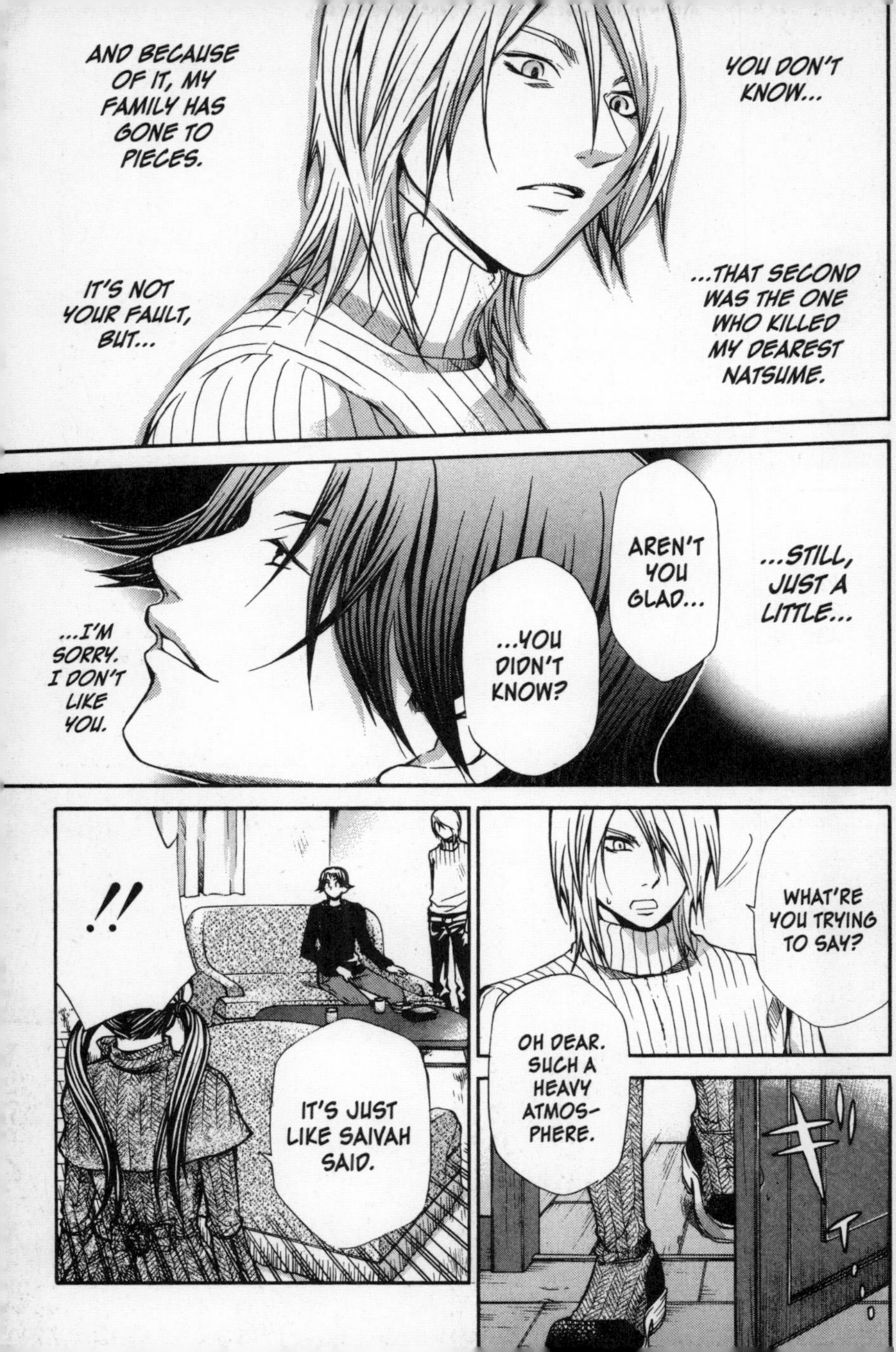
YOU DON'T KNOW...
...THAT SECOND WAS THE ONE WHO KILLED MY DEAREST NATSUME.
AND BECAUSE OF IT, MY FAMILY HAS GONE TO PIECES.
IT'S NOT YOUR FAULT, BUT...
...STILL, JUST A LITTLE...
AREN'T YOU GLAD...
...YOU DIDN'T KNOW?
...I'M SORRY. I DON'T LIKE YOU.
WHAT'RE YOU TRYING TO SAY?
OH DEAR. SUCH A HEAVY ATMOSPHERE.
!!
IT'S JUST LIKE SAIVAH SAID.

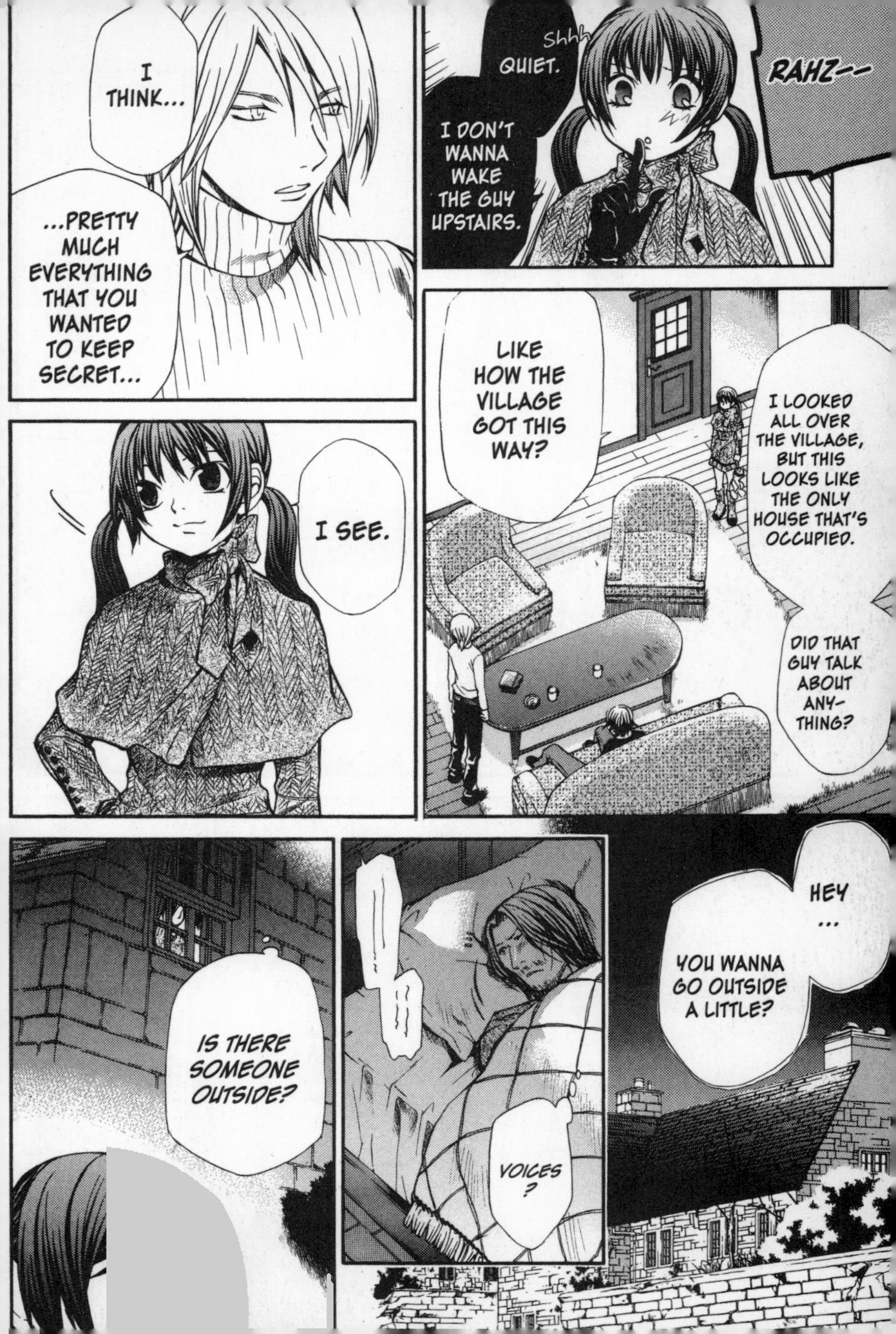
RAHZ--
Shhh
QUIET.
I DON'T WANNA WAKE THE GUY UPSTAIRS.
I THINK...
...PRETTY MUCH EVERYTHING THAT YOU WANTED TO KEEP SECRET...
I LOOKED ALL OVER THE VILLAGE, BUT THIS LOOKS LIKE THE ONLY HOUSE THAT'S OCCUPIED.
DID THAT GUY TALK ABOUT ANYTHING?
LIKE HOW THE VILLAGE GOT THIS WAY?
I SEE.
HEY ...
YOU WANNA GO OUTSIDE A LITTLE?
VOICES ?
IS THERE SOMEONE OUTSIDE?

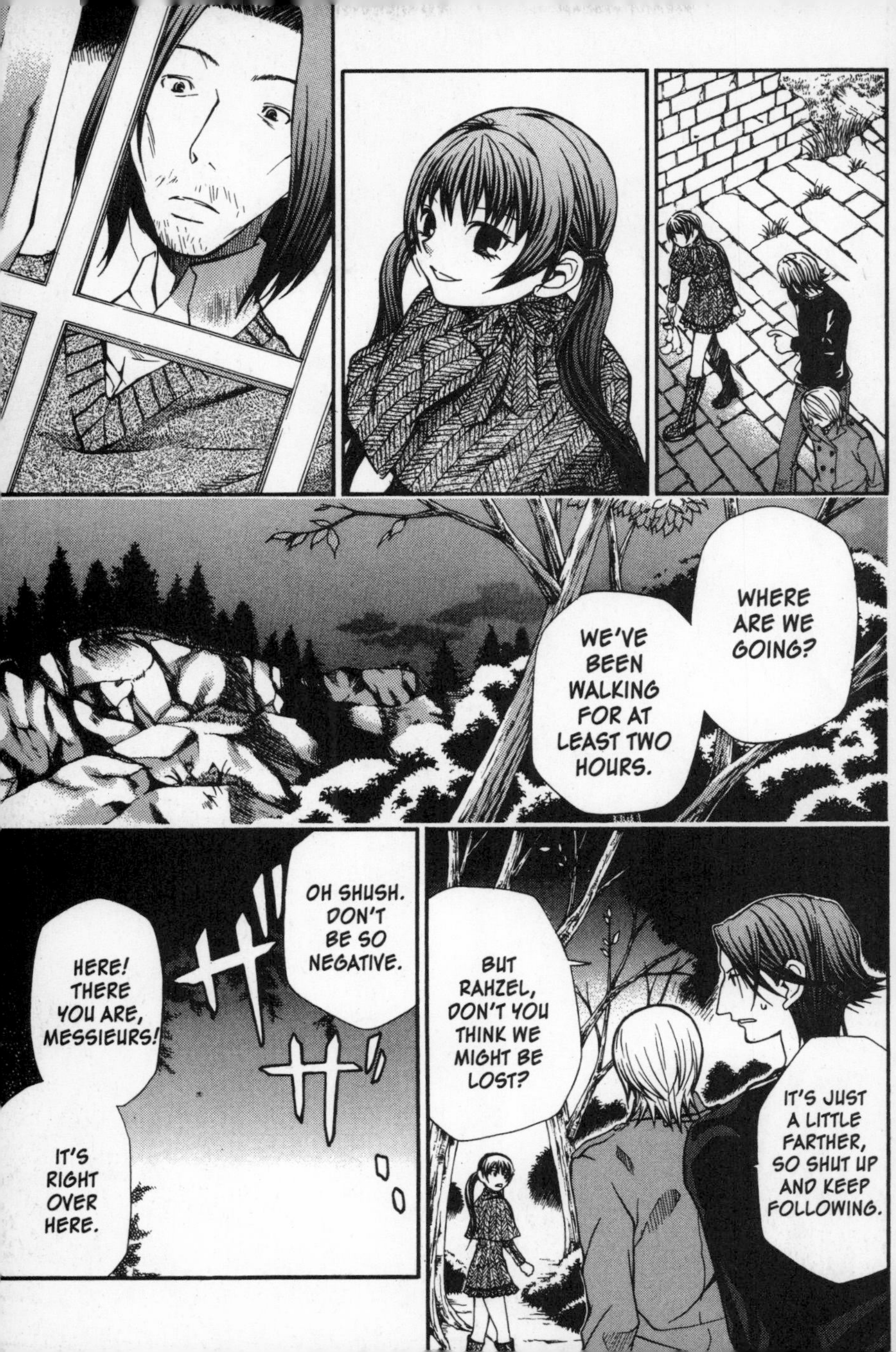
WHERE ARE WE GOING?
WE'VE BEEN WALKING FOR AT LEAST TWO HOURS.
BUT RAHZEL, DON'T YOU THINK WE MIGHT BE LOST?
IT'S JUST A LITTLE FARTHER, SO SHUT UP AND KEEP FOLLOWING.
OH SHUSH. DON'T BE SO NEGATIVE.
HERE! THERE YOU ARE, MESSIEURS!
IT'S RIGHT OVER HERE.

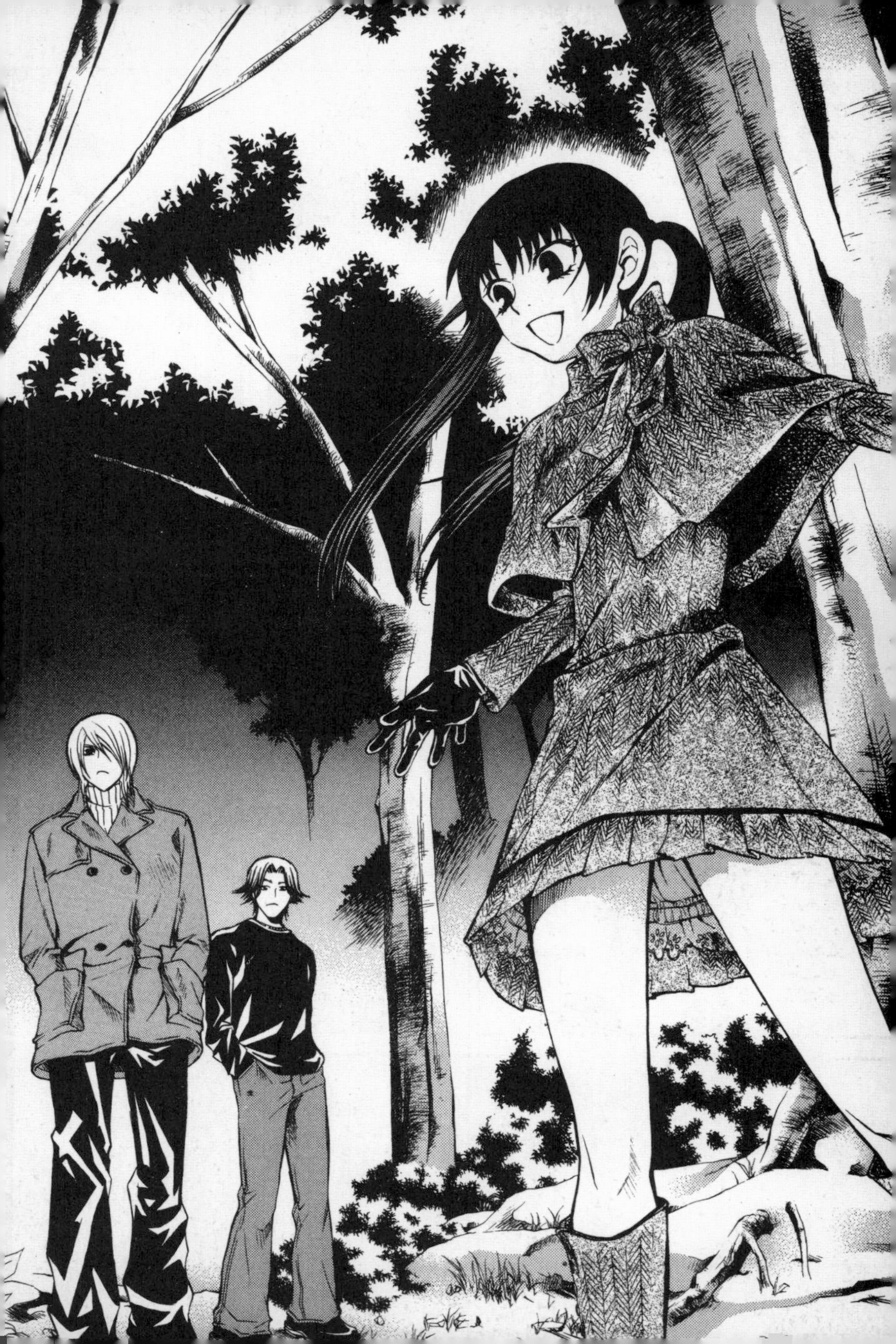

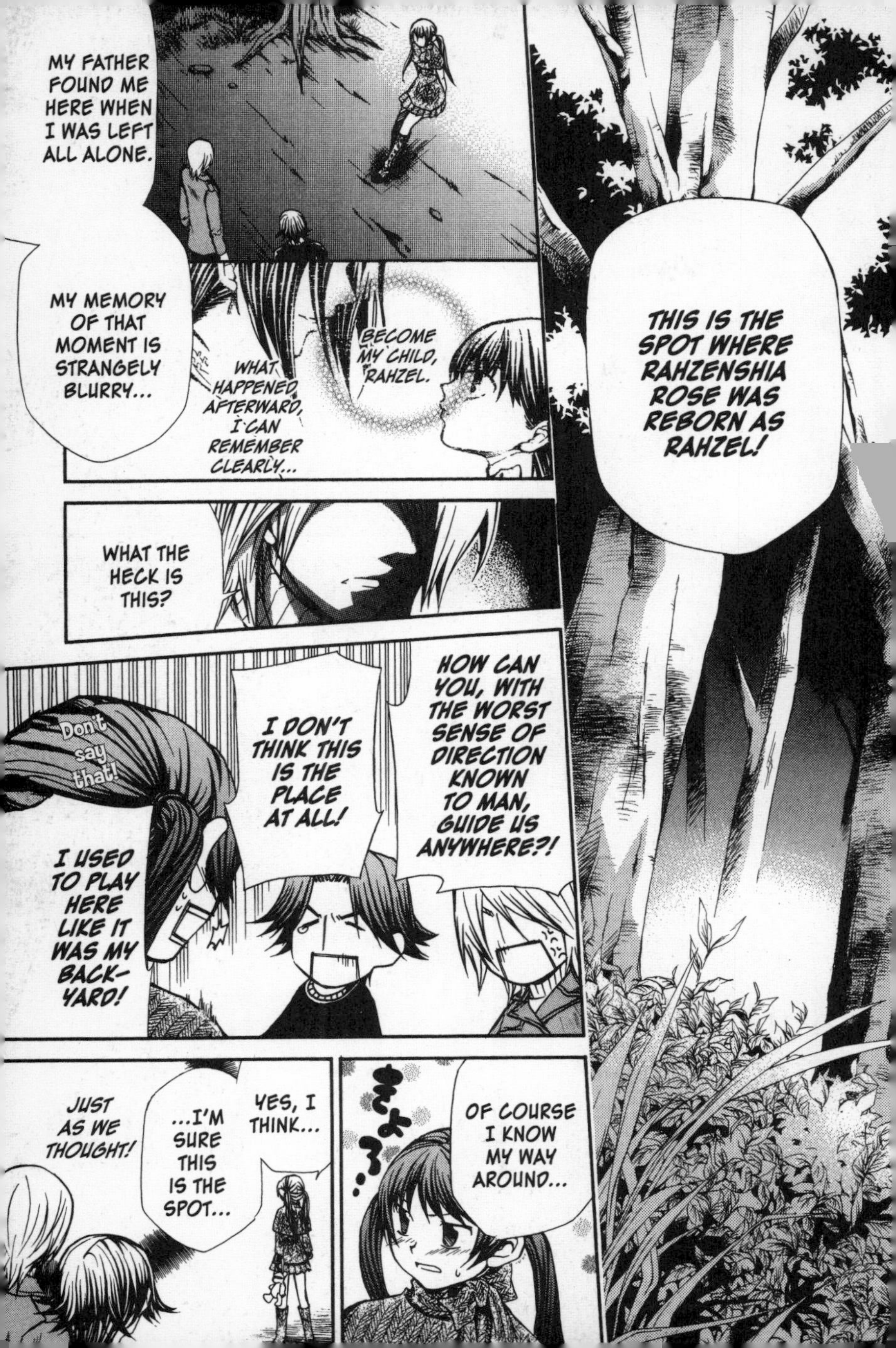
THIS IS THE SPOT WHERE RAHZENSHIA ROSE WAS REBORN AS RAHZEL!
MY FATHER FOUND ME HERE WHEN I WAS LEFT ALL ALONE.
BECOME MY CHILD, RAHZEL.
WHAT HAPPENED AFTERWARD, I CAN REMEMBER CLEARLY...
MY MEMORY OF THAT MOMENT IS STRANGELY BLURRY...
WHAT THE HECK IS THIS?
HOW CAN YOU, WITH THE WORST SENSE OF DIRECTION KNOWN TO MAN, GUIDE US ANYWHERE?!
I DON'T THINK THIS IS THE PLACE AT ALL!
Don't say that!
I USED TO PLAY HERE LIKE IT WAS MY BACK-YARD!
OF COURSE I KNOW MY WAY AROUND...
きょろ...
YES, I THINK...
...I'M SURE THIS IS THE SPOT...
JUST AS WE THOUGHT!

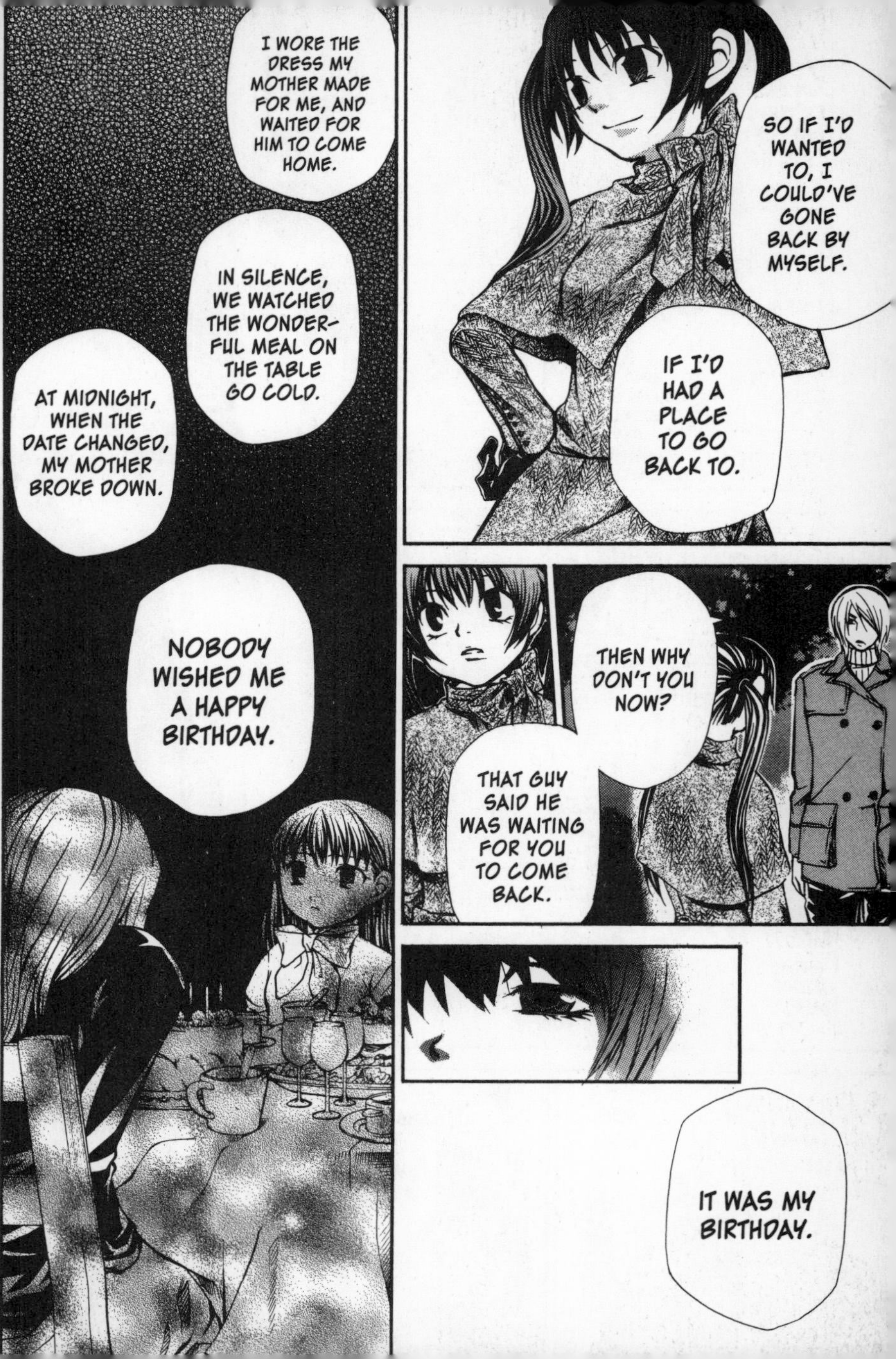
SO IF I'D WANTED TO, I COULD'VE GONE BACK BY MYSELF.
IF I'D HAD A PLACE TO GO BACK TO.
THEN WHY DON'T YOU NOW?
THAT GUY SAID HE WAS WAITING FOR YOU TO COME BACK.
IT WAS MY BIRTHDAY.
I WORE THE DRESS MY MOTHER MADE FOR ME, AND WAITED FOR HIM TO COME HOME.
IN SILENCE, WE WATCHED THE WONDER-FUL MEAL ON THE TABLE GO COLD.
AT MIDNIGHT, WHEN THE DATE CHANGED, MY MOTHER BROKE DOWN.
NOBODY WISHED ME A HAPPY BIRTHDAY.

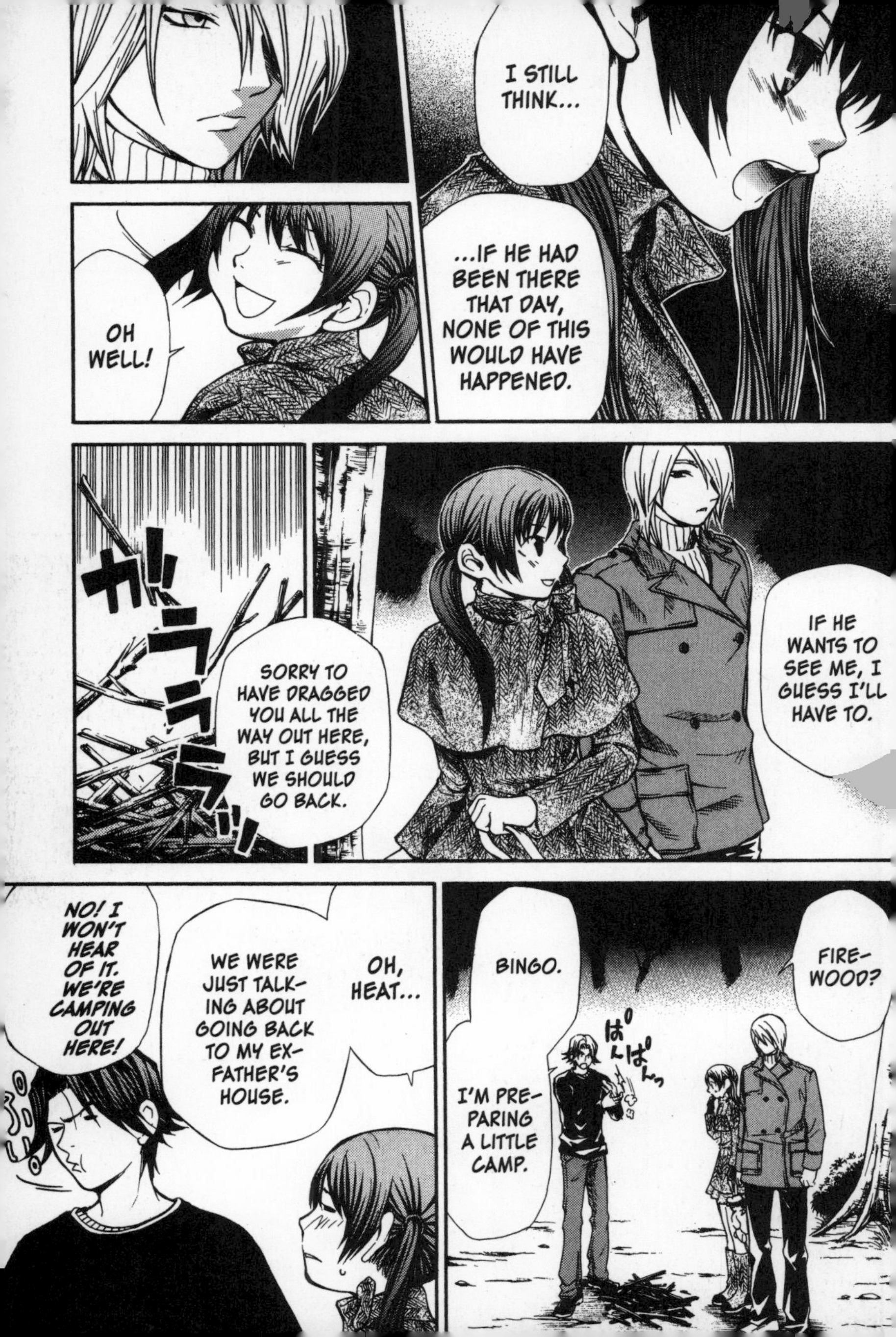
I STILL THINK...
...IF HE HAD BEEN THERE THAT DAY, NONE OF THIS WOULD HAVE HAPPENED.
OH WELL!
IF HE WANTS TO SEE ME, I GUESS I'LL HAVE TO.
SORRY TO HAVE DRAGGED YOU ALL THE WAY OUT HERE, BUT I GUESS WE SHOULD GO BACK.
FIRE-WOOD?
BINGO.
I'M PRE-PARING A LITTLE CAMP.
ぱんぱんっ
OH, HEAT...
WE WERE JUST TALK-ING ABOUT GOING BACK TO MY EX-FATHER'S HOUSE.
NO! I WON'T HEAR OF IT. WE'RE CAMPING OUT HERE!

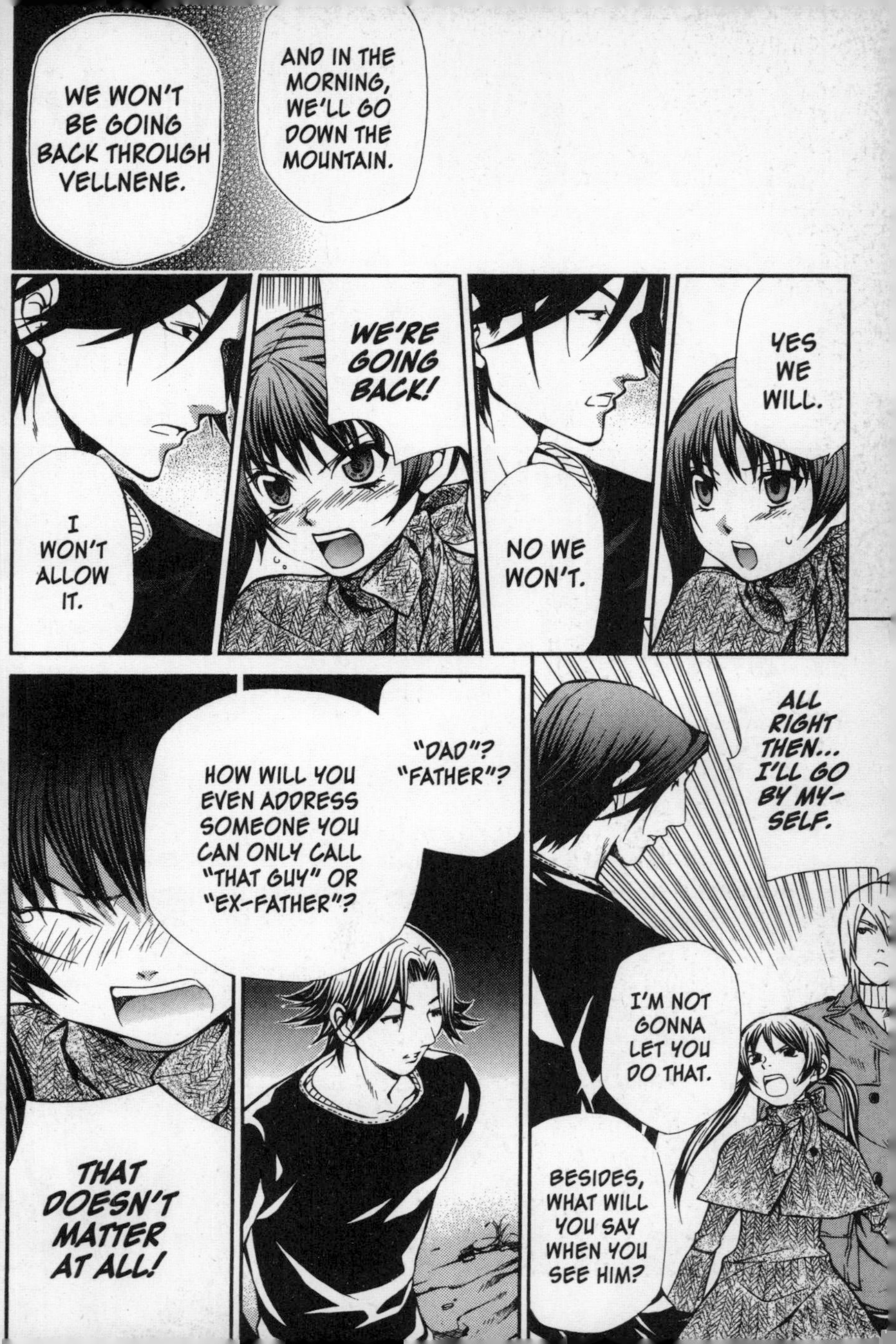
AND IN THE MORNING, WE'LL GO DOWN THE MOUNTAIN.
WE WON'T BE GOING BACK THROUGH VELLNENE.
YES WE WILL.
NO WE WON'T.
WE'RE GOING BACK!
I WON'T ALLOW IT.
ALL RIGHT THEN... I'LL GO BY MY-SELF.
I'M NOT GONNA LET YOU DO THAT.
BESIDES, WHAT WILL YOU SAY WHEN YOU SEE HIM?
"DAD"? "FATHER"?
HOW WILL YOU EVEN ADDRESS SOMEONE YOU CAN ONLY CALL "THAT GUY" OR "EX-FATHER"?
THAT DOESN'T MATTER AT ALL!

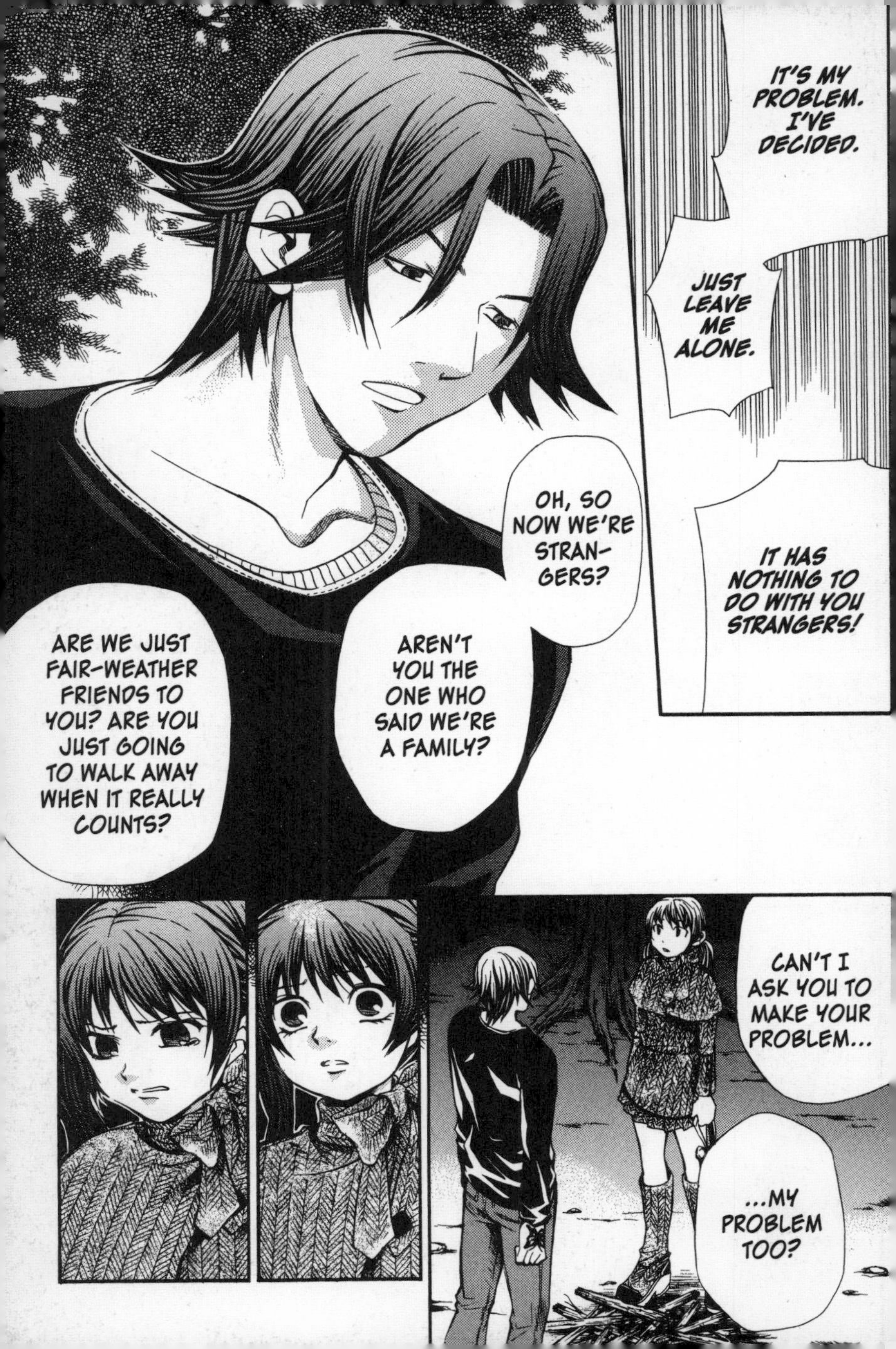
IT'S MY PROBLEM. I'VE DECIDED.
JUST LEAVE ME ALONE.
IT HAS NOTHING TO DO WITH YOU STRANGERS!
OH, SO NOW WE'RE STRAN-GERS?
AREN'T YOU THE ONE WHO SAID WE'RE A FAMILY?
ARE WE JUST FAIR-WEATHER FRIENDS TO YOU? ARE YOU JUST GOING TO WALK AWAY WHEN IT REALLY COUNTS?
CAN'T I ASK YOU TO MAKE YOUR PROBLEM...
...MY PROBLEM TOO?

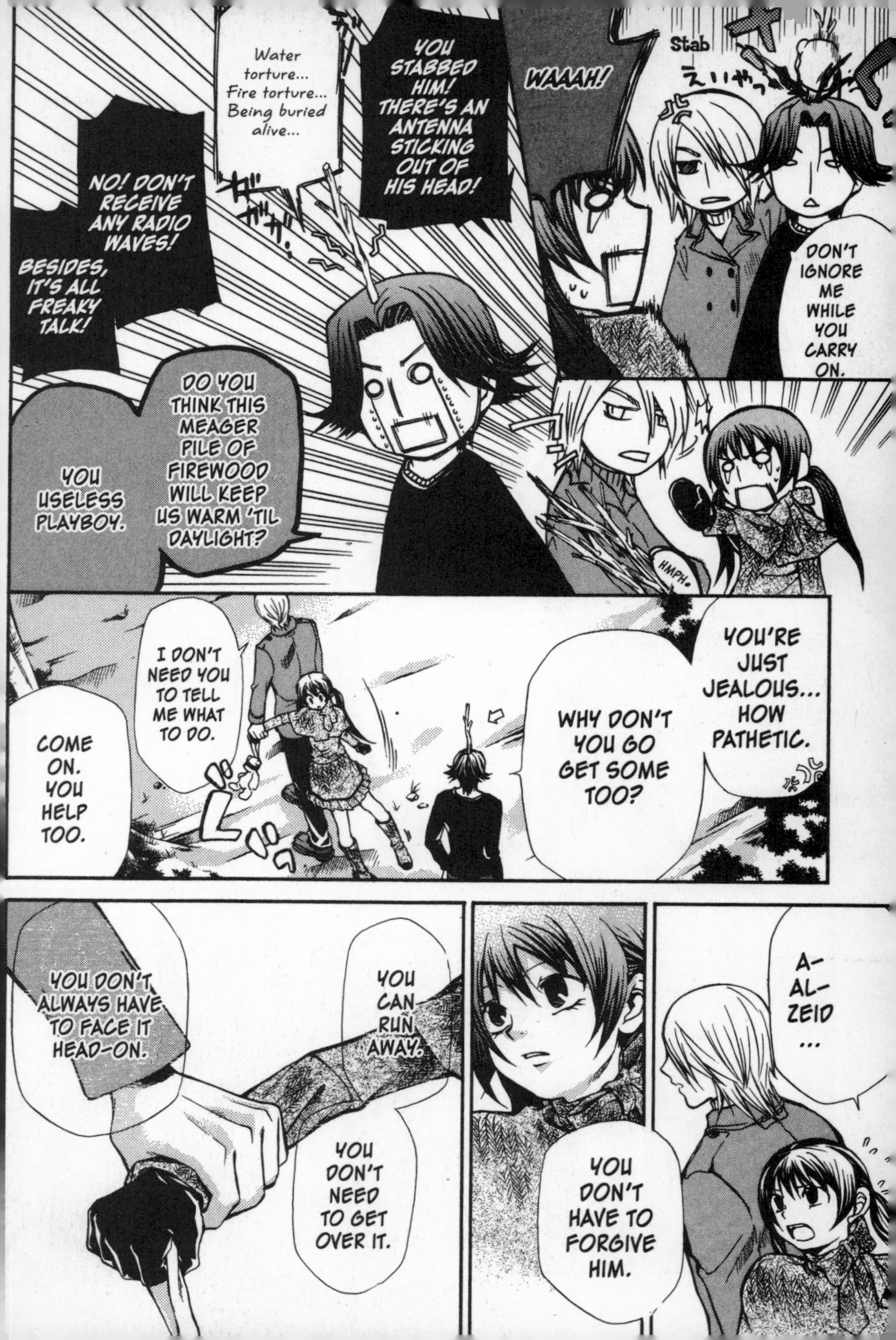

Stab
えいやっ
WAAAH!
YOU STABBED HIM! THERE'S AN ANTENNA STICKING OUT OF HIS HEAD!
Water torture... Fire torture... Being buried alive...
NO! DON'T RECEIVE ANY RADIO WAVES!
BESIDES, IT'S ALL FREAKY TALK!
DON'T IGNORE ME WHILE YOU CARRY ON.
HMPH.
DO YOU THINK THIS MEAGER PILE OF FIREWOOD WILL KEEP US WARM 'TIL DAYLIGHT?
YOU USELESS PLAYBOY.
YOU'RE JUST JEALOUS... HOW PATHETIC.
WHY DON'T YOU GO GET SOME TOO?
I DON'T NEED YOU TO TELL ME WHAT TO DO.
COME ON. YOU HELP TOO.
A-AL-ZEID...
YOU DON'T HAVE TO FORGIVE HIM.
YOU DON'T NEED TO GET OVER IT.
YOU CAN RUN AWAY.
YOU DON'T ALWAYS HAVE TO FACE IT HEAD-ON.

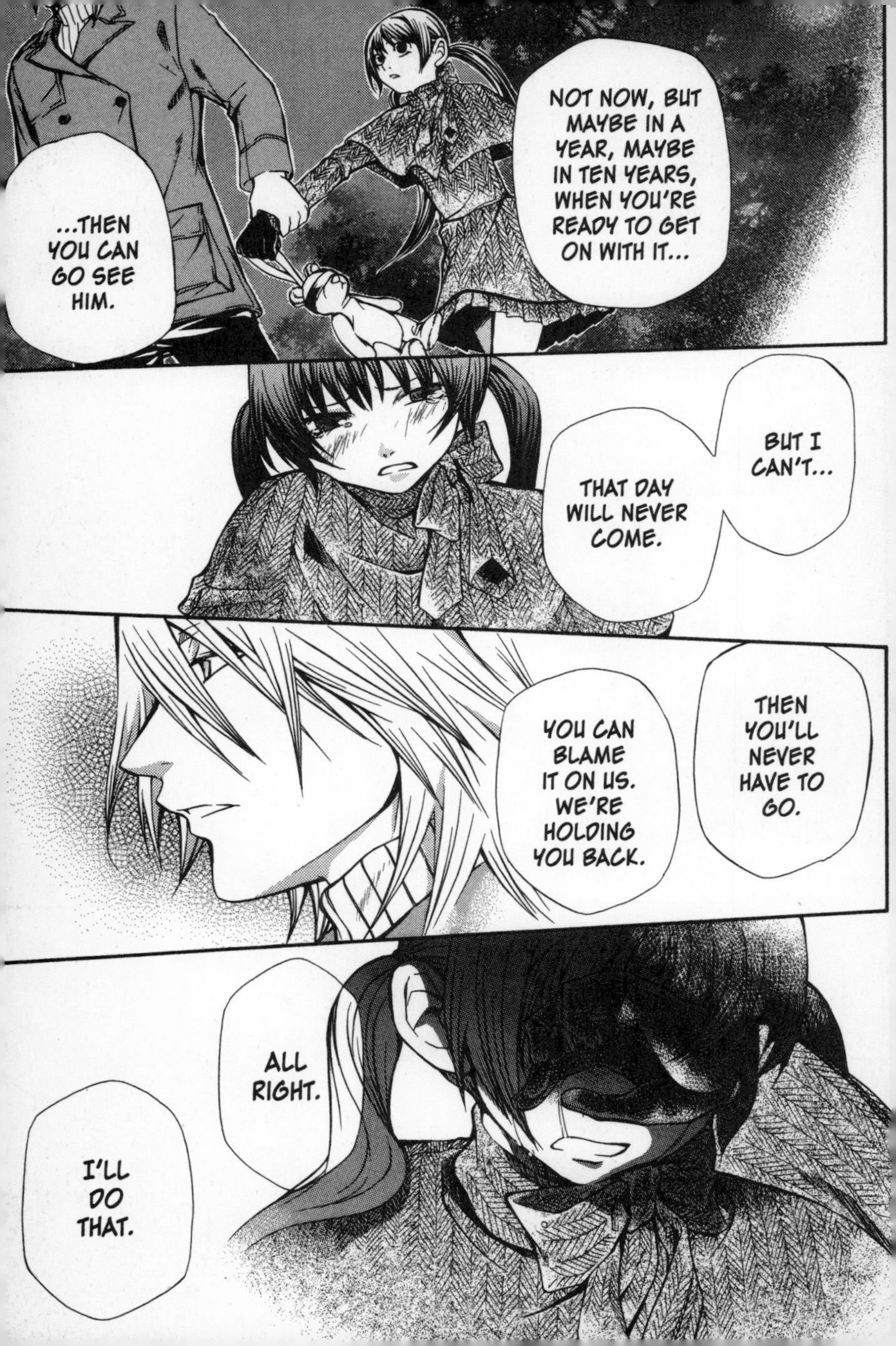
NOT NOW, BUT MAYBE IN A YEAR, MAYBE IN TEN YEARS, WHEN YOU'RE READY TO GET ON WITH IT...
...THEN YOU CAN GO SEE HIM.
BUT I CAN'T...
THAT DAY WILL NEVER COME.
THEN YOU'LL NEVER HAVE TO GO.
YOU CAN BLAME IT ON US. WE'RE HOLDING YOU BACK.
ALL RIGHT.
I'LL DO THAT.

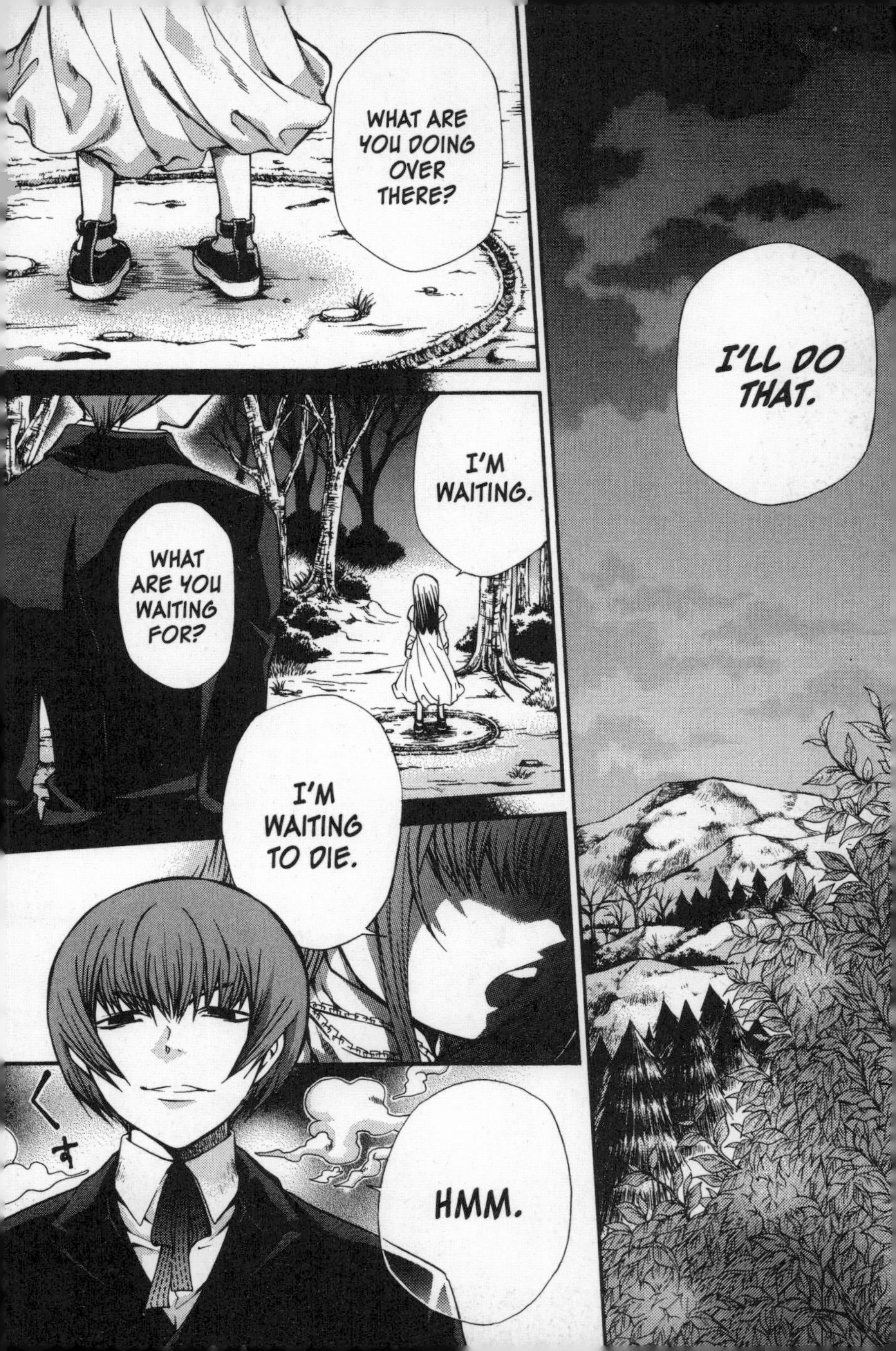
I'LL DO THAT.
WHAT ARE YOU DOING OVER THERE?
I'M WAITING.
WHAT ARE YOU WAITING FOR?
I'M WAITING TO DIE.
HMM.
くす

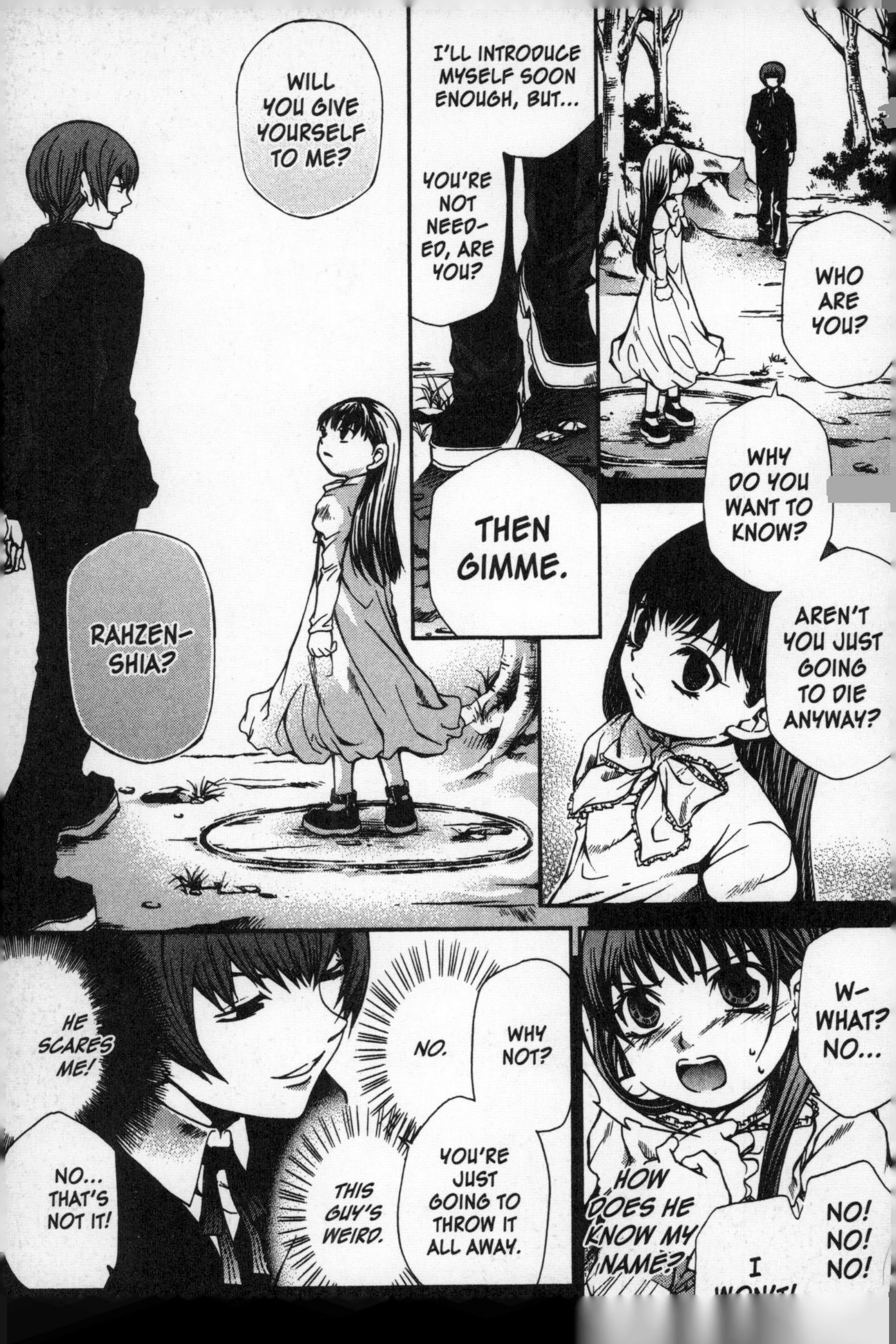
WHO ARE YOU?
WHY DO YOU WANT TO KNOW?
AREN'T YOU JUST GOING TO DIE ANYWAY?
I'LL INTRODUCE MYSELF SOON ENOUGH, BUT...
YOU'RE NOT NEEDED, ARE YOU?
THEN GIMME.
WILL YOU GIVE YOURSELF TO ME?
RAHZEN-SHIA?
W- WHAT? NO...
HOW DOES HE KNOW MY NAME?
NO! NO! NO!
I
WHY NOT?
NO.
YOU'RE JUST GOING TO THROW IT ALL AWAY.
THIS GUY'S WEIRD.
HE SCARES ME!
NO... THAT'S NOT IT!

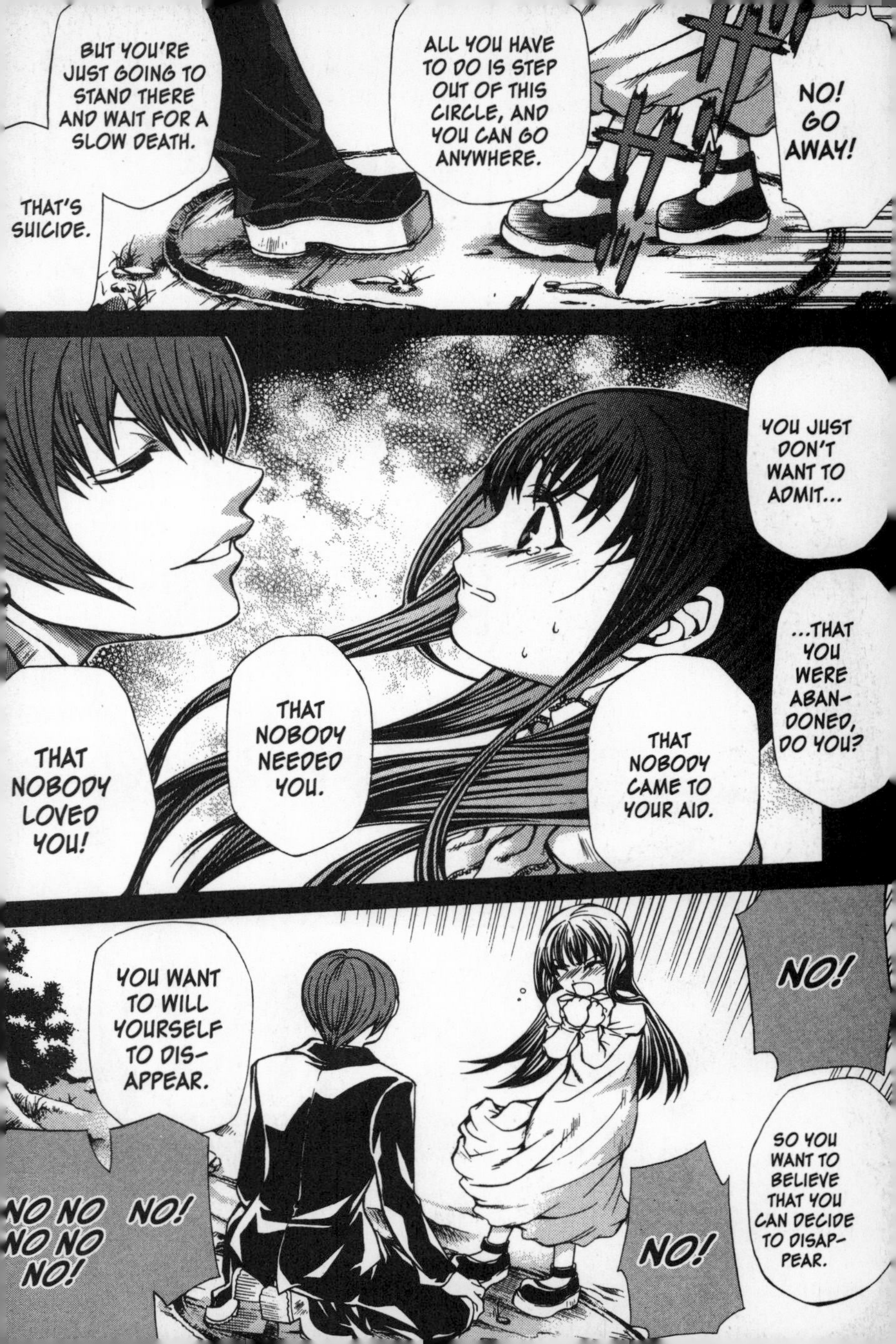
NO! GO AWAY!
ALL YOU HAVE TO DO IS STEP OUT OF THIS CIRCLE, AND YOU CAN GO ANYWHERE.
BUT YOU'RE JUST GOING TO STAND THERE AND WAIT FOR A SLOW DEATH.
THAT'S SUICIDE.
YOU JUST DON'T WANT TO ADMIT...
...THAT YOU WERE ABAN-DONED, DO YOU?
THAT NOBODY CAME TO YOUR AID.
THAT NOBODY NEEDED YOU.
THAT NOBODY LOVED YOU!
NO!
YOU WANT TO WILL YOURSELF TO DIS-APPEAR.
SO YOU WANT TO BELIEVE THAT YOU CAN DECIDE TO DISAP-PEAR.
NO!
NO!
NO NO NO NO NO!

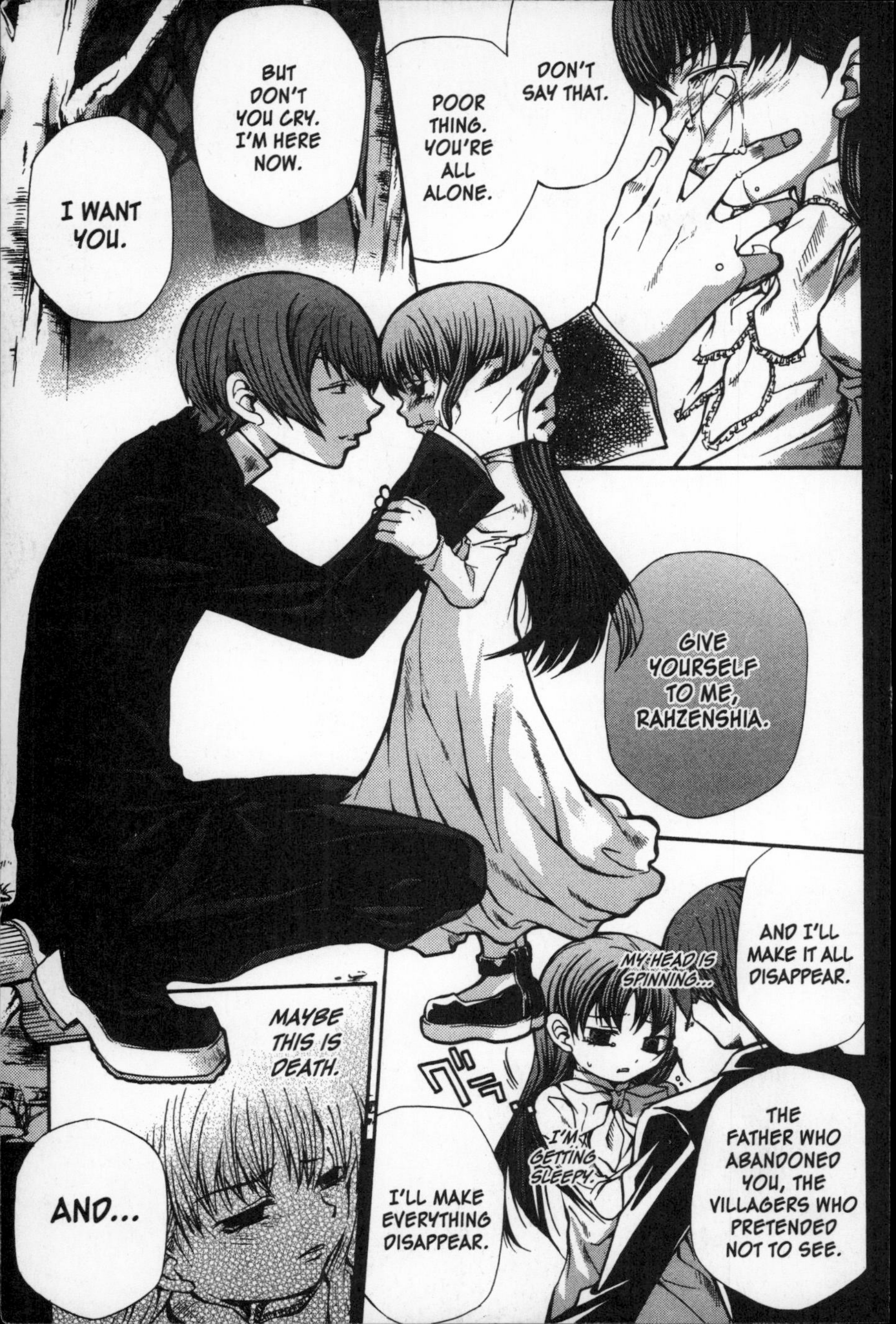
DON'T SAY THAT.
POOR THING. YOU'RE ALL ALONE.
BUT DON'T YOU CRY. I'M HERE NOW.
I WANT YOU.
GIVE YOURSELF TO ME, RAHZENSHIA.
AND I'LL MAKE IT ALL DISAPPEAR.
MY HEAD IS SPINNING...
THE FATHER WHO ABANDONED YOU, THE VILLAGERS WHO PRETENDED NOT TO SEE.
I'M GETTING SLEEPY.
I'LL MAKE EVERYTHING DISAPPEAR.
MAYBE THIS IS DEATH.
AND...

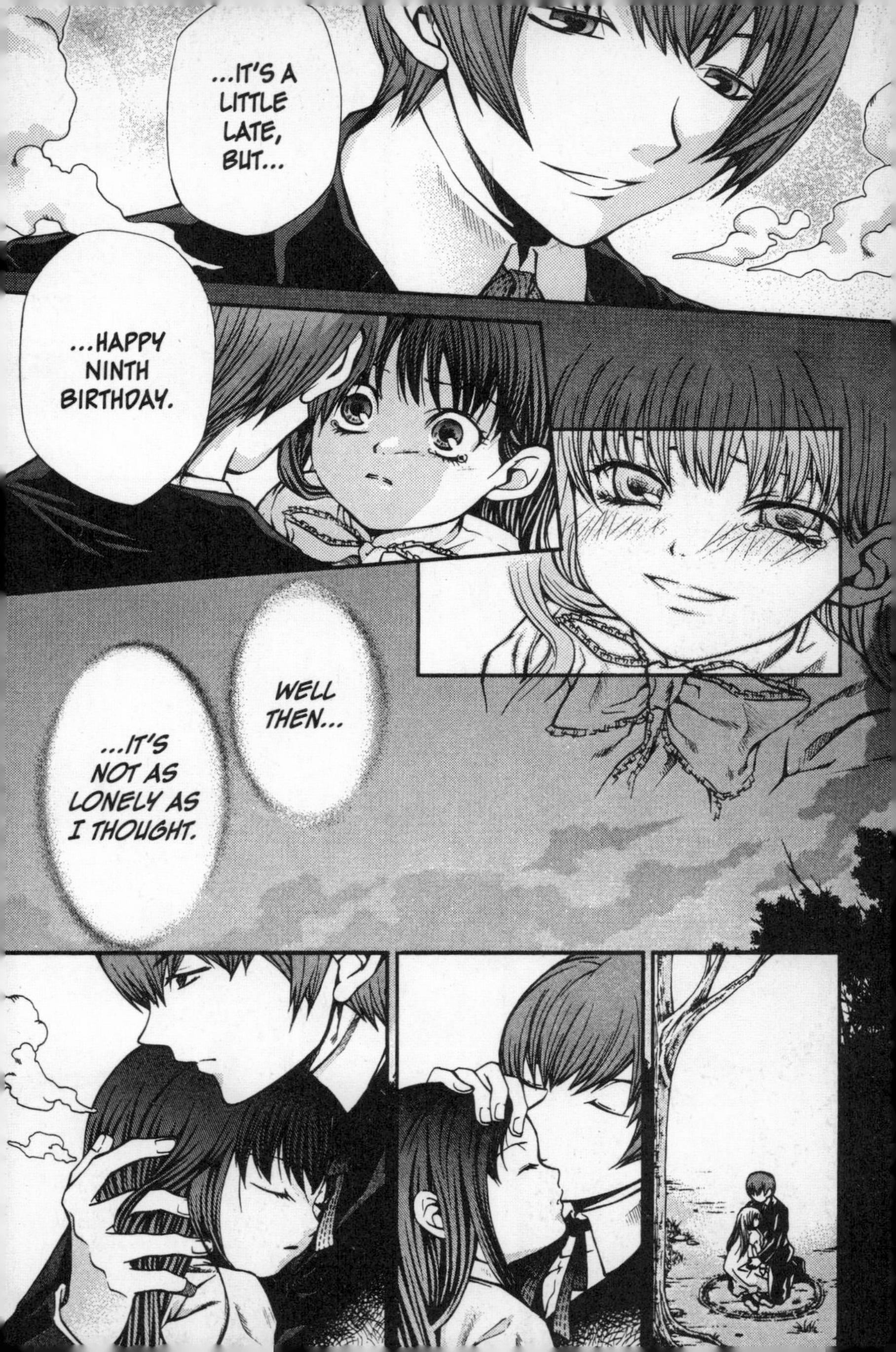
...IT'S A LITTLE LATE, BUT...
...HAPPY NINTH BIRTHDAY.
WELL THEN...
...IT'S NOT AS LONELY AS I THOUGHT.

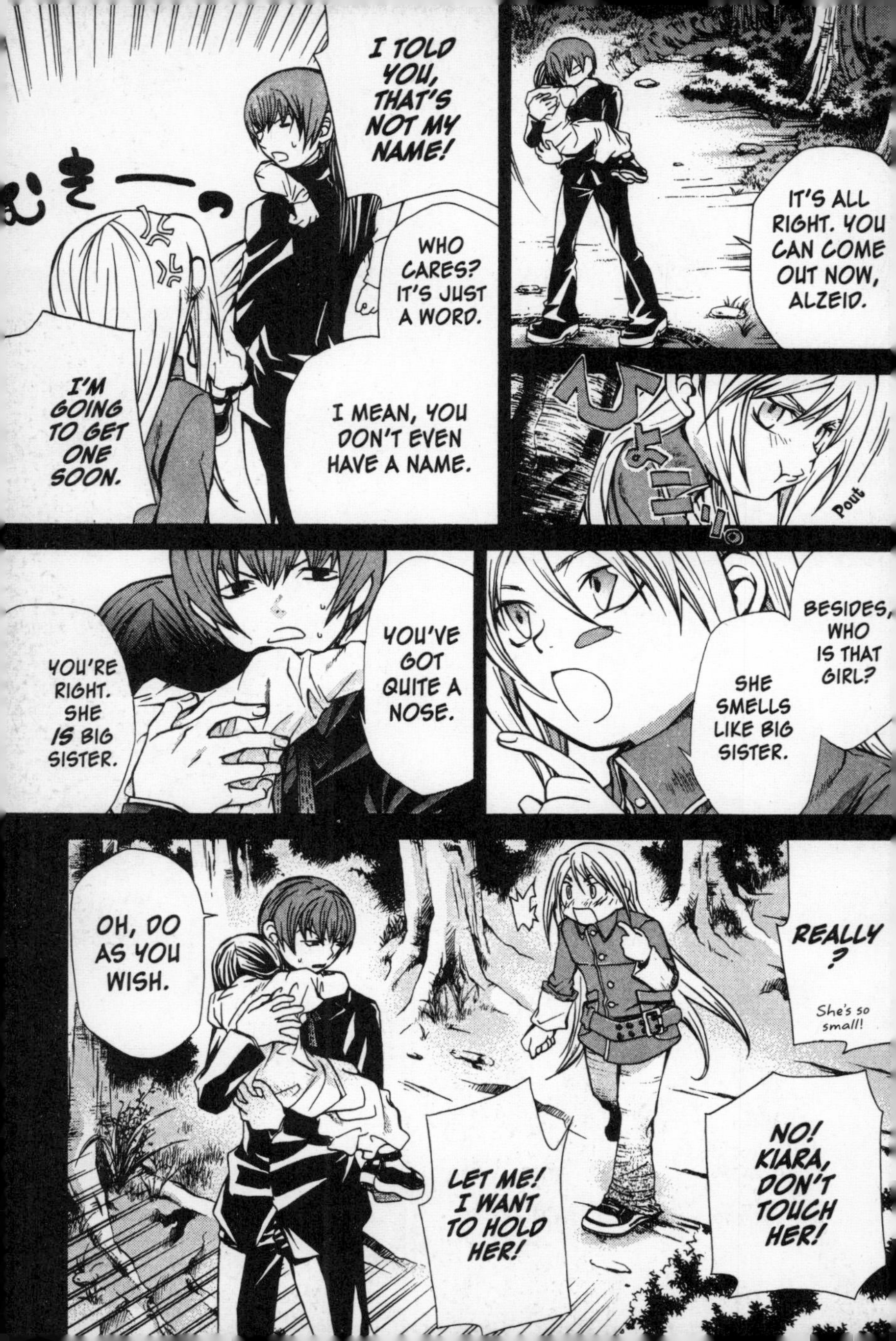
IT'S ALL RIGHT. YOU CAN COME OUT NOW, ALZEID.
Pout
I TOLD YOU, THAT'S NOT MY NAME!
むきーっ
WHO CARES? IT'S JUST A WORD.
I MEAN, YOU DON'T EVEN HAVE A NAME.
I'M GOING TO GET ONE SOON.
BESIDES, WHO IS THAT GIRL?
SHE SMELLS LIKE BIG SISTER.
YOU'VE GOT QUITE A NOSE.
YOU'RE RIGHT. SHE *IS* BIG SISTER.
REALLY?
She's so small!
NO! KIARA, DON'T TOUCH HER!
LET ME! I WANT TO HOLD HER!
OH, DO AS YOU WISH.

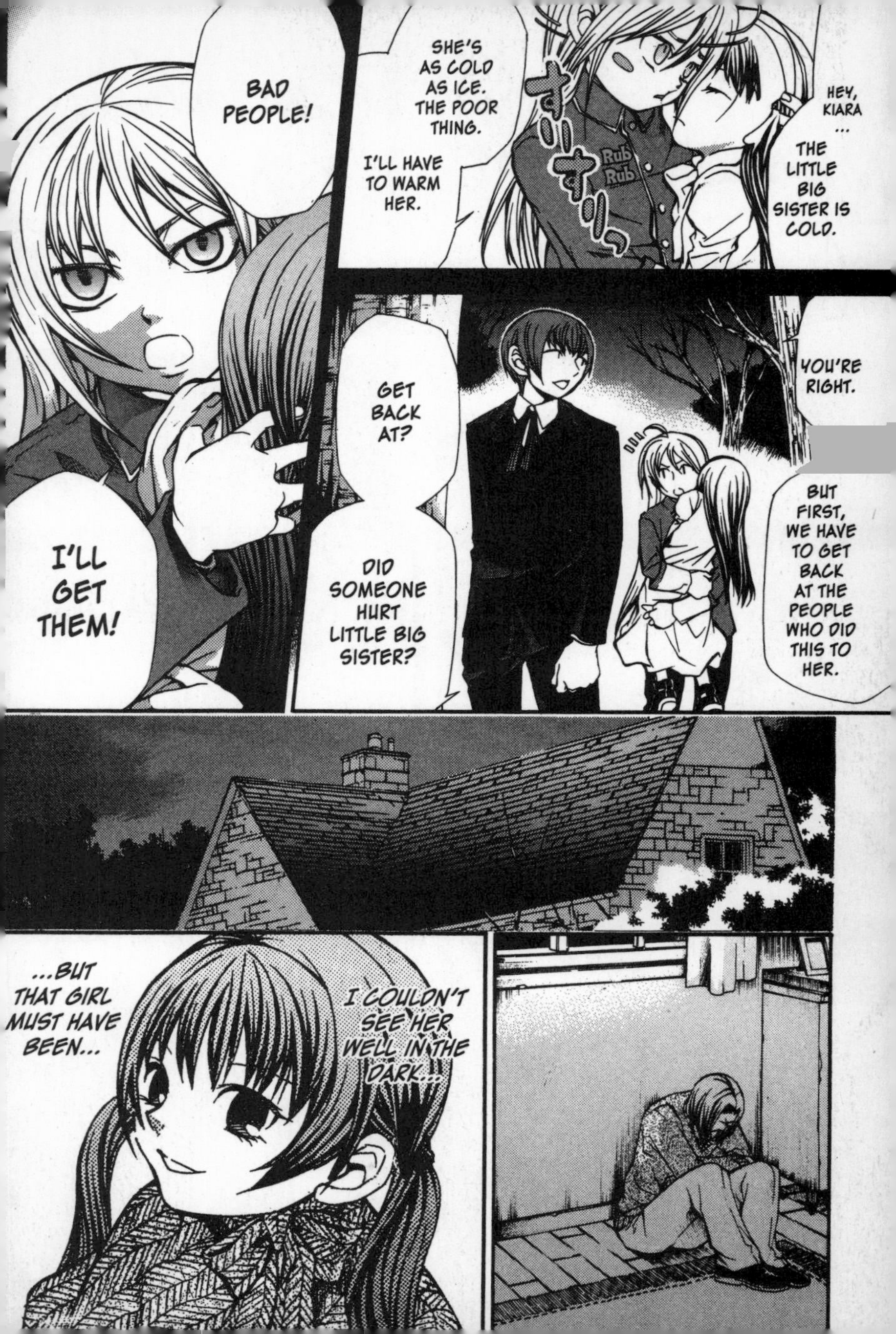
HEY, KIARA...
THE LITTLE BIG SISTER IS COLD.
Rub Rub
SHE'S AS COLD AS ICE. THE POOR THING.
I'LL HAVE TO WARM HER.
YOU'RE RIGHT.
BUT FIRST, WE HAVE TO GET BACK AT THE PEOPLE WHO DID THIS TO HER.
GET BACK AT?
DID SOMEONE HURT LITTLE BIG SISTER?
BAD PEOPLE!
I'LL GET THEM!
I COULDN'T SEE HER WELL IN THE DARK...
...BUT THAT GIRL MUST HAVE BEEN...

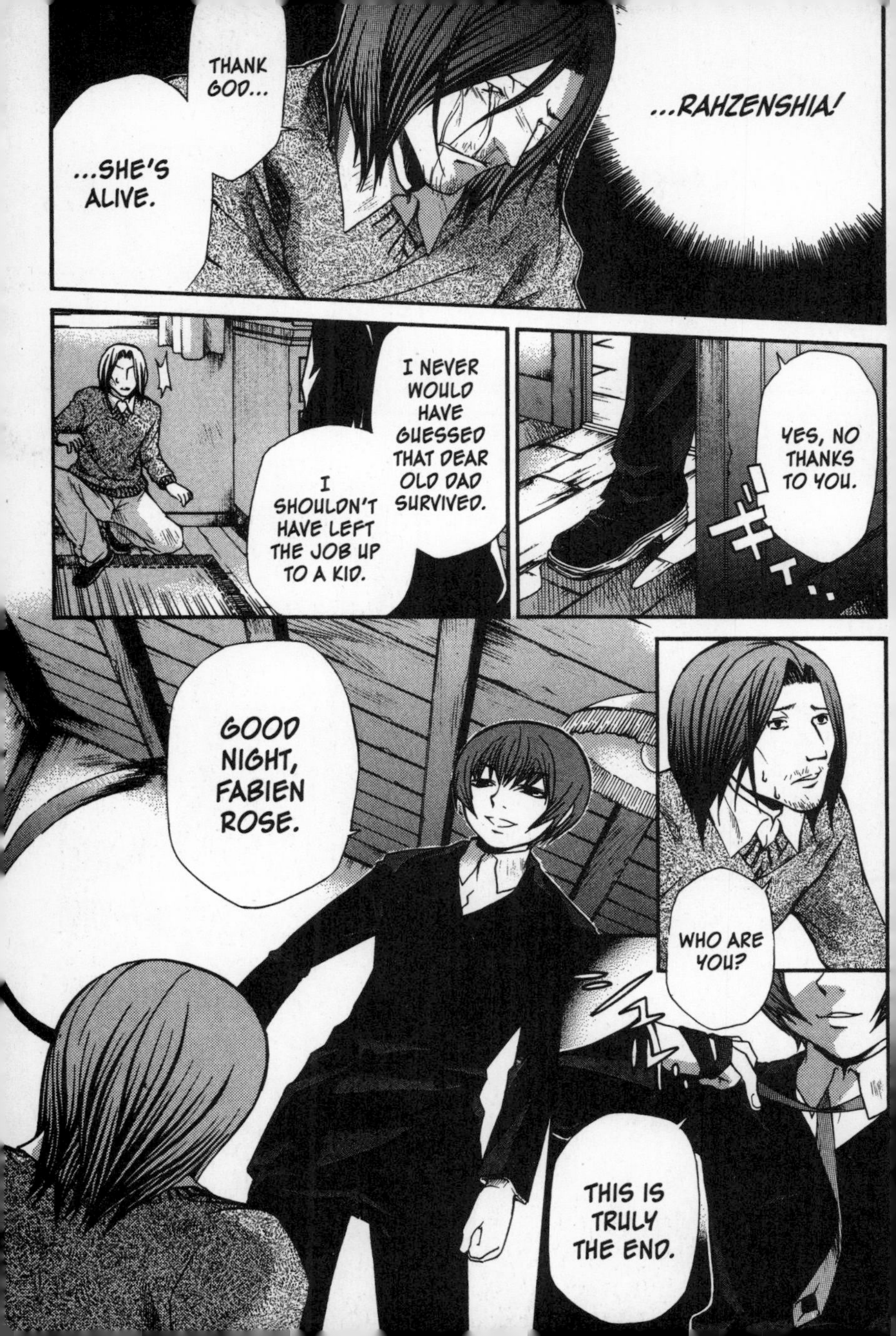
THANK GOD...
...SHE'S ALIVE.
...RAHZENSHIA!
YES, NO THANKS TO YOU.
I NEVER WOULD HAVE GUESSED THAT DEAR OLD DAD SURVIVED.
I SHOULDN'T HAVE LEFT THE JOB UP TO A KID.
WHO ARE YOU?
GOOD NIGHT, FABIEN ROSE.
THIS IS TRULY THE END.

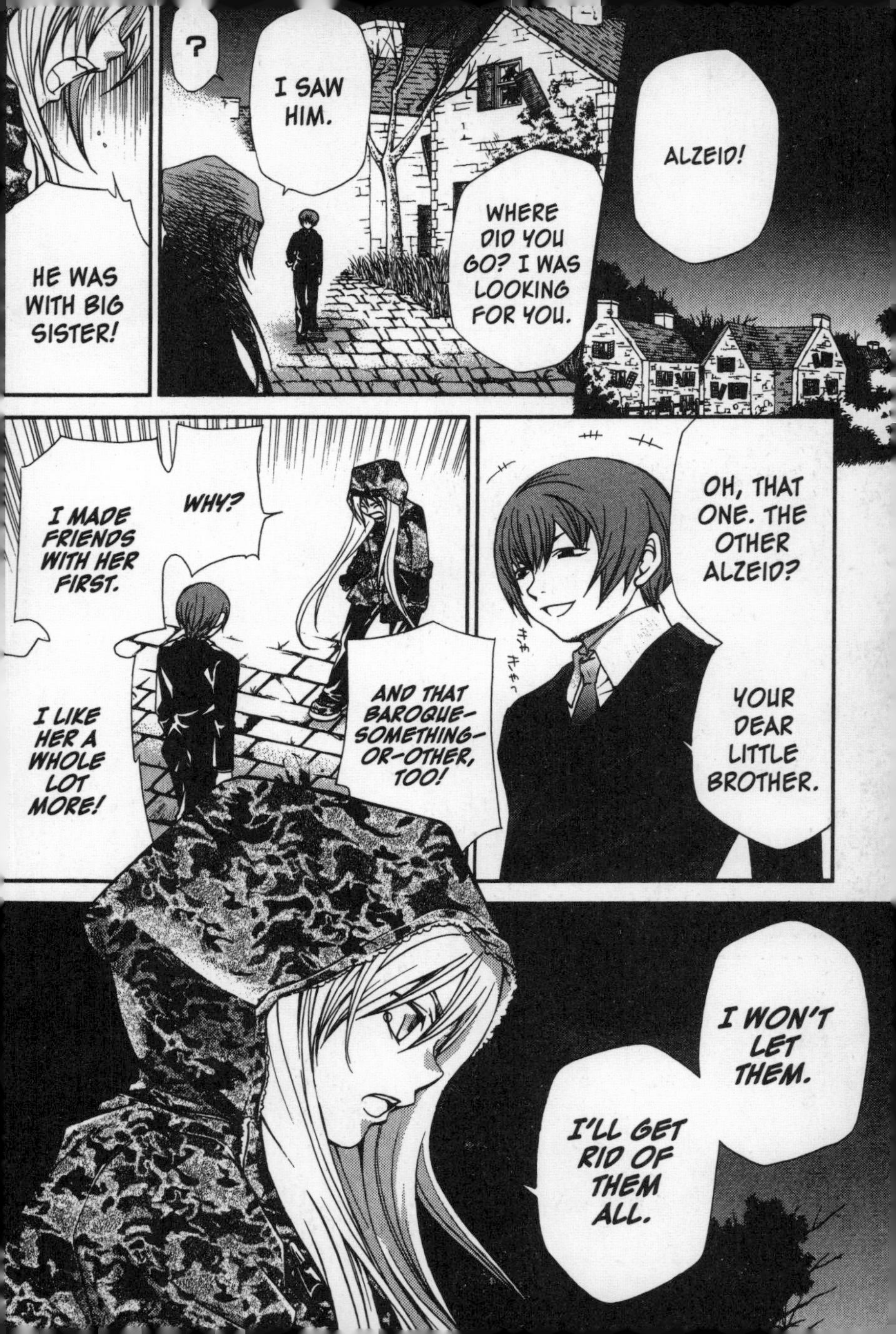

ALZEID!
WHERE DID YOU GO? I WAS LOOKING FOR YOU.
?
I SAW HIM.
HE WAS WITH BIG SISTER!
OH, THAT ONE. THE OTHER ALZEID?
YOUR DEAR LITTLE BROTHER.
WHY?
I MADE FRIENDS WITH HER FIRST.
AND THAT BAROQUE-SOMETHING-OR-OTHER, TOO!
I LIKE HER A WHOLE LOT MORE!
I WON'T LET THEM.
I'LL GET RID OF THEM ALL.

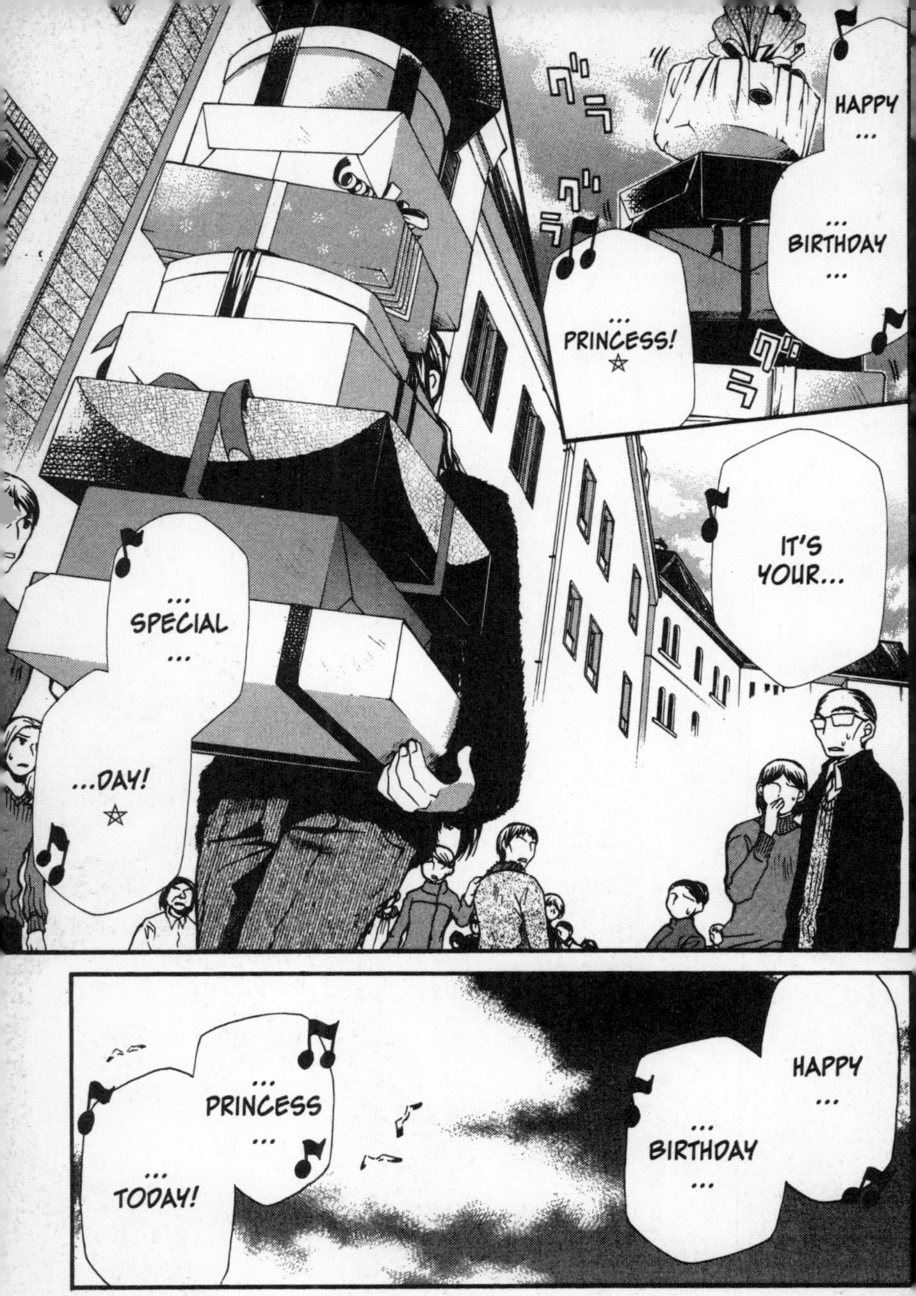
HAPPY ...
... BIRTHDAY ...
... PRINCESS! ☆
IT'S YOUR...
... SPECIAL ...
...DAY! ☆
HAPPY ...
... BIRTHDAY ...
... PRINCESS ...
... TODAY!

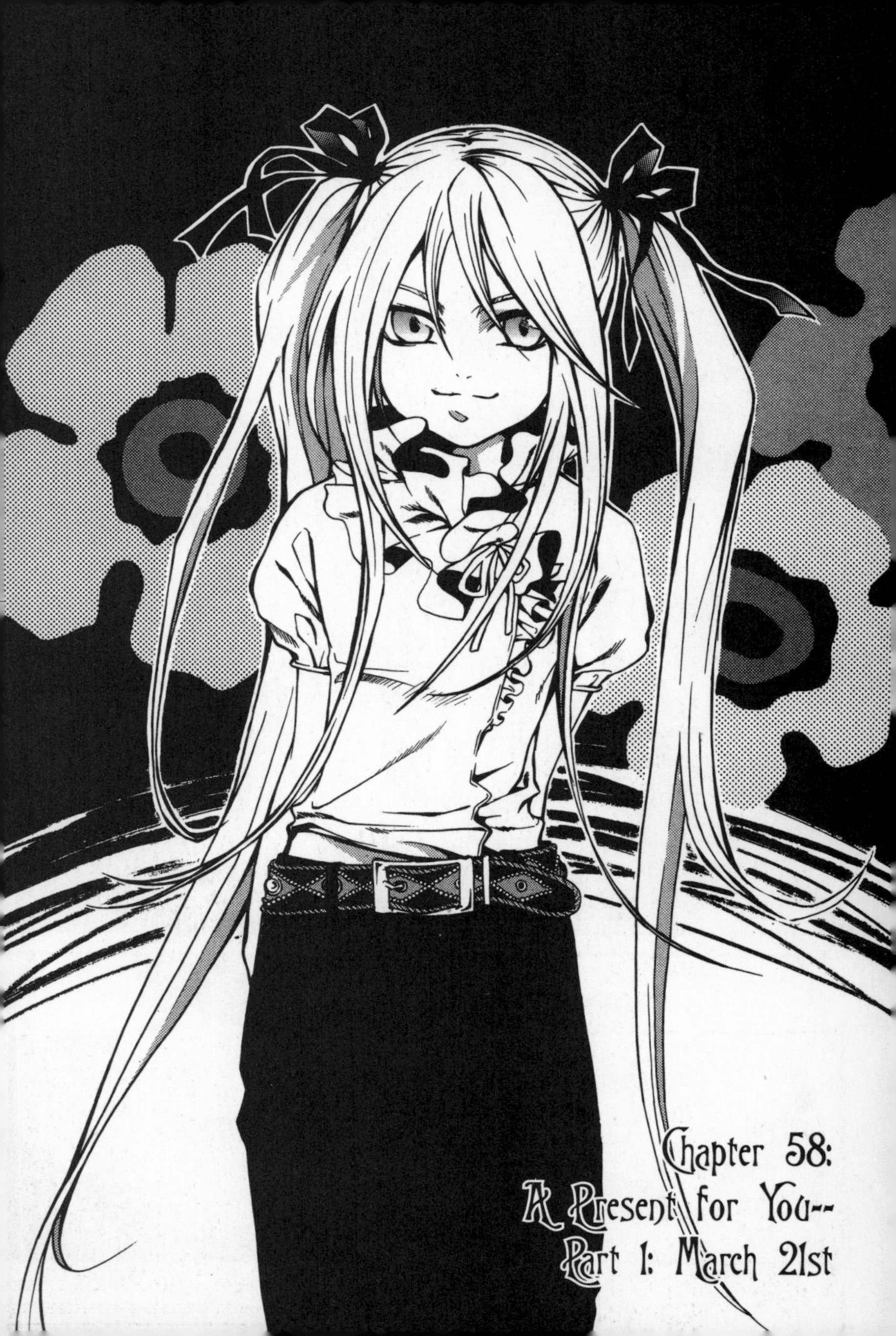
Chapter 58:
A Present for You--
Part 1: March 21st

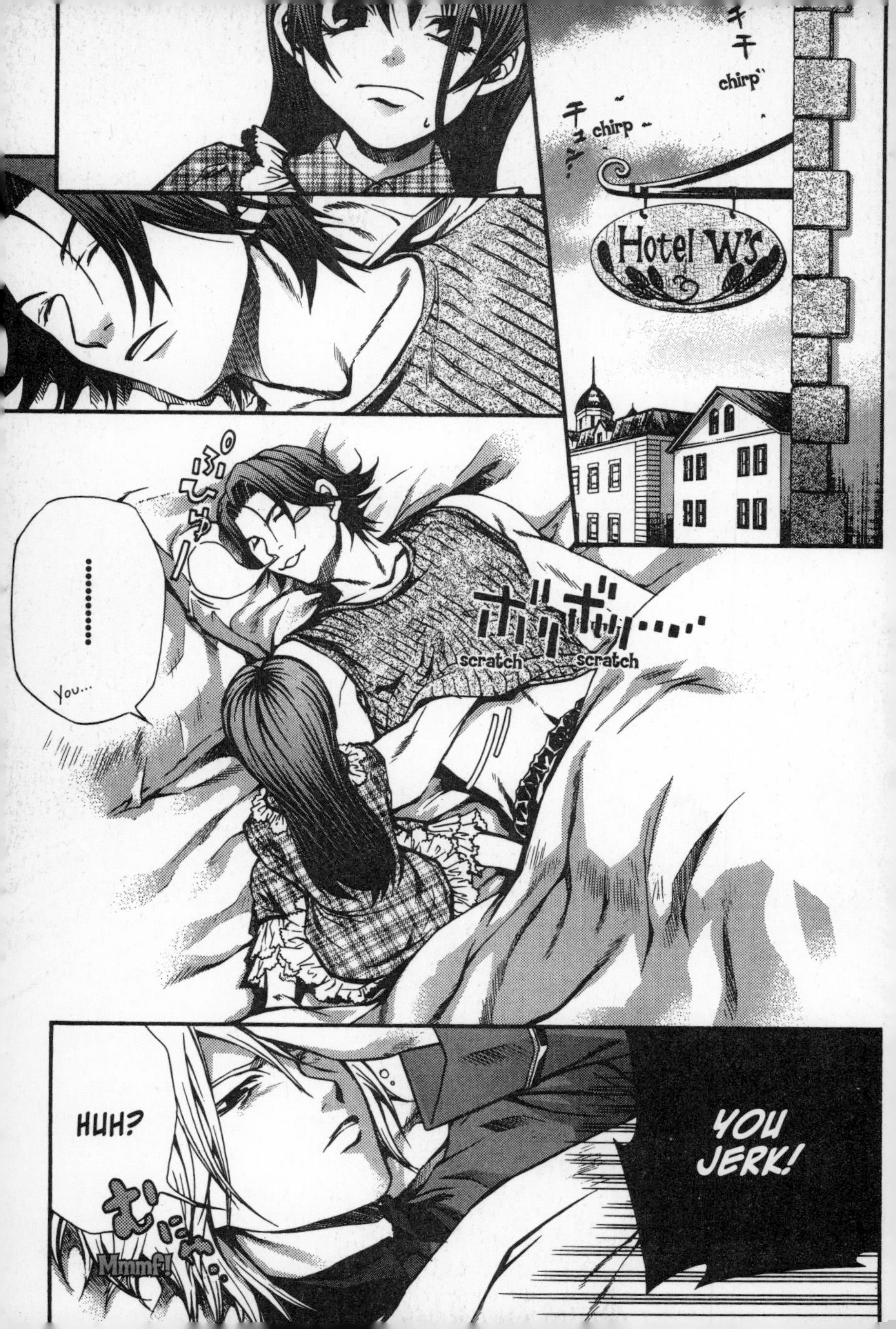

chirp
chirp
Hotel W's
scratch scratch
......
You...
YOU JERK!
HUH?
Mmmf!

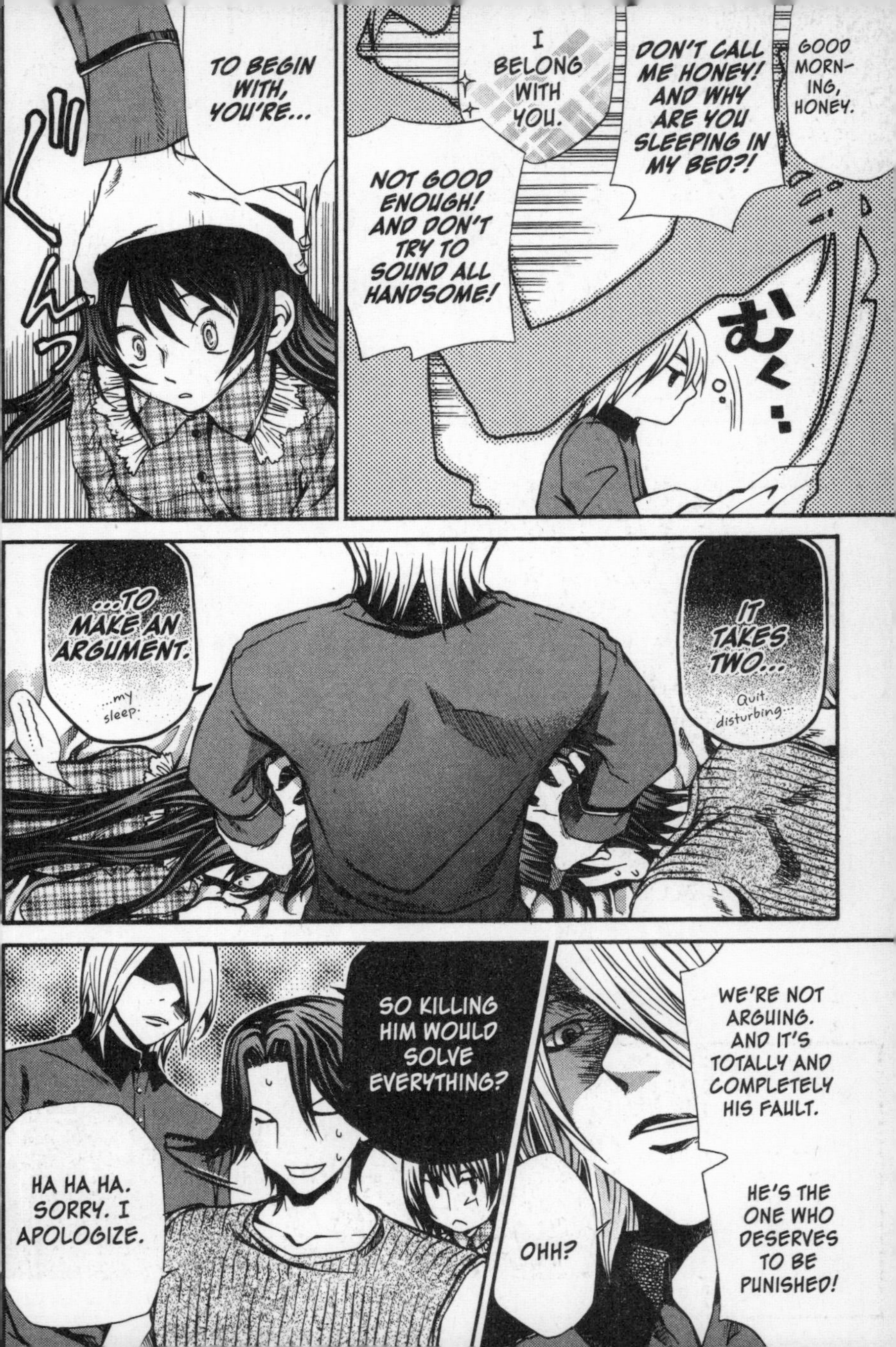
GOOD MORNING, HONEY.
DON'T CALL ME HONEY! AND WHY ARE YOU SLEEPING IN MY BED?!
I BELONG WITH YOU.
NOT GOOD ENOUGH! AND DON'T TRY TO SOUND ALL HANDSOME!
むく
TO BEGIN WITH, YOU'RE...
IT TAKES TWO...
Quit disturbing...
...TO MAKE AN ARGUMENT.
...my sleep.
WE'RE NOT ARGUING. AND IT'S TOTALLY AND COMPLETELY HIS FAULT.
HE'S THE ONE WHO DESERVES TO BE PUNISHED!
OHH?
SO KILLING HIM WOULD SOLVE EVERYTHING?
HA HA HA. SORRY. I APOLOGIZE.

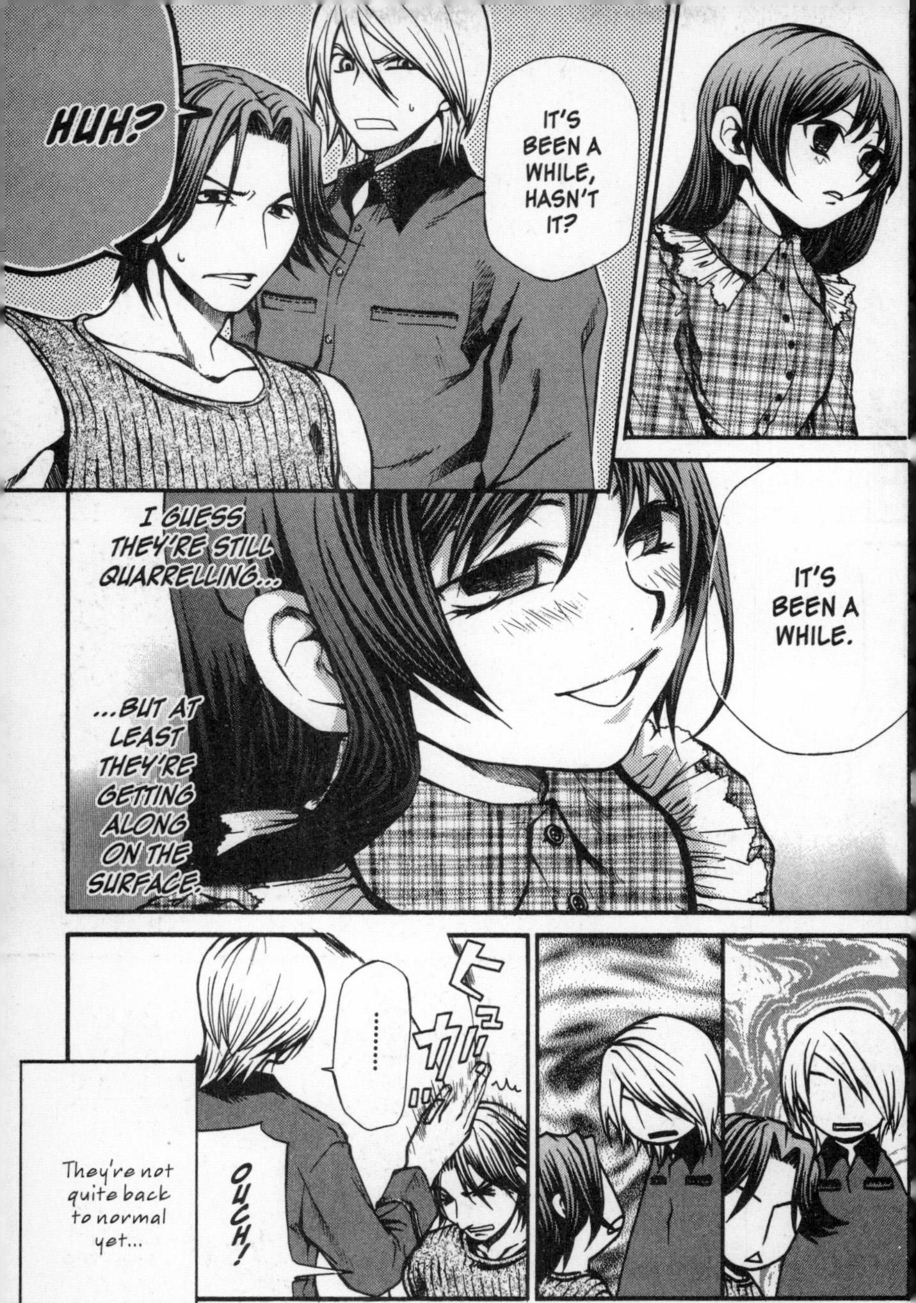
IT'S BEEN A WHILE, HASN'T IT?
HUH?
IT'S BEEN A WHILE.
I GUESS THEY'RE STILL QUARRELLING...
...BUT AT LEAST THEY'RE GETTING ALONG ON THE SURFACE.
......
OUCH!
They're not quite back to normal yet...

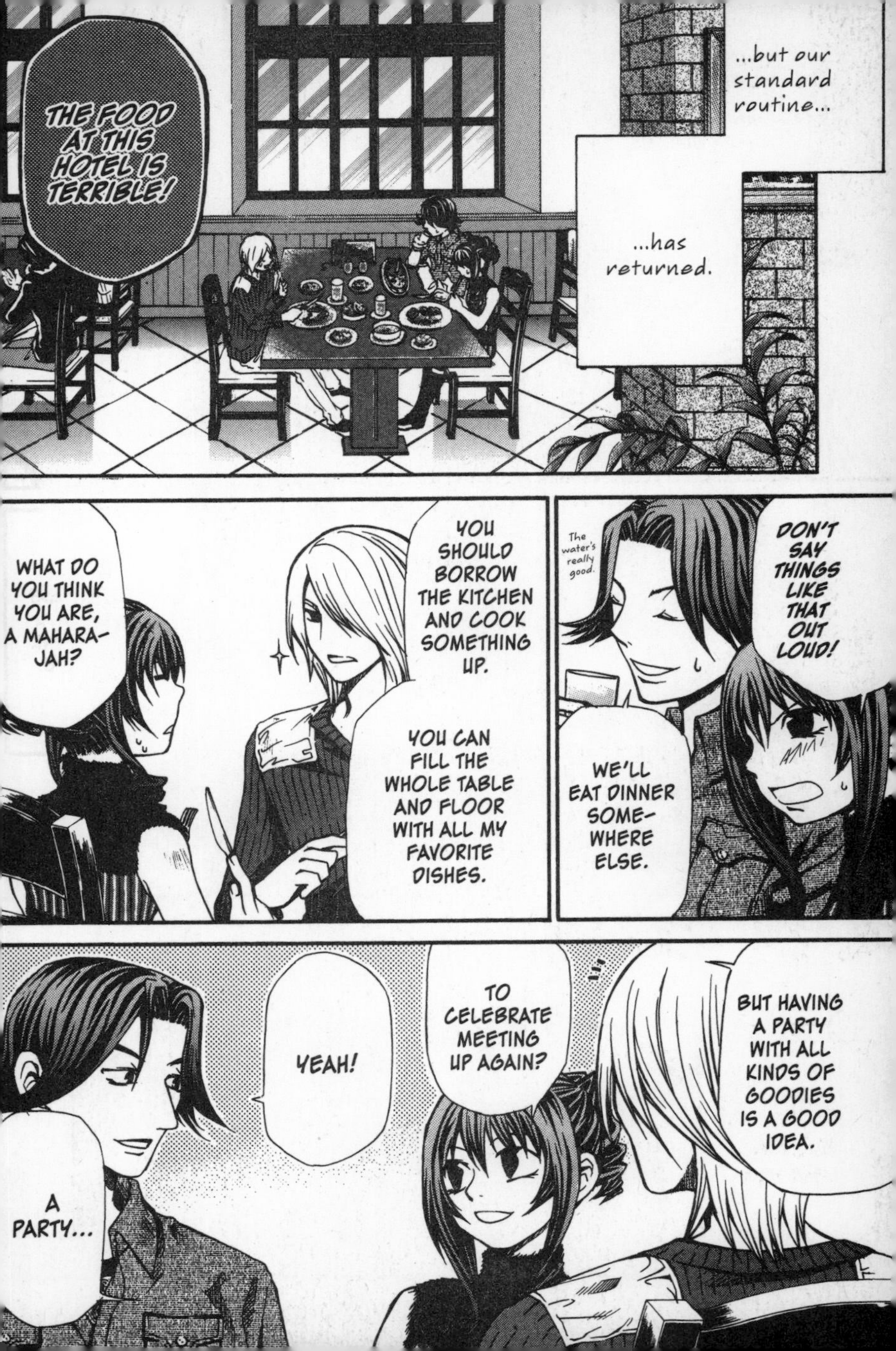
...but our standard routine...
...has returned.
THE FOOD AT THIS HOTEL IS TERRIBLE!
DON'T SAY THINGS LIKE THAT OUT LOUD!
The water's really good.
WE'LL EAT DINNER SOMEWHERE ELSE.
YOU SHOULD BORROW THE KITCHEN AND COOK SOMETHING UP.
WHAT DO YOU THINK YOU ARE, A MAHARAJAH?
YOU CAN FILL THE WHOLE TABLE AND FLOOR WITH ALL MY FAVORITE DISHES.
BUT HAVING A PARTY WITH ALL KINDS OF GOODIES IS A GOOD IDEA.
TO CELEBRATE MEETING UP AGAIN?
YEAH!
A PARTY...

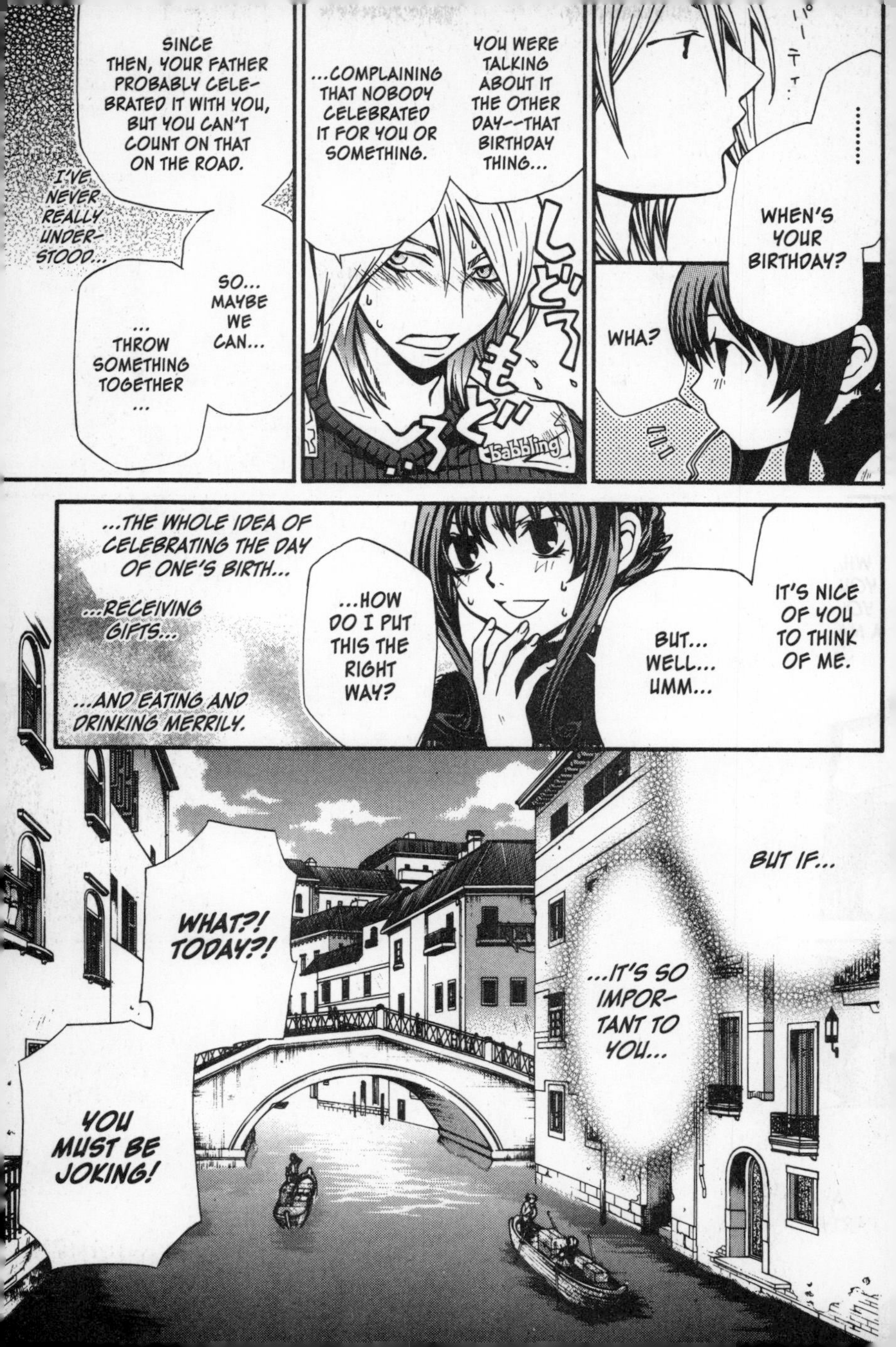

......
WHEN'S YOUR BIRTHDAY?
WHA?
YOU WERE TALKING ABOUT IT THE OTHER DAY--THAT BIRTHDAY THING...
...COMPLAINING THAT NOBODY CELEBRATED IT FOR YOU OR SOMETHING.
しどろもどろ
babbling
SINCE THEN, YOUR FATHER PROBABLY CELE-BRATED IT WITH YOU, BUT YOU CAN'T COUNT ON THAT ON THE ROAD.
SO... MAYBE WE CAN...
... THROW SOMETHING TOGETHER ...
I'VE NEVER REALLY UNDER-STOOD...
IT'S NICE OF YOU TO THINK OF ME.
BUT... WELL... UMM...
...HOW DO I PUT THIS THE RIGHT WAY?
...THE WHOLE IDEA OF CELEBRATING THE DAY OF ONE'S BIRTH...
...RECEIVING GIFTS...
...AND EATING AND DRINKING MERRILY.
BUT IF...
...IT'S SO IMPOR-TANT TO YOU...
WHAT?! TODAY?!
YOU MUST BE JOKING!

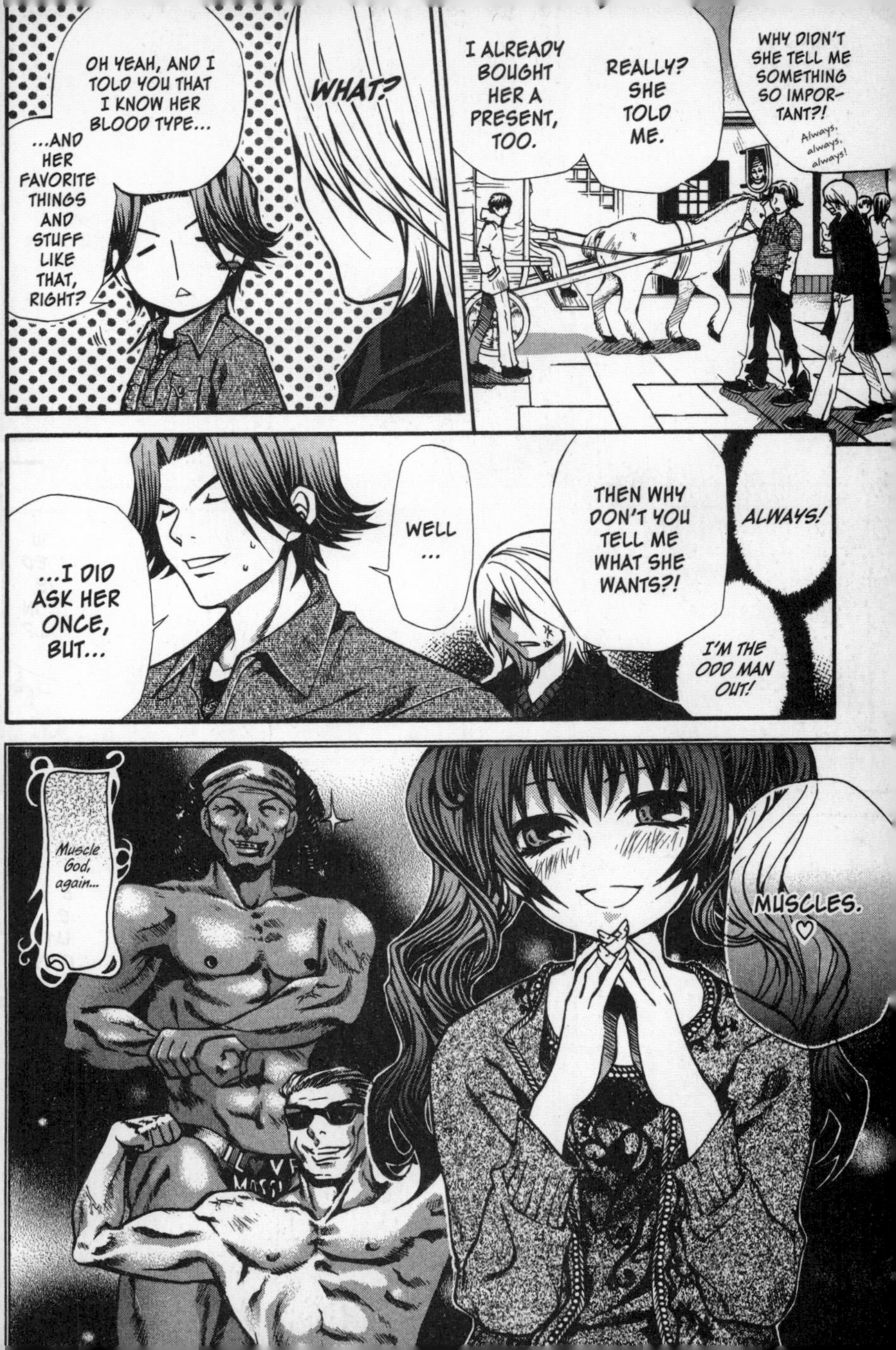
WHY DIDN'T SHE TELL ME SOMETHING SO IMPORTANT?!
Always, always, always!
REALLY? SHE TOLD ME.
I ALREADY BOUGHT HER A PRESENT, TOO.
WHAT?
OH YEAH, AND I TOLD YOU THAT I KNOW HER BLOOD TYPE...
...AND HER FAVORITE THINGS AND STUFF LIKE THAT, RIGHT?
ALWAYS!
I'M THE ODD MAN OUT!
THEN WHY DON'T YOU TELL ME WHAT SHE WANTS?!
WELL...
...I DID ASK HER ONCE, BUT...
MUSCLES. ♡
Muscle God, again...

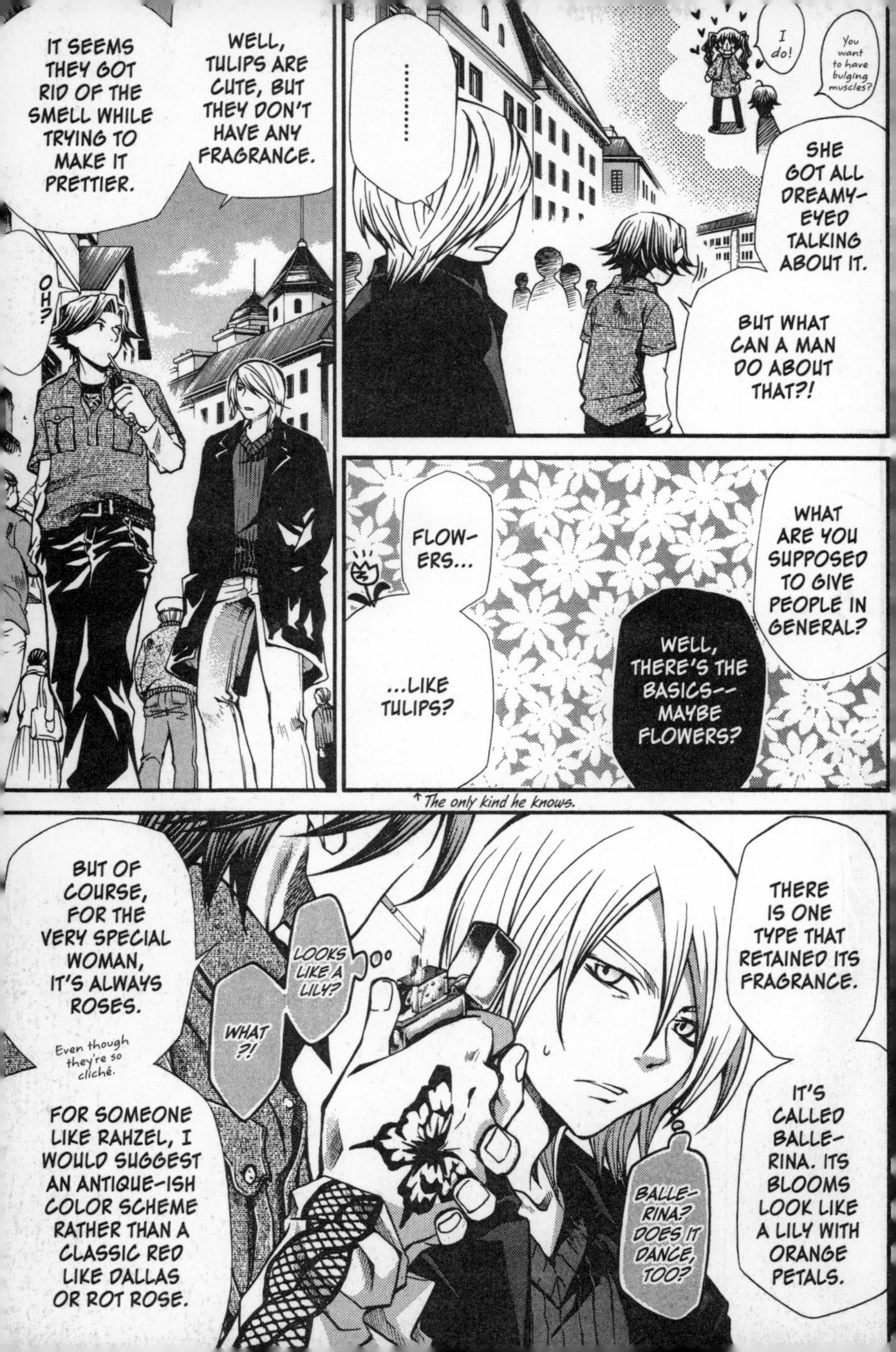
You want to have bulging muscles?
I do!
SHE GOT ALL DREAMY-EYED TALKING ABOUT IT.
BUT WHAT CAN A MAN DO ABOUT THAT?!
......
WHAT ARE YOU SUPPOSED TO GIVE PEOPLE IN GENERAL?
WELL, THERE'S THE BASICS--MAYBE FLOWERS?
FLOWERS...
...LIKE TULIPS?
↑The only kind he knows.
WELL, TULIPS ARE CUTE, BUT THEY DON'T HAVE ANY FRAGRANCE.
IT SEEMS THEY GOT RID OF THE SMELL WHILE TRYING TO MAKE IT PRETTIER.
OH?
THERE IS ONE TYPE THAT RETAINED ITS FRAGRANCE.
IT'S CALLED BALLERINA. ITS BLOOMS LOOK LIKE A LILY WITH ORANGE PETALS.
BALLERINA? DOES IT DANCE, TOO?
LOOKS LIKE A LILY?
WHAT?!
BUT OF COURSE, FOR THE VERY SPECIAL WOMAN, IT'S ALWAYS ROSES.
Even though they're so cliché.
FOR SOMEONE LIKE RAHZEL, I WOULD SUGGEST AN ANTIQUE-ISH COLOR SCHEME RATHER THAN A CLASSIC RED LIKE DALLAS OR ROT ROSE.

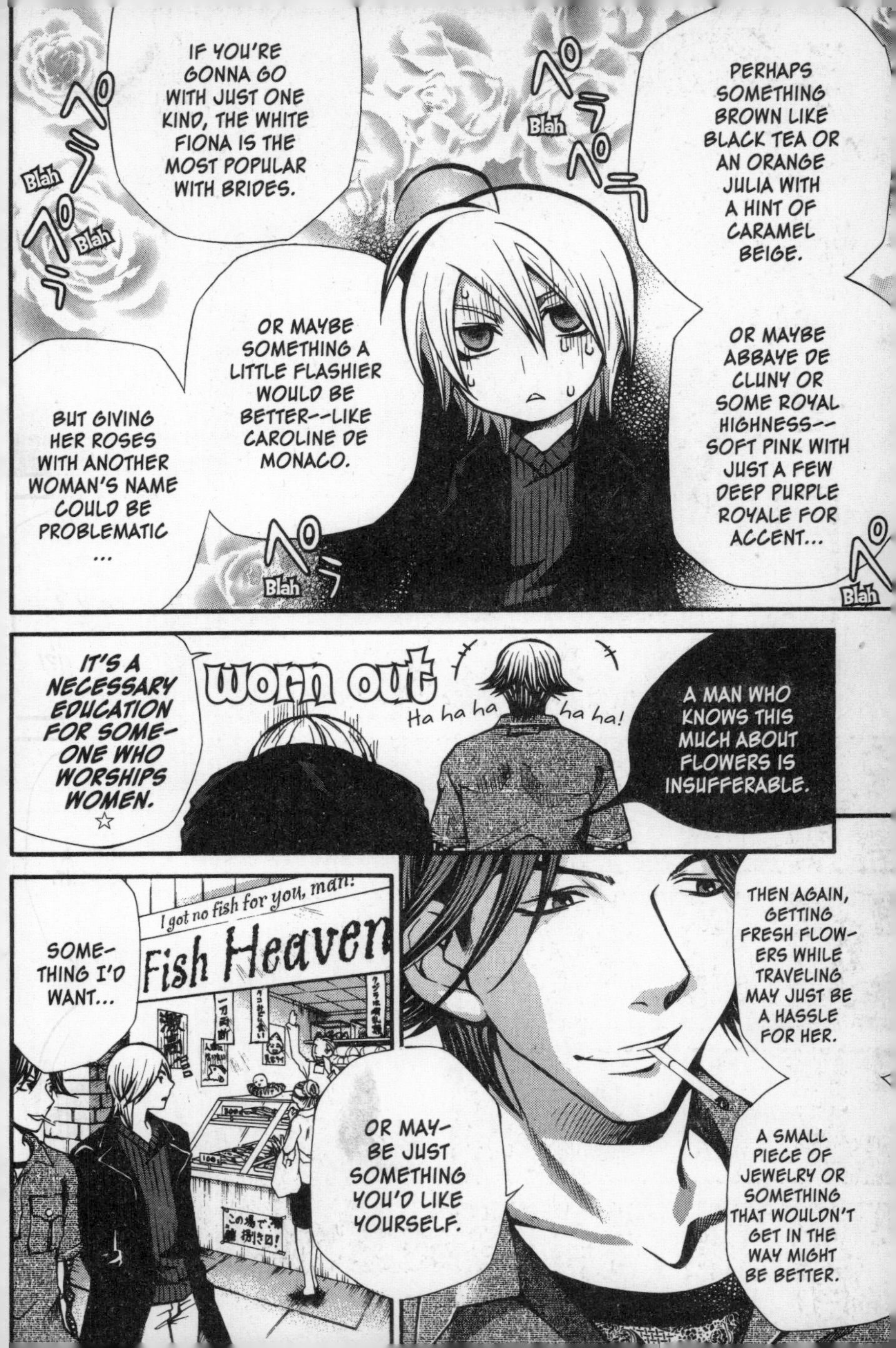
PERHAPS SOMETHING BROWN LIKE BLACK TEA OR AN ORANGE JULIA WITH A HINT OF CARAMEL BEIGE.
Blah
IF YOU'RE GONNA GO WITH JUST ONE KIND, THE WHITE FIONA IS THE MOST POPULAR WITH BRIDES.
Blah
Blah
OR MAYBE ABBAYE DE CLUNY OR SOME ROYAL HIGHNESS--SOFT PINK WITH JUST A FEW DEEP PURPLE ROYALE FOR ACCENT...
Blah
OR MAYBE SOMETHING A LITTLE FLASHIER WOULD BE BETTER--LIKE CAROLINE DE MONACO.
BUT GIVING HER ROSES WITH ANOTHER WOMAN'S NAME COULD BE PROBLEMATIC...
Blah
A MAN WHO KNOWS THIS MUCH ABOUT FLOWERS IS INSUFFERABLE.
ha ha!
Ha ha ha
worn out
IT'S A NECESSARY EDUCATION FOR SOMEONE WHO WORSHIPS WOMEN. ☆
THEN AGAIN, GETTING FRESH FLOWERS WHILE TRAVELING MAY JUST BE A HASSLE FOR HER.
A SMALL PIECE OF JEWELRY OR SOMETHING THAT WOULDN'T GET IN THE WAY MIGHT BE BETTER.
OR MAYBE JUST SOMETHING YOU'D LIKE YOURSELF.
I got no fish for you, man!
Fish Heaven
SOMETHING I'D WANT...

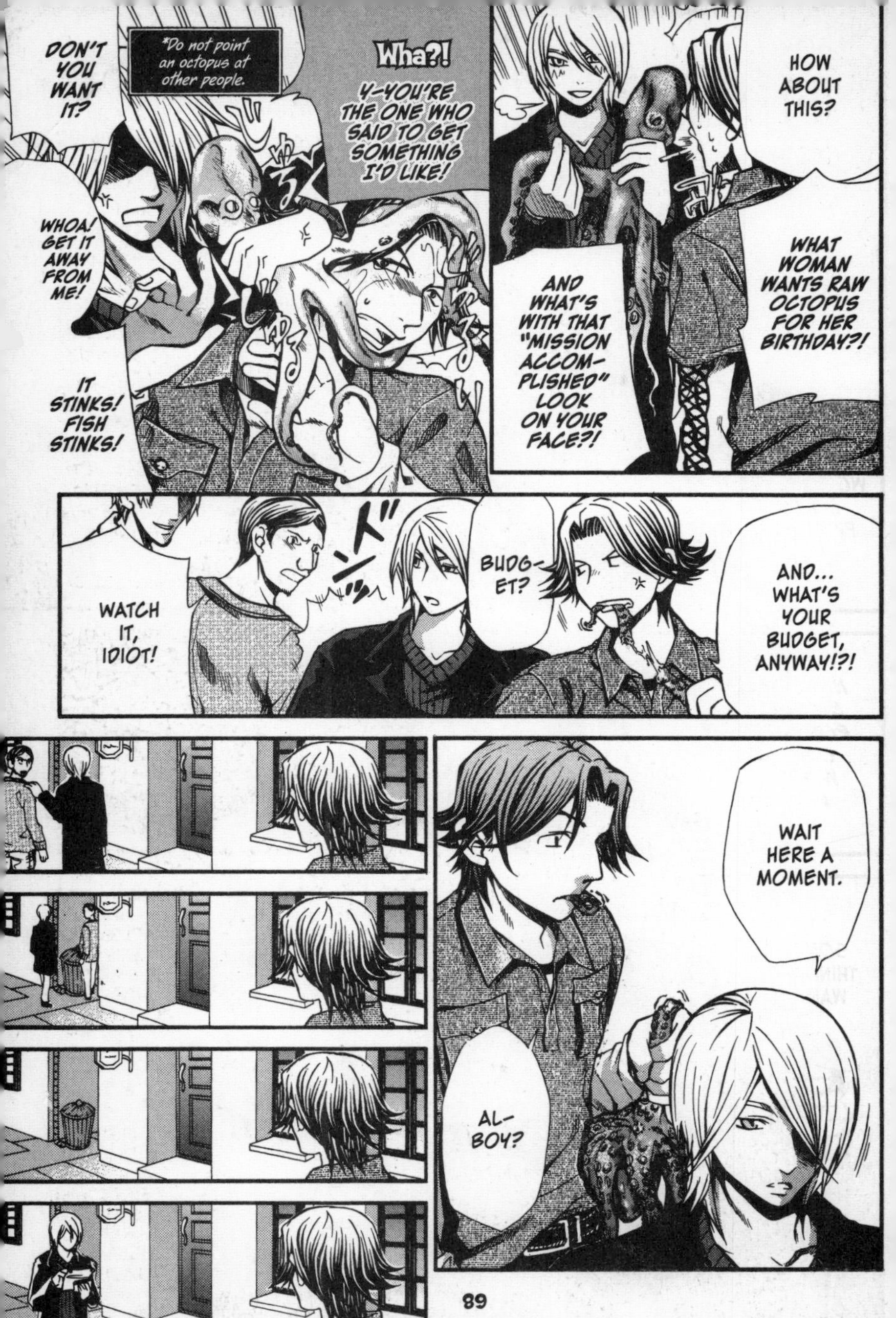
HOW ABOUT THIS?
WHAT WOMAN WANTS RAW OCTOPUS FOR HER BIRTHDAY?!
AND WHAT'S WITH THAT "MISSION ACCOMPLISHED" LOOK ON YOUR FACE?!
Wha?!
Y-YOU'RE THE ONE WHO SAID TO GET SOMETHING I'D LIKE!
*Do not point an octopus at other people.
DON'T YOU WANT IT?
WHOA! GET IT AWAY FROM ME!
IT STINKS! FISH STINKS!
AND... WHAT'S YOUR BUDGET, ANYWAY!?!
BUDG-ET?
WATCH IT, IDIOT!
WAIT HERE A MOMENT.
AL-BOY?

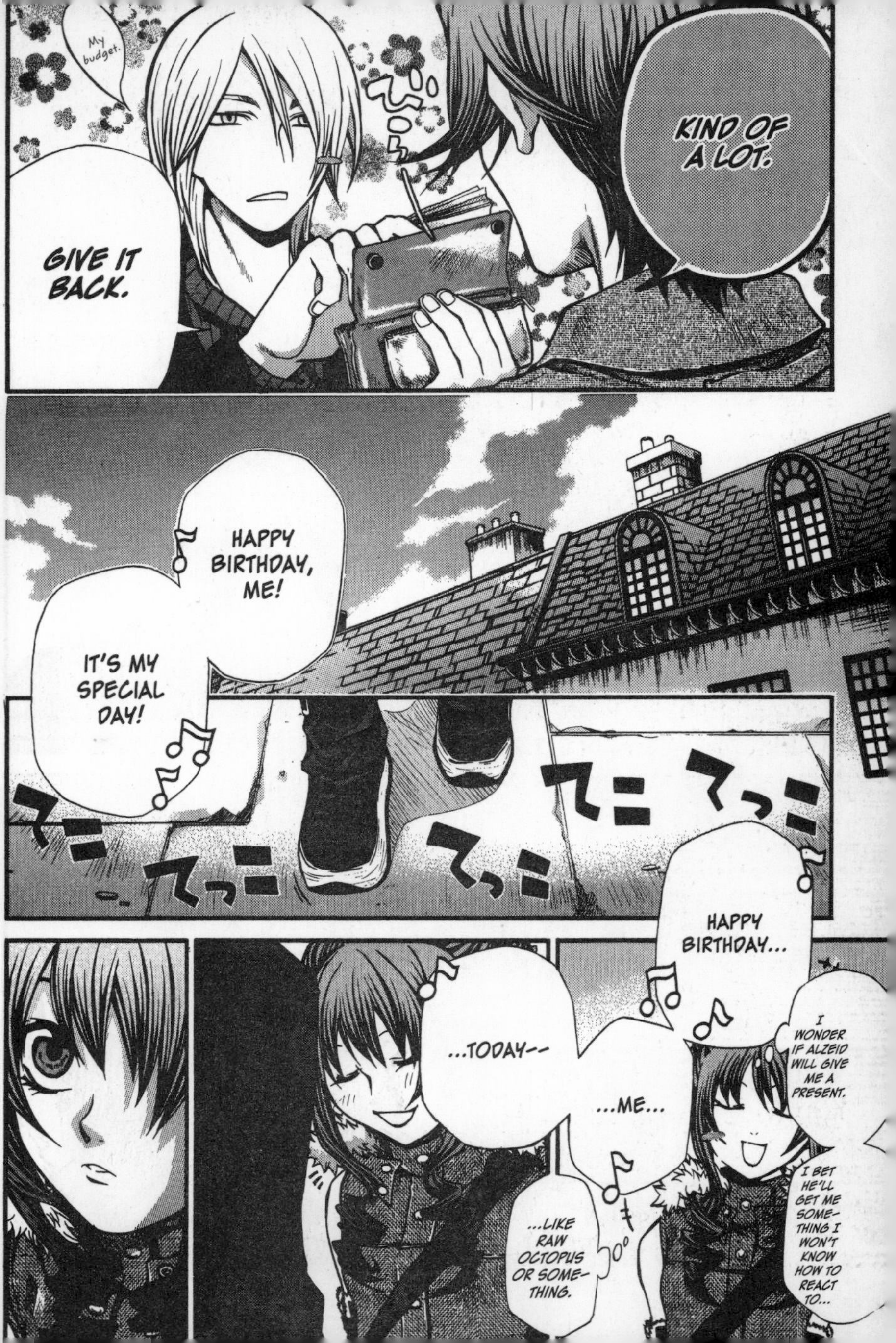
KIND OF A LOT.
My budget.
GIVE IT BACK.
HAPPY BIRTHDAY, ME!
IT'S MY SPECIAL DAY!
てっこ てっこ てっこ てっこ
HAPPY BIRTHDAY...
...TODAY--
...ME...
I WONDER IF ALZEID WILL GIVE ME A PRESENT.
I BET HE'LL GET ME SOME-THING I WON'T KNOW HOW TO REACT TO...
...LIKE RAW OCTOPUS OR SOME-THING.

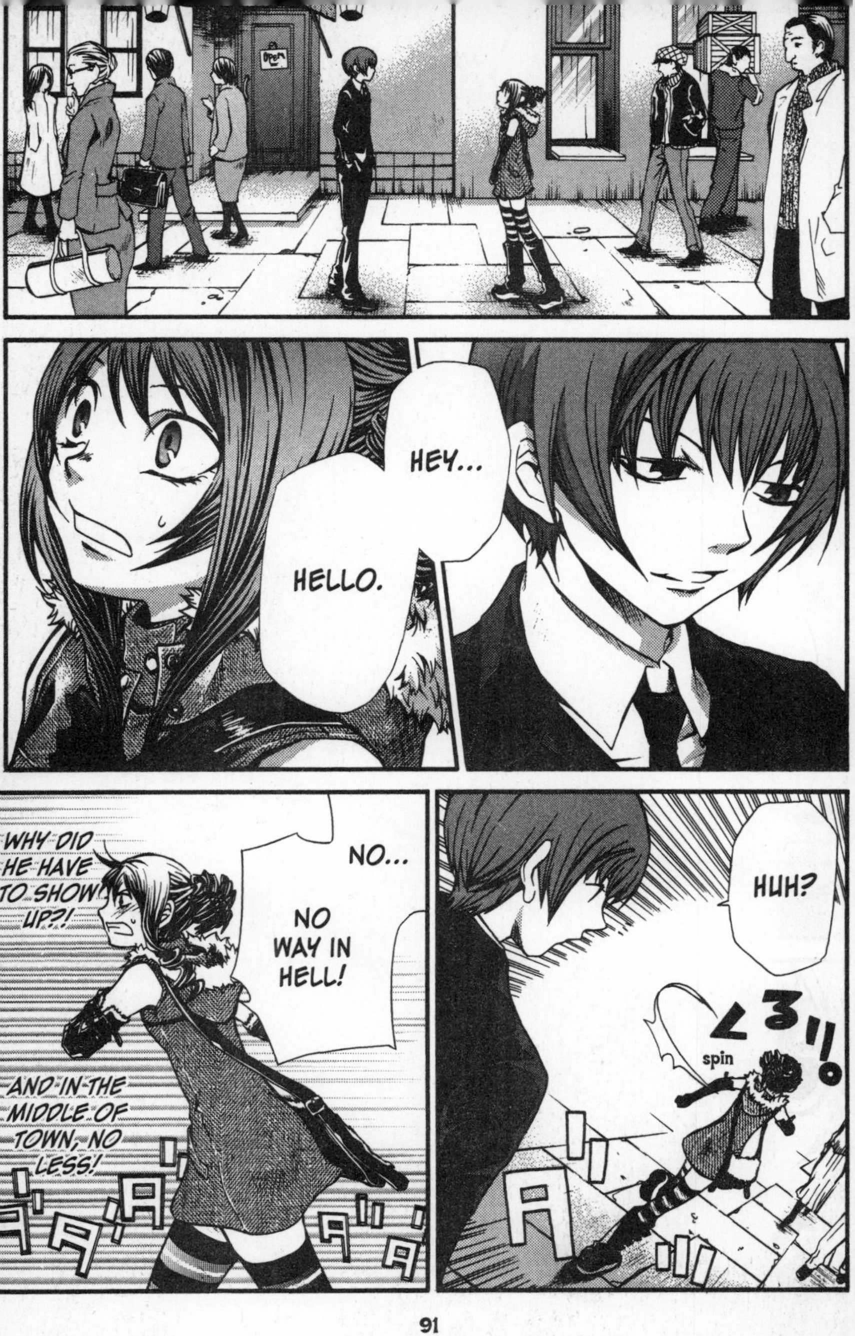
HEY...
HELLO.
HUH?
くるり
spin
NO...
NO WAY IN HELL!
WHY DID HE HAVE TO SHOW UP?!
AND IN THE MIDDLE OF TOWN, NO LESS!

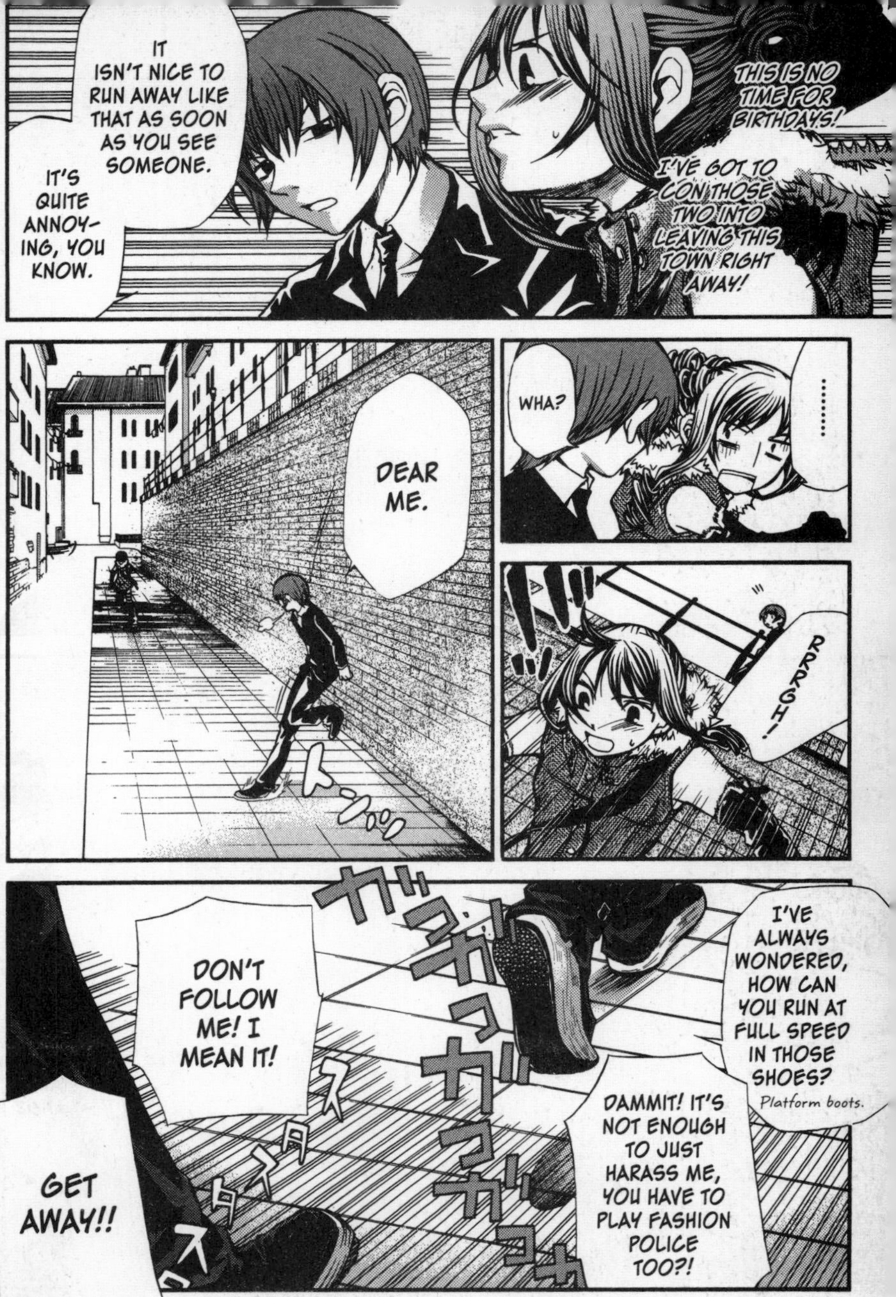
THIS IS NO TIME FOR BIRTHDAYS!
I'VE GOT TO CON THOSE TWO INTO LEAVING THIS TOWN RIGHT AWAY!
IT ISN'T NICE TO RUN AWAY LIKE THAT AS SOON AS YOU SEE SOMEONE.
IT'S QUITE ANNOY-ING, YOU KNOW.
....
WHA?
RRRGH!
DEAR ME.
I'VE ALWAYS WONDERED, HOW CAN YOU RUN AT FULL SPEED IN THOSE SHOES?
Platform boots.
DAMMIT! IT'S NOT ENOUGH TO JUST HARASS ME, YOU HAVE TO PLAY FASHION POLICE TOO?!
DON'T FOLLOW ME! I MEAN IT!
GET AWAY!!

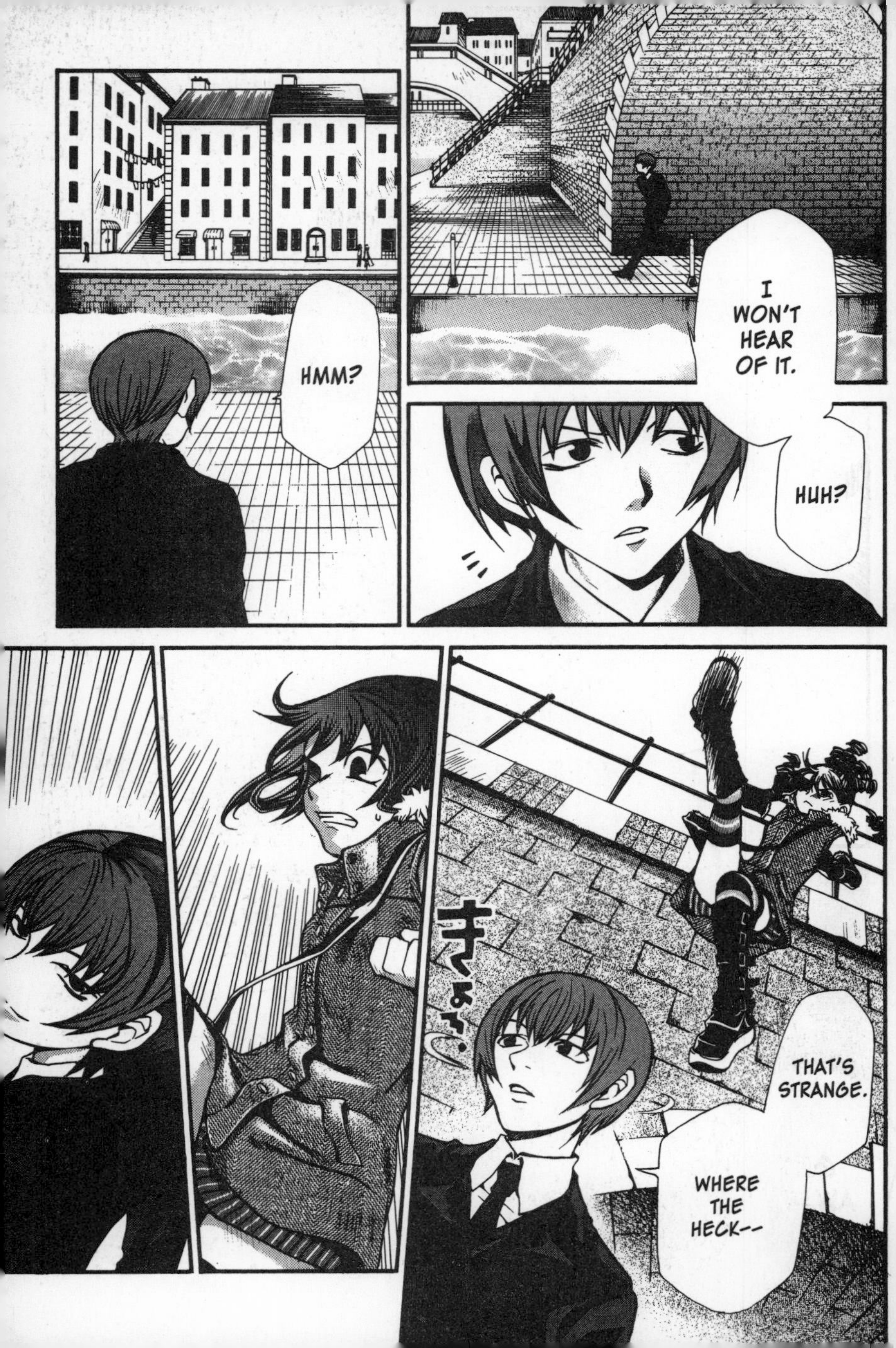
I WON'T HEAR OF IT.
HUH?
HMM?
THAT'S STRANGE.
WHERE THE HECK--

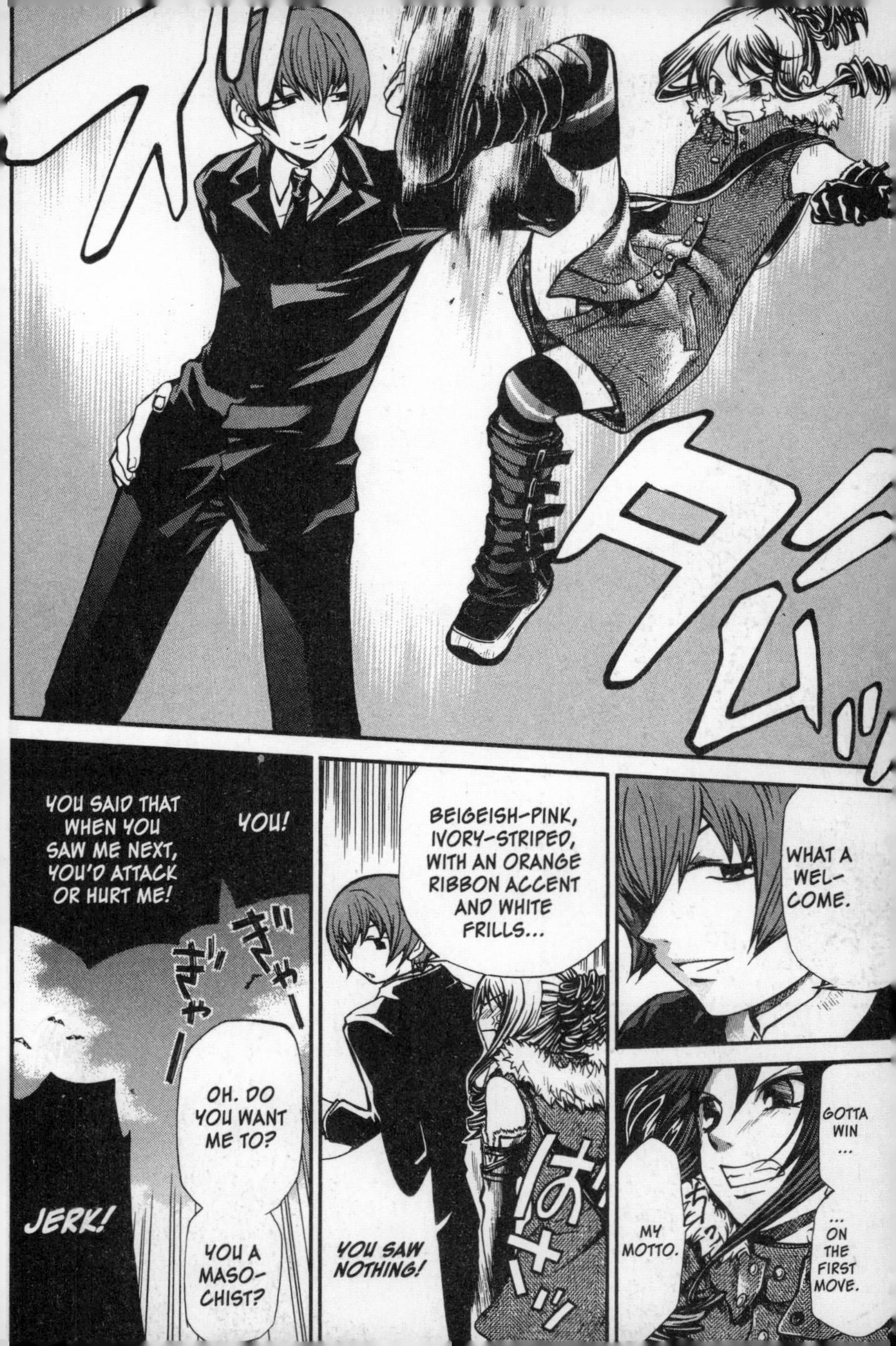
WHAT A WEL-COME.
GOTTA WIN ...
... ON THE FIRST MOVE.
MY MOTTO.
BEIGEISH-PINK, IVORY-STRIPED, WITH AN ORANGE RIBBON ACCENT AND WHITE FRILLS...
YOU SAW NOTHING!
YOU!
YOU SAID THAT WHEN YOU SAW ME NEXT, YOU'D ATTACK OR HURT ME!
OH. DO YOU WANT ME TO?
YOU A MASO-CHIST?
JERK!

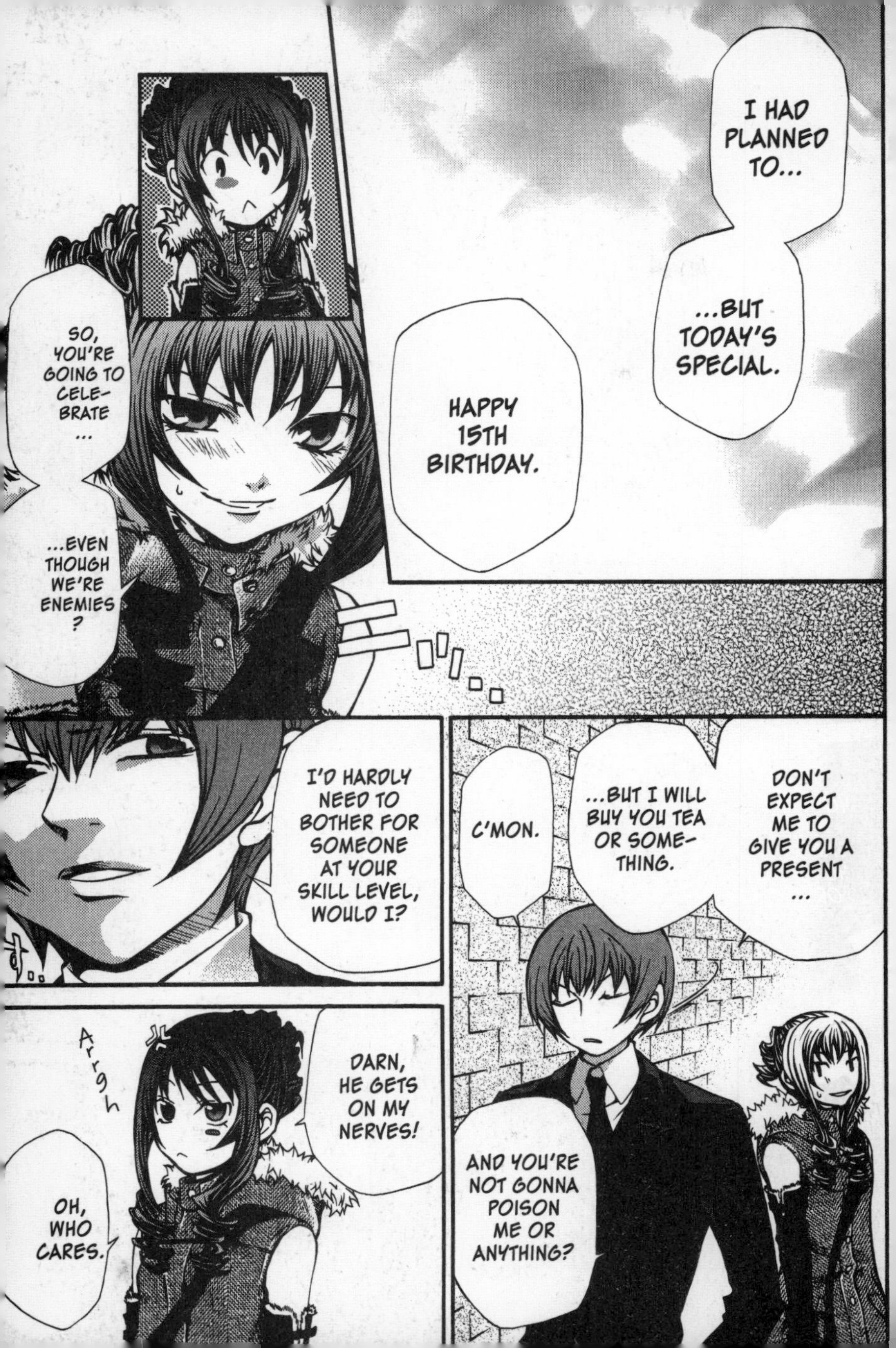
I HAD PLANNED TO...
...BUT TODAY'S SPECIAL.
HAPPY 15TH BIRTHDAY.
SO, YOU'RE GOING TO CELE-BRATE...
...EVEN THOUGH WE'RE ENEMIES?
DON'T EXPECT ME TO GIVE YOU A PRESENT...
...BUT I WILL BUY YOU TEA OR SOME-THING.
C'MON.
AND YOU'RE NOT GONNA POISON ME OR ANYTHING?
I'D HARDLY NEED TO BOTHER FOR SOMEONE AT YOUR SKILL LEVEL, WOULD I?
Arrgh
DARN, HE GETS ON MY NERVES!
OH, WHO CARES.

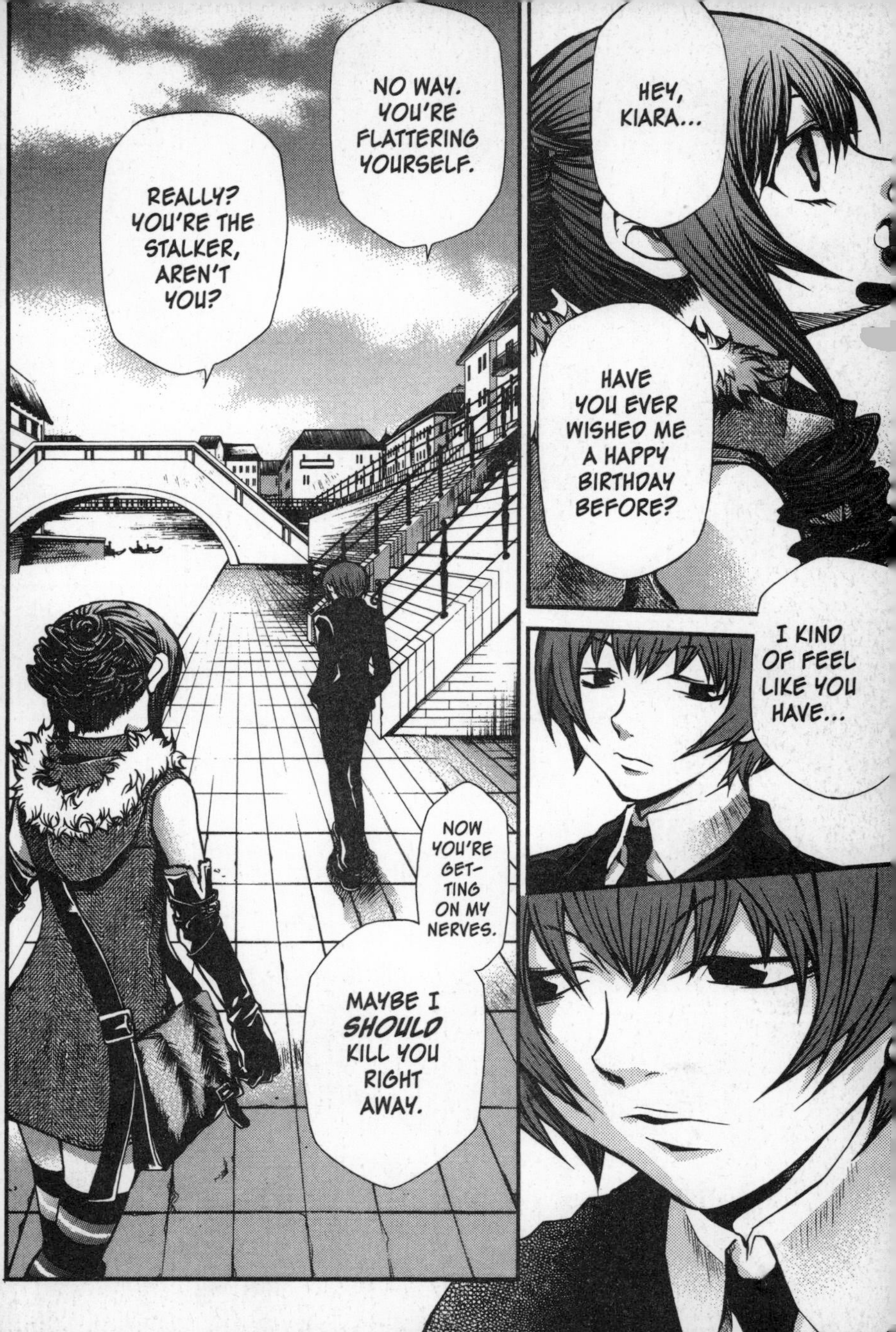
HEY, KIARA...
HAVE YOU EVER WISHED ME A HAPPY BIRTHDAY BEFORE?
I KIND OF FEEL LIKE YOU HAVE...
NO WAY. YOU'RE FLATTERING YOURSELF.
REALLY? YOU'RE THE STALKER, AREN'T YOU?
NOW YOU'RE GET-TING ON MY NERVES.
MAYBE I *SHOULD* KILL YOU RIGHT AWAY.

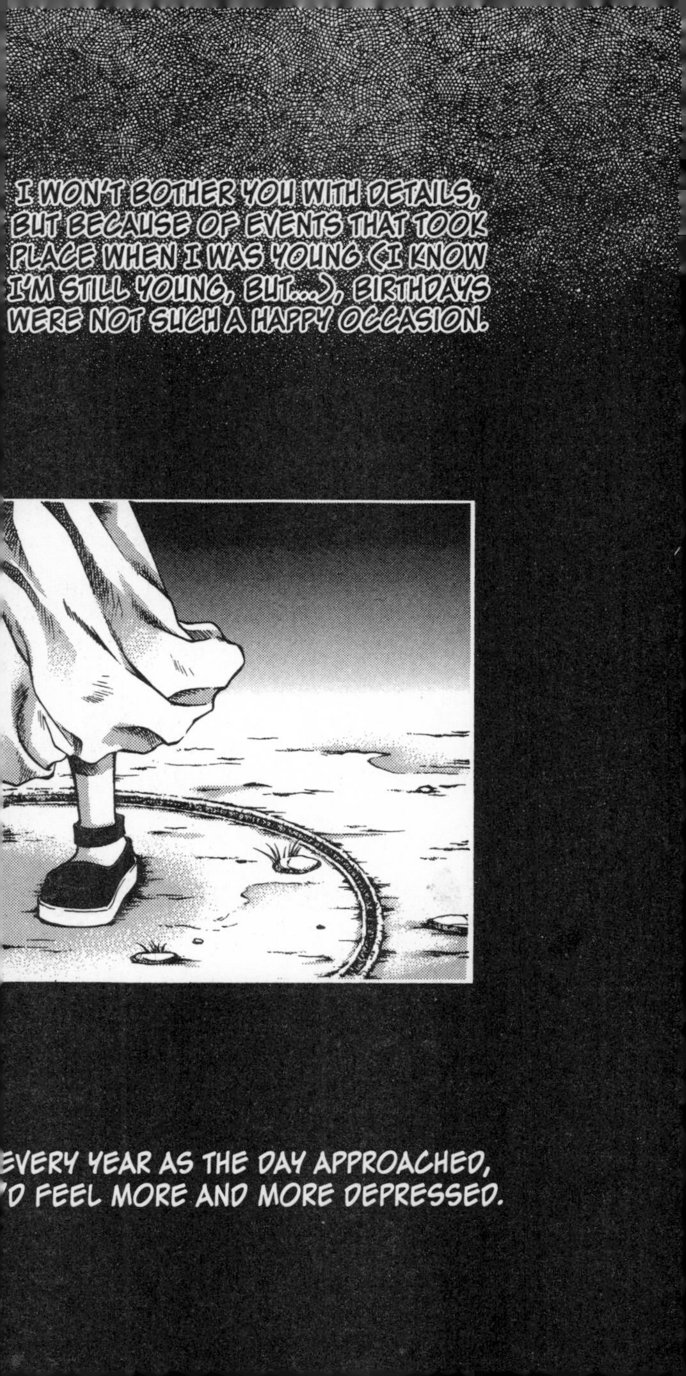

I WON'T BOTHER YOU WITH DETAILS, BUT BECAUSE OF EVENTS THAT TOOK PLACE WHEN I WAS YOUNG (I KNOW I'M STILL YOUNG, BUT...), BIRTHDAYS WERE NOT SUCH A HAPPY OCCASION.
EVERY YEAR AS THE DAY APPROACHED,
D FEEL MORE AND MORE DEPRESSED.

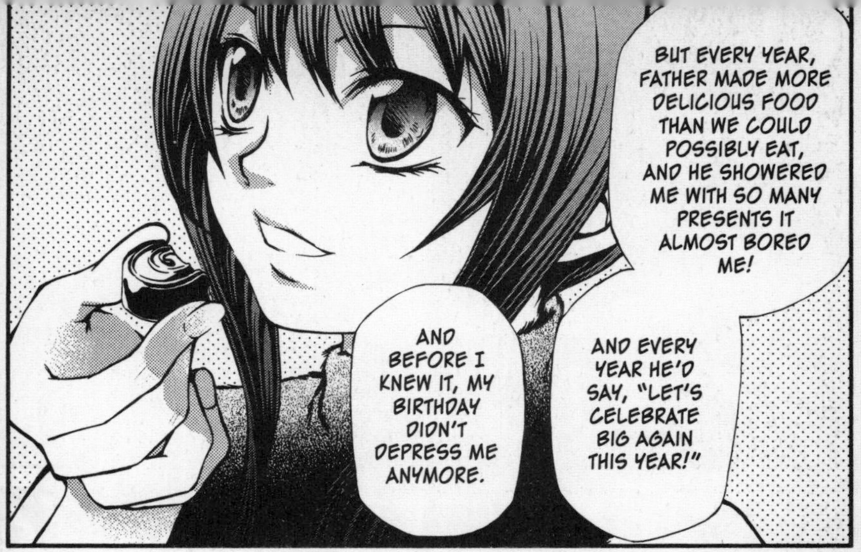
BUT EVERY YEAR, FATHER MADE MORE DELICIOUS FOOD THAN WE COULD POSSIBLY EAT, AND HE SHOWERED ME WITH SO MANY PRESENTS IT ALMOST BORED ME!
AND EVERY YEAR HE'D SAY, "LET'S CELEBRATE BIG AGAIN THIS YEAR!"
AND BEFORE I KNEW IT, MY BIRTHDAY DIDN'T DEPRESS ME ANYMORE.

Chapter 59:
A Present for You--Part 2:
Reunion and a Premonition of Parting

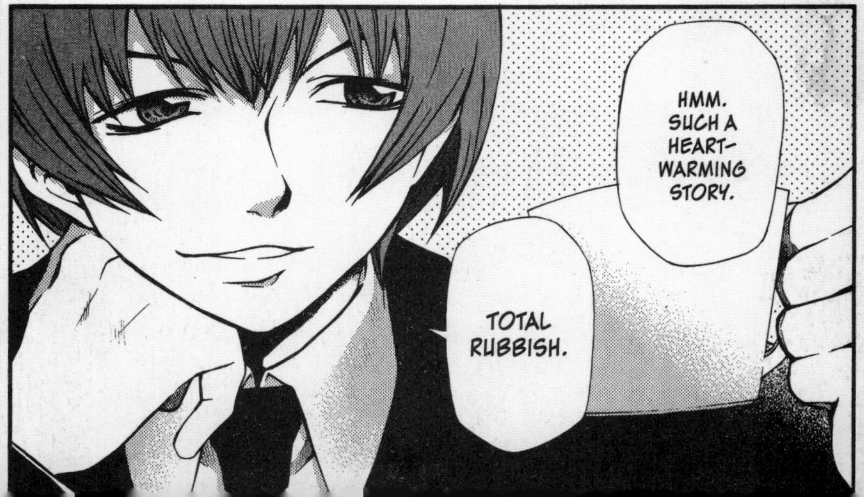
HMM. SUCH A HEART-WARMING STORY.
TOTAL RUBBISH.

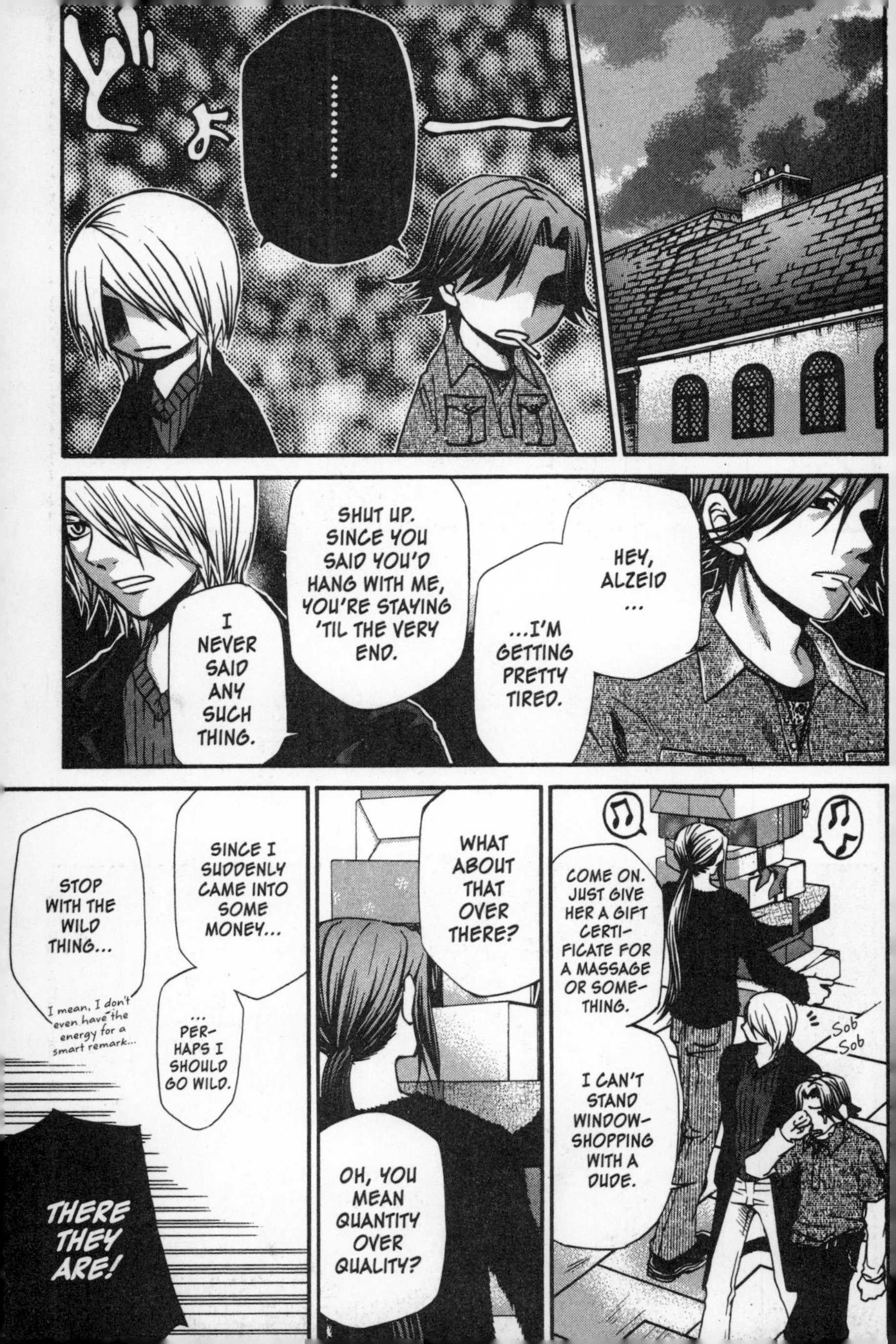
どよ
......
HEY, ALZEID ...
...I'M GETTING PRETTY TIRED.
SHUT UP. SINCE YOU SAID YOU'D HANG WITH ME, YOU'RE STAYING 'TIL THE VERY END.
I NEVER SAID ANY SUCH THING.
COME ON. JUST GIVE HER A GIFT CERTIFICATE FOR A MASSAGE OR SOMETHING.
Sob Sob
I CAN'T STAND WINDOW-SHOPPING WITH A DUDE.
WHAT ABOUT THAT OVER THERE?
OH, YOU MEAN QUANTITY OVER QUALITY?
SINCE I SUDDENLY CAME INTO SOME MONEY...
...PERHAPS I SHOULD GO WILD.
STOP WITH THE WILD THING...
I mean, I don't even have the energy for a smart remark...
THERE THEY ARE!

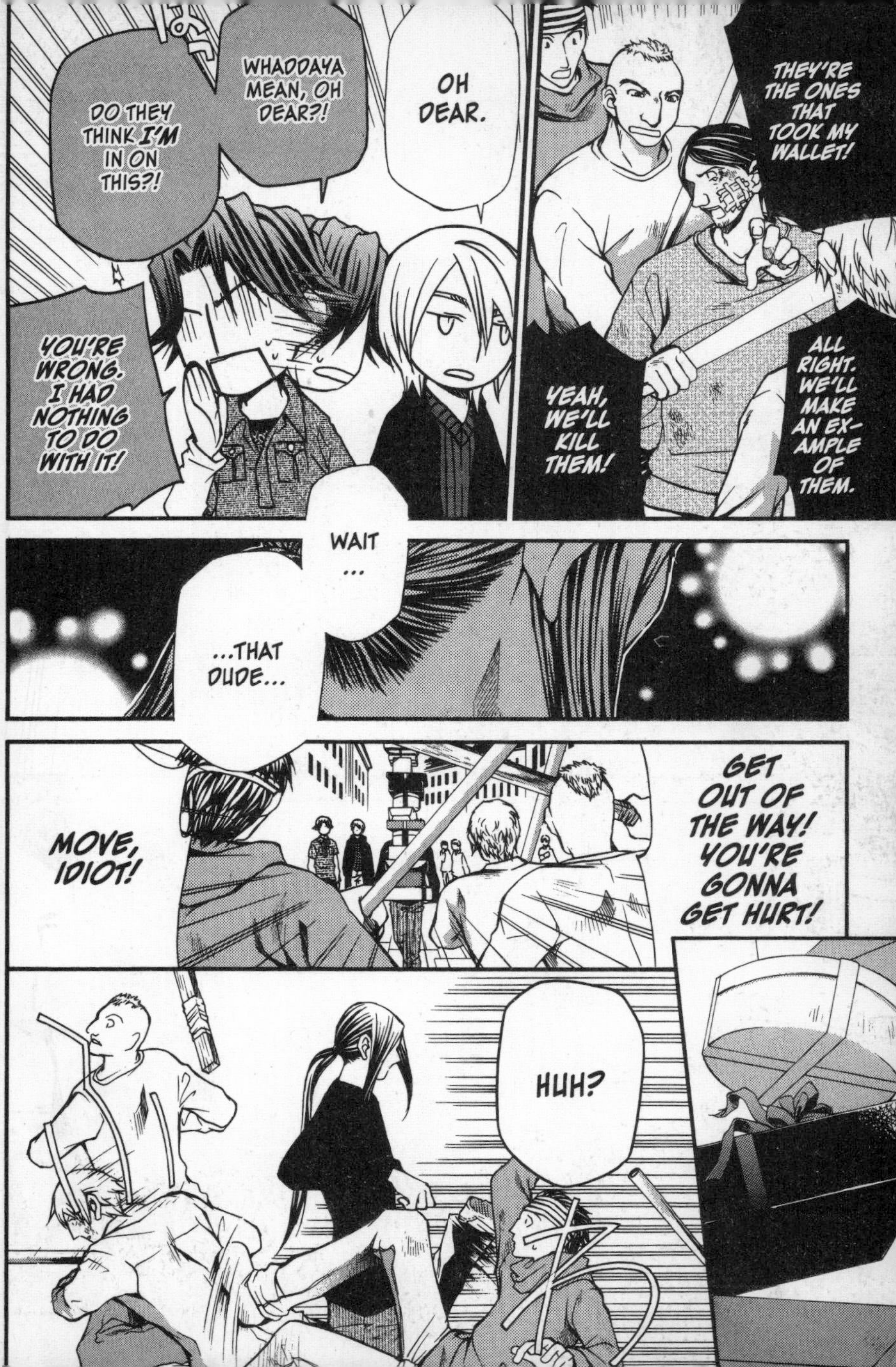
THEY'RE THE ONES THAT TOOK MY WALLET!
ALL RIGHT. WE'LL MAKE AN EX-AMPLE OF THEM.
YEAH, WE'LL KILL THEM!
OH DEAR.
WHADDAYA MEAN, OH DEAR?!
DO THEY THINK I'M IN ON THIS?!
YOU'RE WRONG. I HAD NOTHING TO DO WITH IT!
WAIT ...
...THAT DUDE...
GET OUT OF THE WAY! YOU'RE GONNA GET HURT!
MOVE, IDIOT!
HUH?

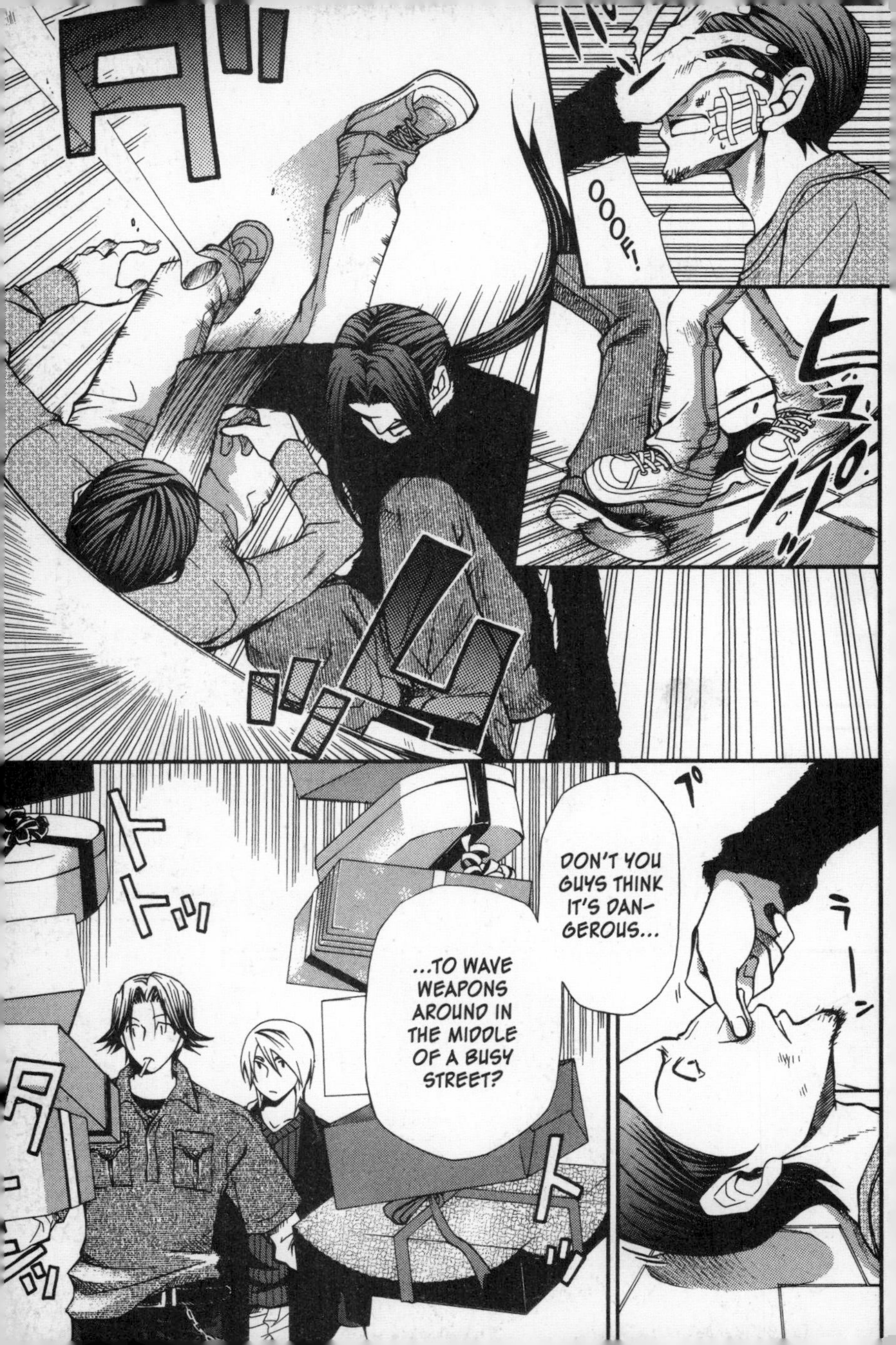
OOOF!
DON'T YOU GUYS THINK IT'S DAN-GEROUS...
...TO WAVE WEAPONS AROUND IN THE MIDDLE OF A BUSY STREET?

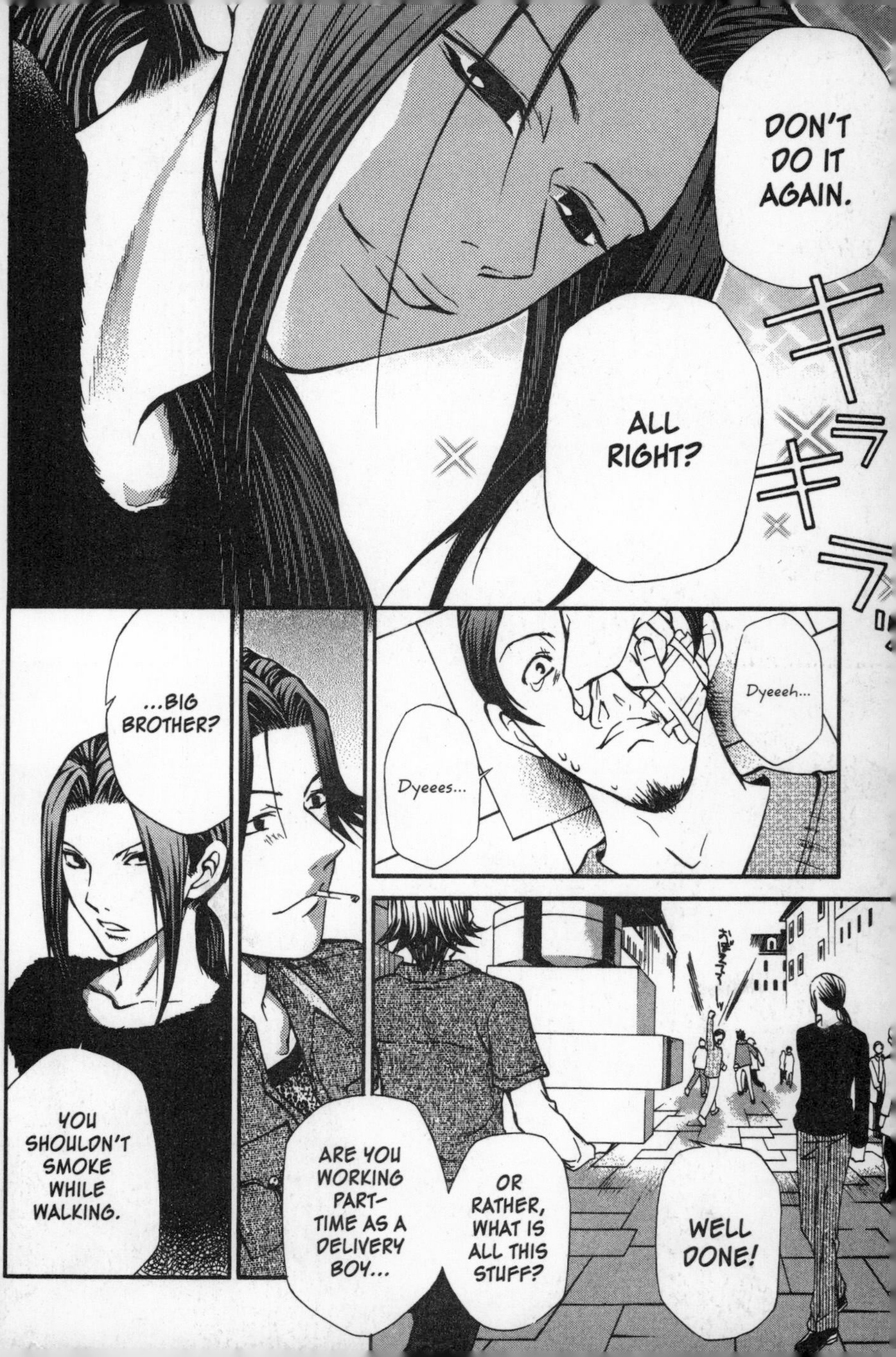
DON'T DO IT AGAIN.
ALL RIGHT?
キラキラッ
Dyeeeh...
Dyeees...
WELL DONE!
ARE YOU WORKING PART-TIME AS A DELIVERY BOY...
OR RATHER, WHAT IS ALL THIS STUFF?
...BIG BROTHER?
YOU SHOULDN'T SMOKE WHILE WALKING.

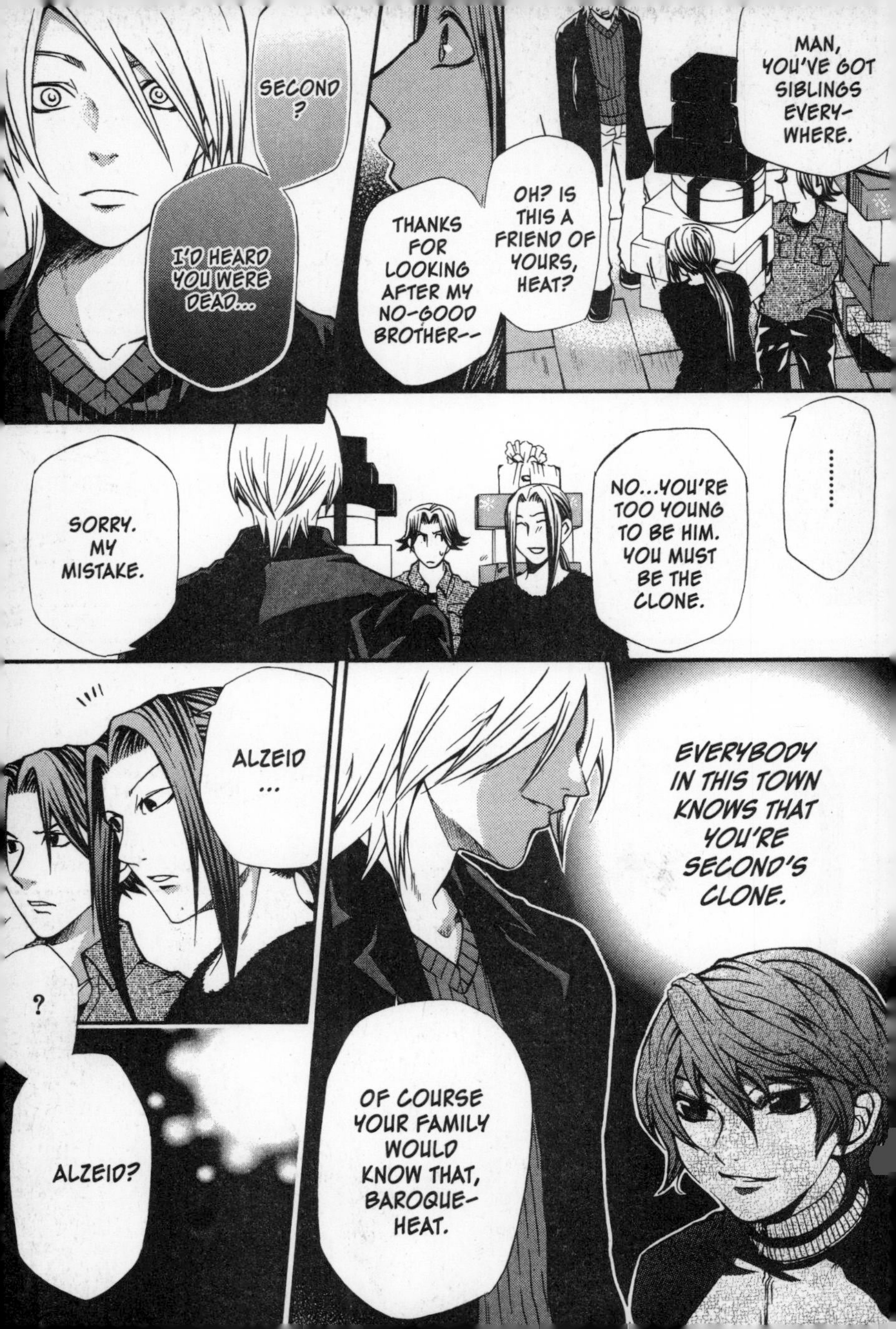
MAN, YOU'VE GOT SIBLINGS EVERY-WHERE.
OH? IS THIS A FRIEND OF YOURS, HEAT?
THANKS FOR LOOKING AFTER MY NO-GOOD BROTHER--
SECOND ?
I'D HEARD YOU WERE DEAD...
......
NO...YOU'RE TOO YOUNG TO BE HIM. YOU MUST BE THE CLONE.
SORRY. MY MISTAKE.
EVERYBODY IN THIS TOWN KNOWS THAT YOU'RE SECOND'S CLONE.
OF COURSE YOUR FAMILY WOULD KNOW THAT, BAROQUE-HEAT.
ALZEID ...
?
ALZEID?

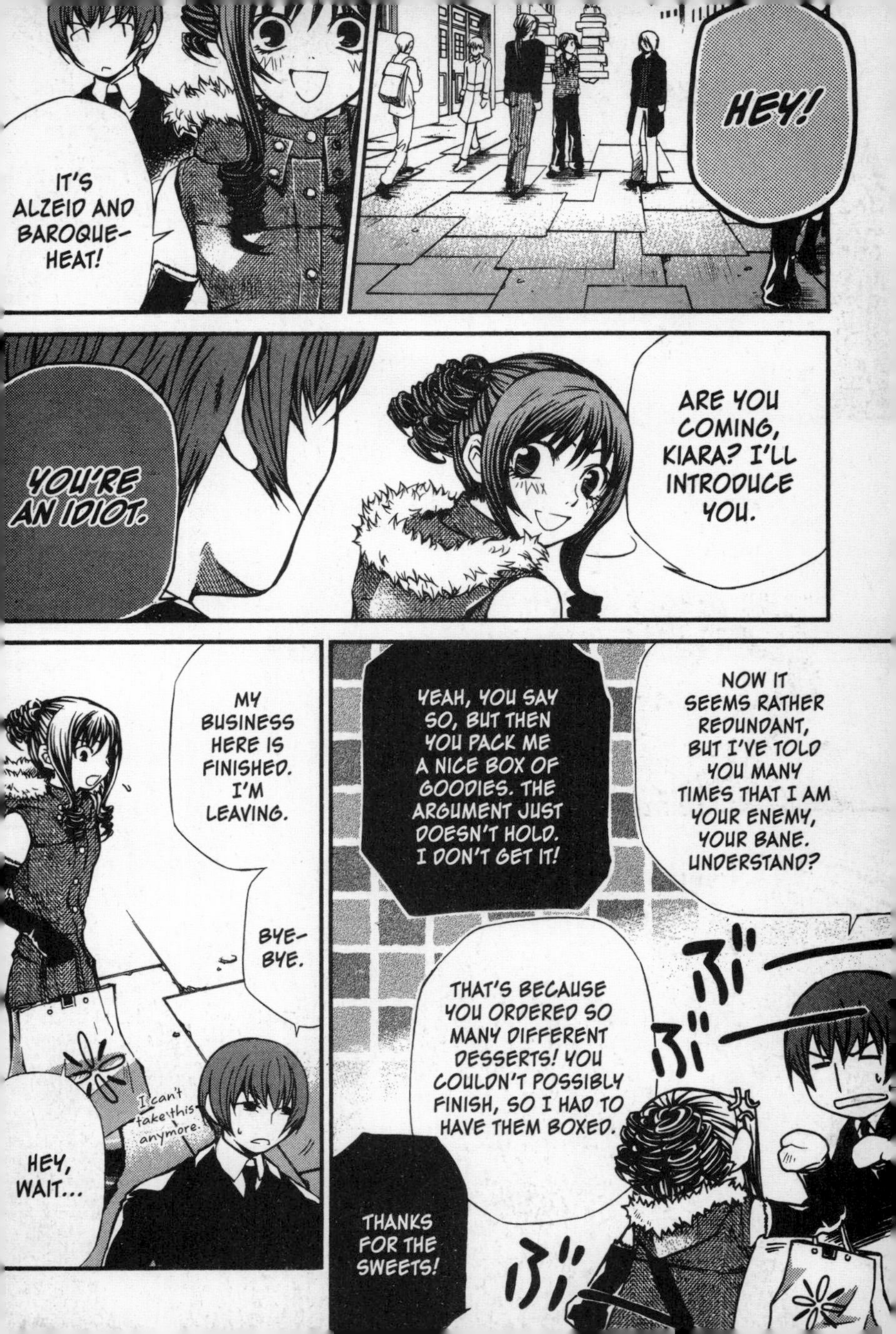
HEY!
IT'S ALZEID AND BAROQUE-HEAT!
ARE YOU COMING, KIARA? I'LL INTRODUCE YOU.
YOU'RE AN IDIOT.
NOW IT SEEMS RATHER REDUNDANT, BUT I'VE TOLD YOU MANY TIMES THAT I AM YOUR ENEMY, YOUR BANE. UNDERSTAND?
YEAH, YOU SAY SO, BUT THEN YOU PACK ME A NICE BOX OF GOODIES. THE ARGUMENT JUST DOESN'T HOLD. I DON'T GET IT!
THAT'S BECAUSE YOU ORDERED SO MANY DIFFERENT DESSERTS! YOU COULDN'T POSSIBLY FINISH, SO I HAD TO HAVE THEM BOXED.
ぶー
ぶー
ぶ
THANKS FOR THE SWEETS!
MY BUSINESS HERE IS FINISHED. I'M LEAVING.
BYE-BYE.
I can't take this anymore.
HEY, WAIT...

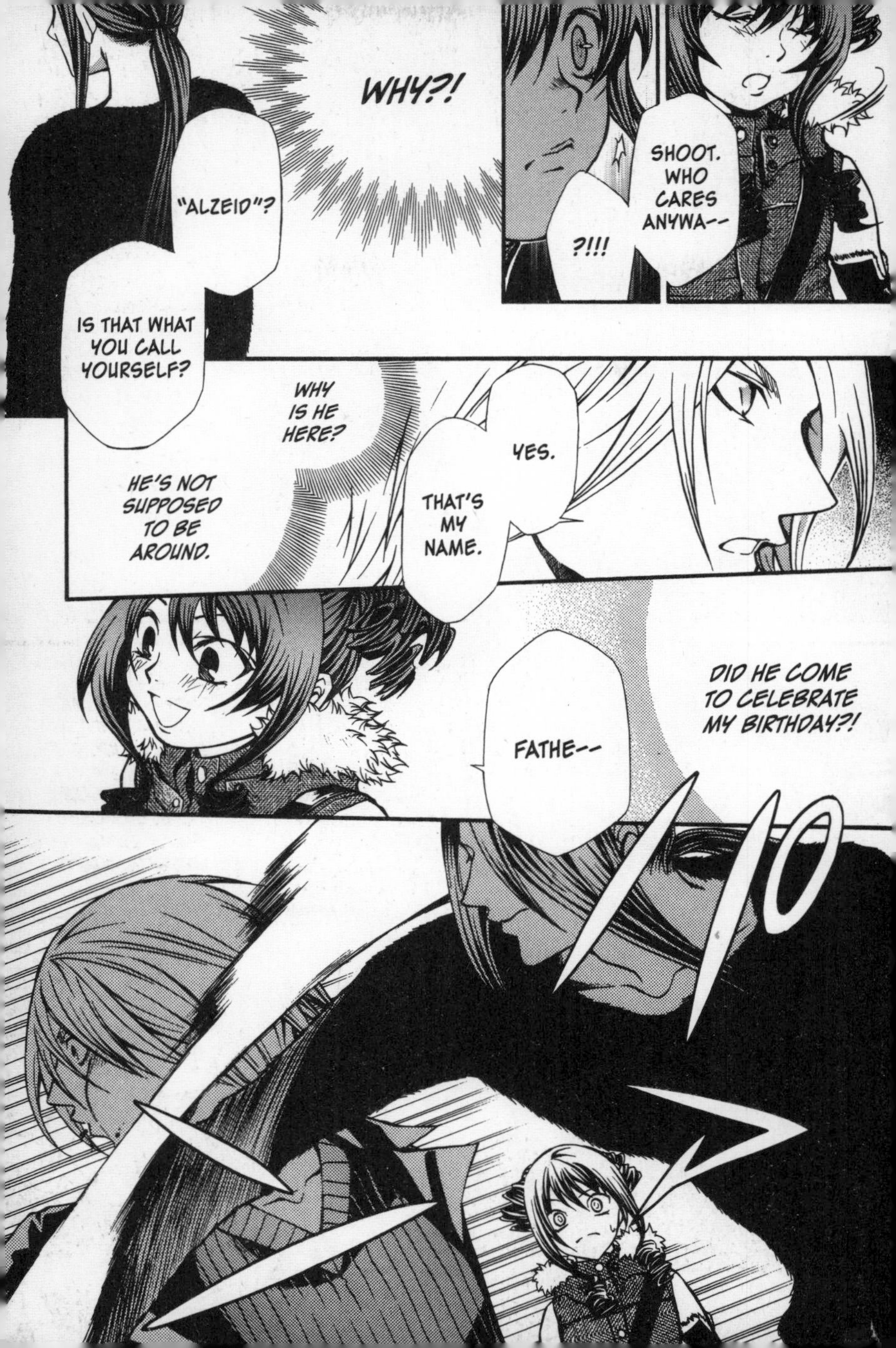
SHOOT. WHO CARES ANYWA--
?!!!
WHY?!
"ALZEID"?
IS THAT WHAT YOU CALL YOURSELF?
YES.
THAT'S MY NAME.
WHY IS HE HERE?
HE'S NOT SUPPOSED TO BE AROUND.
DID HE COME TO CELEBRATE MY BIRTHDAY?!
FATHE--

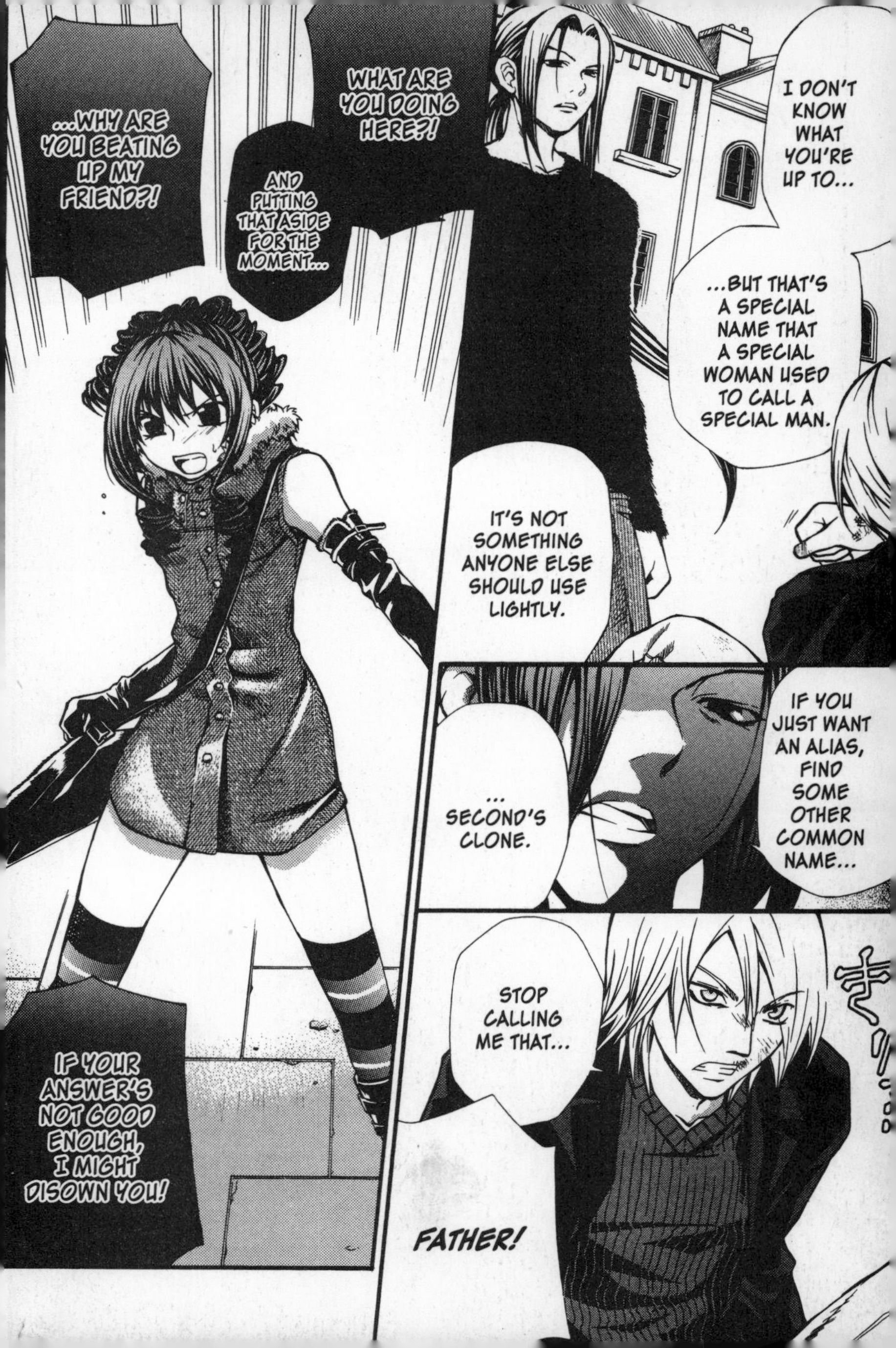

I DON'T KNOW WHAT YOU'RE UP TO...
...BUT THAT'S A SPECIAL NAME THAT A SPECIAL WOMAN USED TO CALL A SPECIAL MAN.
IT'S NOT SOMETHING ANYONE ELSE SHOULD USE LIGHTLY.
IF YOU JUST WANT AN ALIAS, FIND SOME OTHER COMMON NAME...
... SECOND'S CLONE.
STOP CALLING ME THAT...
FATHER!
WHAT ARE YOU DOING HERE?!
AND PUTTING THAT ASIDE FOR THE MOMENT...
...WHY ARE YOU BEATING UP MY FRIEND?!
IF YOUR ANSWER'S NOT GOOD ENOUGH, I MIGHT DISOWN YOU!

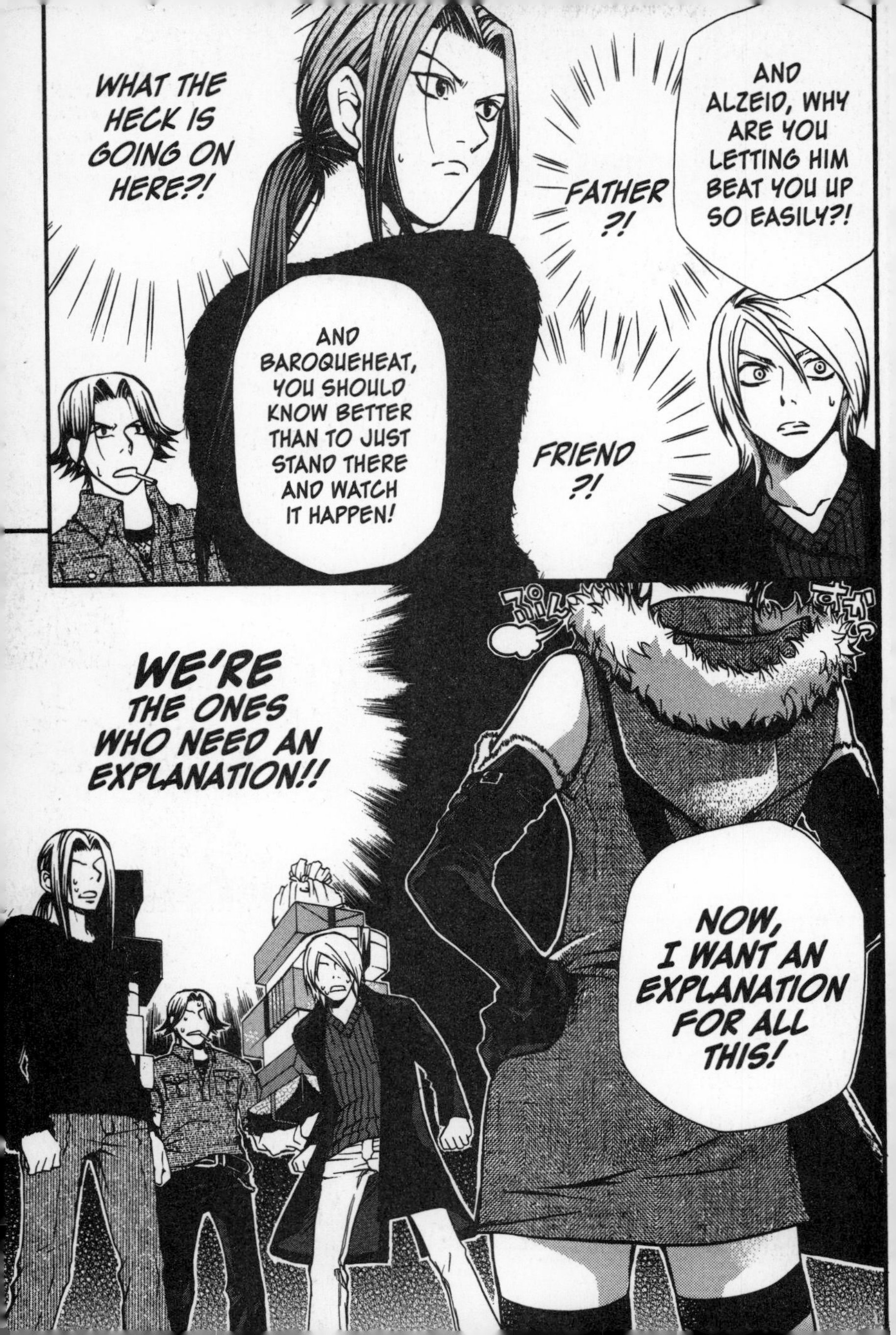
AND ALZEID, WHY ARE YOU LETTING HIM BEAT YOU UP SO EASILY?!
FATHER ?!
WHAT THE HECK IS GOING ON HERE?!
AND BAROQUEHEAT, YOU SHOULD KNOW BETTER THAN TO JUST STAND THERE AND WATCH IT HAPPEN!
FRIEND ?!
NOW, I WANT AN EXPLANATION FOR ALL THIS!
WE'RE THE ONES WHO NEED AN EXPLANATION!!

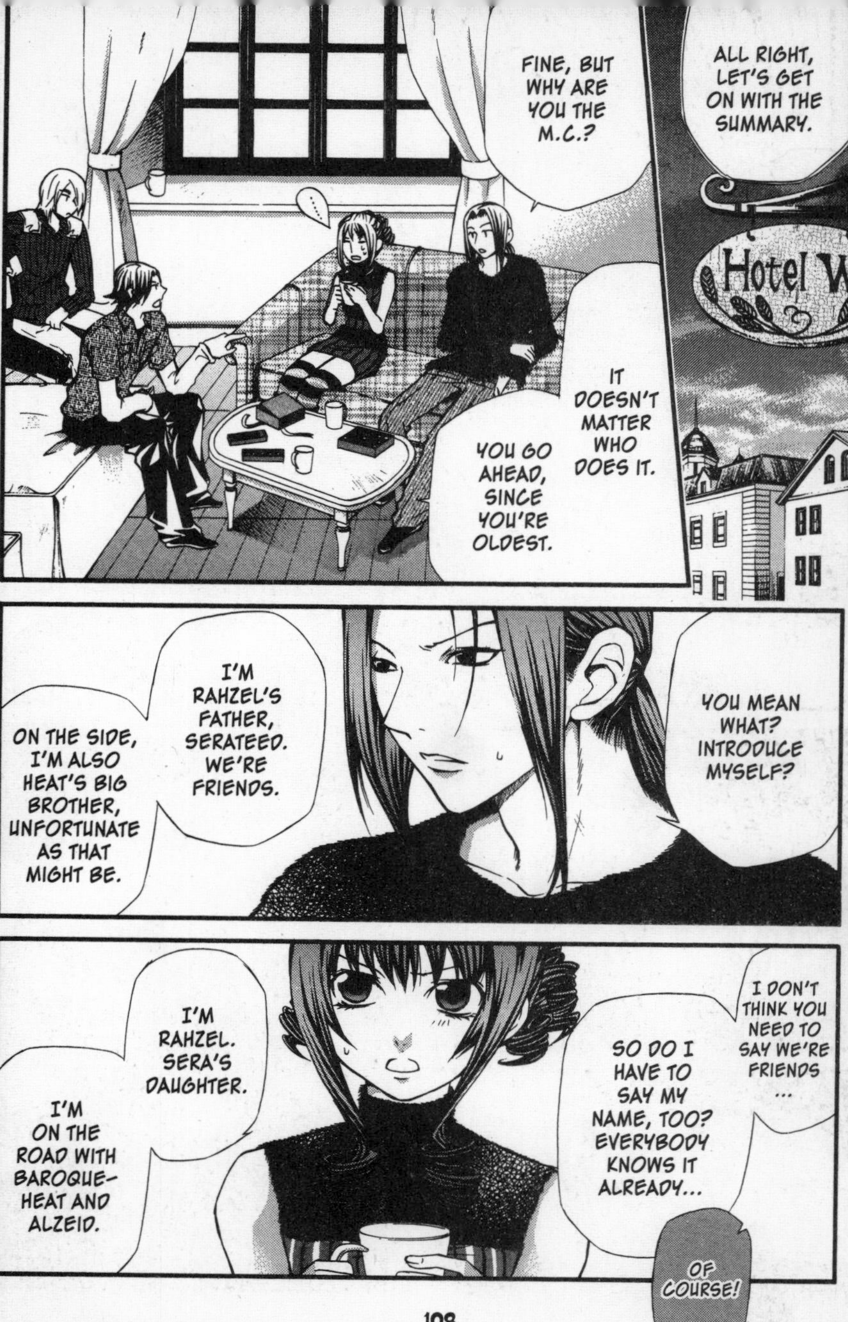
ALL RIGHT, LET'S GET ON WITH THE SUMMARY.
Hotel W's
FINE, BUT WHY ARE YOU THE M.C.?
...
IT DOESN'T MATTER WHO DOES IT.
YOU GO AHEAD, SINCE YOU'RE OLDEST.
YOU MEAN WHAT? INTRODUCE MYSELF?
I'M RAHZEL'S FATHER, SERATEED. WE'RE FRIENDS.
ON THE SIDE, I'M ALSO HEAT'S BIG BROTHER, UNFORTUNATE AS THAT MIGHT BE.
I DON'T THINK YOU NEED TO SAY WE'RE FRIENDS ...
SO DO I HAVE TO SAY MY NAME, TOO? EVERYBODY KNOWS IT ALREADY...
OF COURSE!
I'M RAHZEL. SERA'S DAUGHTER.
I'M ON THE ROAD WITH BAROQUE-HEAT AND ALZEID.

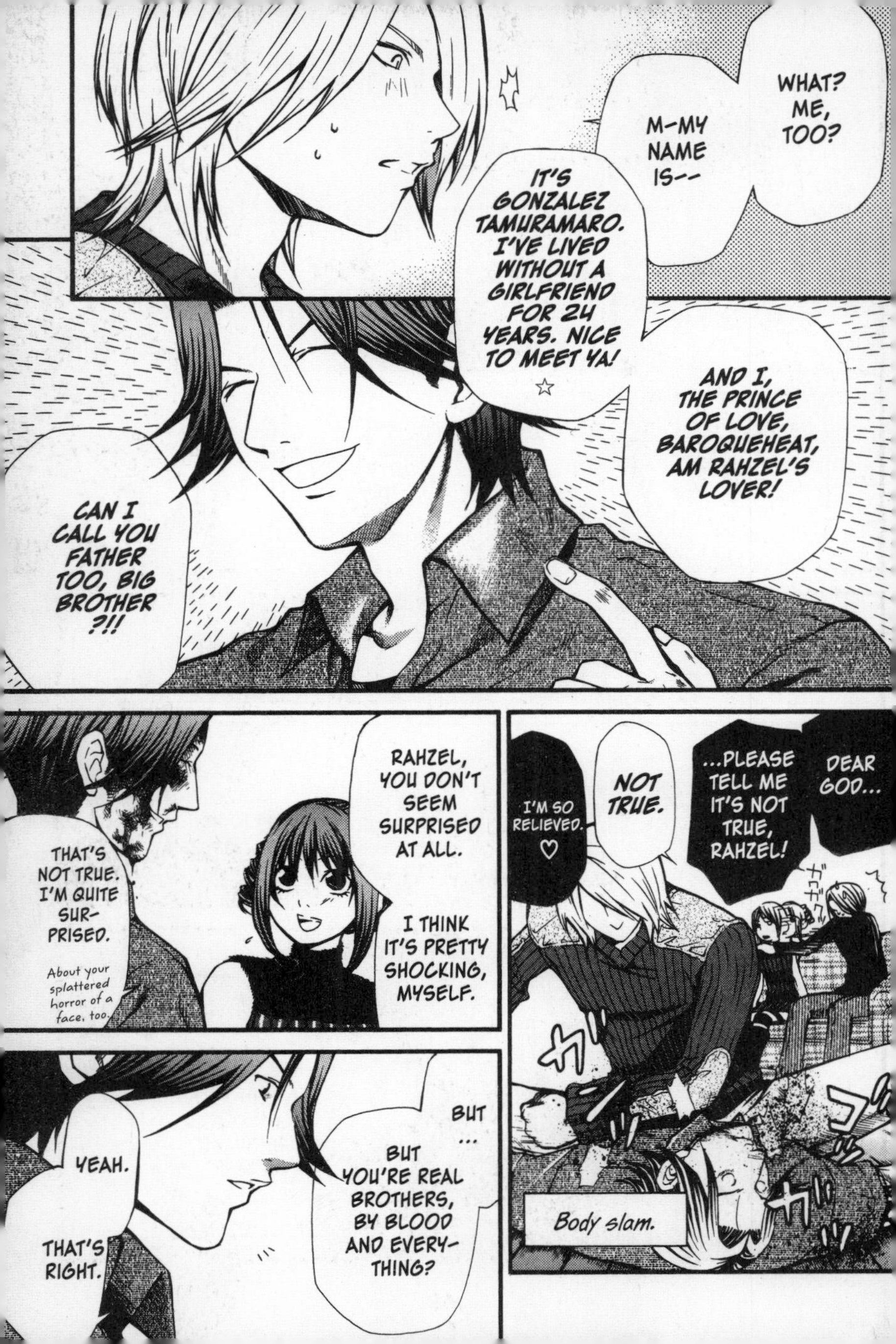
WHAT? ME, TOO?
M-MY NAME IS--
IT'S GONZALEZ TAMURAMARO. I'VE LIVED WITHOUT A GIRLFRIEND FOR 24 YEARS. NICE TO MEET YA! ☆
AND I, THE PRINCE OF LOVE, BAROQUEHEAT, AM RAHZEL'S LOVER!
CAN I CALL YOU FATHER TOO, BIG BROTHER?!!
DEAR GOD...
...PLEASE TELL ME IT'S NOT TRUE, RAHZEL!
NOT TRUE.
I'M SO RELIEVED. ♡
Body slam.
RAHZEL, YOU DON'T SEEM SURPRISED AT ALL.
I THINK IT'S PRETTY SHOCKING, MYSELF.
THAT'S NOT TRUE. I'M QUITE SURPRISED.
About your splattered horror of a face, too.
BUT ...
BUT YOU'RE REAL BROTHERS, BY BLOOD AND EVERYTHING?
YEAH.
THAT'S RIGHT.

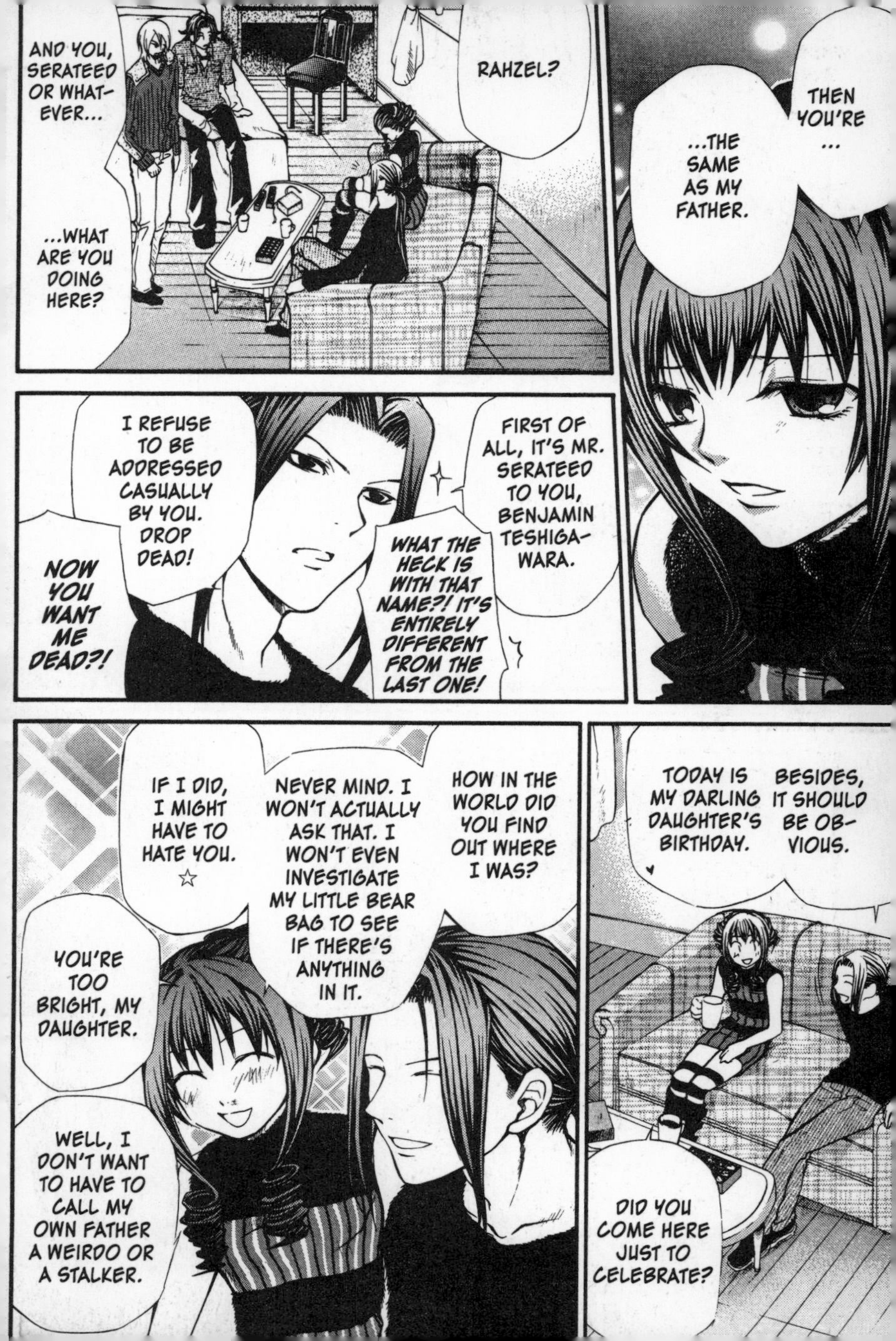
THEN YOU'RE ...
...THE SAME AS MY FATHER.
RAHZEL?
AND YOU, SERATEED OR WHAT-EVER...
...WHAT ARE YOU DOING HERE?
FIRST OF ALL, IT'S MR. SERATEED TO YOU, BENJAMIN TESHIGA-WARA.
WHAT THE HECK IS WITH THAT NAME?! IT'S ENTIRELY DIFFERENT FROM THE LAST ONE!
I REFUSE TO BE ADDRESSED CASUALLY BY YOU. DROP DEAD!
NOW YOU WANT ME DEAD?!
BESIDES, IT SHOULD BE OB-VIOUS.
TODAY IS MY DARLING DAUGHTER'S BIRTHDAY. ♥
DID YOU COME HERE JUST TO CELEBRATE?
HOW IN THE WORLD DID YOU FIND OUT WHERE I WAS?
NEVER MIND. I WON'T ACTUALLY ASK THAT. I WON'T EVEN INVESTIGATE MY LITTLE BEAR BAG TO SEE IF THERE'S ANYTHING IN IT.
IF I DID, I MIGHT HAVE TO HATE YOU. ☆
YOU'RE TOO BRIGHT, MY DAUGHTER.
WELL, I DON'T WANT TO HAVE TO CALL MY OWN FATHER A WEIRDO OR A STALKER.

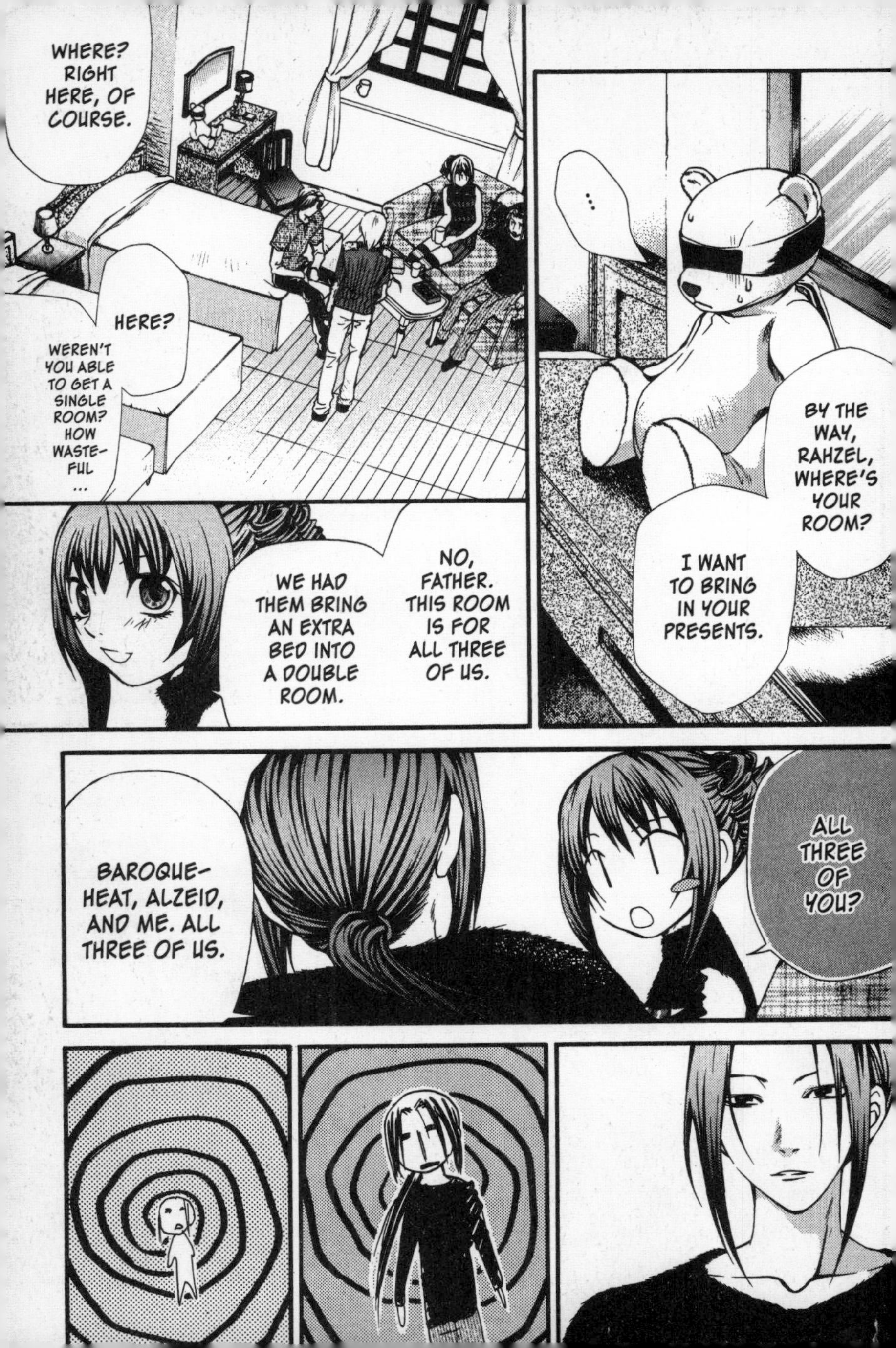
...
BY THE WAY, RAHZEL, WHERE'S YOUR ROOM?
I WANT TO BRING IN YOUR PRESENTS.
WHERE? RIGHT HERE, OF COURSE.
HERE? WEREN'T YOU ABLE TO GET A SINGLE ROOM? HOW WASTEFUL ...
NO, FATHER. THIS ROOM IS FOR ALL THREE OF US.
WE HAD THEM BRING AN EXTRA BED INTO A DOUBLE ROOM.
ALL THREE OF YOU?
BAROQUE-HEAT, ALZEID, AND ME. ALL THREE OF US.

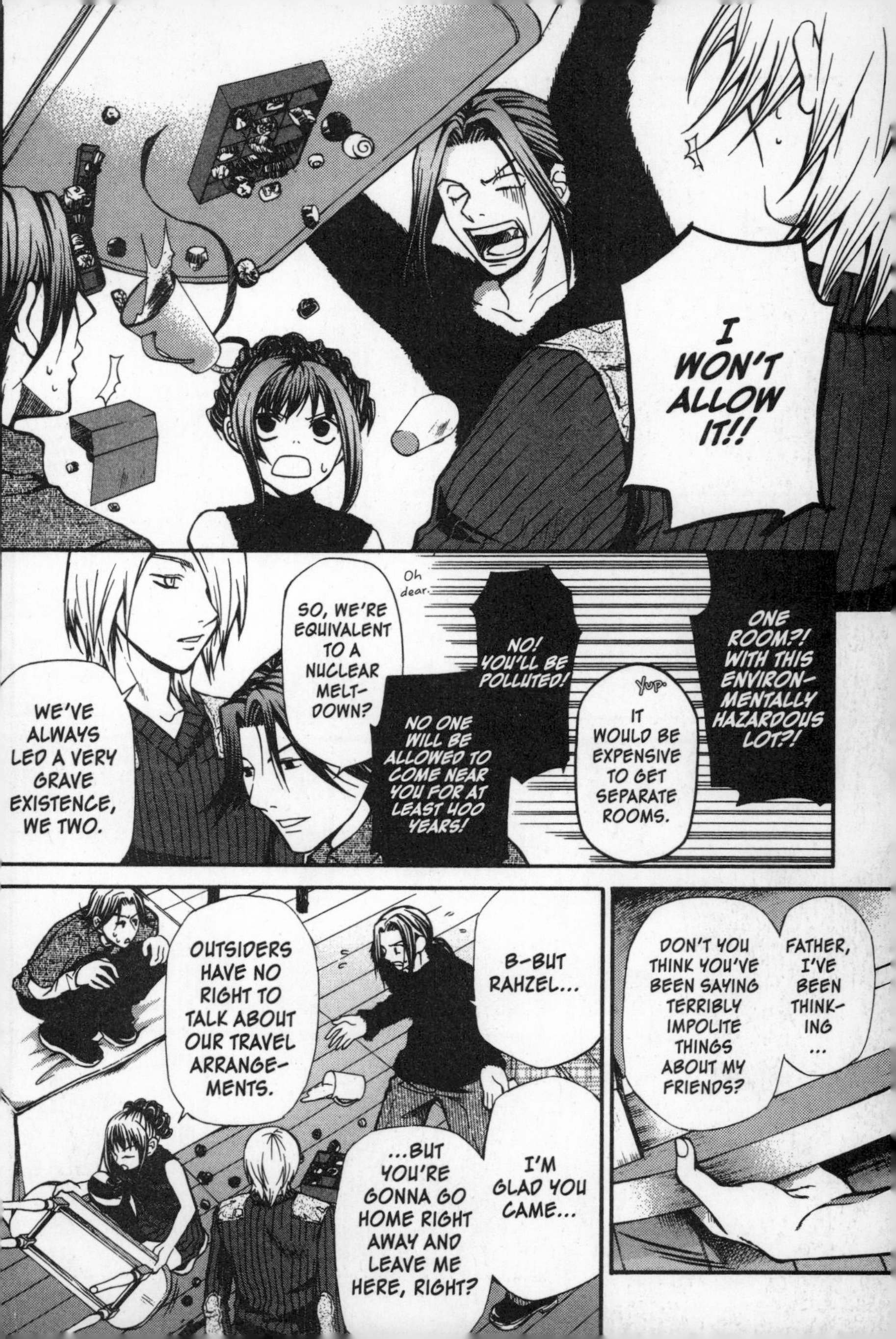

I WON'T ALLOW IT!!
ONE ROOM?! WITH THIS ENVIRON-MENTALLY HAZARDOUS LOT?!
Yup.
IT WOULD BE EXPENSIVE TO GET SEPARATE ROOMS.
NO! YOU'LL BE POLLUTED!
NO ONE WILL BE ALLOWED TO COME NEAR YOU FOR AT LEAST 400 YEARS!
Oh dear.
SO, WE'RE EQUIVALENT TO A NUCLEAR MELT-DOWN?
WE'VE ALWAYS LED A VERY GRAVE EXISTENCE, WE TWO.
FATHER, I'VE BEEN THINK-ING...
DON'T YOU THINK YOU'VE BEEN SAYING TERRIBLY IMPOLITE THINGS ABOUT MY FRIENDS?
B-BUT RAHZEL...
OUTSIDERS HAVE NO RIGHT TO TALK ABOUT OUR TRAVEL ARRANGE-MENTS.
I'M GLAD YOU CAME...
...BUT YOU'RE GONNA GO HOME RIGHT AWAY AND LEAVE ME HERE, RIGHT?

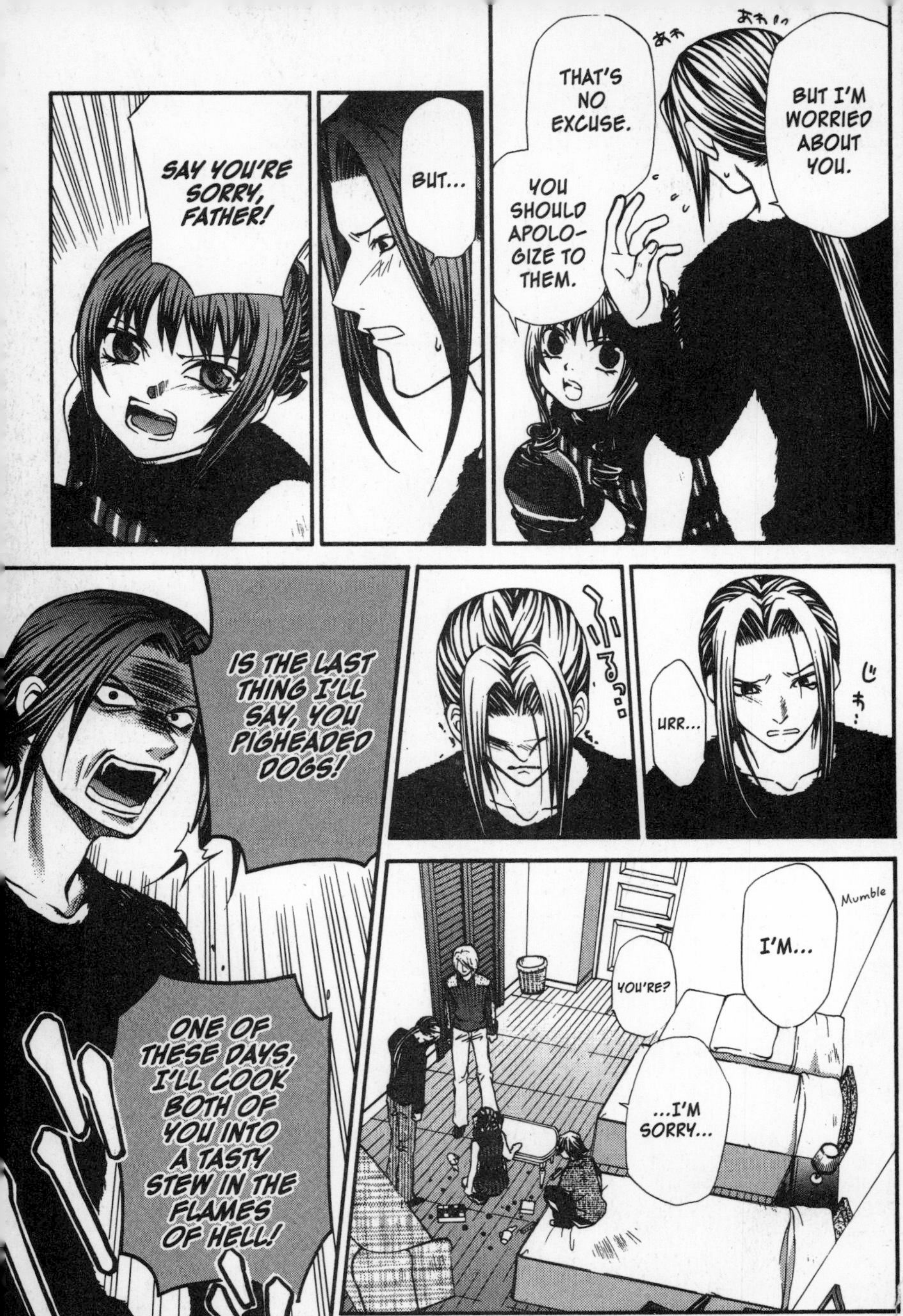

BUT I'M WORRIED ABOUT YOU.
THAT'S NO EXCUSE.
YOU SHOULD APOLOGIZE TO THEM.
BUT...
SAY YOU'RE SORRY, FATHER!
URR...
Mumble
I'M...
YOU'RE?
...I'M SORRY...
IS THE LAST THING I'LL SAY, YOU PIGHEADED DOGS!
ONE OF THESE DAYS, I'LL COOK BOTH OF YOU INTO A TASTY STEW IN THE FLAMES OF HELL!

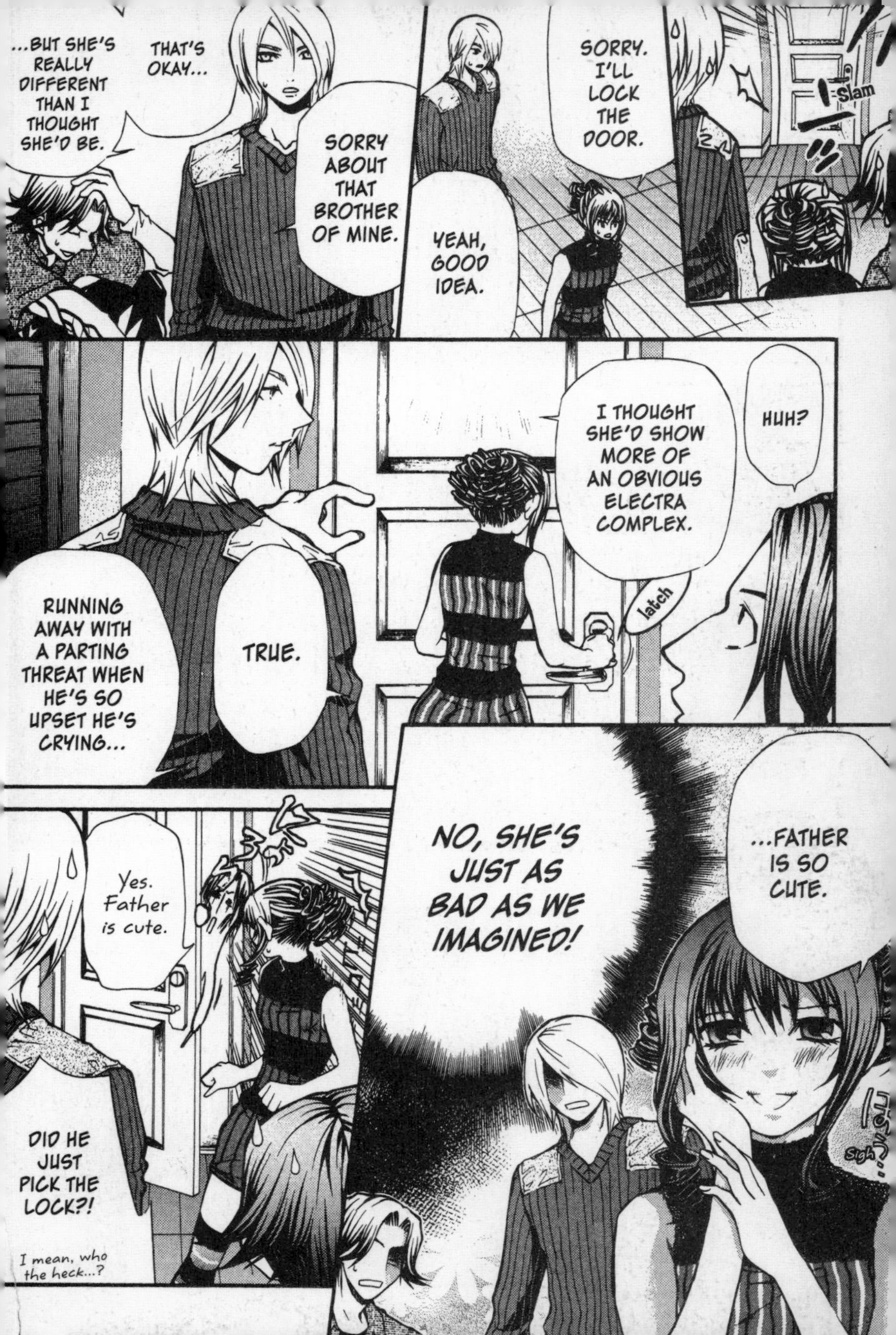
Slam
SORRY. I'LL LOCK THE DOOR.
YEAH, GOOD IDEA.
SORRY ABOUT THAT BROTHER OF MINE.
THAT'S OKAY...
...BUT SHE'S REALLY DIFFERENT THAN I THOUGHT SHE'D BE.
HUH?
I THOUGHT SHE'D SHOW MORE OF AN OBVIOUS ELECTRA COMPLEX.
latch
TRUE.
RUNNING AWAY WITH A PARTING THREAT WHEN HE'S SO UPSET HE'S CRYING...
...FATHER IS SO CUTE.
Sigh
NO, SHE'S JUST AS BAD AS WE IMAGINED!
Yes. Father is cute.
DID HE JUST PICK THE LOCK?!
I mean, who the heck...?

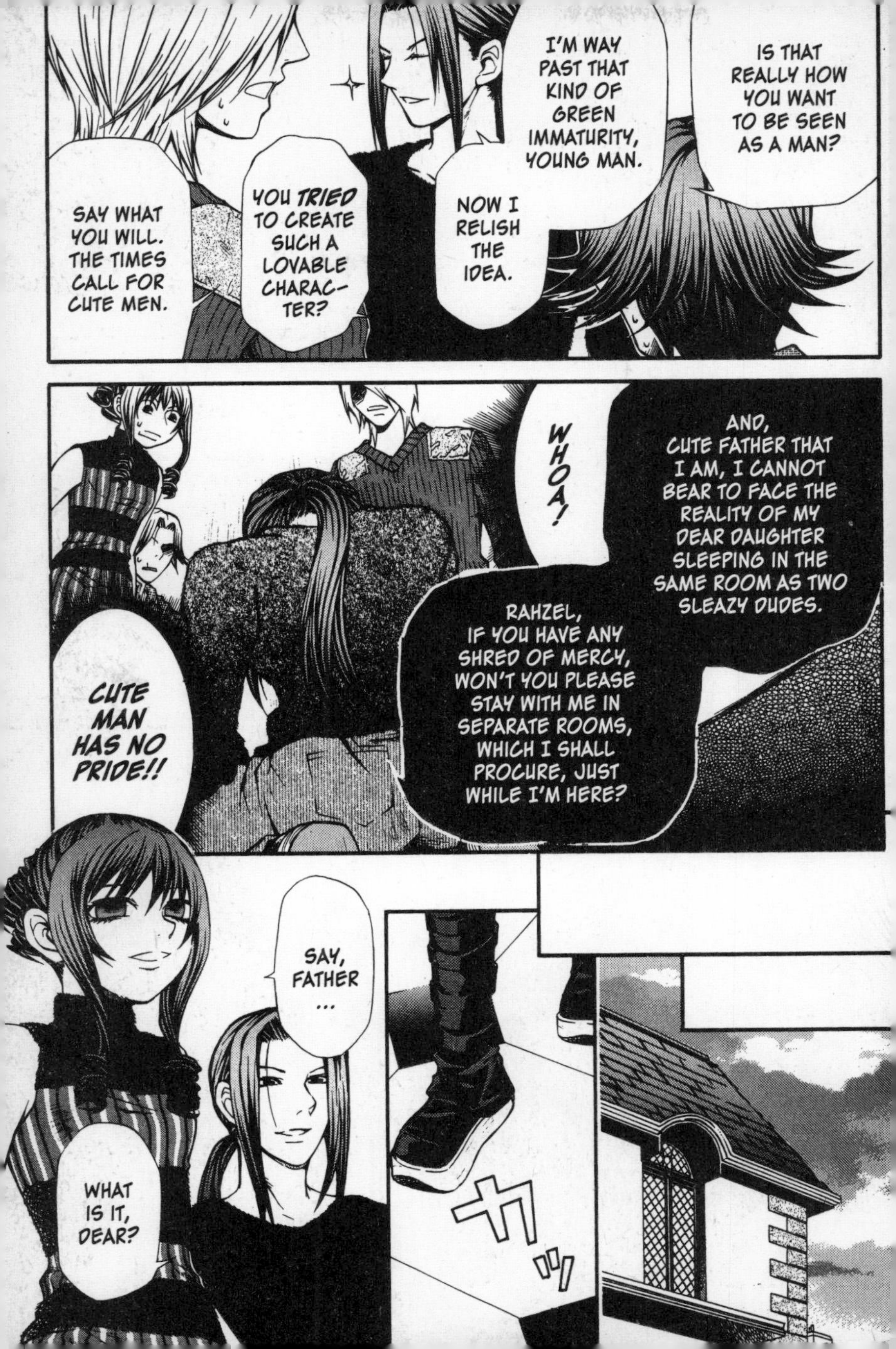
IS THAT REALLY HOW YOU WANT TO BE SEEN AS A MAN?
I'M WAY PAST THAT KIND OF GREEN IMMATURITY, YOUNG MAN.
NOW I RELISH THE IDEA.
YOU *TRIED* TO CREATE SUCH A LOVABLE CHARAC-TER?
SAY WHAT YOU WILL. THE TIMES CALL FOR CUTE MEN.
AND, CUTE FATHER THAT I AM, I CANNOT BEAR TO FACE THE REALITY OF MY DEAR DAUGHTER SLEEPING IN THE SAME ROOM AS TWO SLEAZY DUDES.
WHOA!
RAHZEL, IF YOU HAVE ANY SHRED OF MERCY, WON'T YOU PLEASE STAY WITH ME IN SEPARATE ROOMS, WHICH I SHALL PROCURE, JUST WHILE I'M HERE?
CUTE MAN HAS NO PRIDE!!
SAY, FATHER ...
WHAT IS IT, DEAR?

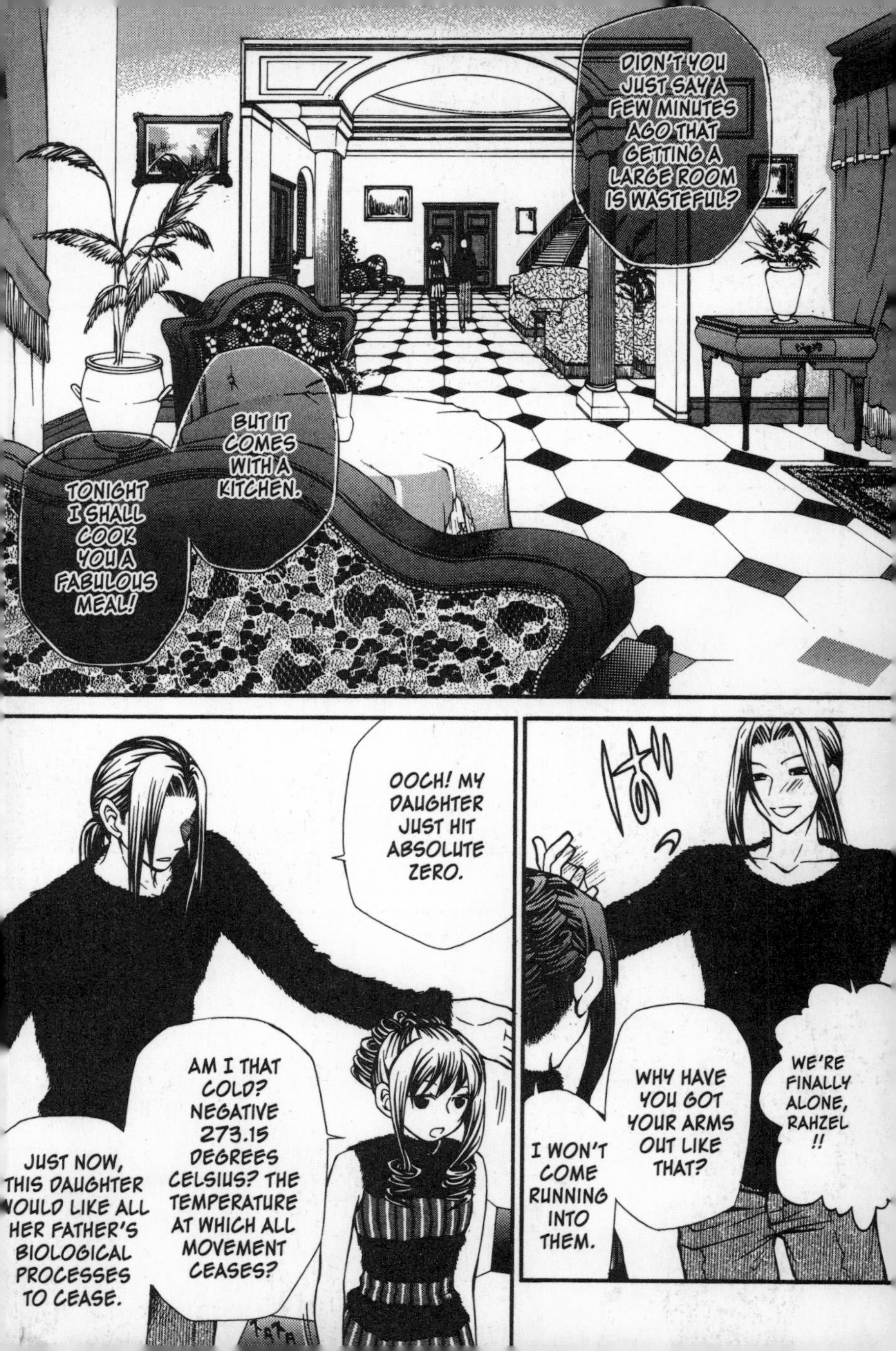
DIDN'T YOU JUST SAY A FEW MINUTES AGO THAT GETTING A LARGE ROOM IS WASTEFUL?
BUT IT COMES WITH A KITCHEN.
TONIGHT I SHALL COOK YOU A FABULOUS MEAL!
WE'RE FINALLY ALONE, RAHZEL !!
WHY HAVE YOU GOT YOUR ARMS OUT LIKE THAT?
I WON'T COME RUNNING INTO THEM.
OOCH! MY DAUGHTER JUST HIT ABSOLUTE ZERO.
AM I THAT COLD? NEGATIVE 273.15 DEGREES CELSIUS? THE TEMPERATURE AT WHICH ALL MOVEMENT CEASES?
JUST NOW, THIS DAUGHTER WOULD LIKE ALL HER FATHER'S BIOLOGICAL PROCESSES TO CEASE.

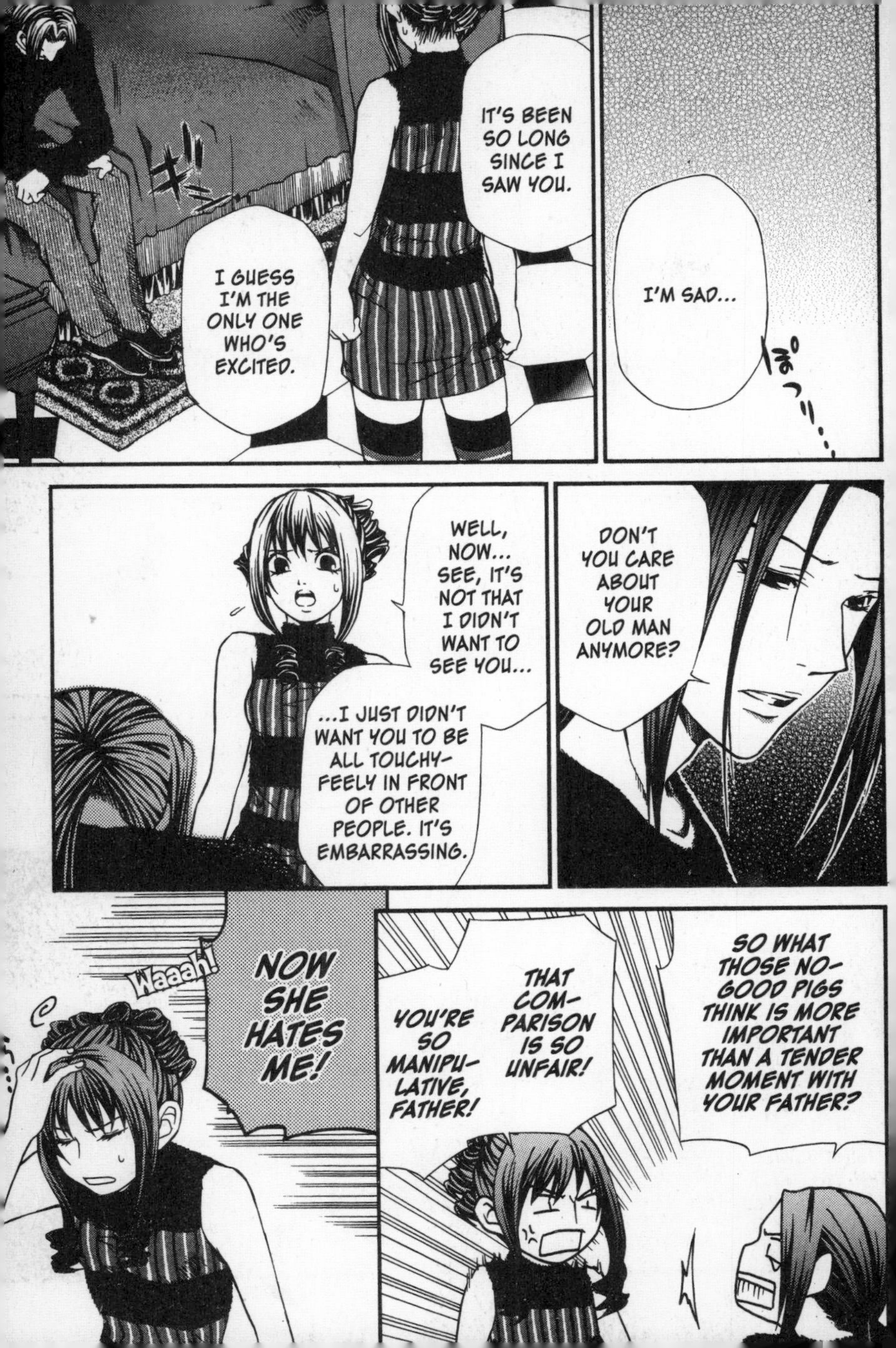
I'M SAD...
ぽつり...
IT'S BEEN SO LONG SINCE I SAW YOU.
I GUESS I'M THE ONLY ONE WHO'S EXCITED.
DON'T YOU CARE ABOUT YOUR OLD MAN ANYMORE?
WELL, NOW... SEE, IT'S NOT THAT I DIDN'T WANT TO SEE YOU...
...I JUST DIDN'T WANT YOU TO BE ALL TOUCHY-FEELY IN FRONT OF OTHER PEOPLE. IT'S EMBARRASSING.
SO WHAT THOSE NO-GOOD PIGS THINK IS MORE IMPORTANT THAN A TENDER MOMENT WITH YOUR FATHER?
THAT COM-PARISON IS SO UNFAIR!
YOU'RE SO MANIPU-LATIVE, FATHER!
Waaah!
NOW SHE HATES ME!

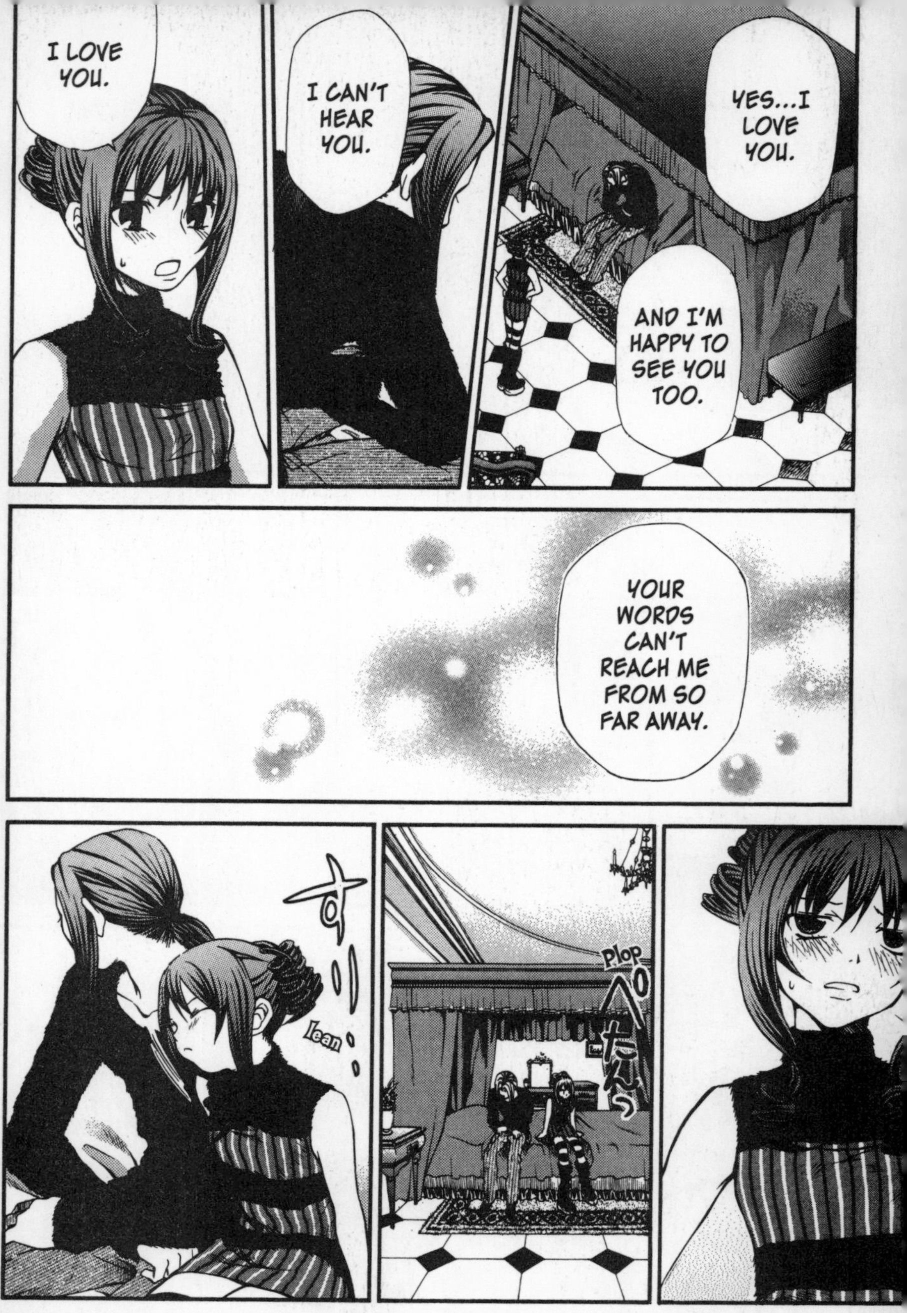
YES...I LOVE YOU.
AND I'M HAPPY TO SEE YOU TOO.
I CAN'T HEAR YOU.
I LOVE YOU.
YOUR WORDS CAN'T REACH ME FROM SO FAR AWAY.
Plop
lean

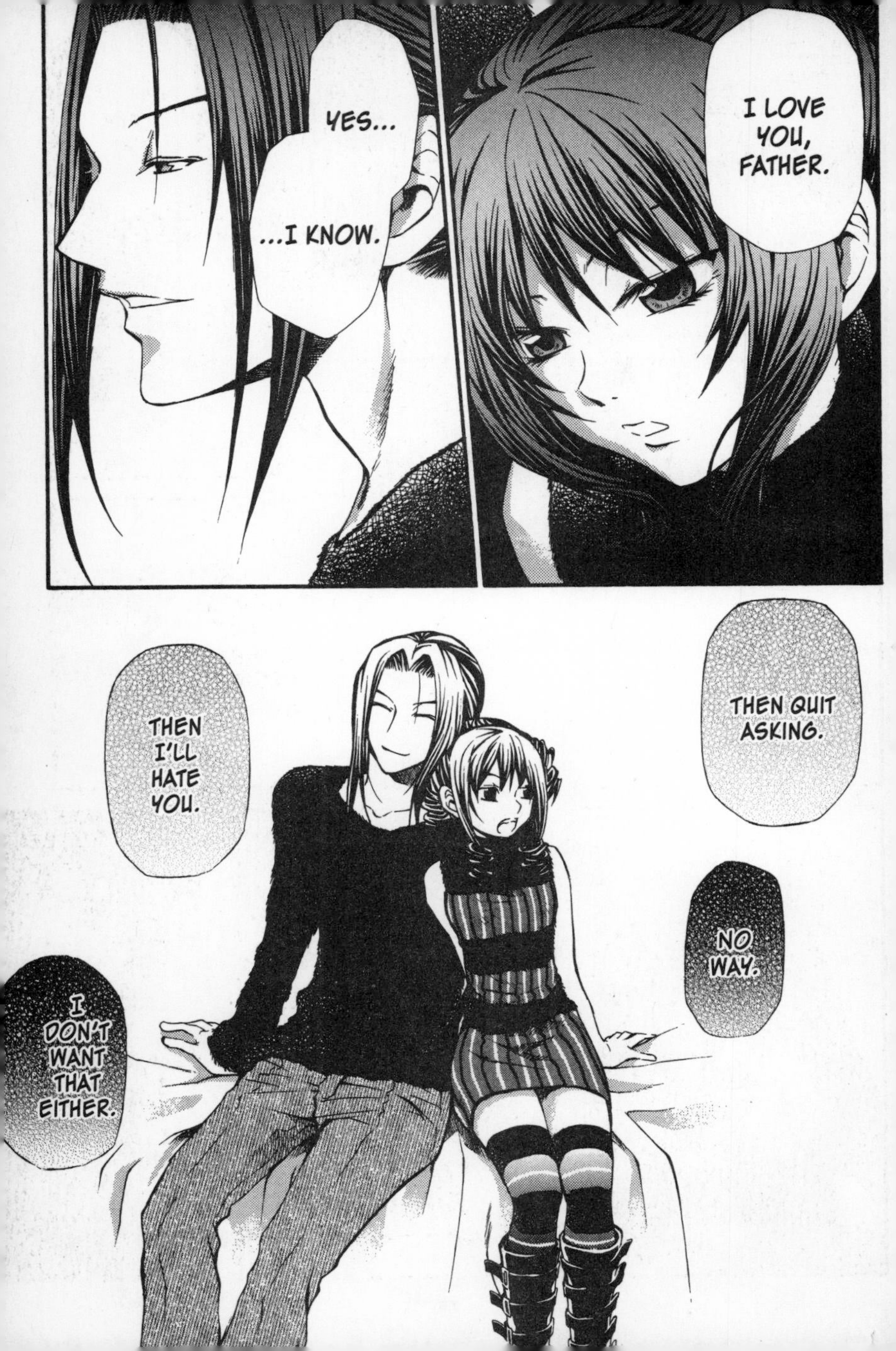
I LOVE YOU, FATHER.
YES...
...I KNOW.
THEN QUIT ASKING.
THEN I'LL HATE YOU.
NO WAY.
I DON'T WANT THAT EITHER.

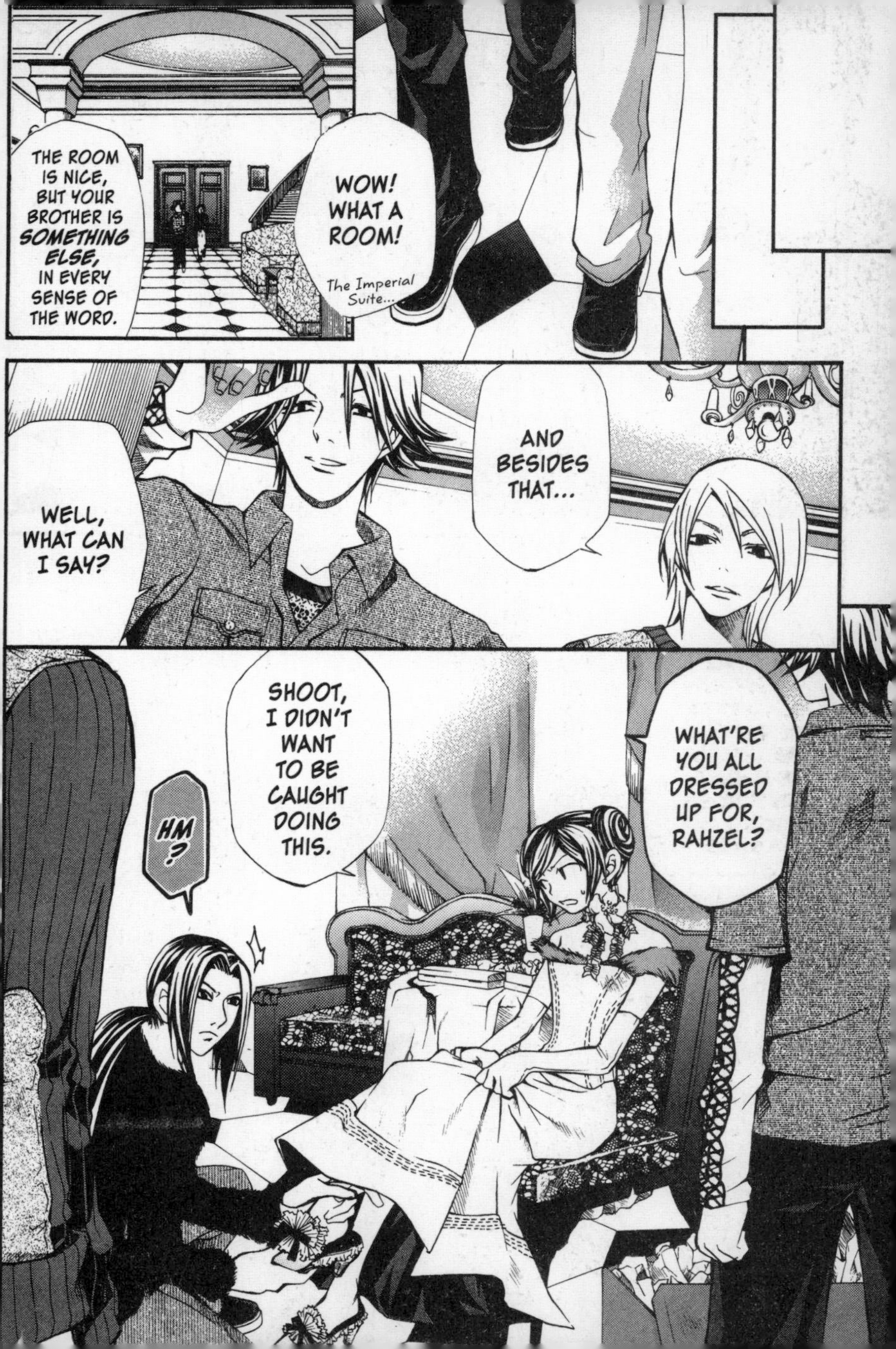
WOW! WHAT A ROOM!
The Imperial Suite...
THE ROOM IS NICE, BUT YOUR BROTHER IS *SOMETHING ELSE,* IN EVERY SENSE OF THE WORD.
AND BESIDES THAT...
WELL, WHAT CAN I SAY?
WHAT'RE YOU ALL DRESSED UP FOR, RAHZEL?
SHOOT, I DIDN'T WANT TO BE CAUGHT DOING THIS.
HM?

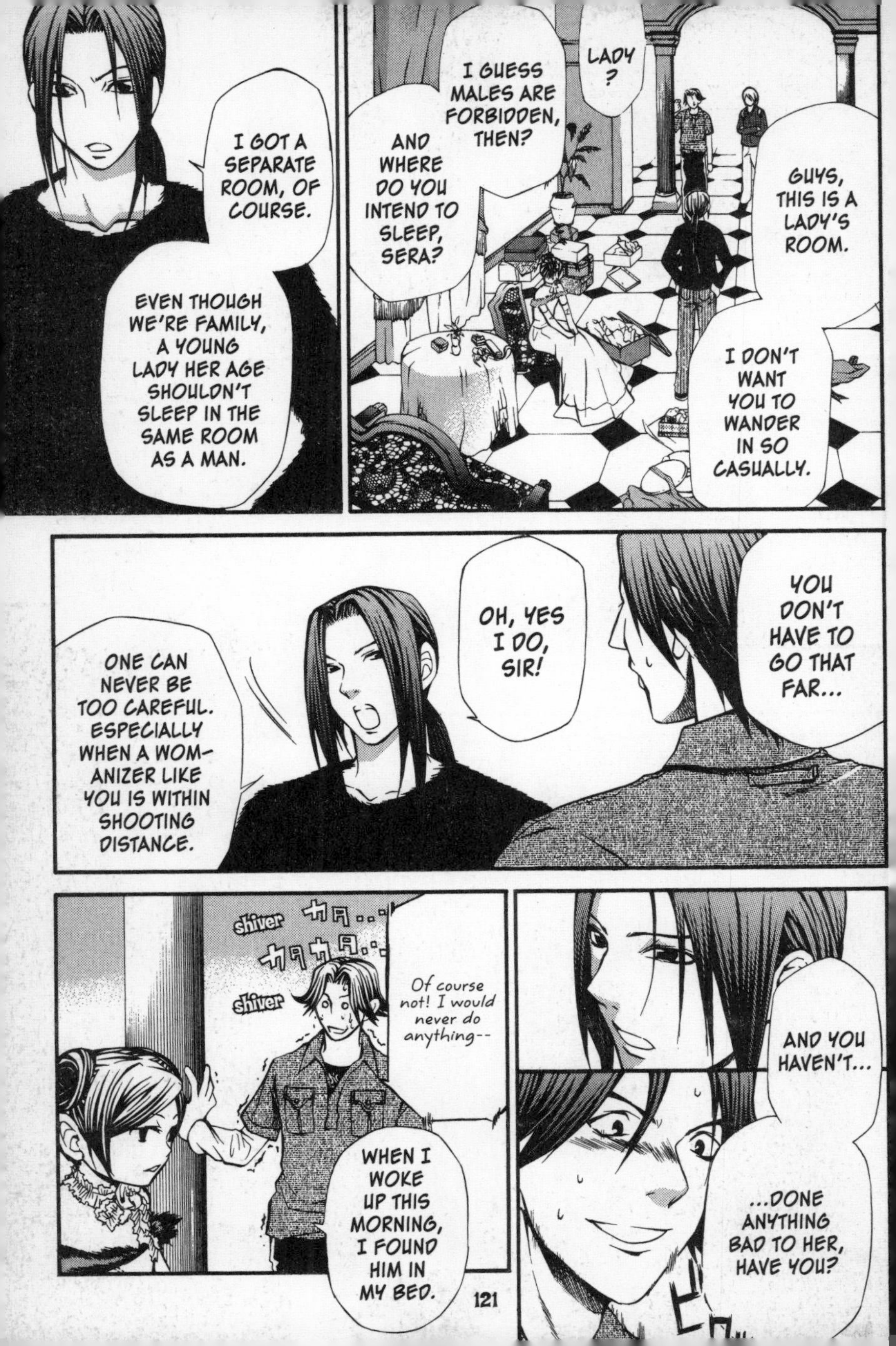

GUYS, THIS IS A LADY'S ROOM.
I DON'T WANT YOU TO WANDER IN SO CASUALLY.
LADY?
I GUESS MALES ARE FORBIDDEN, THEN?
AND WHERE DO YOU INTEND TO SLEEP, SERA?
I GOT A SEPARATE ROOM, OF COURSE.
EVEN THOUGH WE'RE FAMILY, A YOUNG LADY HER AGE SHOULDN'T SLEEP IN THE SAME ROOM AS A MAN.
YOU DON'T HAVE TO GO THAT FAR...
OH, YES I DO, SIR!
ONE CAN NEVER BE TOO CAREFUL. ESPECIALLY WHEN A WOM-ANIZER LIKE YOU IS WITHIN SHOOTING DISTANCE.
AND YOU HAVEN'T...
...DONE ANYTHING BAD TO HER, HAVE YOU?
Of course not! I would never do anything--
shiver
shiver
WHEN I WOKE UP THIS MORNING, I FOUND HIM IN MY BED.

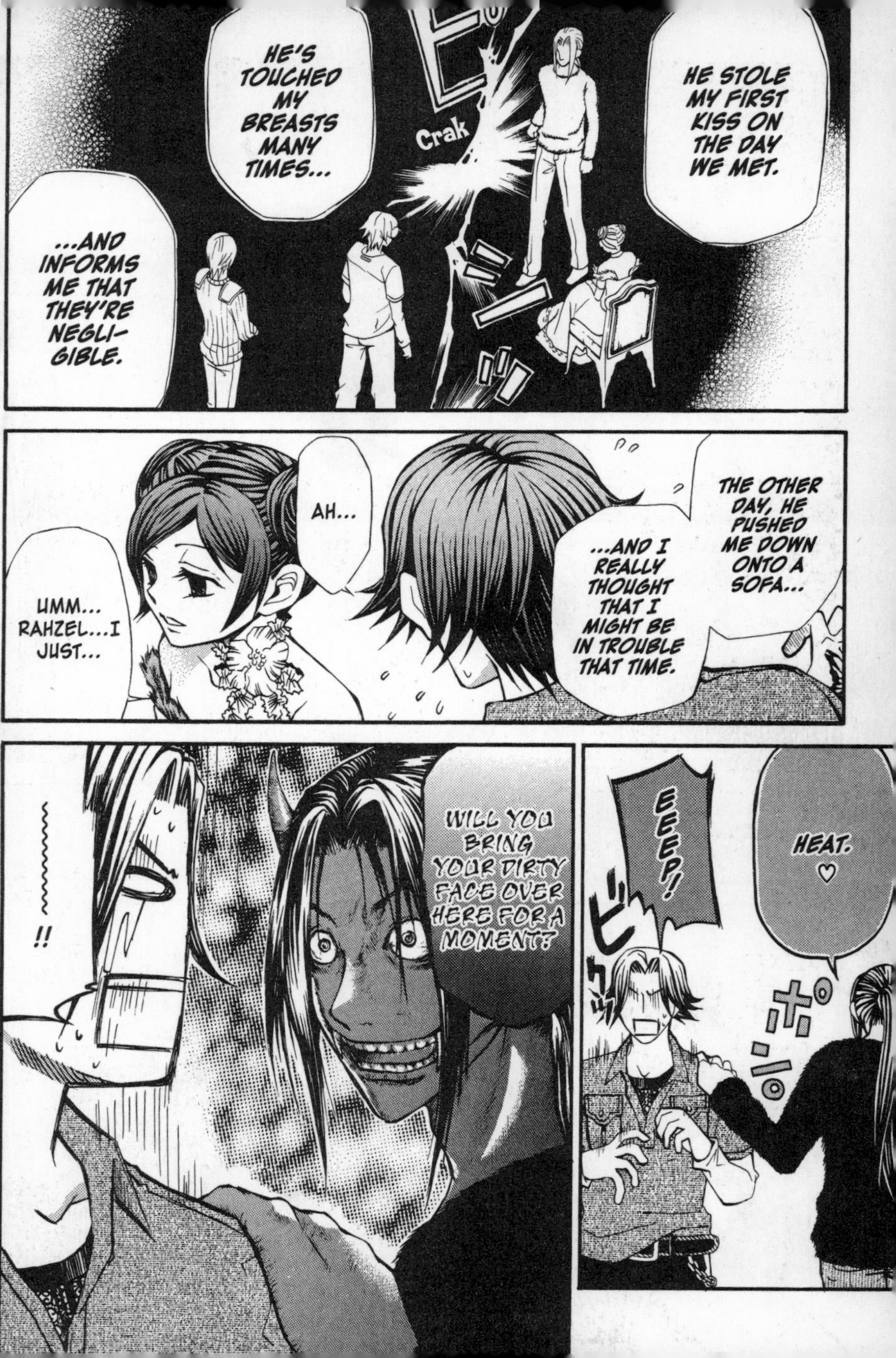
HE STOLE MY FIRST KISS ON THE DAY WE MET.
HE'S TOUCHED MY BREASTS MANY TIMES...
Crak
...AND INFORMS ME THAT THEY'RE NEGLI-GIBLE.
THE OTHER DAY, HE PUSHED ME DOWN ONTO A SOFA...
...AND I REALLY THOUGHT THAT I MIGHT BE IN TROUBLE THAT TIME.
AH...
UMM... RAHZEL...I JUST...
HEAT. ♡
EEEP!
WILL YOU BRING YOUR DIRTY FACE OVER HERE FOR A MOMENT?
!!

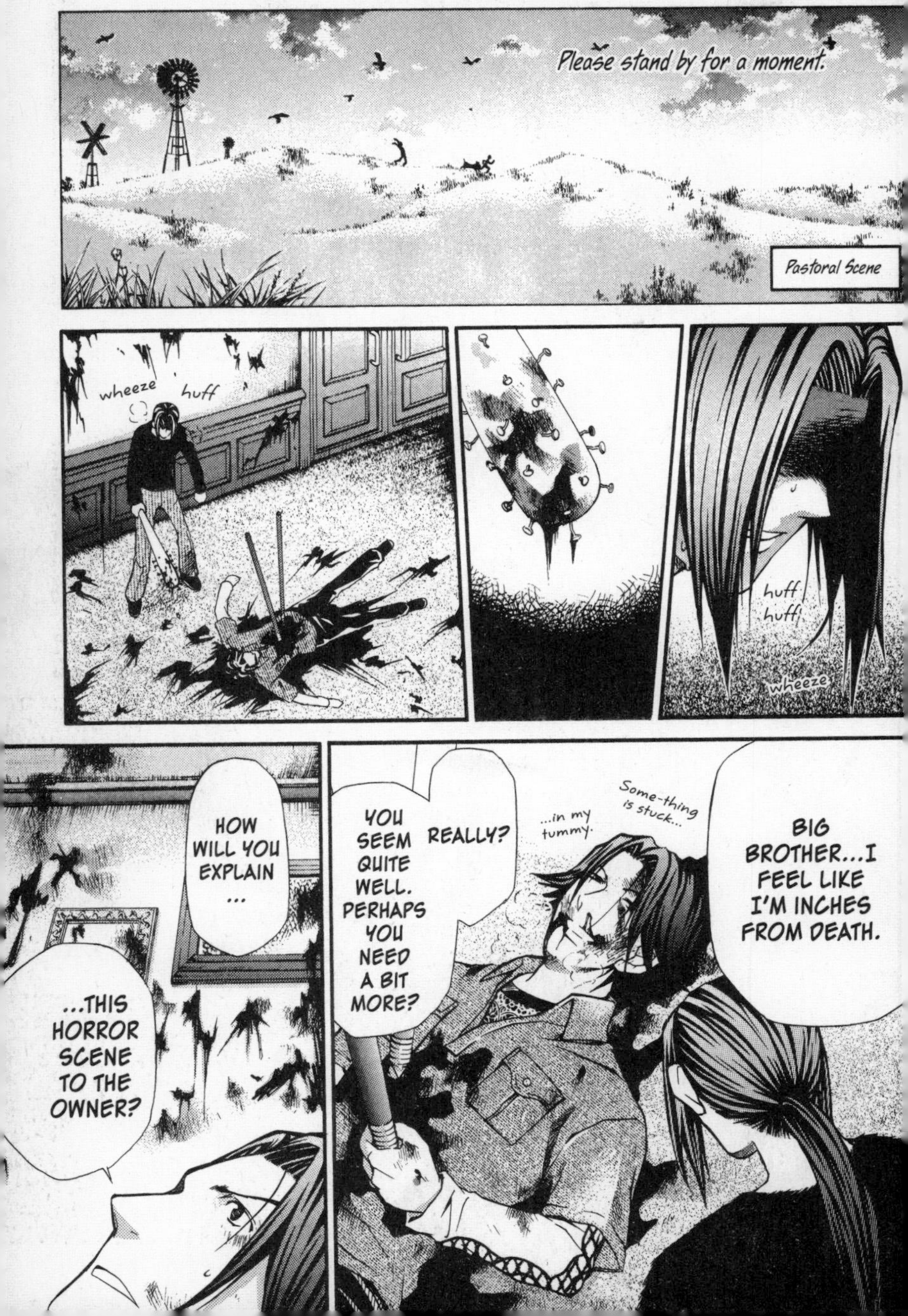
Please stand by for a moment.
Pastoral Scene
huff huff
wheeze
wheeze
huff
BIG BROTHER...I FEEL LIKE I'M INCHES FROM DEATH.
Some-thing is stuck...
...in my tummy.
REALLY?
YOU SEEM QUITE WELL. PERHAPS YOU NEED A BIT MORE?
HOW WILL YOU EXPLAIN ...
...THIS HORROR SCENE TO THE OWNER?

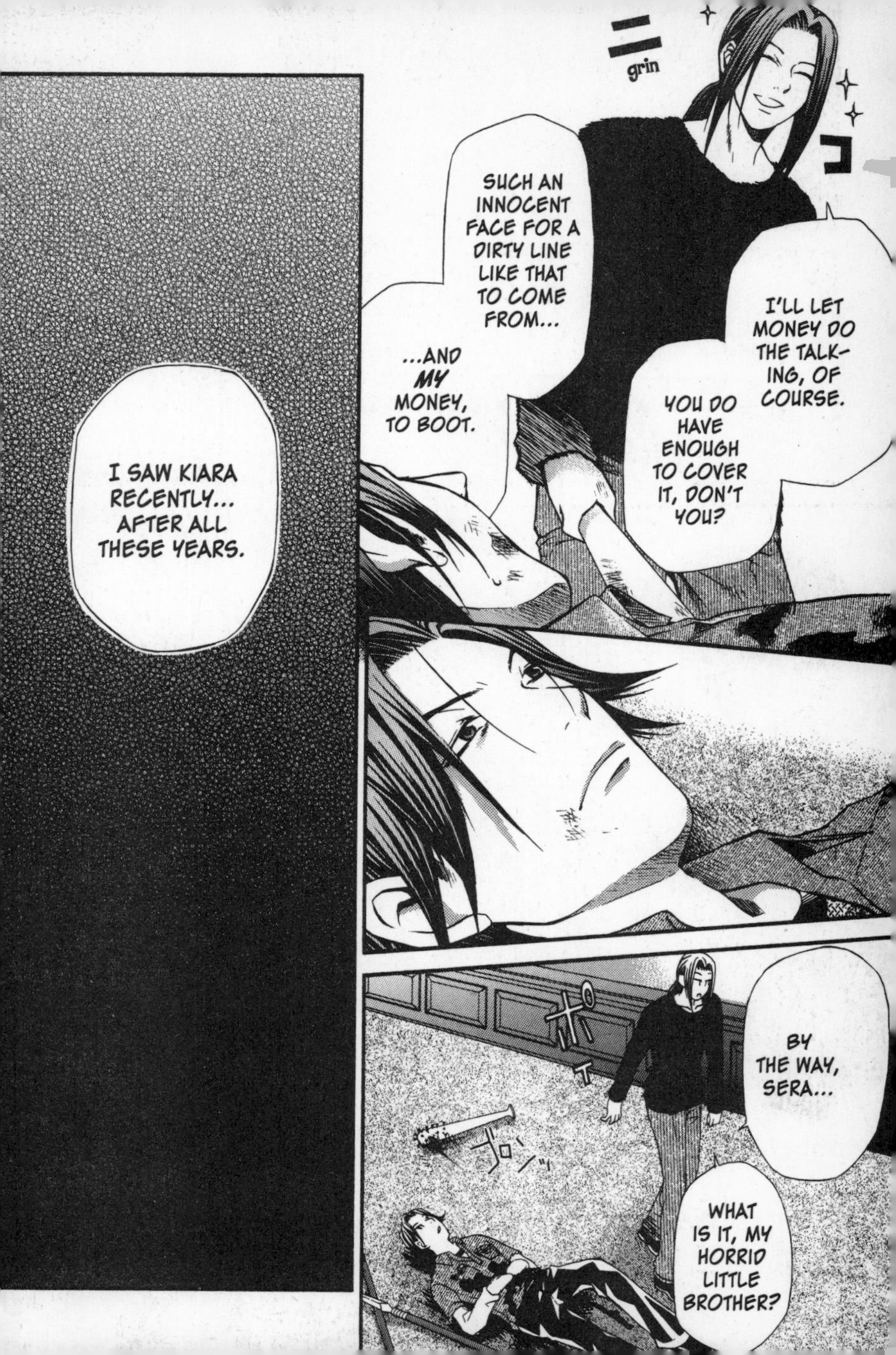
grin
I'LL LET MONEY DO THE TALKING, OF COURSE.
YOU DO HAVE ENOUGH TO COVER IT, DON'T YOU?
SUCH AN INNOCENT FACE FOR A DIRTY LINE LIKE THAT TO COME FROM...
...AND MY MONEY, TO BOOT.
BY THE WAY, SERA...
WHAT IS IT, MY HORRID LITTLE BROTHER?
I SAW KIARA RECENTLY... AFTER ALL THESE YEARS.

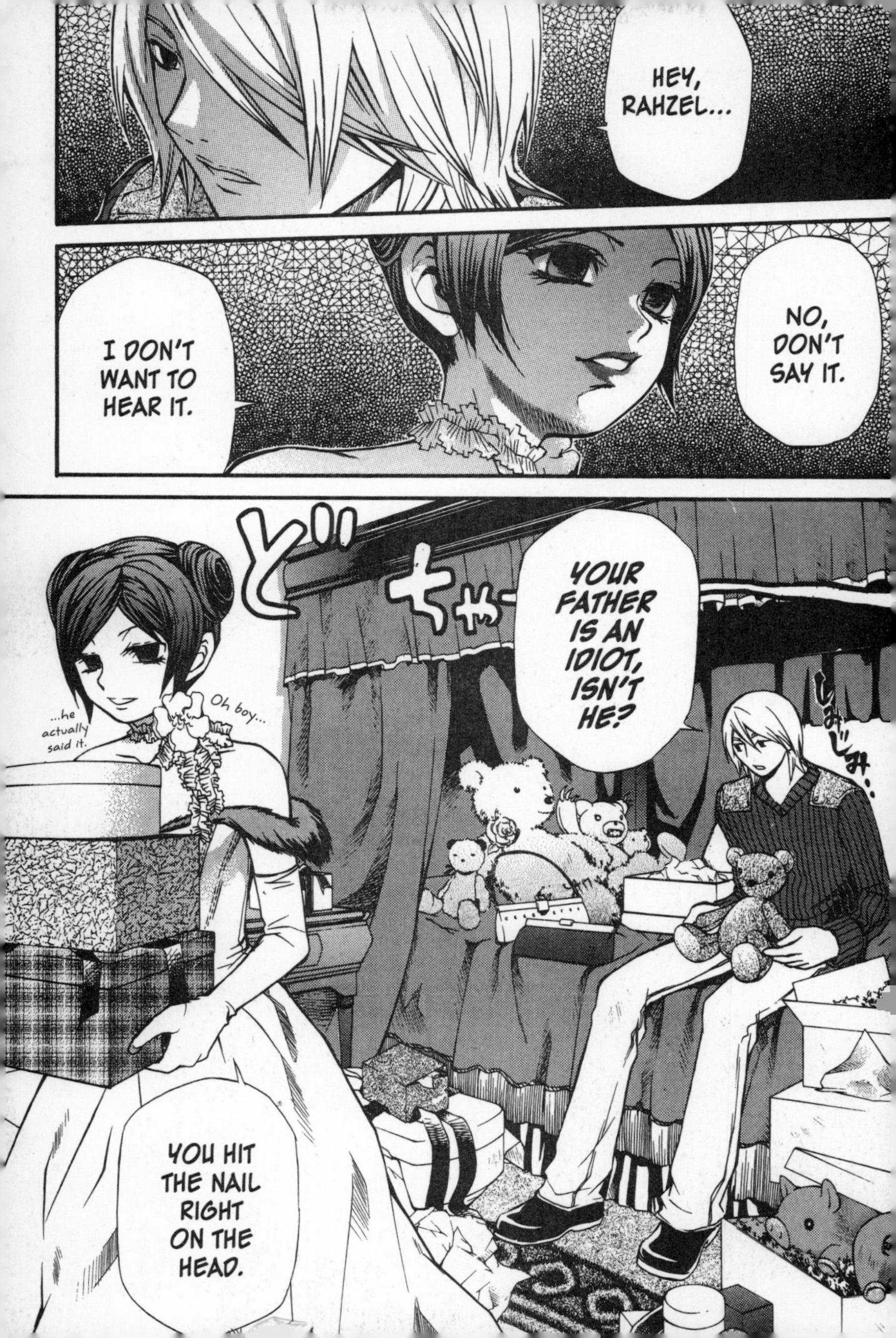
HEY, RAHZEL...
NO, DON'T SAY IT.
I DON'T WANT TO HEAR IT.
しみじみ…
YOUR FATHER IS AN IDIOT, ISN'T HE?
Oh boy...
...he actually said it.
YOU HIT THE NAIL RIGHT ON THE HEAD.

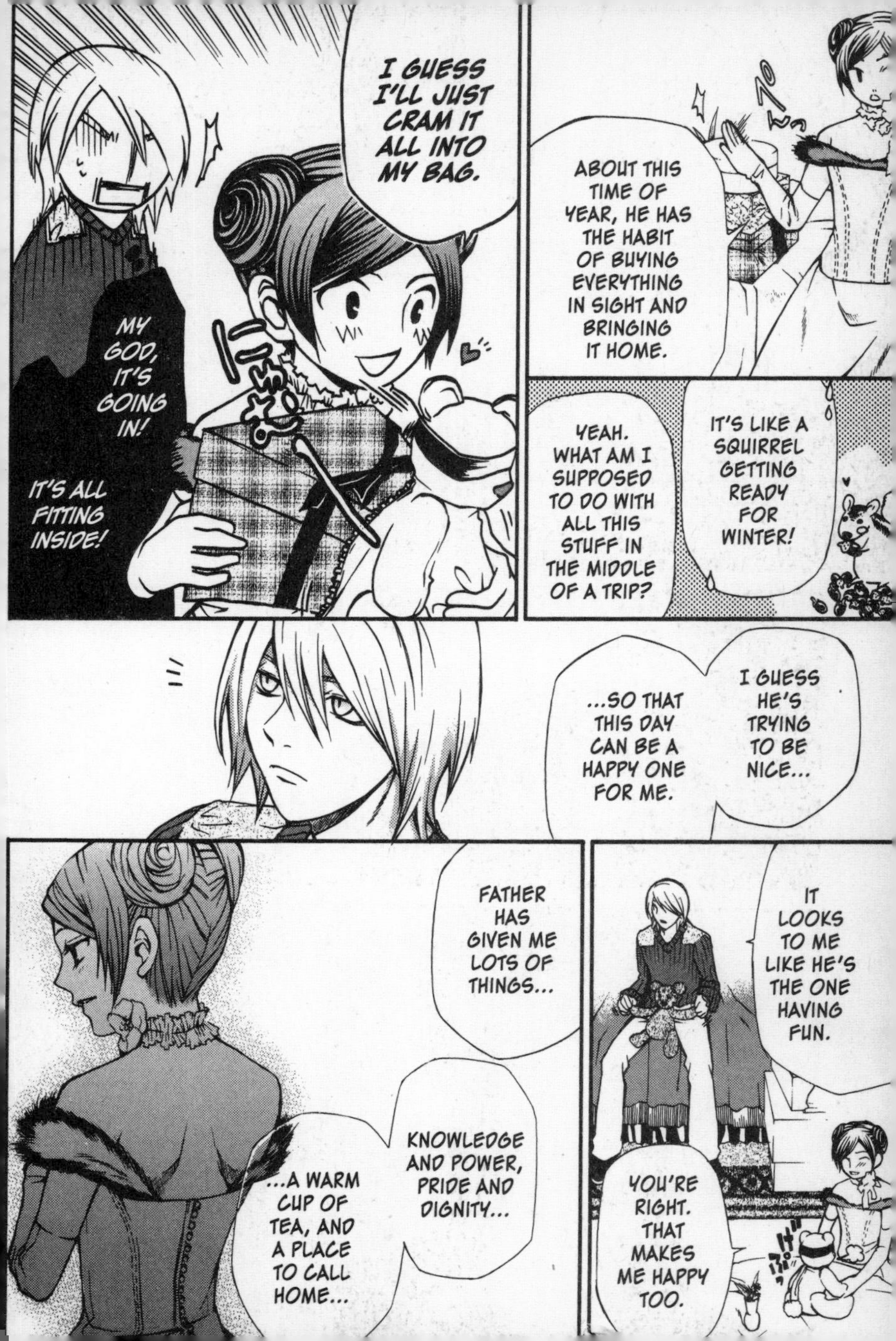
ABOUT THIS TIME OF YEAR, HE HAS THE HABIT OF BUYING EVERYTHING IN SIGHT AND BRINGING IT HOME.
IT'S LIKE A SQUIRREL GETTING READY FOR WINTER!
YEAH. WHAT AM I SUPPOSED TO DO WITH ALL THIS STUFF IN THE MIDDLE OF A TRIP?
I GUESS I'LL JUST CRAM IT ALL INTO MY BAG.
MY GOD, IT'S GOING IN!
IT'S ALL FITTING INSIDE!
I GUESS HE'S TRYING TO BE NICE...
...SO THAT THIS DAY CAN BE A HAPPY ONE FOR ME.
IT LOOKS TO ME LIKE HE'S THE ONE HAVING FUN.
YOU'RE RIGHT. THAT MAKES ME HAPPY TOO.
FATHER HAS GIVEN ME LOTS OF THINGS...
KNOWLEDGE AND POWER, PRIDE AND DIGNITY...
...A WARM CUP OF TEA, AND A PLACE TO CALL HOME...

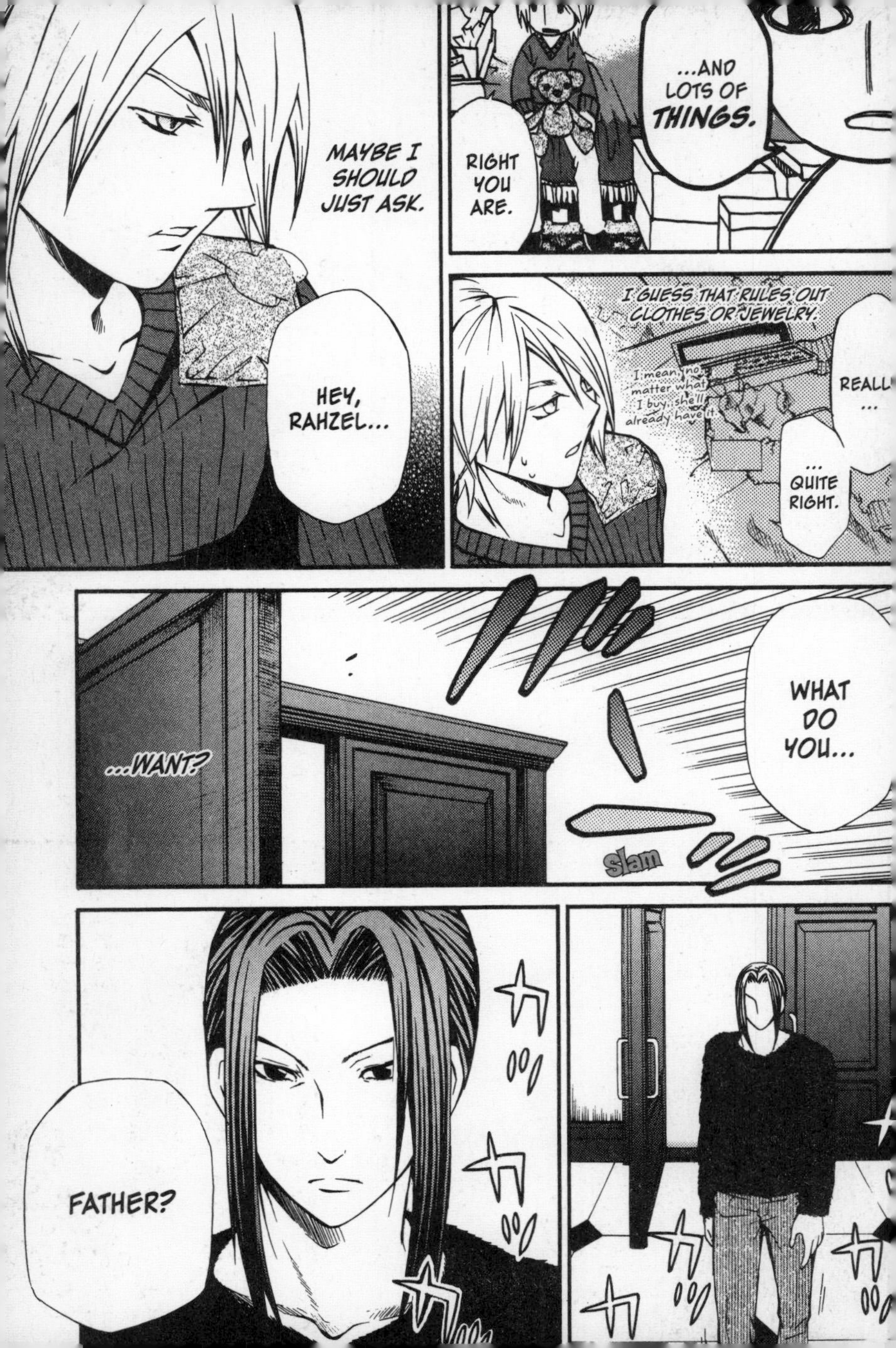
...AND LOTS OF THINGS.
RIGHT YOU ARE.
I GUESS THAT RULES OUT CLOTHES OR JEWELRY.
I mean, no matter what I buy, she'll already have it.
REALL ...
... QUITE RIGHT.
MAYBE I SHOULD JUST ASK.
HEY, RAHZEL...
WHAT DO YOU...
slam
...WANT?
FATHER?

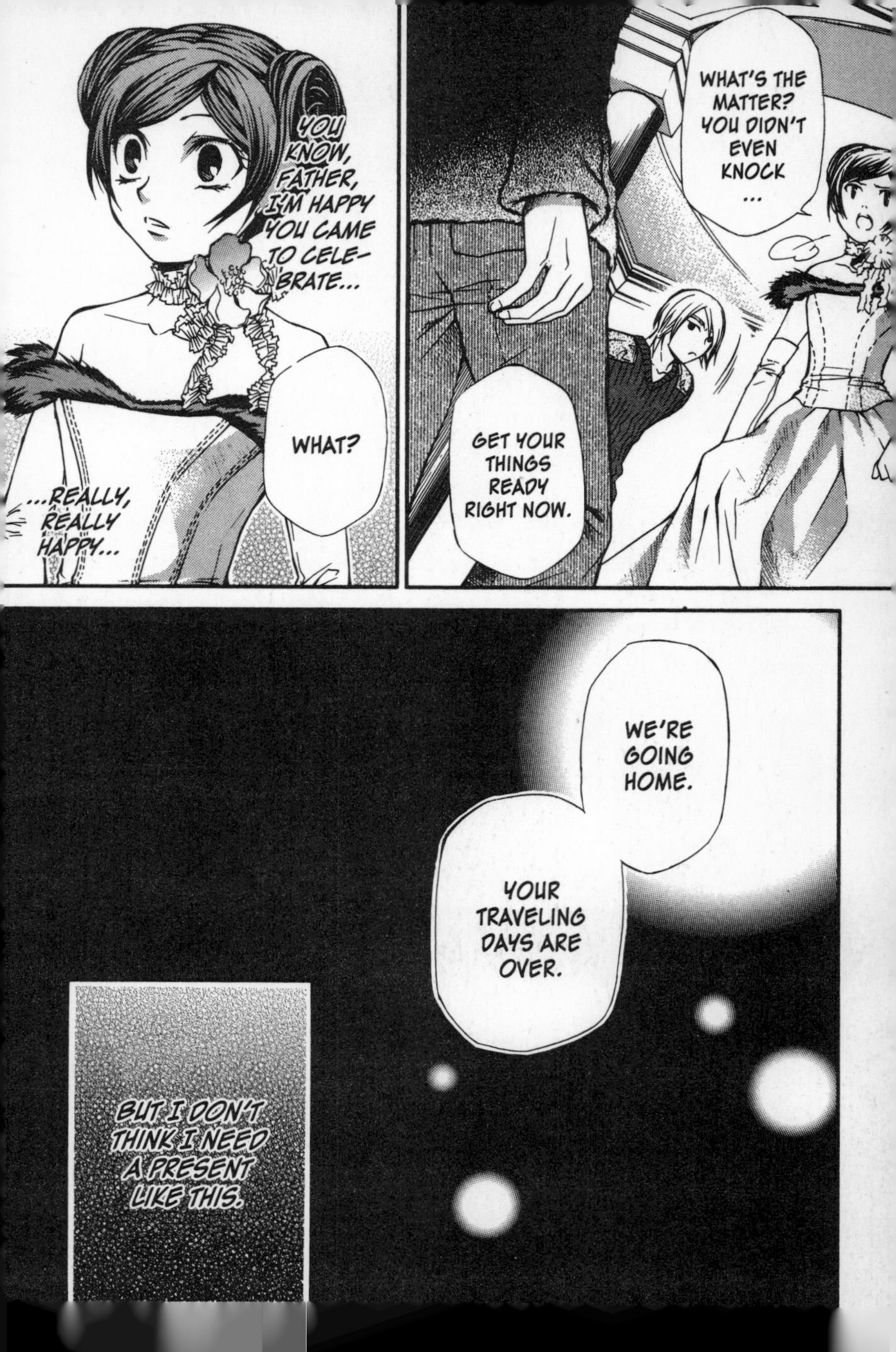
WHAT'S THE MATTER? YOU DIDN'T EVEN KNOCK ...
GET YOUR THINGS READY RIGHT NOW.
YOU KNOW, FATHER, I'M HAPPY YOU CAME TO CELE-BRATE...
WHAT?
...REALLY, REALLY HAPPY...
WE'RE GOING HOME.
YOUR TRAVELING DAYS ARE OVER.
BUT I DON'T THINK I NEED A PRESENT LIKE THIS.

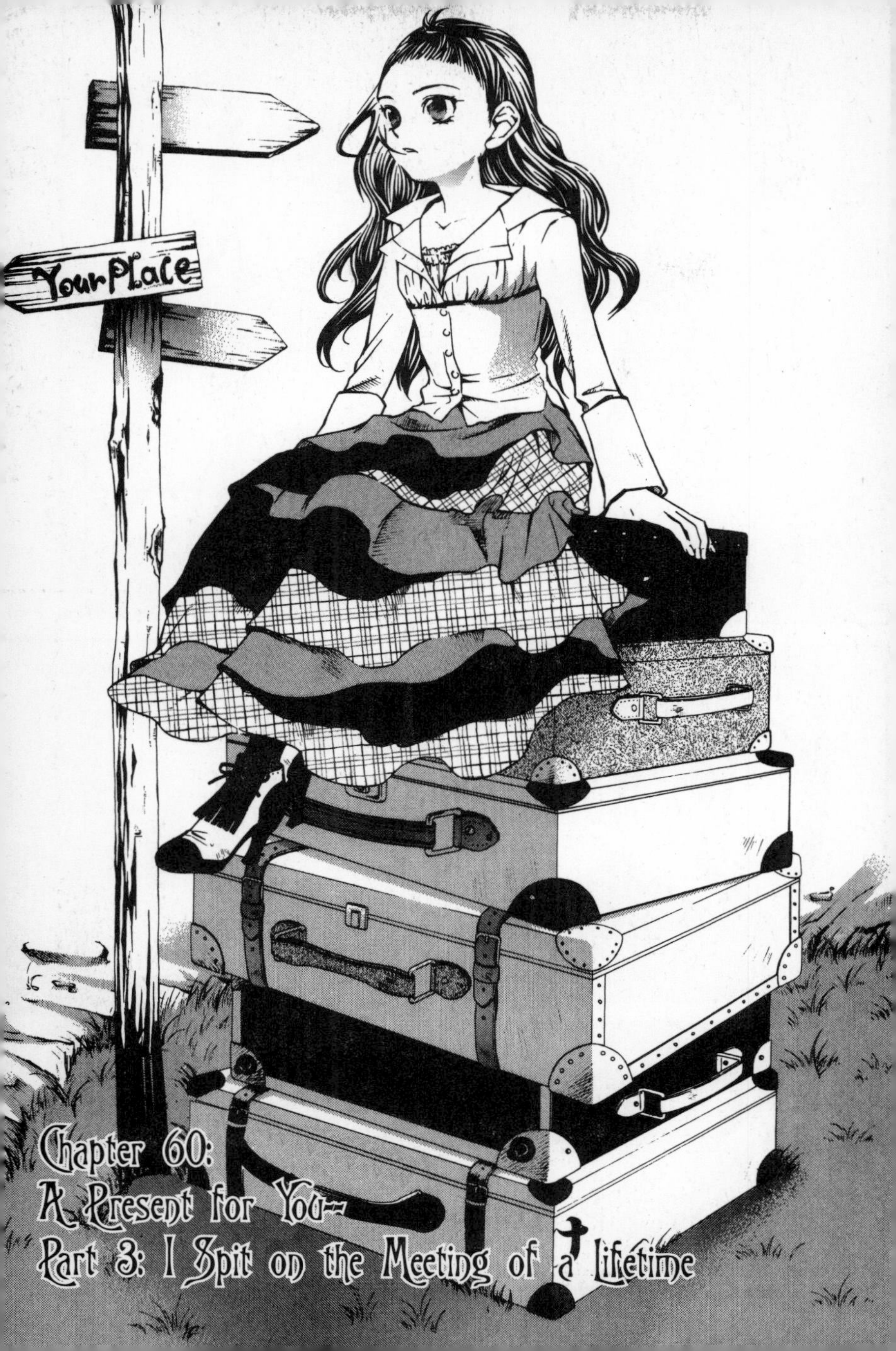
YOUR PLACE

Chapter 60: A Present for You-- Part 3: I Spit on the Meeting of a Lifetime

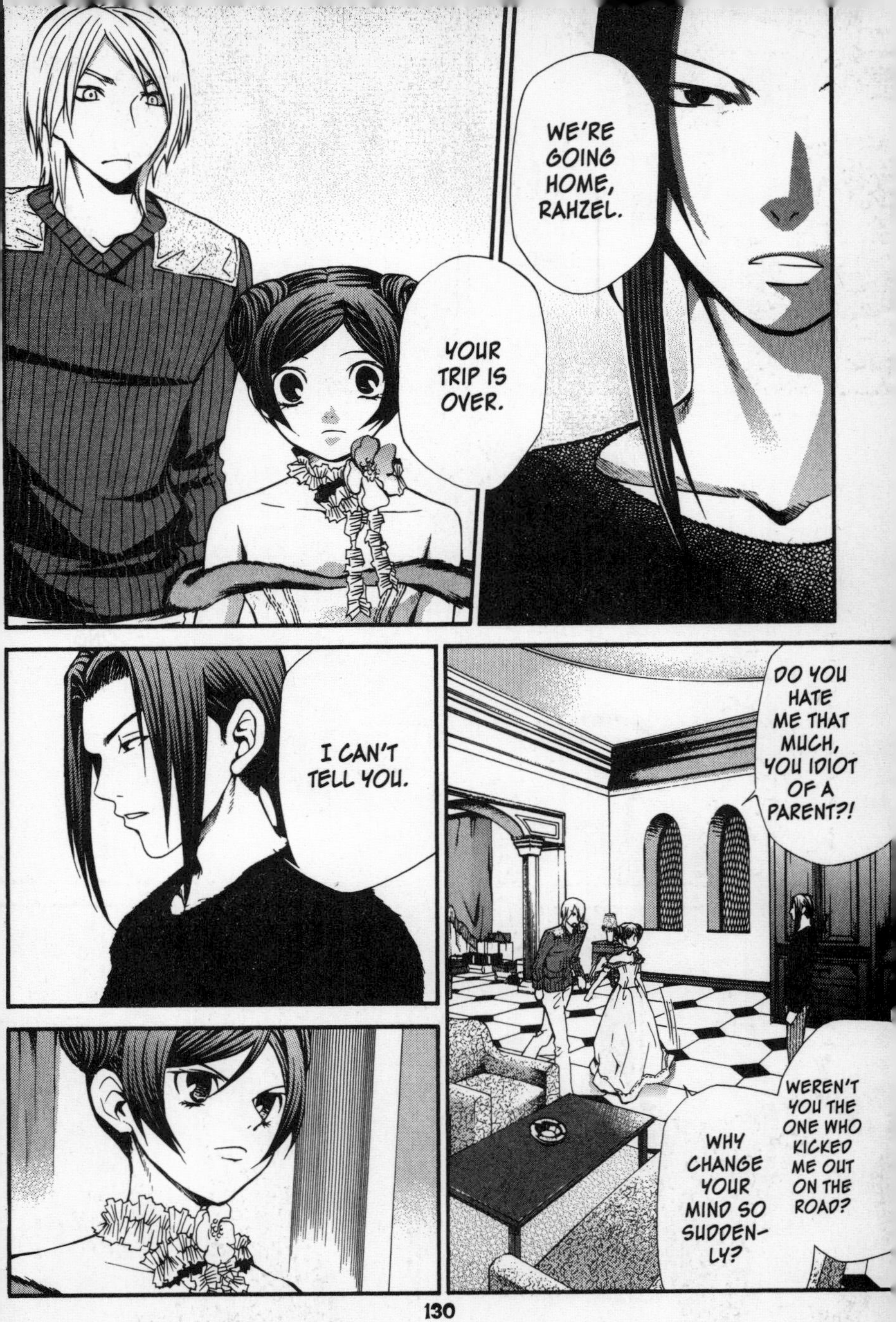
WE'RE GOING HOME, RAHZEL.
YOUR TRIP IS OVER.
DO YOU HATE ME THAT MUCH, YOU IDIOT OF A PARENT?!
WEREN'T YOU THE ONE WHO KICKED ME OUT ON THE ROAD?
WHY CHANGE YOUR MIND SO SUDDEN-LY?
I CAN'T TELL YOU.

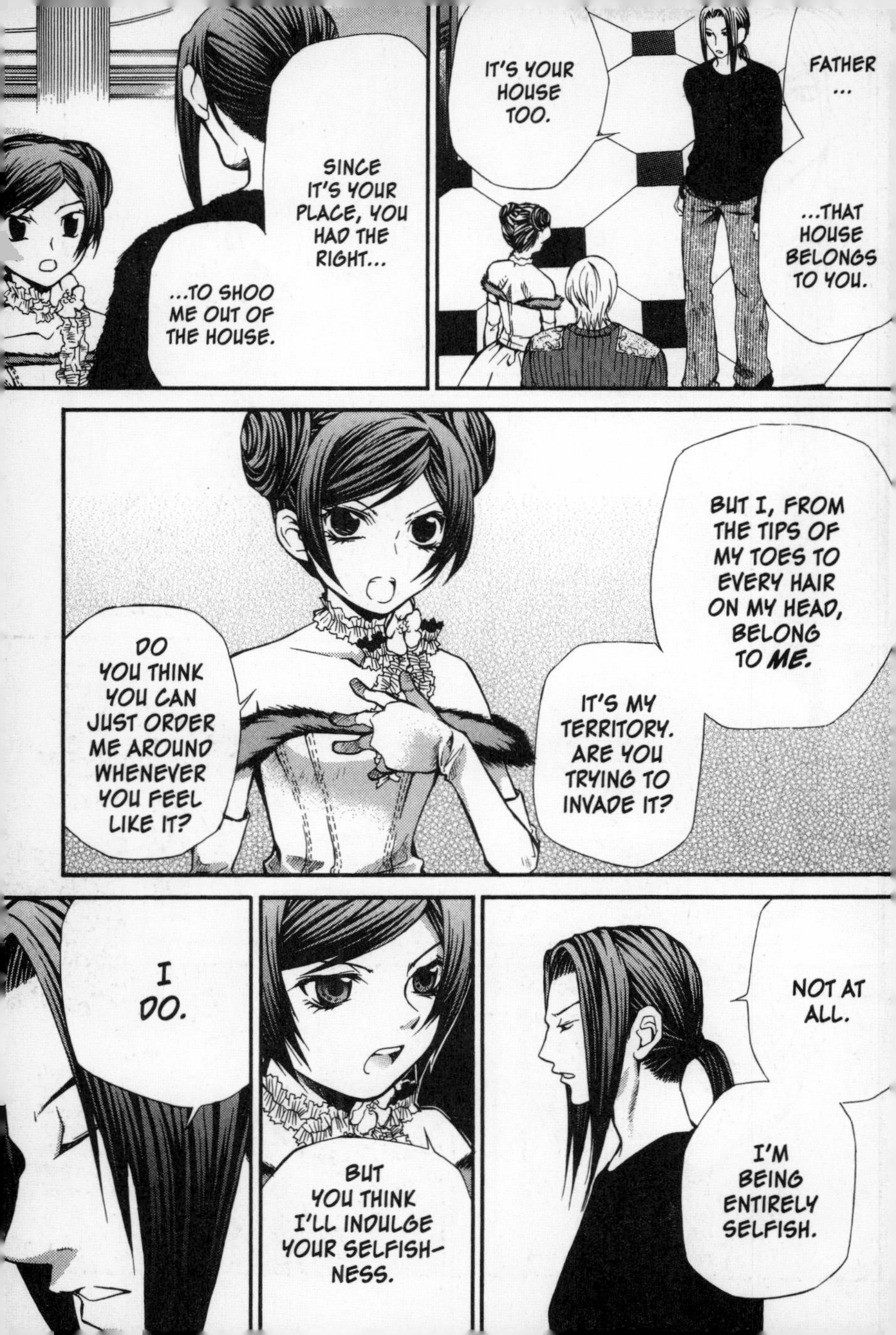
FATHER ...
...THAT HOUSE BELONGS TO YOU.
IT'S YOUR HOUSE TOO.
SINCE IT'S YOUR PLACE, YOU HAD THE RIGHT...
...TO SHOO ME OUT OF THE HOUSE.
BUT I, FROM THE TIPS OF MY TOES TO EVERY HAIR ON MY HEAD, BELONG TO *ME.*
IT'S MY TERRITORY. ARE YOU TRYING TO INVADE IT?
DO YOU THINK YOU CAN JUST ORDER ME AROUND WHENEVER YOU FEEL LIKE IT?
NOT AT ALL.
I'M BEING ENTIRELY SELFISH.
BUT YOU THINK I'LL INDULGE YOUR SELFISH-NESS.
I DO.

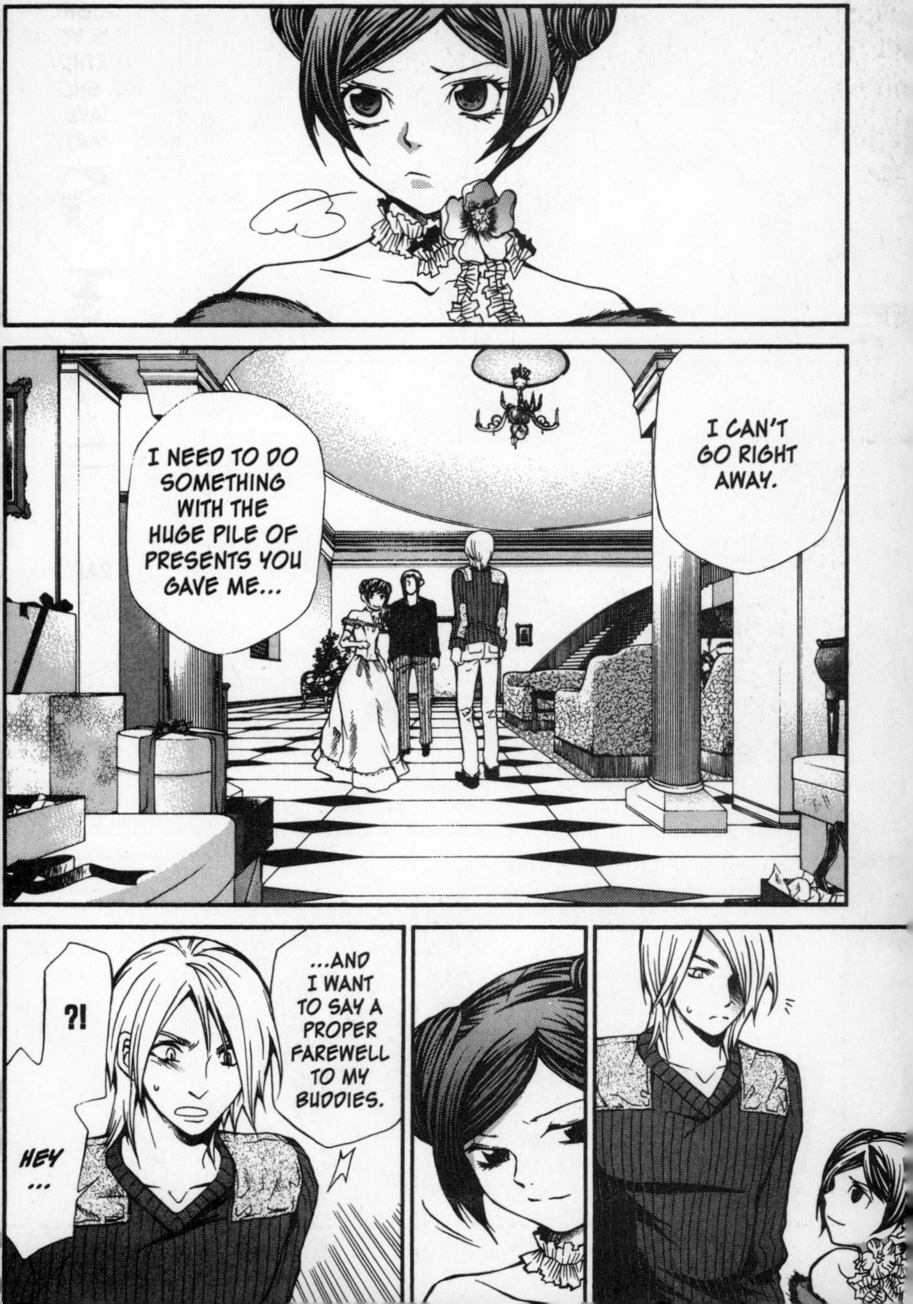
I CAN'T GO RIGHT AWAY.
I NEED TO DO SOMETHING WITH THE HUGE PILE OF PRESENTS YOU GAVE ME...
...AND I WANT TO SAY A PROPER FAREWELL TO MY BUDDIES.
?!
HEY ...

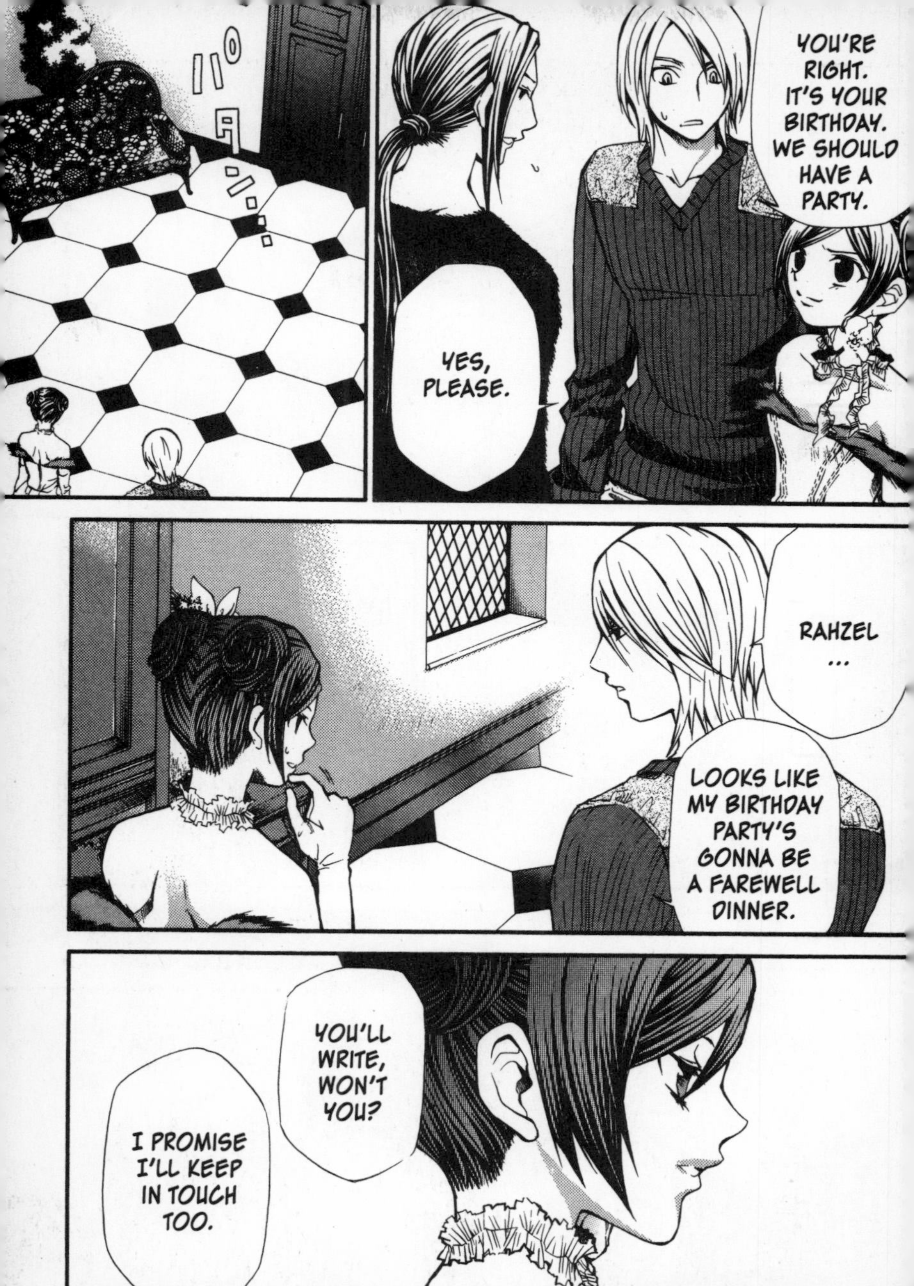
YOU'RE RIGHT. IT'S YOUR BIRTHDAY. WE SHOULD HAVE A PARTY.
YES, PLEASE.
RAHZEL ...
LOOKS LIKE MY BIRTHDAY PARTY'S GONNA BE A FAREWELL DINNER.
YOU'LL WRITE, WON'T YOU?
I PROMISE I'LL KEEP IN TOUCH TOO.

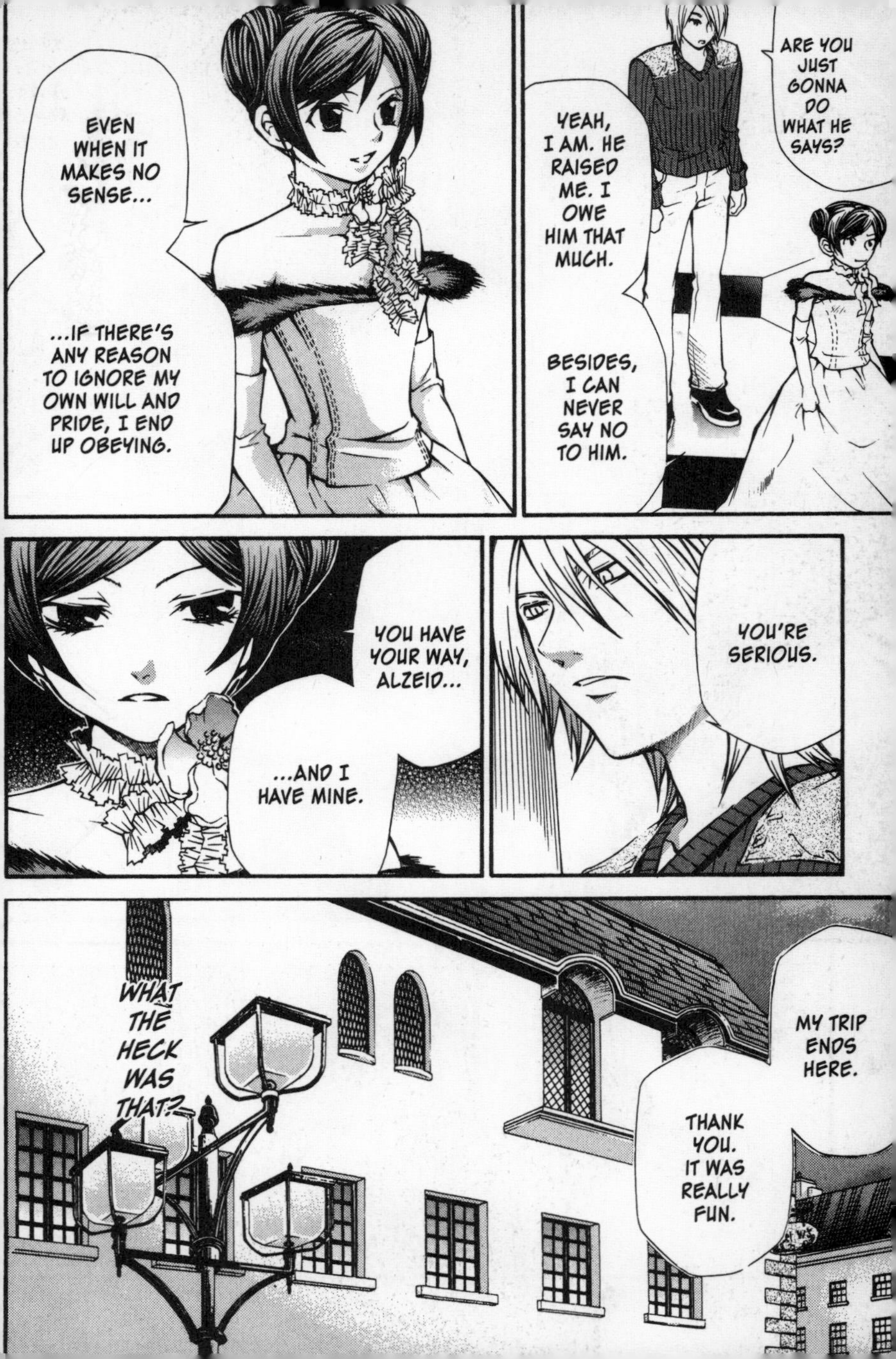
ARE YOU JUST GONNA DO WHAT HE SAYS?
YEAH, I AM. HE RAISED ME. I OWE HIM THAT MUCH.
BESIDES, I CAN NEVER SAY NO TO HIM.
EVEN WHEN IT MAKES NO SENSE...
...IF THERE'S ANY REASON TO IGNORE MY OWN WILL AND PRIDE, I END UP OBEYING.
YOU'RE SERIOUS.
YOU HAVE YOUR WAY, ALZEID...
...AND I HAVE MINE.
MY TRIP ENDS HERE.
THANK YOU. IT WAS REALLY FUN.
WHAT THE HECK WAS THAT?

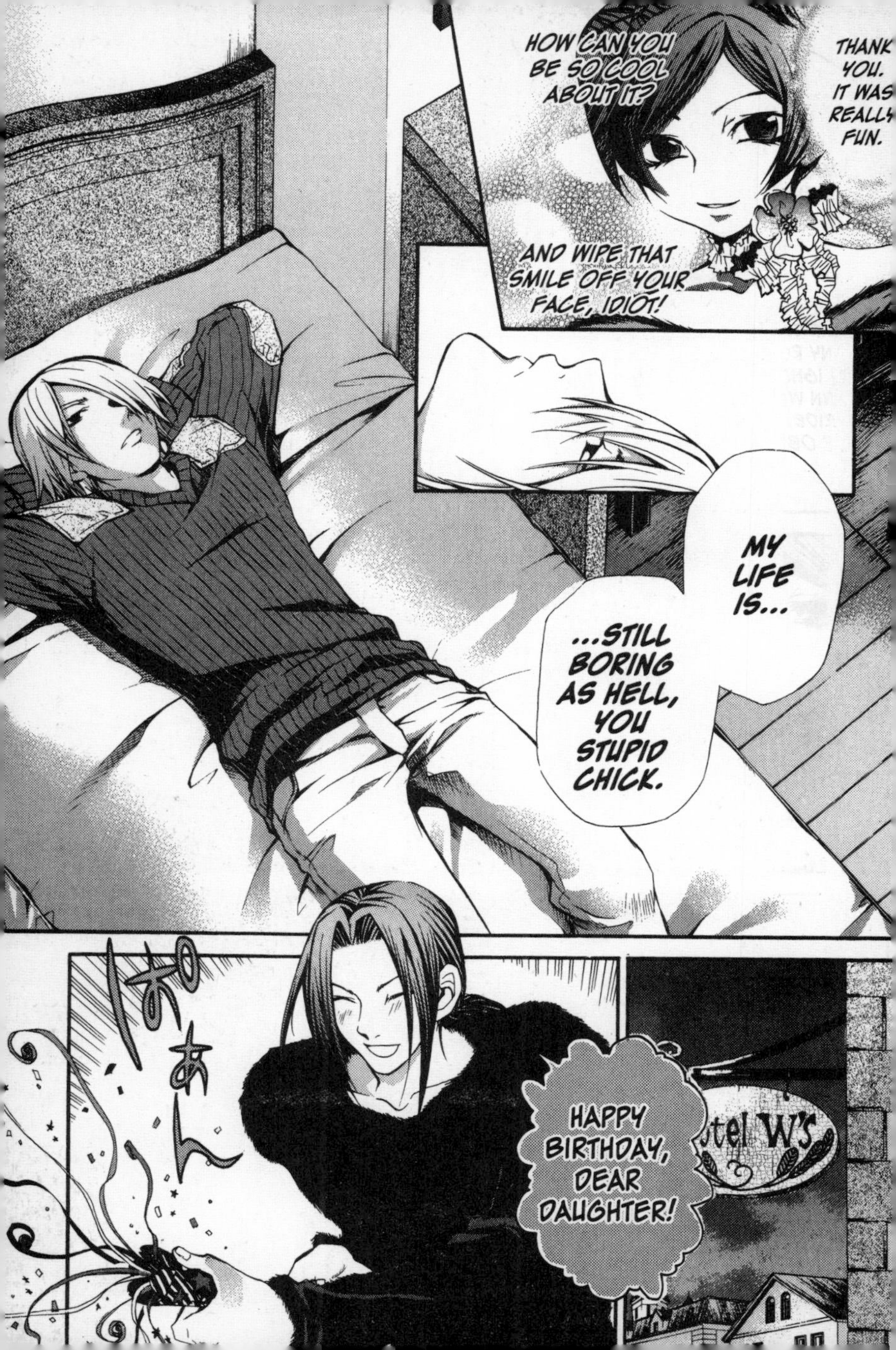
THANK YOU. IT WAS REALLY FUN.
HOW CAN YOU BE SO COOL ABOUT IT?
AND WIPE THAT SMILE OFF YOUR FACE, IDIOT!
MY LIFE IS...
...STILL BORING AS HELL, YOU STUPID CHICK.
HAPPY BIRTHDAY, DEAR DAUGHTER!
ぱぁん

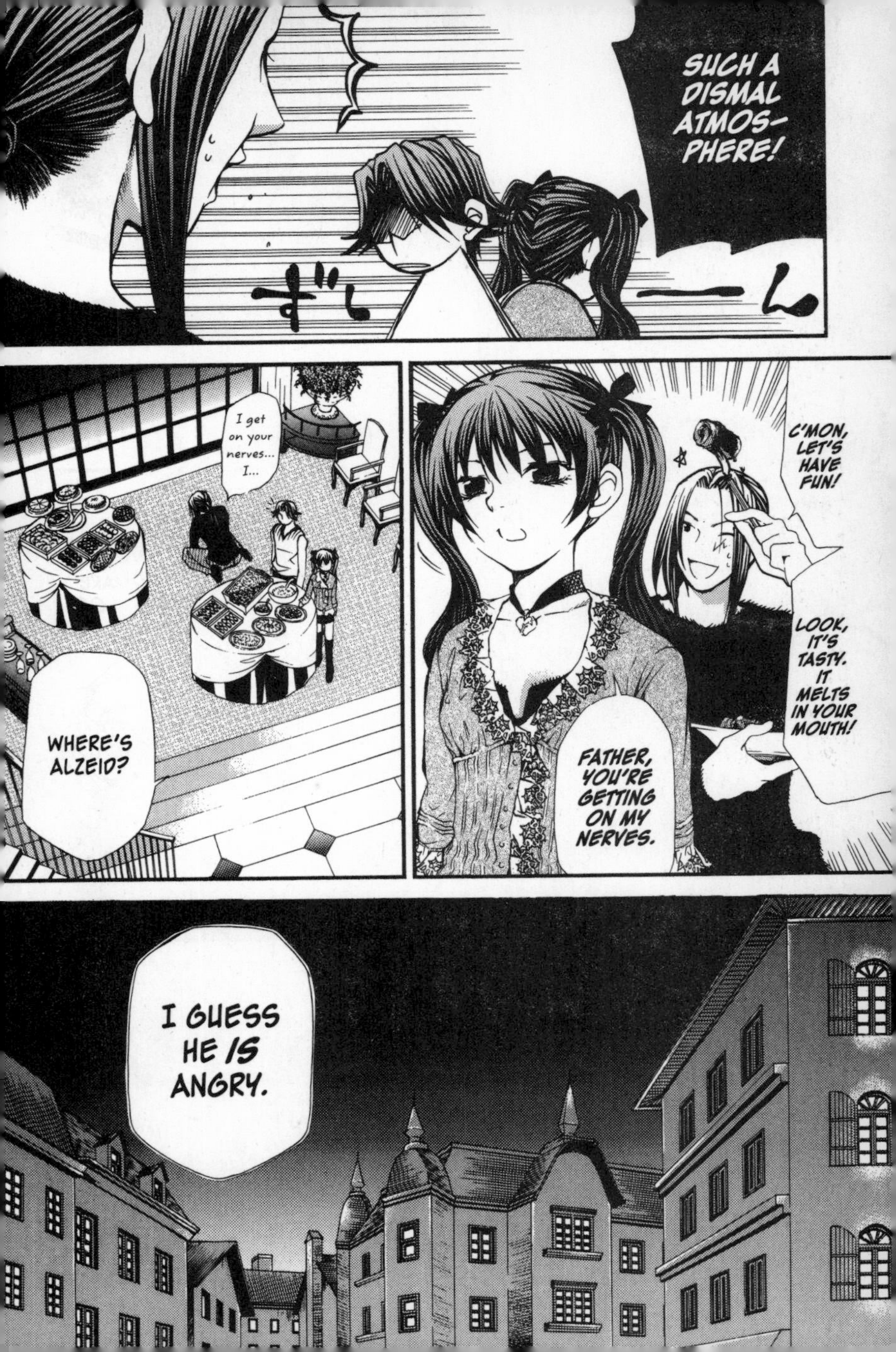
SUCH A DISMAL ATMOSPHERE!
ずーん
C'MON, LET'S HAVE FUN!
LOOK, IT'S TASTY. IT MELTS IN YOUR MOUTH!
FATHER, YOU'RE GETTING ON MY NERVES.
I get on your nerves... I...
WHERE'S ALZEID?
I GUESS HE IS ANGRY.

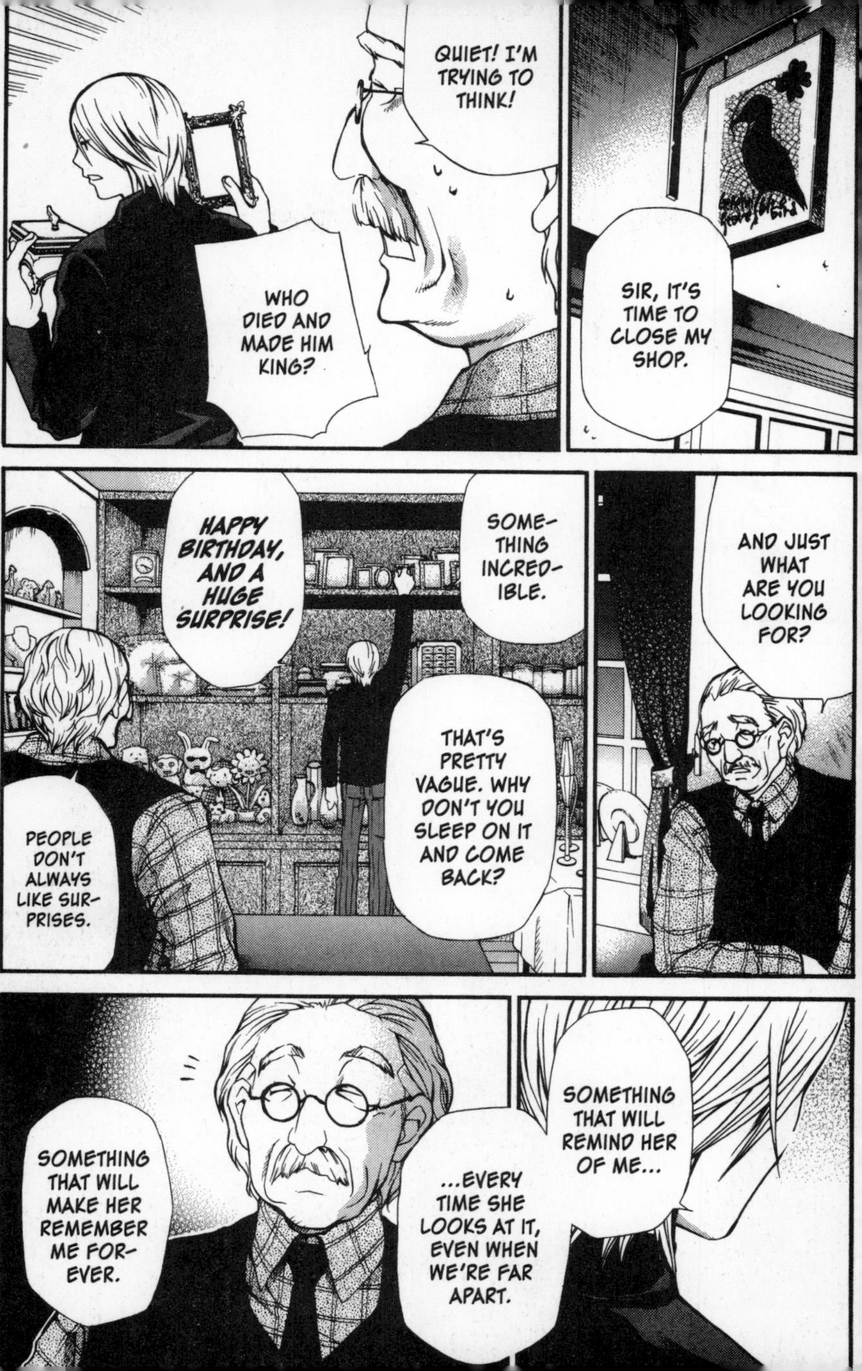
SIR, IT'S TIME TO CLOSE MY SHOP.
QUIET! I'M TRYING TO THINK!
WHO DIED AND MADE HIM KING?
AND JUST WHAT ARE YOU LOOKING FOR?
SOMETHING INCREDIBLE.
HAPPY BIRTHDAY, AND A HUGE SURPRISE!
THAT'S PRETTY VAGUE. WHY DON'T YOU SLEEP ON IT AND COME BACK?
PEOPLE DON'T ALWAYS LIKE SURPRISES.
SOMETHING THAT WILL REMIND HER OF ME...
...EVERY TIME SHE LOOKS AT IT, EVEN WHEN WE'RE FAR APART.
SOMETHING THAT WILL MAKE HER REMEMBER ME FOREVER.

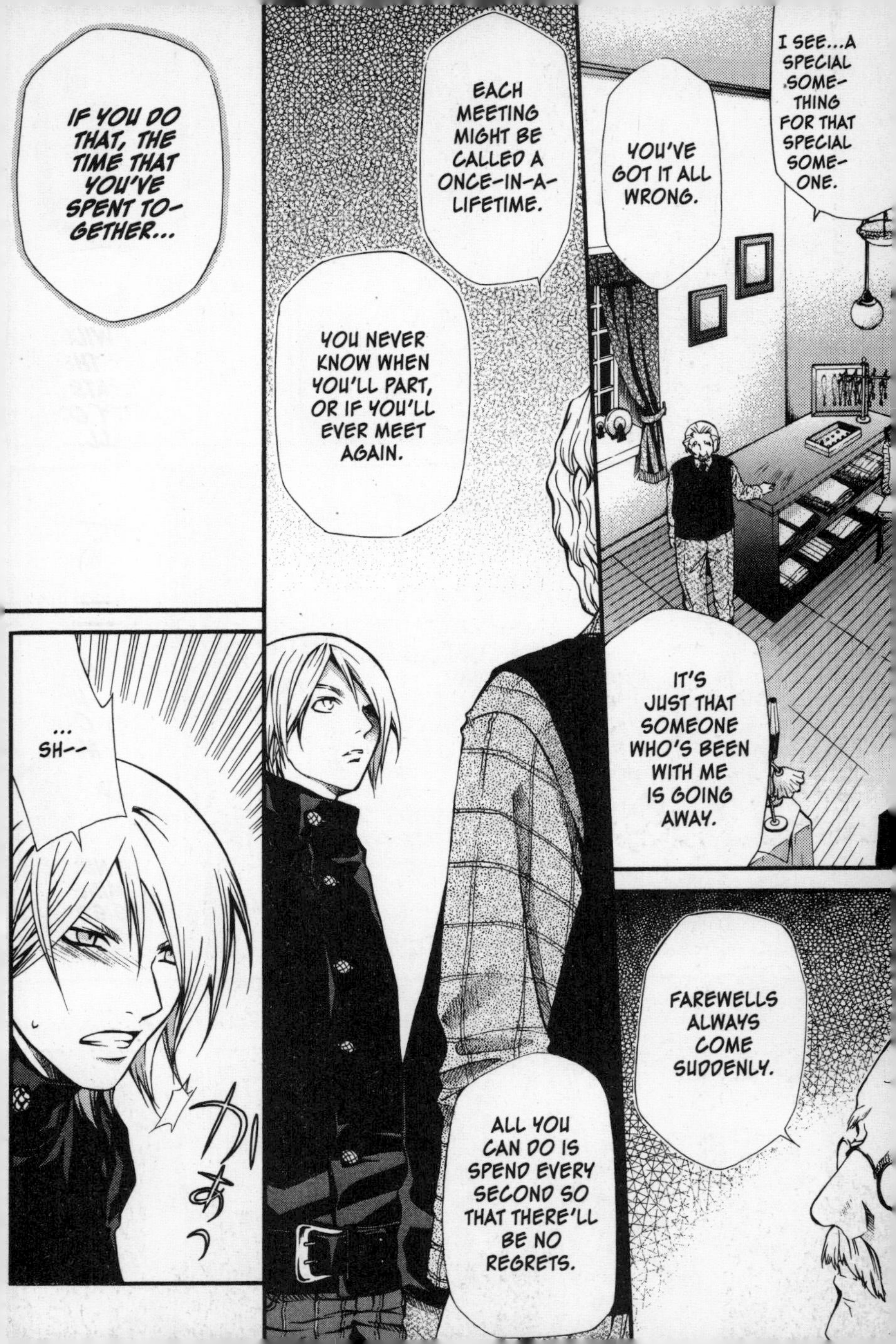
I SEE...A SPECIAL SOMETHING FOR THAT SPECIAL SOMEONE.
YOU'VE GOT IT ALL WRONG.
IT'S JUST THAT SOMEONE WHO'S BEEN WITH ME IS GOING AWAY.
FAREWELLS ALWAYS COME SUDDENLY.
EACH MEETING MIGHT BE CALLED A ONCE-IN-A-LIFETIME.
YOU NEVER KNOW WHEN YOU'LL PART, OR IF YOU'LL EVER MEET AGAIN.
ALL YOU CAN DO IS SPEND EVERY SECOND SO THAT THERE'LL BE NO REGRETS.
IF YOU DO THAT, THE TIME THAT YOU'VE SPENT TOGETHER...
... SH--
かぁっ

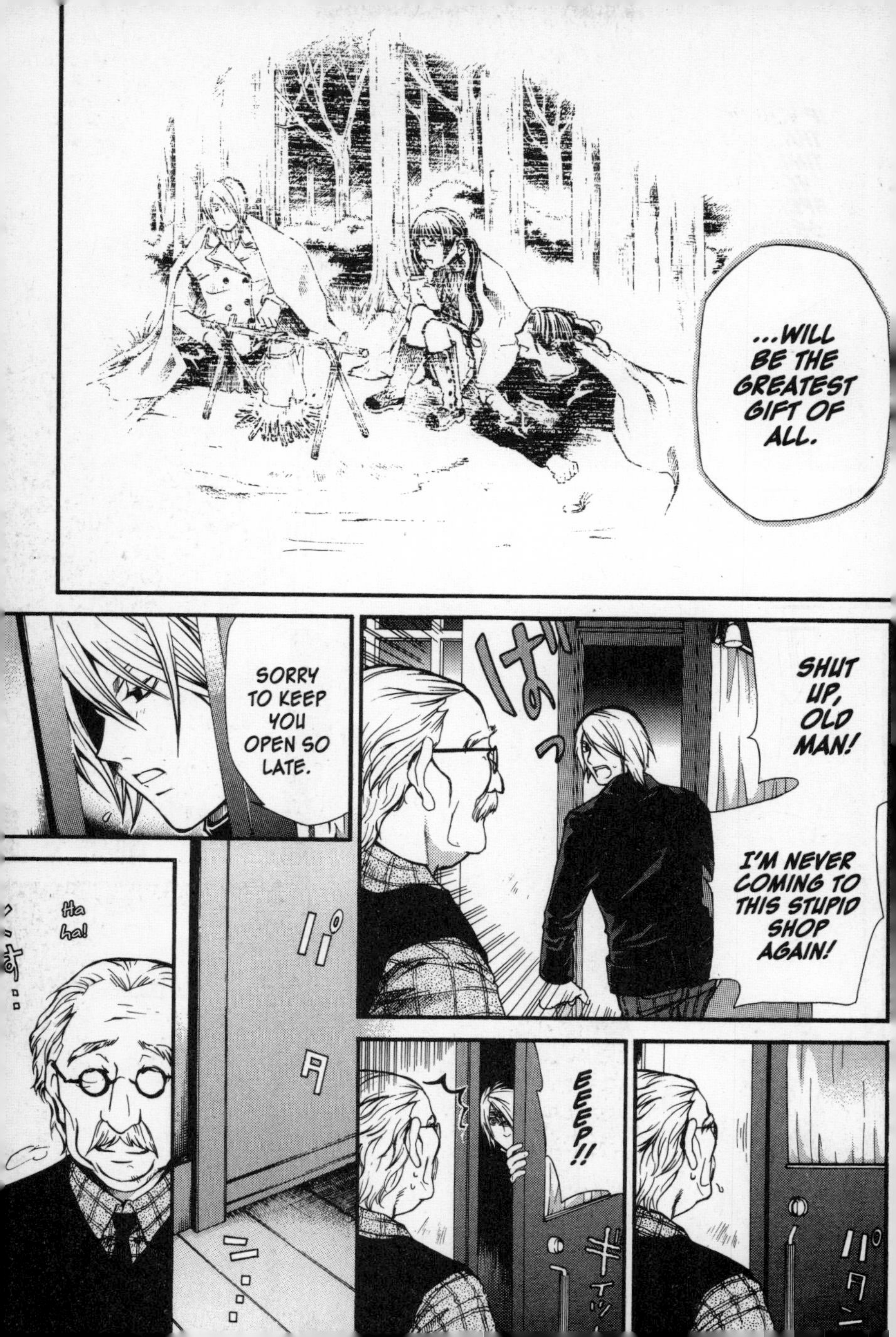
...WILL BE THE GREATEST GIFT OF ALL.
ぱっ
SHUT UP, OLD MAN!
I'M NEVER COMING TO THIS STUPID SHOP AGAIN!
パタン
ギイッ
EEEP!!
SORRY TO KEEP YOU OPEN SO LATE.
パタ
Ha ha!

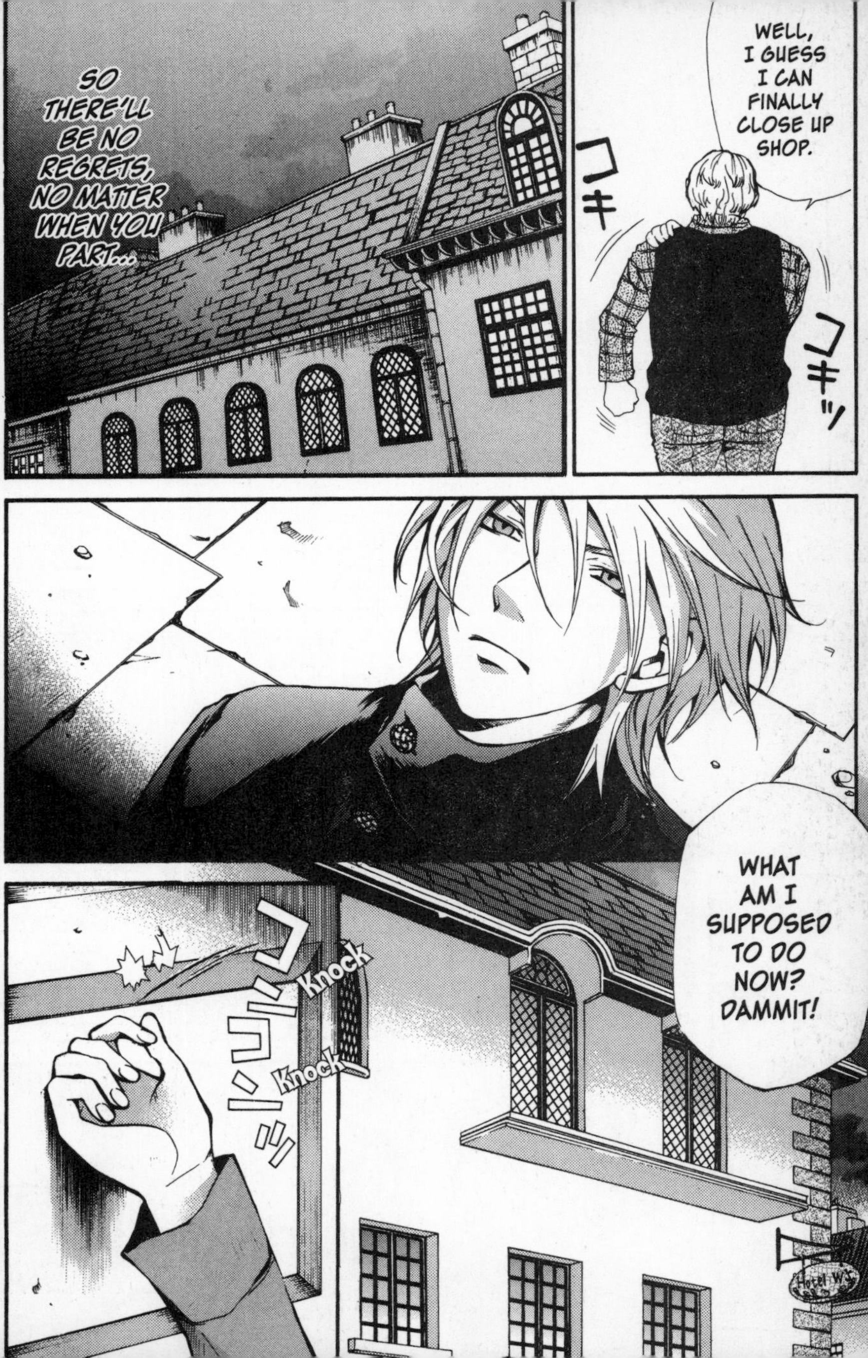
WELL, I GUESS I CAN FINALLY CLOSE UP SHOP.
コキ
コキッ
SO THERE'LL BE NO REGRETS, NO MATTER WHEN YOU PART...
WHAT AM I SUPPOSED TO DO NOW? DAMMIT!
Knock
Knock

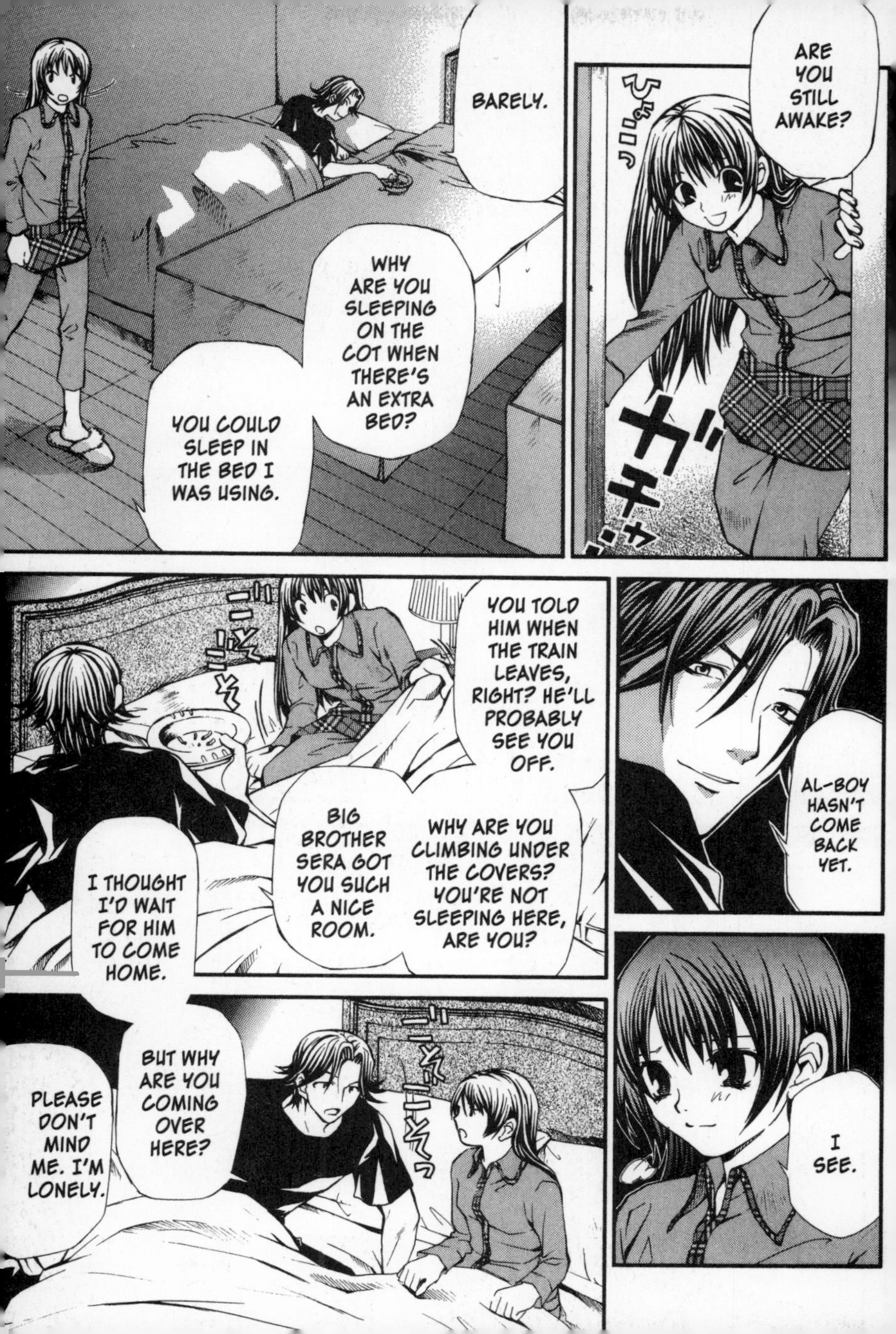
ARE YOU STILL AWAKE?
BARELY.
WHY ARE YOU SLEEPING ON THE COT WHEN THERE'S AN EXTRA BED?
YOU COULD SLEEP IN THE BED I WAS USING.
AL-BOY HASN'T COME BACK YET.
I SEE.
YOU TOLD HIM WHEN THE TRAIN LEAVES, RIGHT? HE'LL PROBABLY SEE YOU OFF.
BIG BROTHER SERA GOT YOU SUCH A NICE ROOM.
WHY ARE YOU CLIMBING UNDER THE COVERS? YOU'RE NOT SLEEPING HERE, ARE YOU?
I THOUGHT I'D WAIT FOR HIM TO COME HOME.
BUT WHY ARE YOU COMING OVER HERE?
PLEASE DON'T MIND ME. I'M LONELY.

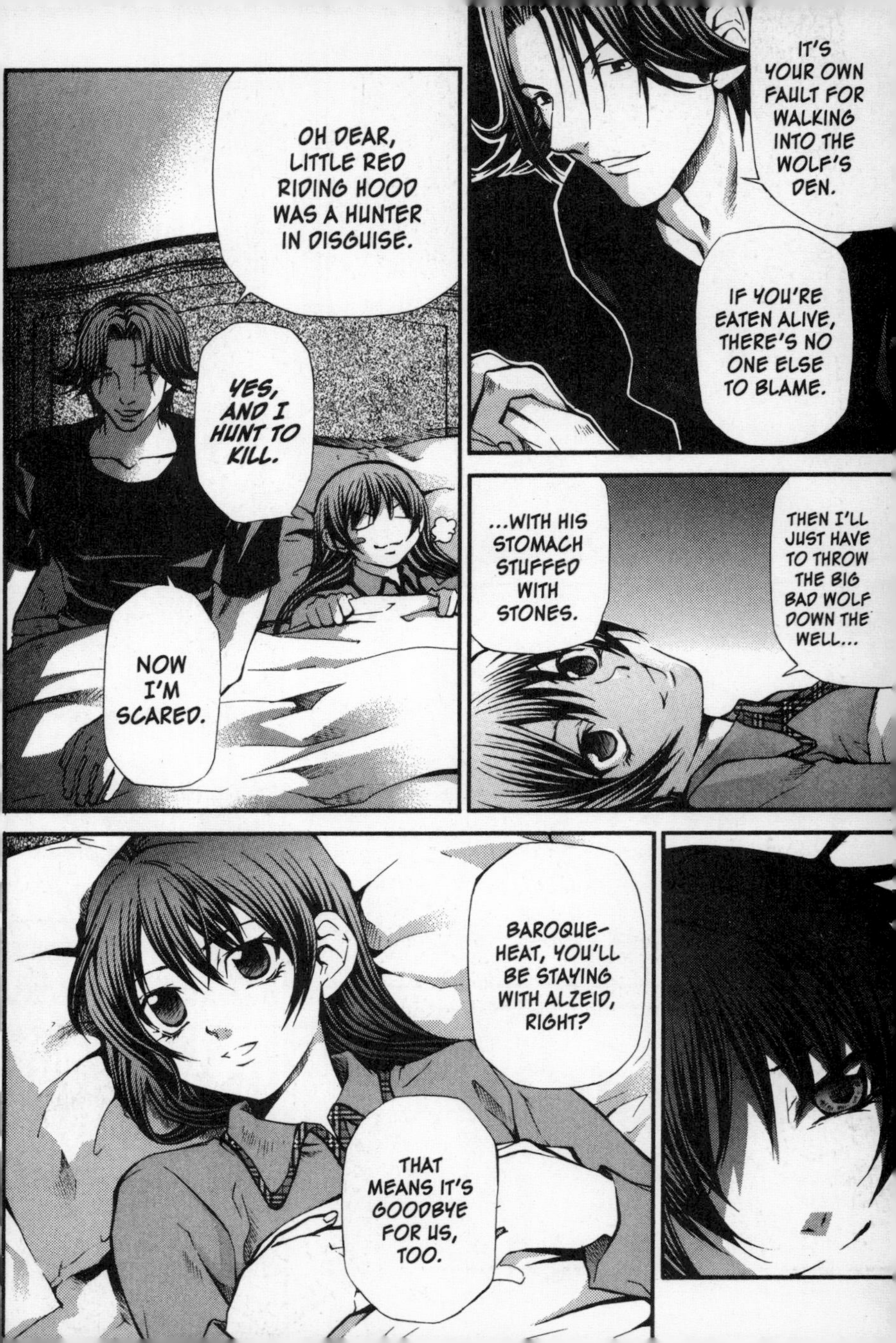
IT'S YOUR OWN FAULT FOR WALKING INTO THE WOLF'S DEN.
IF YOU'RE EATEN ALIVE, THERE'S NO ONE ELSE TO BLAME.
THEN I'LL JUST HAVE TO THROW THE BIG BAD WOLF DOWN THE WELL...
...WITH HIS STOMACH STUFFED WITH STONES.
OH DEAR, LITTLE RED RIDING HOOD WAS A HUNTER IN DISGUISE.
YES, AND I HUNT TO KILL.
NOW I'M SCARED.
BAROQUE-HEAT, YOU'LL BE STAYING WITH ALZEID, RIGHT?
THAT MEANS IT'S GOODBYE FOR US, TOO.

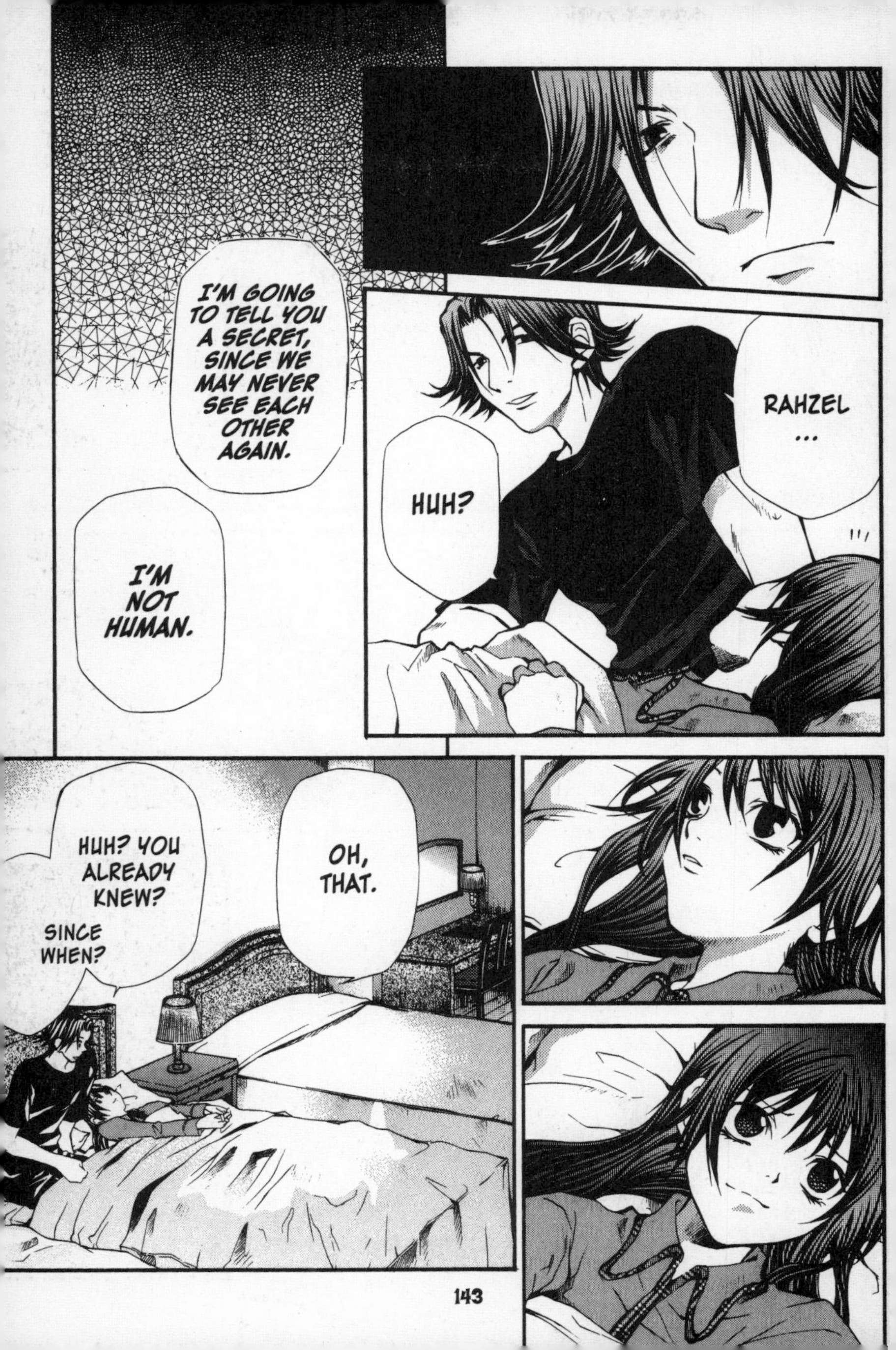
RAHZEL ...
HUH?
I'M GOING TO TELL YOU A SECRET, SINCE WE MAY NEVER SEE EACH OTHER AGAIN.
I'M NOT HUMAN.
OH, THAT.
HUH? YOU ALREADY KNEW?
SINCE WHEN?

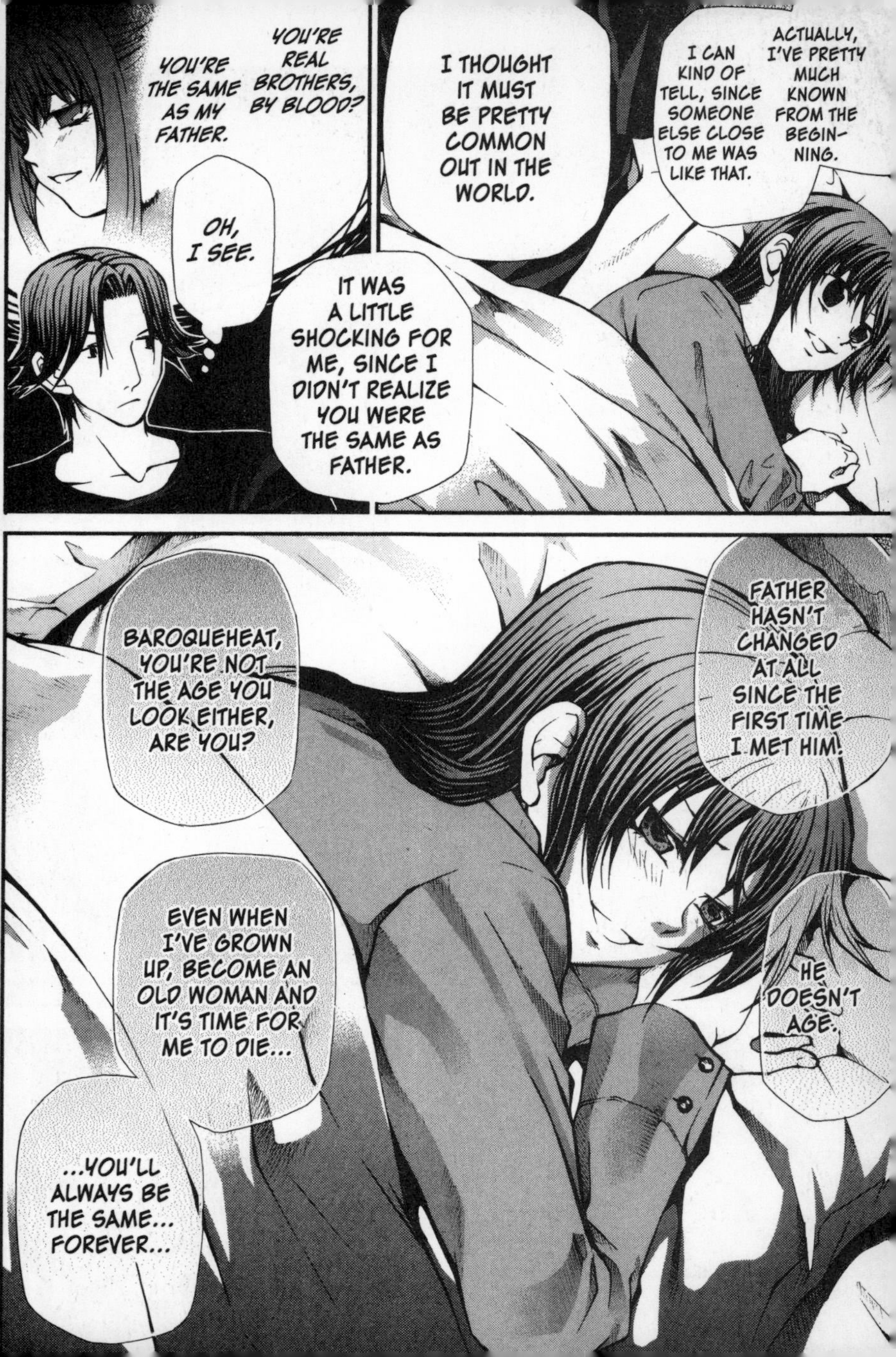
ACTUALLY, I'VE PRETTY MUCH KNOWN FROM THE BEGIN-NING.
I CAN KIND OF TELL, SINCE SOMEONE ELSE CLOSE TO ME WAS LIKE THAT.
I THOUGHT IT MUST BE PRETTY COMMON OUT IN THE WORLD.
IT WAS A LITTLE SHOCKING FOR ME, SINCE I DIDN'T REALIZE YOU WERE THE SAME AS FATHER.
YOU'RE REAL BROTHERS, BY BLOOD?
YOU'RE THE SAME AS MY FATHER.
OH, I SEE.
FATHER HASN'T CHANGED AT ALL SINCE THE FIRST TIME I MET HIM.
HE DOESN'T AGE.
BAROQUEHEAT, YOU'RE NOT THE AGE YOU LOOK EITHER, ARE YOU?
EVEN WHEN I'VE GROWN UP, BECOME AN OLD WOMAN AND IT'S TIME FOR ME TO DIE...
...YOU'LL ALWAYS BE THE SAME... FOREVER...

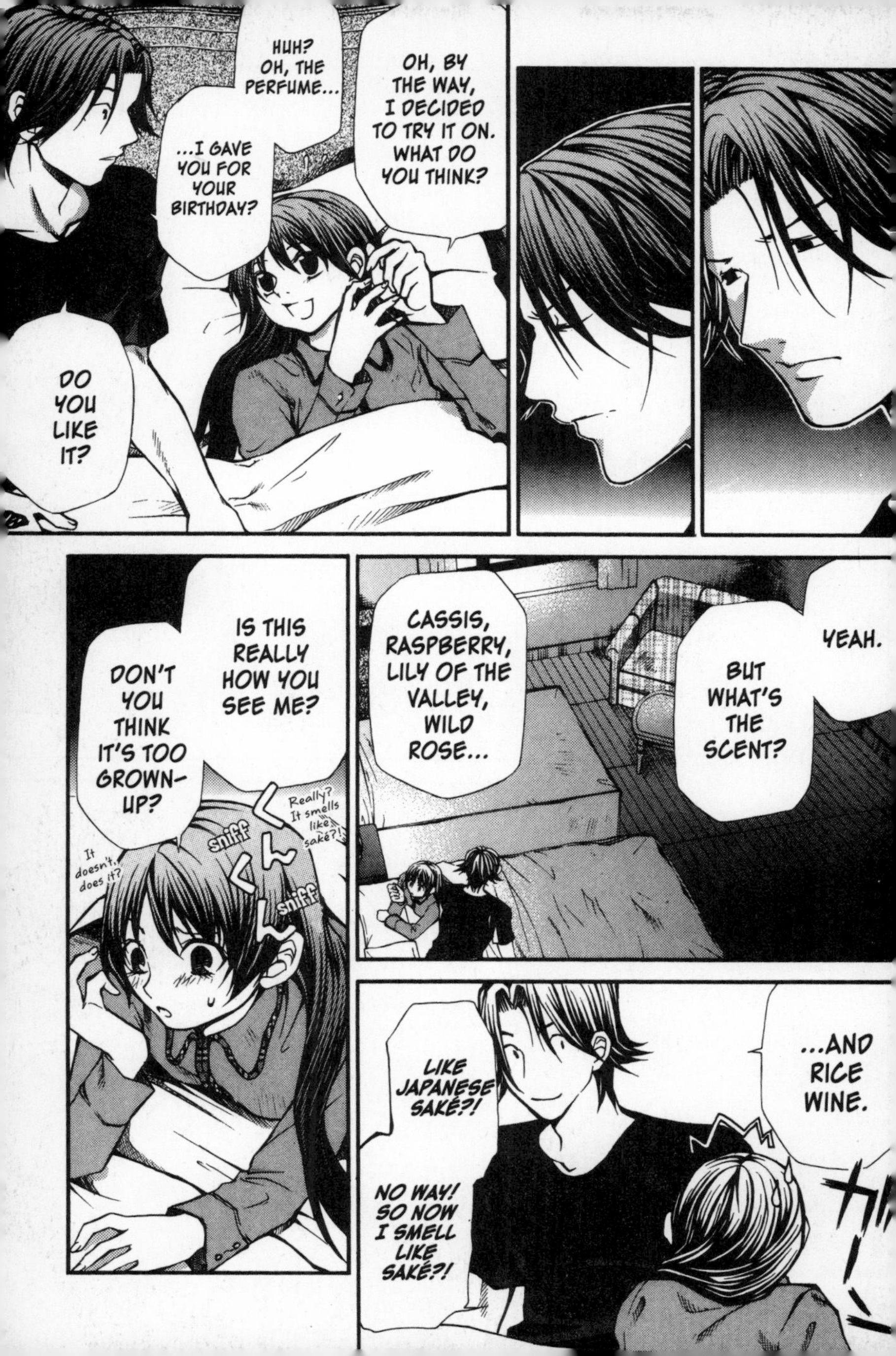
OH, BY THE WAY, I DECIDED TO TRY IT ON. WHAT DO YOU THINK?
HUH? OH, THE PERFUME...
...I GAVE YOU FOR YOUR BIRTHDAY?
DO YOU LIKE IT?
YEAH.
BUT WHAT'S THE SCENT?
CASSIS, RASPBERRY, LILY OF THE VALLEY, WILD ROSE...
...AND RICE WINE.
LIKE JAPANESE SAKÉ?!
NO WAY! SO NOW I SMELL LIKE SAKÉ?!
IS THIS REALLY HOW YOU SEE ME?
DON'T YOU THINK IT'S TOO GROWN-UP?
Really? It smells like saké?!
sniff
It doesn't, does it?
sniff

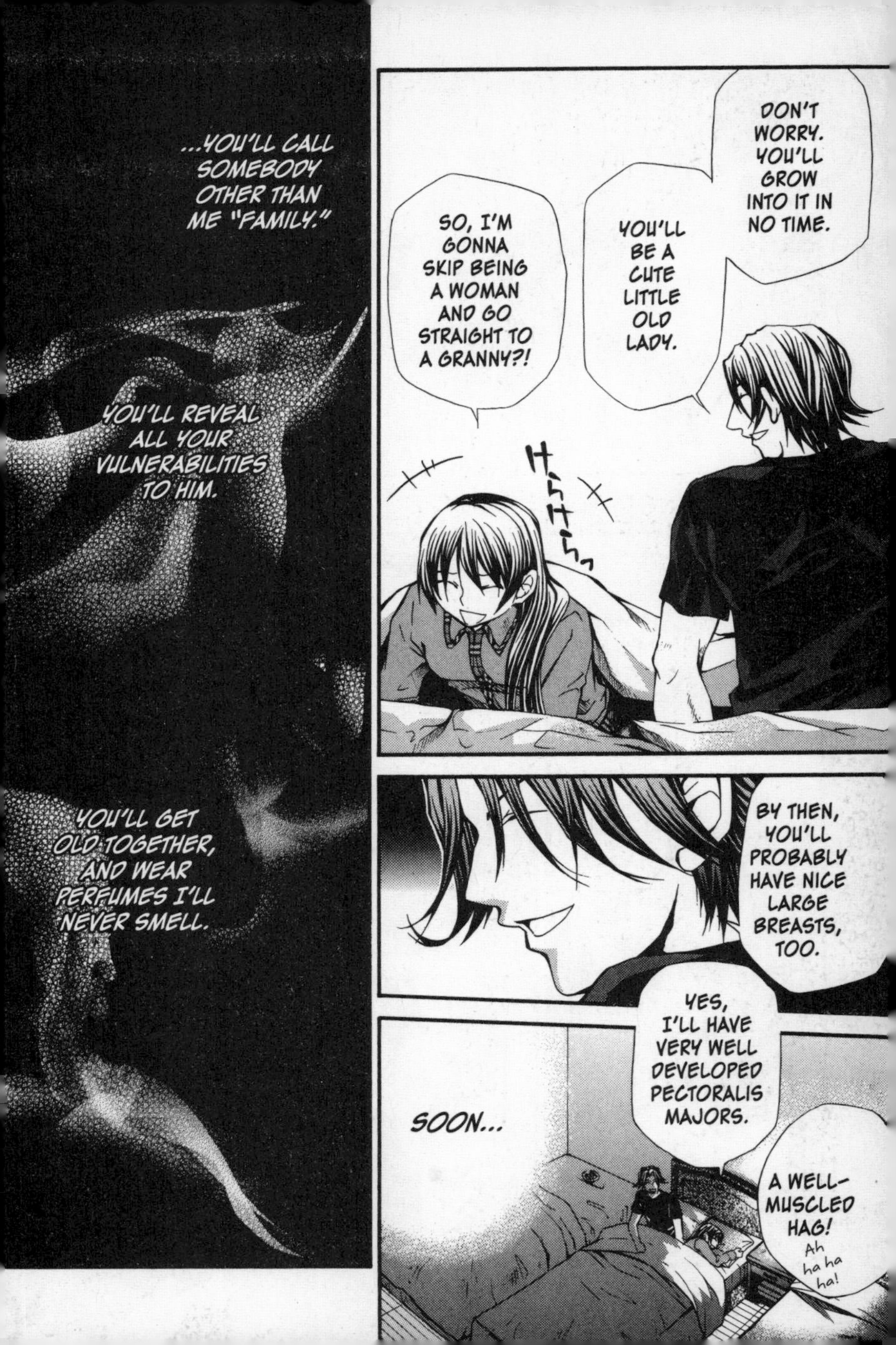
DON'T WORRY. YOU'LL GROW INTO IT IN NO TIME.
YOU'LL BE A CUTE LITTLE OLD LADY.
SO, I'M GONNA SKIP BEING A WOMAN AND GO STRAIGHT TO A GRANNY?!
けらけら
BY THEN, YOU'LL PROBABLY HAVE NICE LARGE BREASTS, TOO.
YES, I'LL HAVE VERY WELL DEVELOPED PECTORALIS MAJORS.
A WELL-MUSCLED HAG!
Ah ha ha ha!
SOON...
...YOU'LL CALL SOMEBODY OTHER THAN ME "FAMILY."
YOU'LL REVEAL ALL YOUR VULNERABILITIES TO HIM.
YOU'LL GET OLD TOGETHER, AND WEAR PERFUMES I'LL NEVER SMELL.

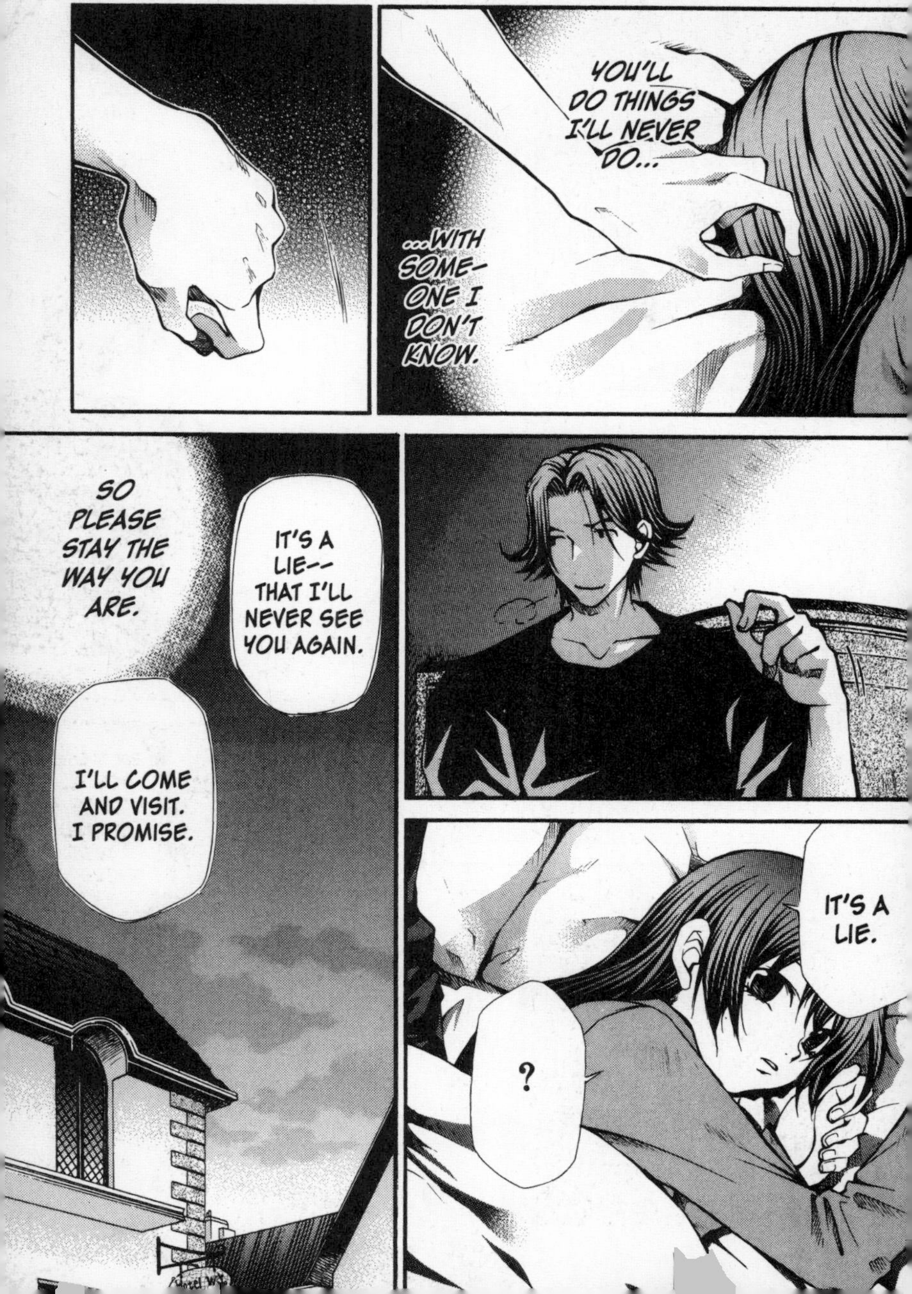
YOU'LL DO THINGS I'LL NEVER DO...
...WITH SOMEONE I DON'T KNOW.
IT'S A LIE.
?
SO PLEASE STAY THE WAY YOU ARE.
IT'S A LIE-- THAT I'LL NEVER SEE YOU AGAIN.
I'LL COME AND VISIT. I PROMISE.

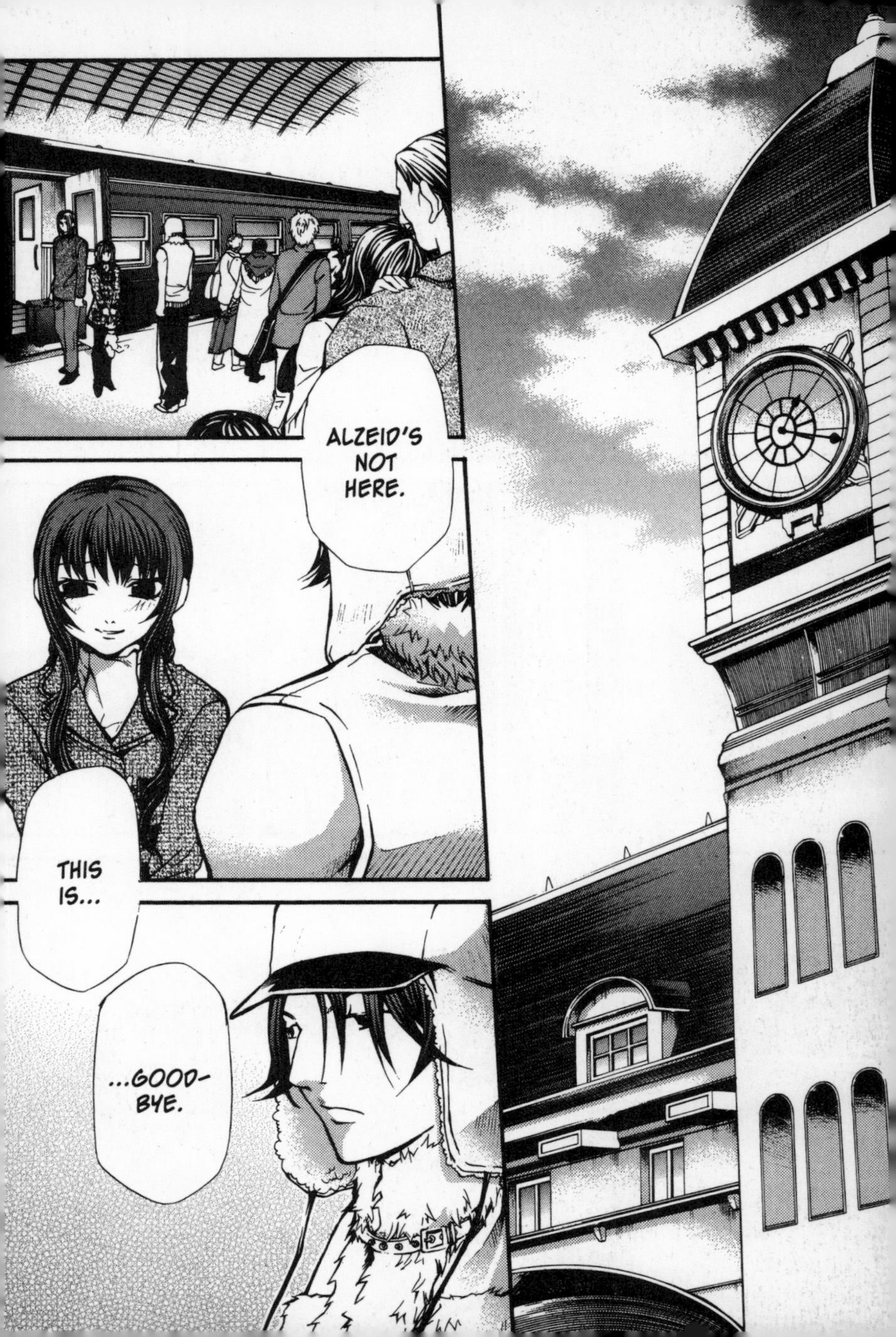
ALZEID'S NOT HERE.
THIS IS...
...GOOD-BYE.

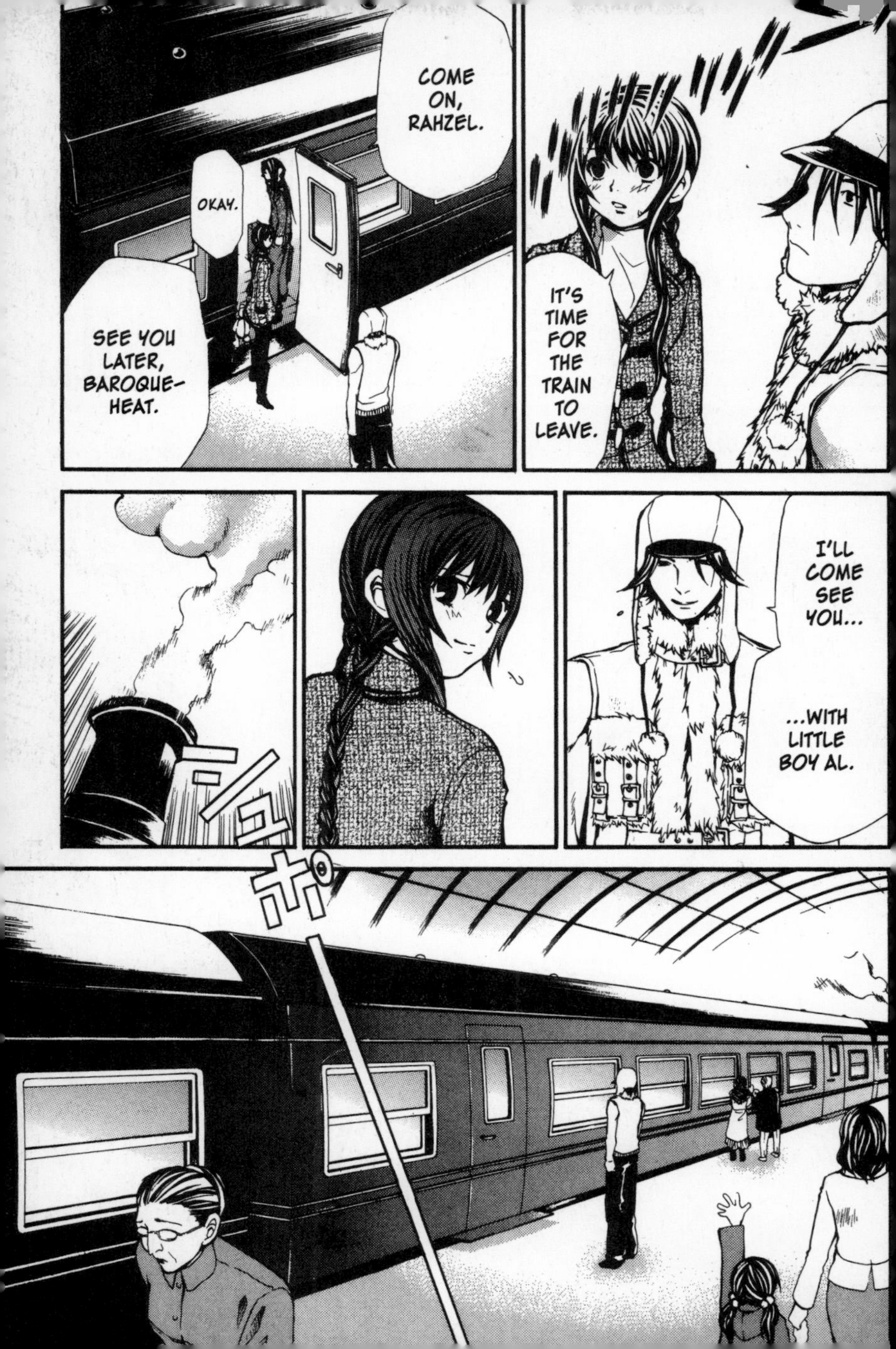
IT'S TIME FOR THE TRAIN TO LEAVE.
COME ON, RAHZEL.
OKAY.
SEE YOU LATER, BAROQUE-HEAT.
I'LL COME SEE YOU...
...WITH LITTLE BOY AL.
ポ

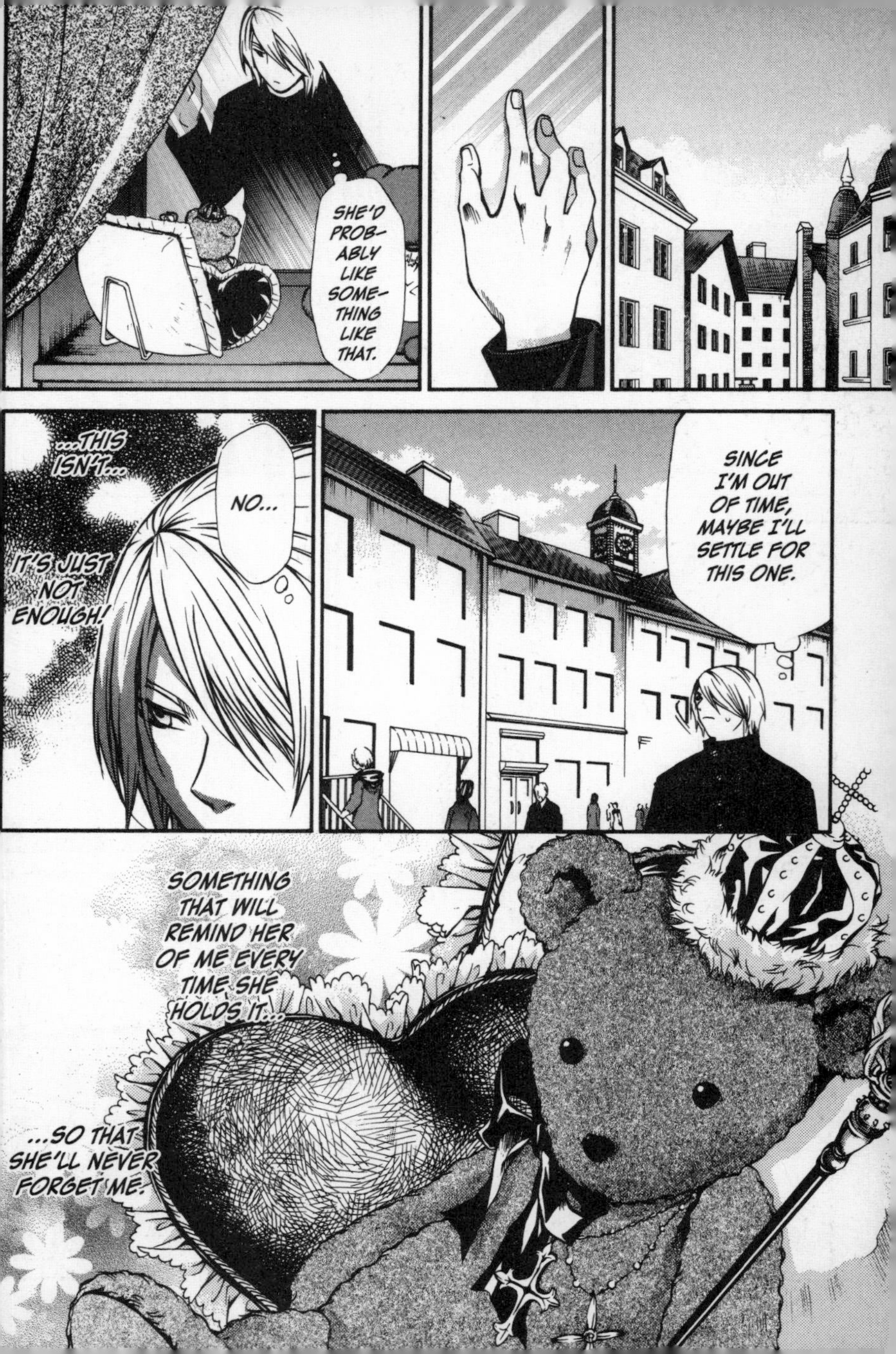
SHE'D PROBABLY LIKE SOMETHING LIKE THAT.
SINCE I'M OUT OF TIME, MAYBE I'LL SETTLE FOR THIS ONE.
NO...
...THIS ISN'T...
IT'S JUST NOT ENOUGH!
SOMETHING THAT WILL REMIND HER OF ME EVERY TIME SHE HOLDS IT...
...SO THAT SHE'LL NEVER FORGET ME.

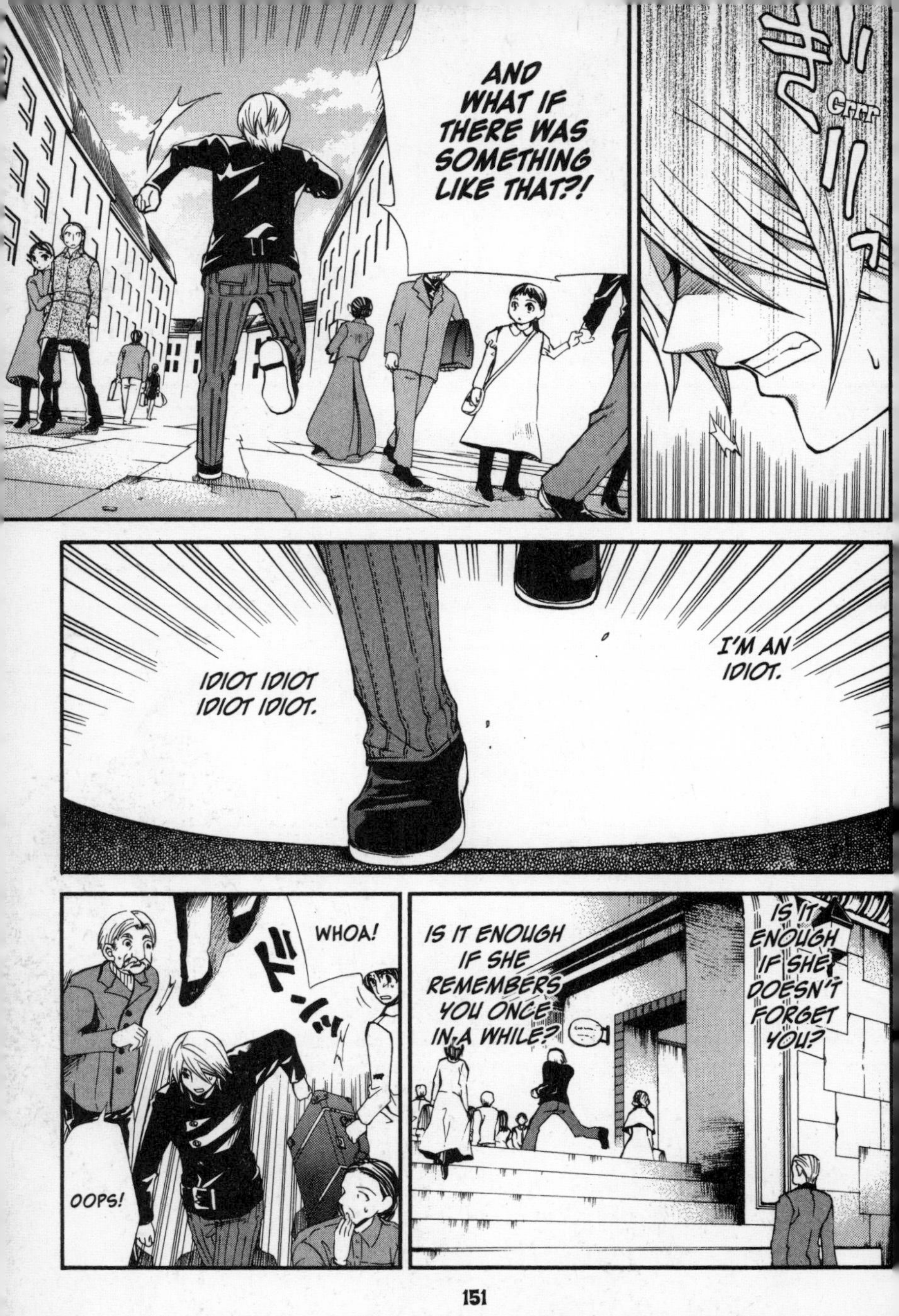
Grrr
AND WHAT IF THERE WAS SOMETHING LIKE THAT?!
I'M AN IDIOT.
IDIOT IDIOT IDIOT IDIOT.
IS IT ENOUGH IF SHE DOESN'T FORGET YOU?
IS IT ENOUGH IF SHE REMEMBERS YOU ONCE IN A WHILE?
WHOA!
OOPS!

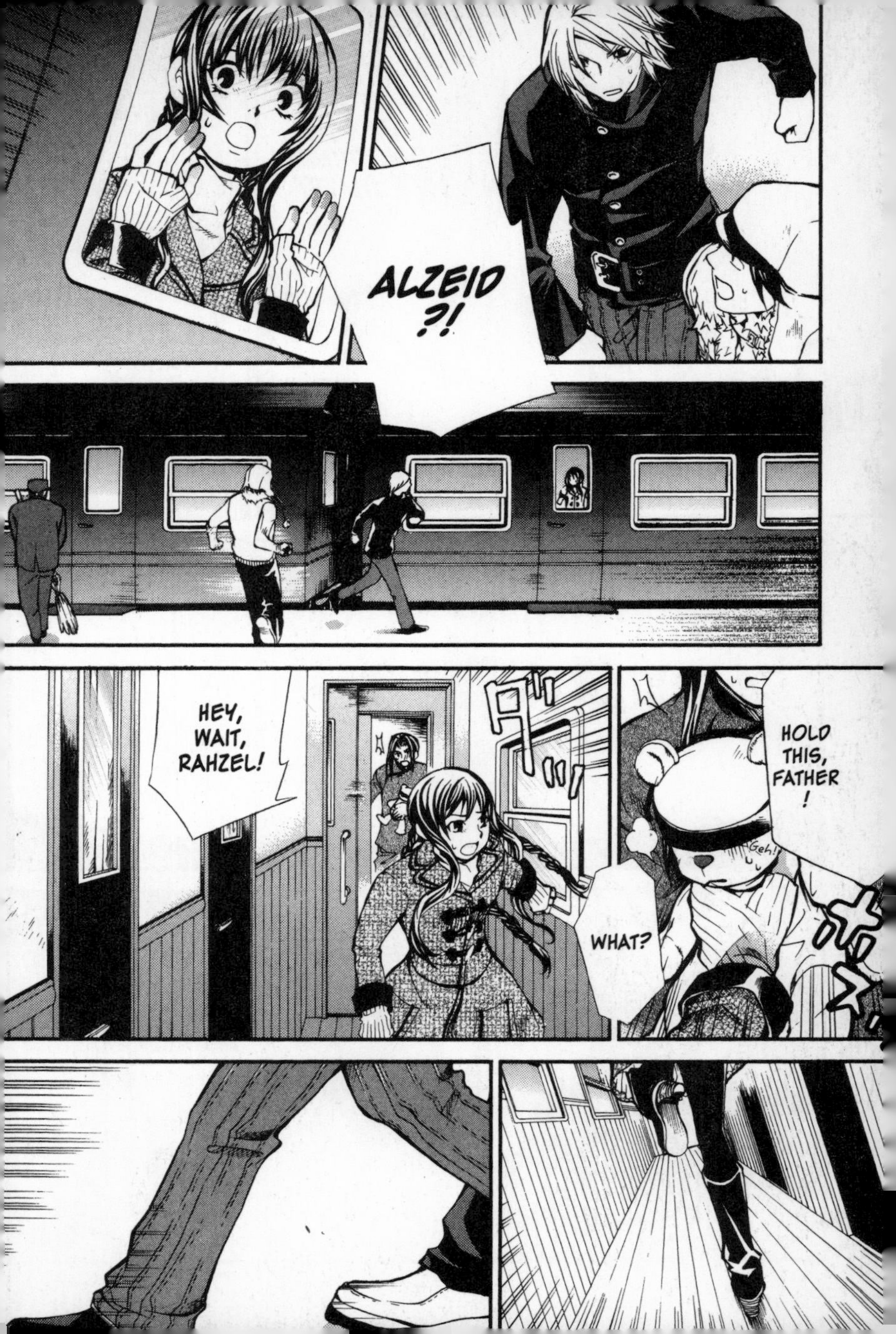
ALZEID ?!
HOLD THIS, FATHER!
Geh!
WHAT?
HEY, WAIT, RAHZEL!

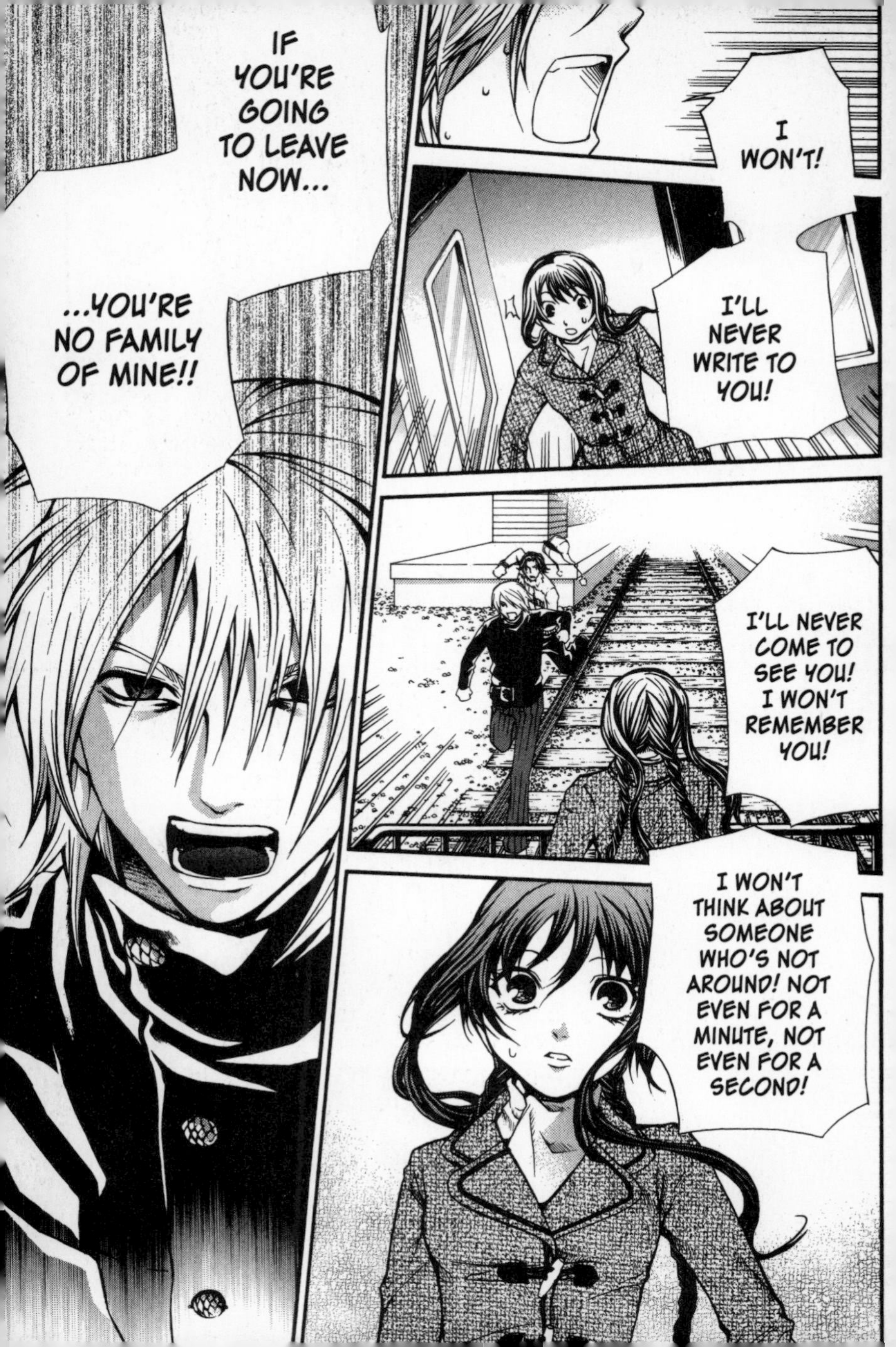
I WON'T!
I'LL NEVER WRITE TO YOU!
I'LL NEVER COME TO SEE YOU! I WON'T REMEMBER YOU!
I WON'T THINK ABOUT SOMEONE WHO'S NOT AROUND! NOT EVEN FOR A MINUTE, NOT EVEN FOR A SECOND!
IF YOU'RE GOING TO LEAVE NOW...
...YOU'RE NO FAMILY OF MINE!!

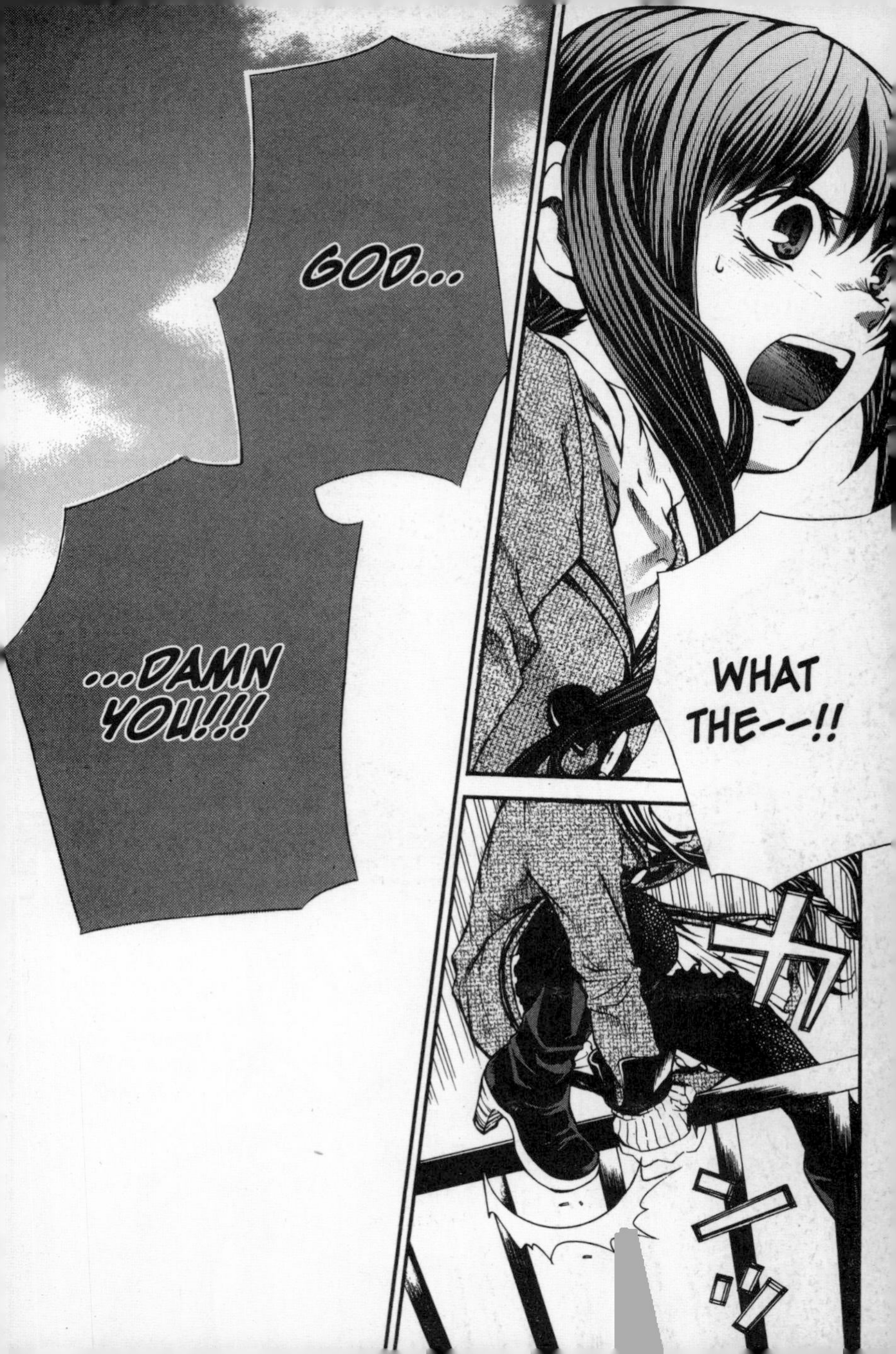
WHAT THE--!!
GOD...
...DAMN YOU!!!

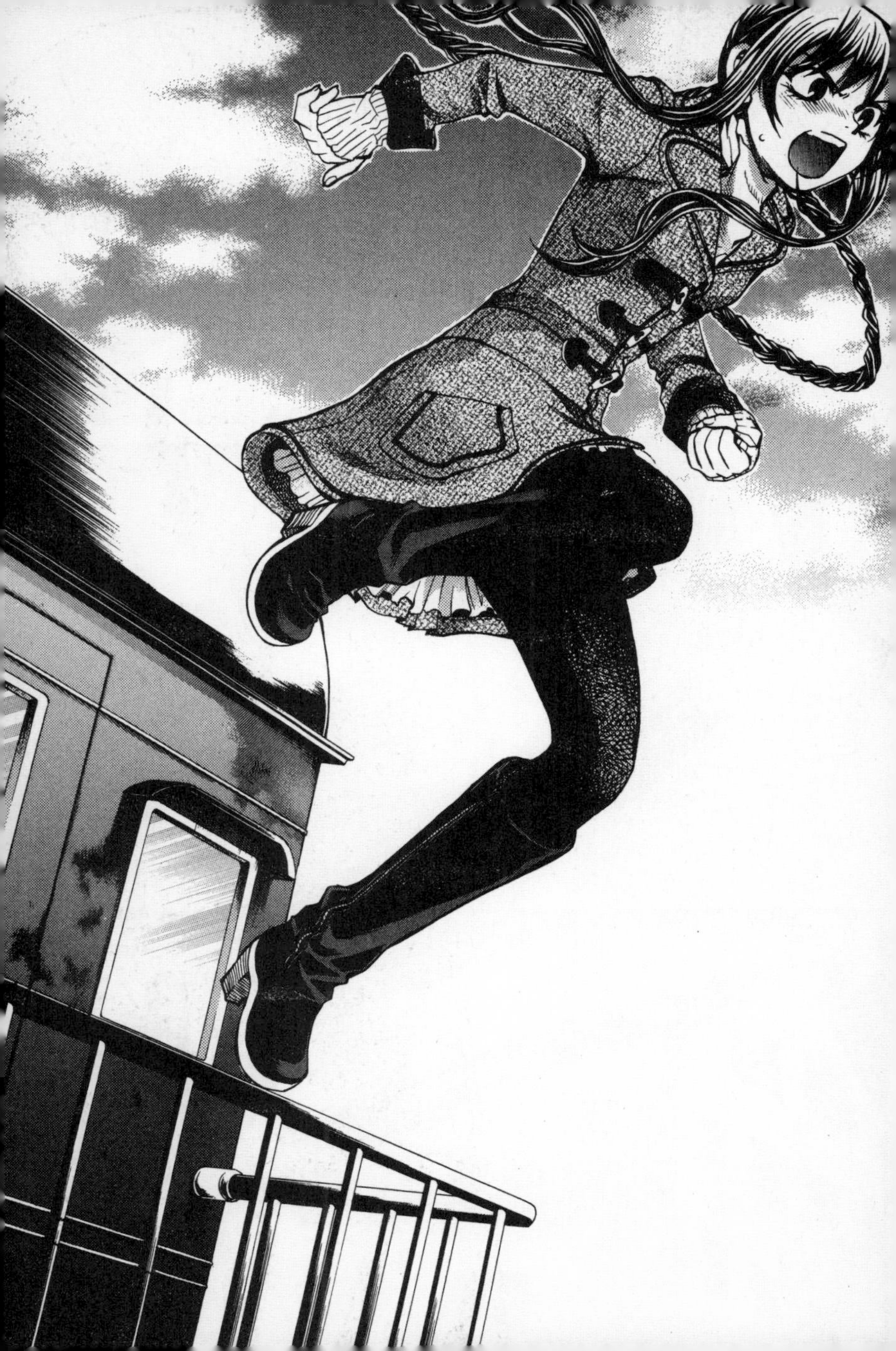

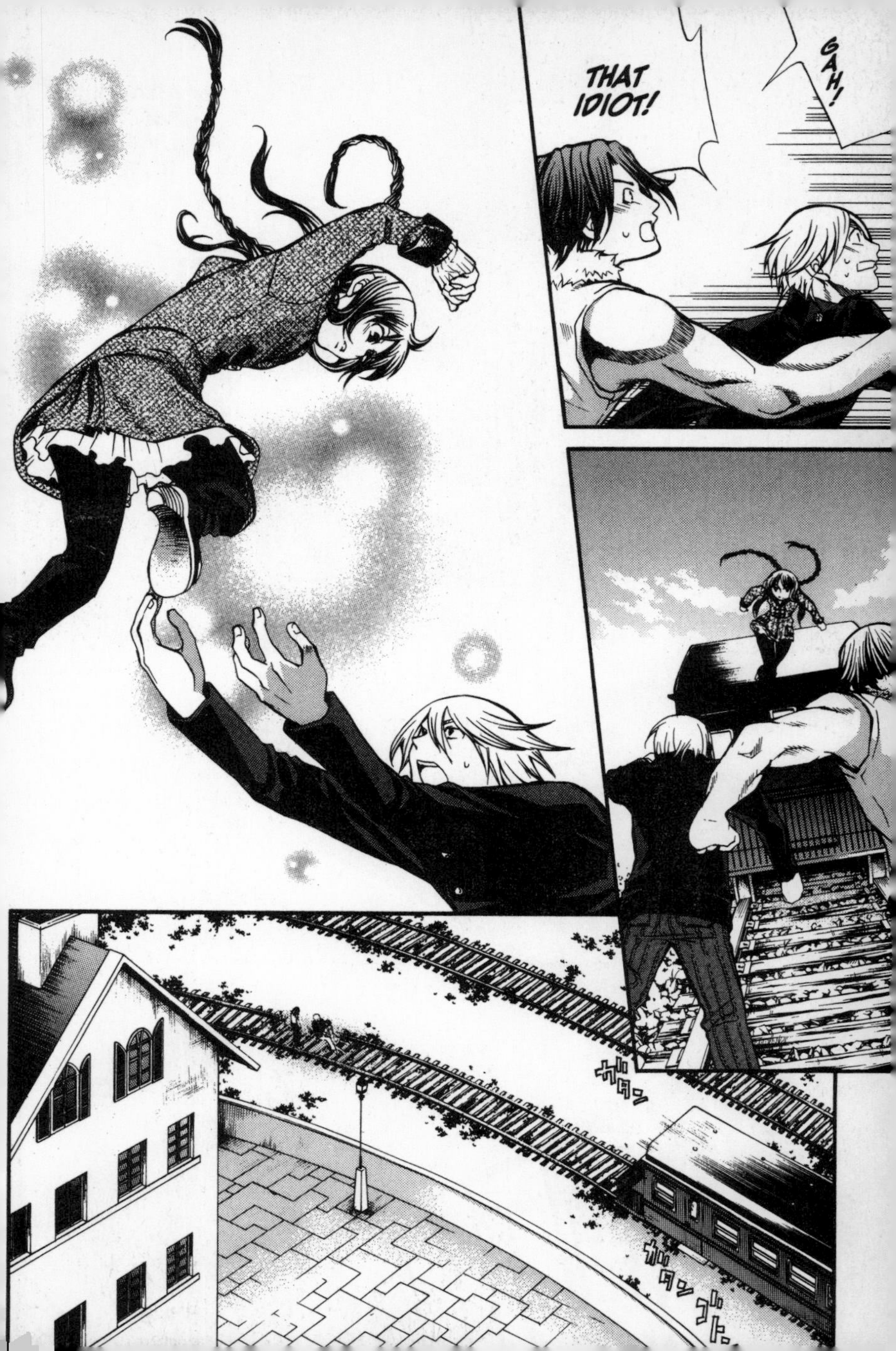
GAH!
THAT IDIOT!
ガタン
ガタンゴトー

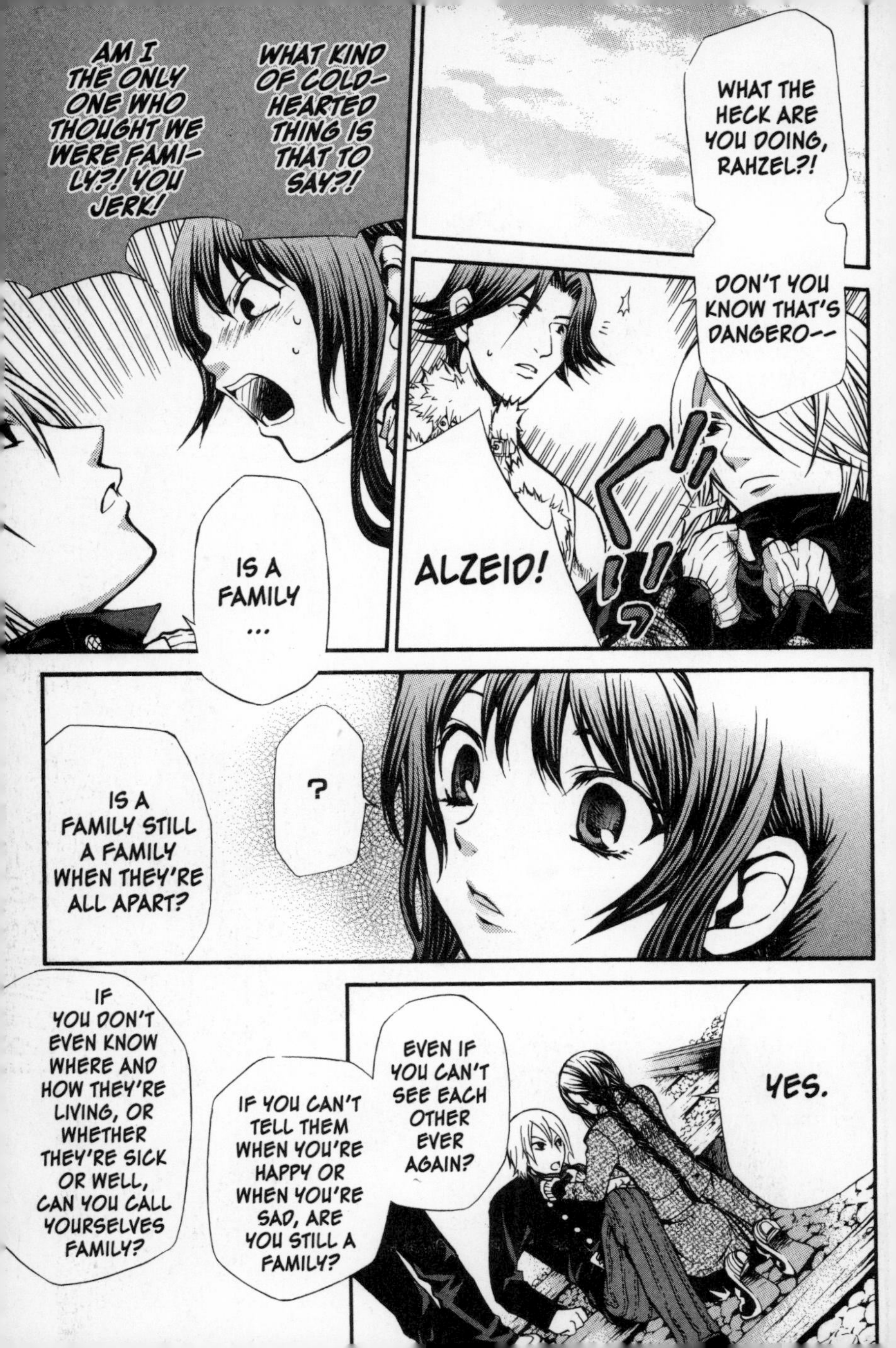
WHAT THE HECK ARE YOU DOING, RAHZEL?!
DON'T YOU KNOW THAT'S DANGERO--
ALZEID!
WHAT KIND OF COLD-HEARTED THING IS THAT TO SAY?!
AM I THE ONLY ONE WHO THOUGHT WE WERE FAMI-LY?! YOU JERK!
IS A FAMILY ...
?
IS A FAMILY STILL A FAMILY WHEN THEY'RE ALL APART?
YES.
EVEN IF YOU CAN'T SEE EACH OTHER EVER AGAIN?
IF YOU CAN'T TELL THEM WHEN YOU'RE HAPPY OR WHEN YOU'RE SAD, ARE YOU STILL A FAMILY?
IF YOU DON'T EVEN KNOW WHERE AND HOW THEY'RE LIVING, OR WHETHER THEY'RE SICK OR WELL, CAN YOU CALL YOURSELVES FAMILY?

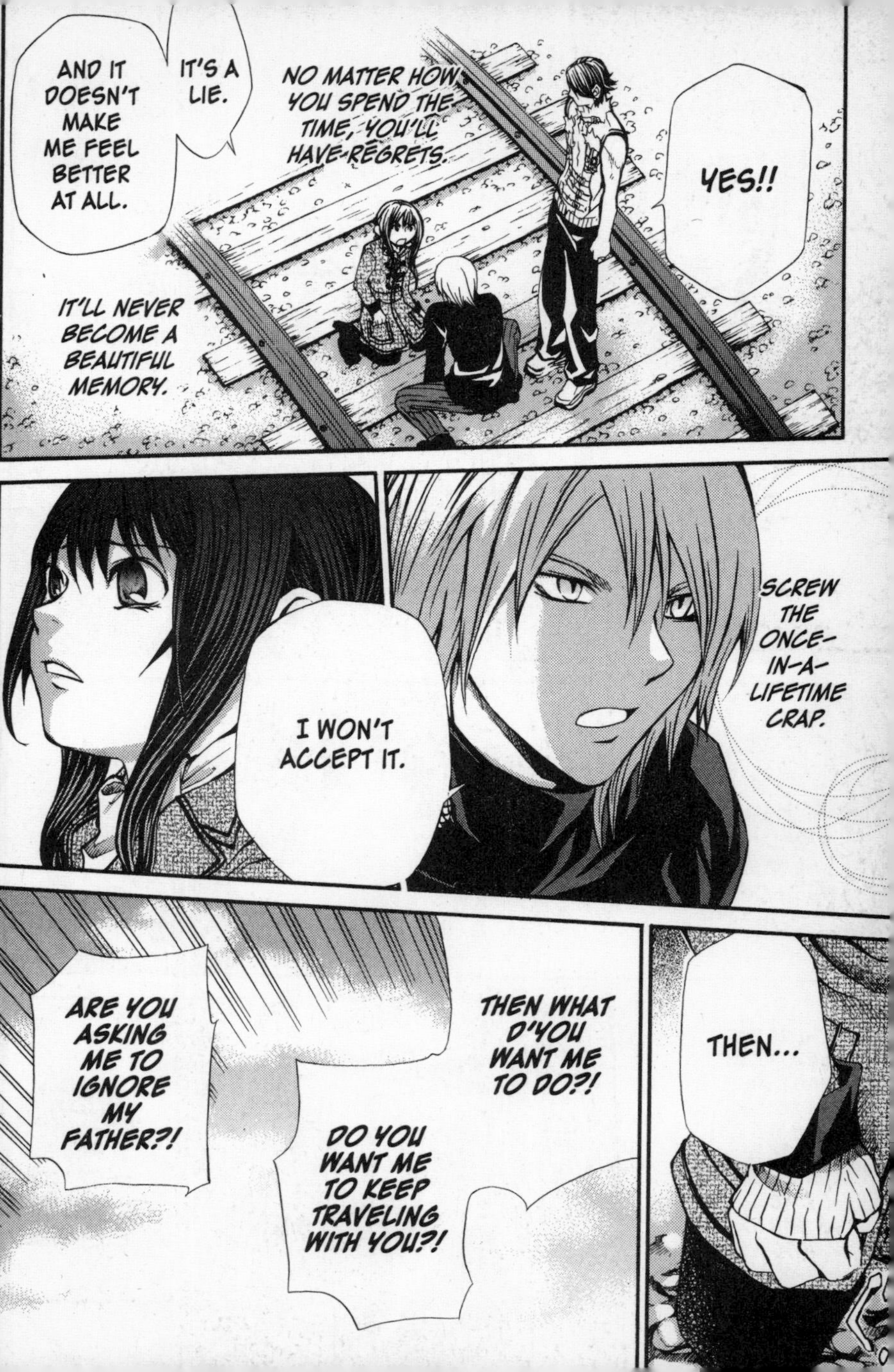

YES!!
NO MATTER HOW YOU SPEND THE TIME, YOU'LL HAVE REGRETS.
IT'S A LIE.
AND IT DOESN'T MAKE ME FEEL BETTER AT ALL.
IT'LL NEVER BECOME A BEAUTIFUL MEMORY.
SCREW THE ONCE-IN-A-LIFETIME CRAP.
I WON'T ACCEPT IT.
THEN...
THEN WHAT D'YOU WANT ME TO DO?!
ARE YOU ASKING ME TO IGNORE MY FATHER?!
DO YOU WANT ME TO KEEP TRAVELING WITH YOU?!

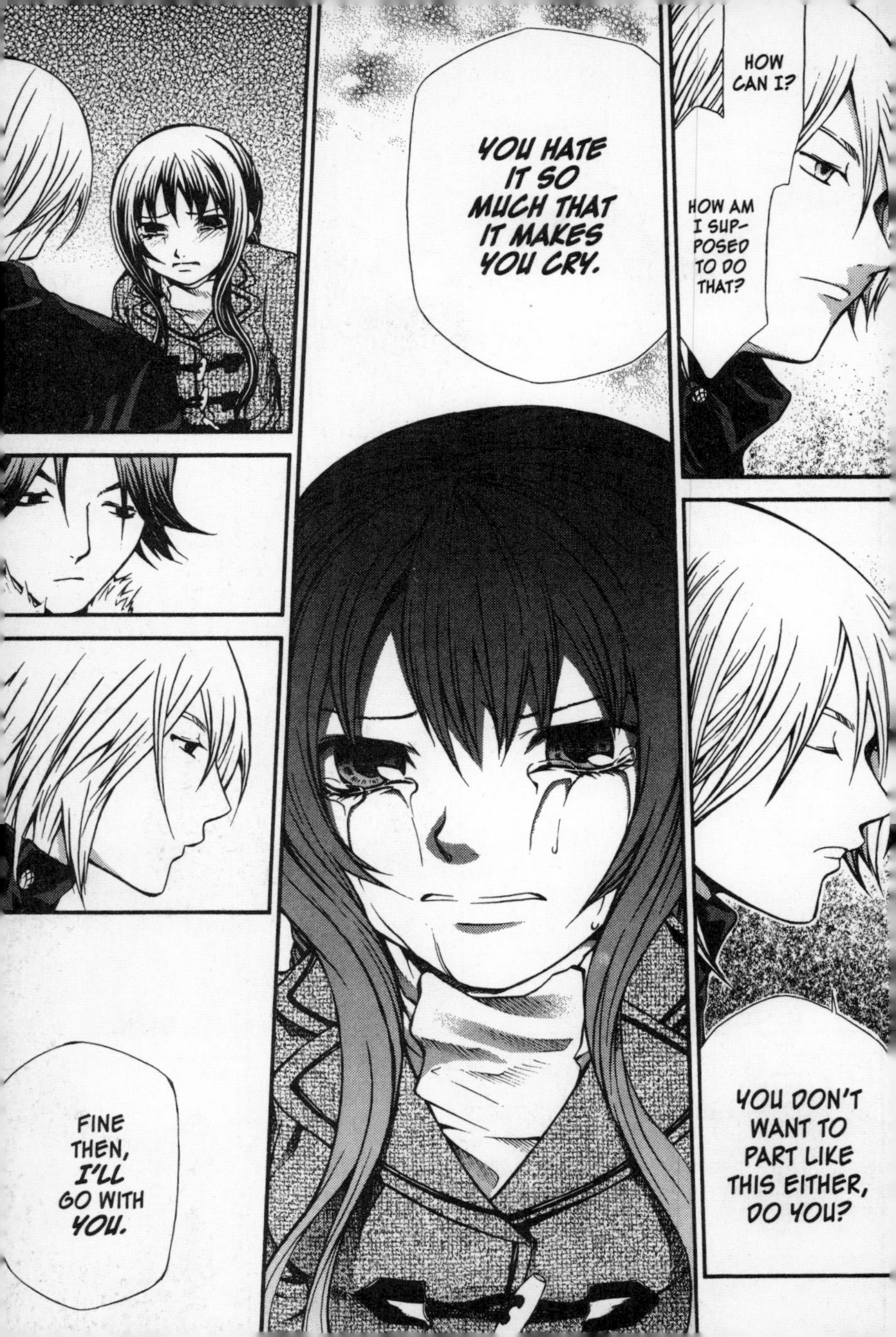
HOW CAN I?
HOW AM I SUP-POSED TO DO THAT?
YOU HATE IT SO MUCH THAT IT MAKES YOU CRY.
YOU DON'T WANT TO PART LIKE THIS EITHER, DO YOU?
FINE THEN, I'LL GO WITH YOU.

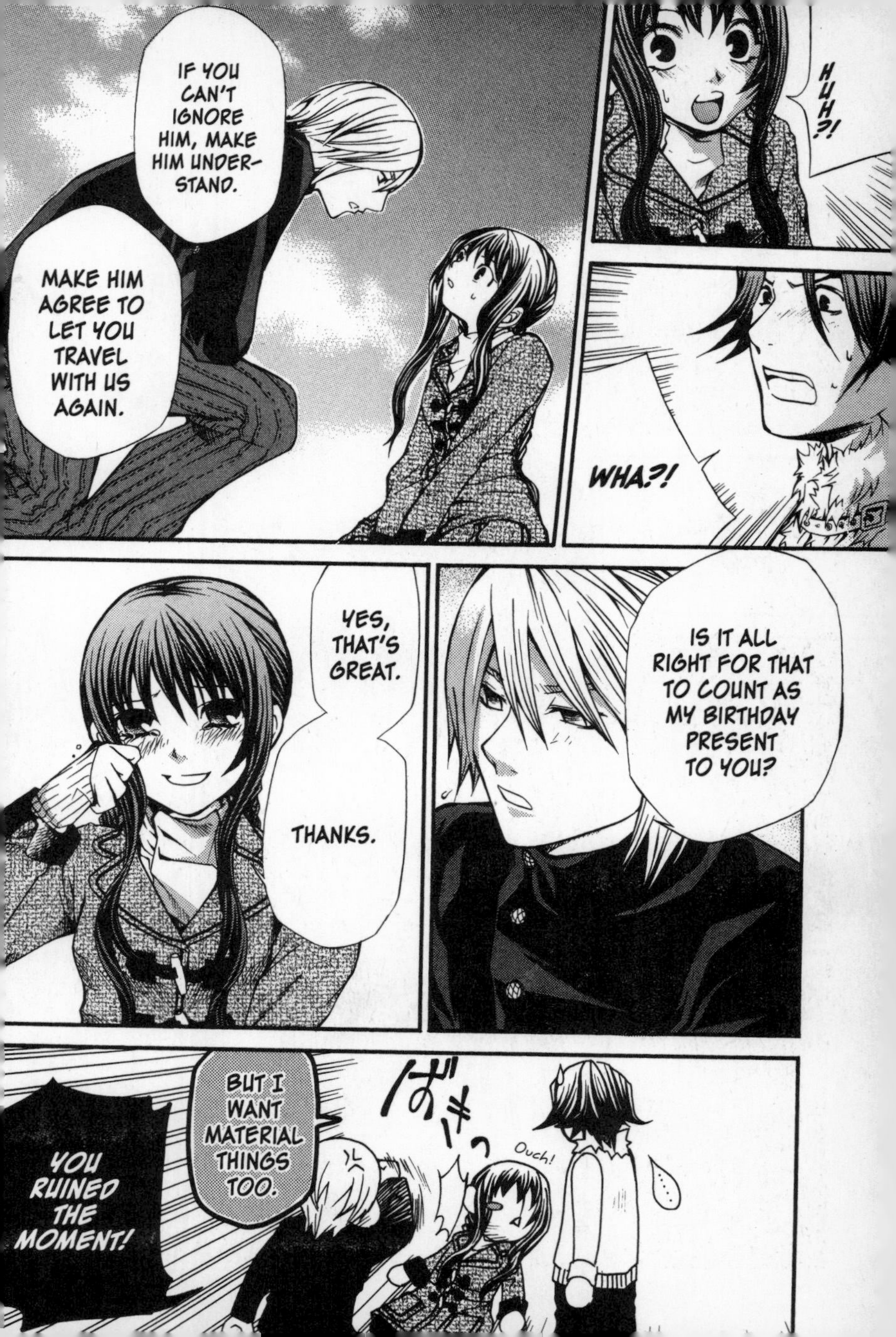
HUH?!
WHA?!
IF YOU CAN'T IGNORE HIM, MAKE HIM UNDER-STAND.
MAKE HIM AGREE TO LET YOU TRAVEL WITH US AGAIN.
IS IT ALL RIGHT FOR THAT TO COUNT AS MY BIRTHDAY PRESENT TO YOU?
YES, THAT'S GREAT.
THANKS.
...
Ouch!
ばきっ
BUT I WANT MATERIAL THINGS TOO.
YOU RUINED THE MOMENT!

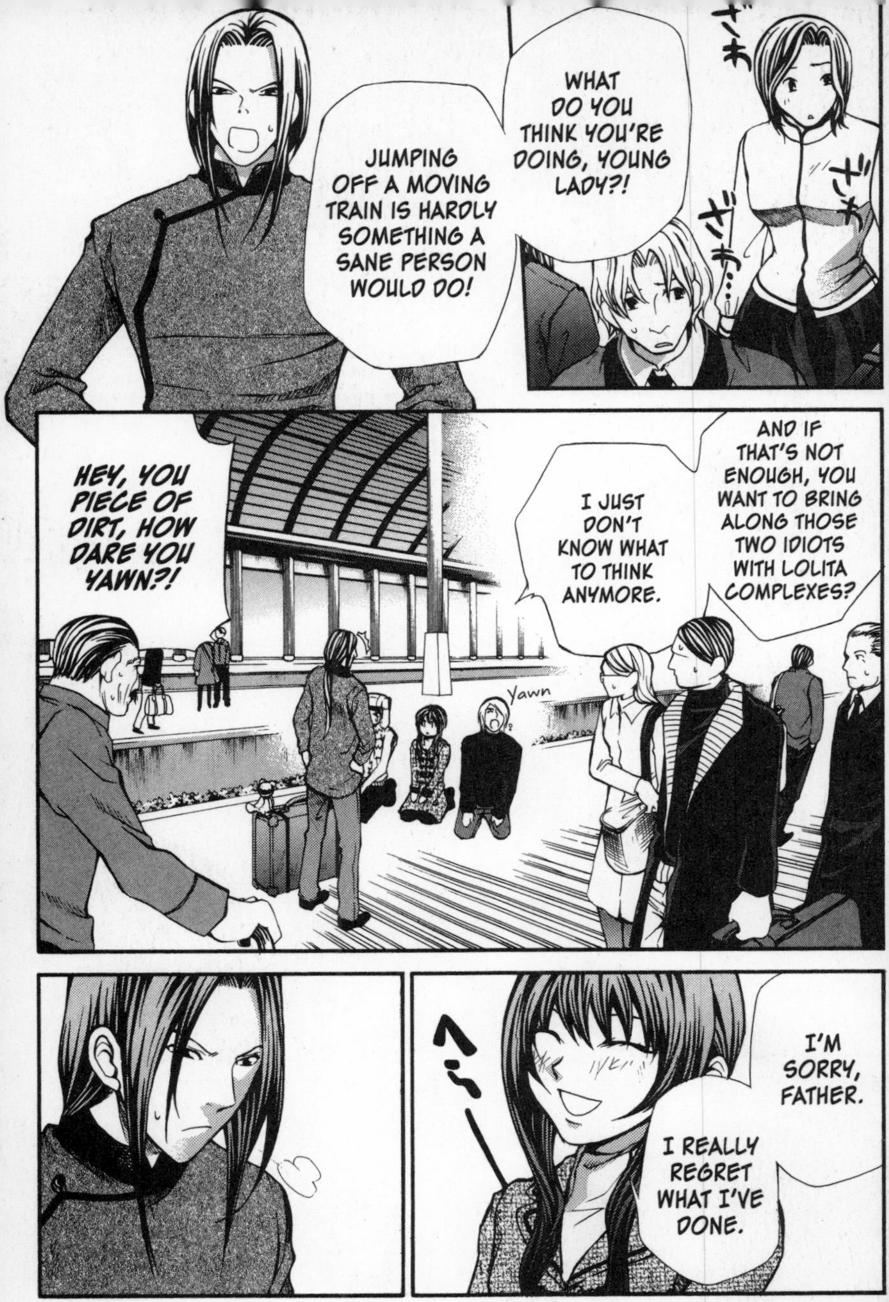
ざわ
ざわ
ざわ…
WHAT DO YOU THINK YOU'RE DOING, YOUNG LADY?!
JUMPING OFF A MOVING TRAIN IS HARDLY SOMETHING A SANE PERSON WOULD DO!
AND IF THAT'S NOT ENOUGH, YOU WANT TO BRING ALONG THOSE TWO IDIOTS WITH LOLITA COMPLEXES?
I JUST DON'T KNOW WHAT TO THINK ANYMORE.
Yawn
HEY, YOU PIECE OF DIRT, HOW DARE YOU YAWN?!
I'M SORRY, FATHER.
I REALLY REGRET WHAT I'VE DONE.

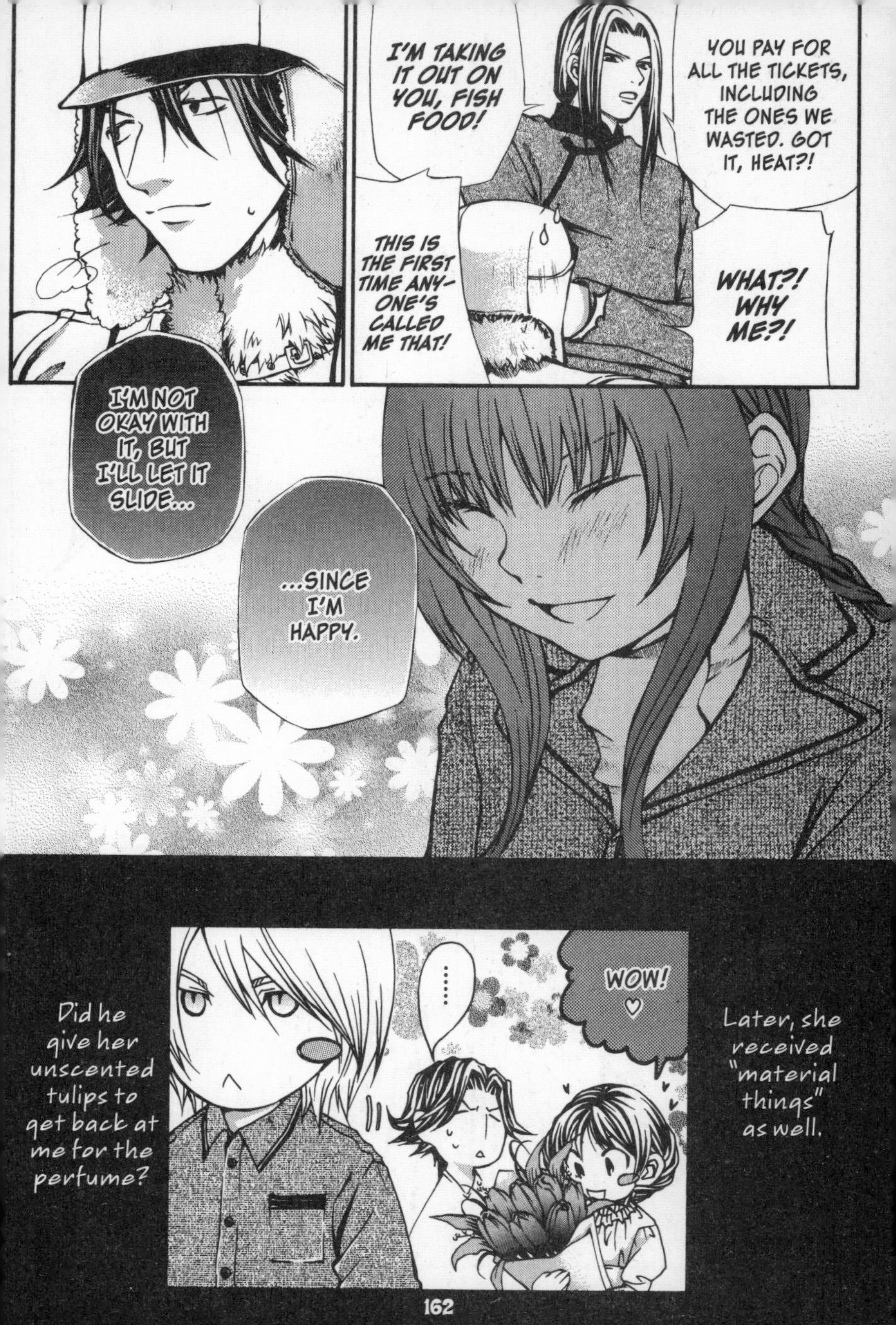
YOU PAY FOR ALL THE TICKETS, INCLUDING THE ONES WE WASTED. GOT IT, HEAT?!
I'M TAKING IT OUT ON YOU, FISH FOOD!
WHAT?! WHY ME?!
THIS IS THE FIRST TIME ANYONE'S CALLED ME THAT!
I'M NOT OKAY WITH IT, BUT I'LL LET IT SLIDE...
...SINCE I'M HAPPY.
Later, she received "material things" as well.
WOW! ♡
......
Did he give her unscented tulips to get back at me for the perfume?

Chapter 61:
Such a Cold Night's Hand--
Part 1: At the End of a Trip

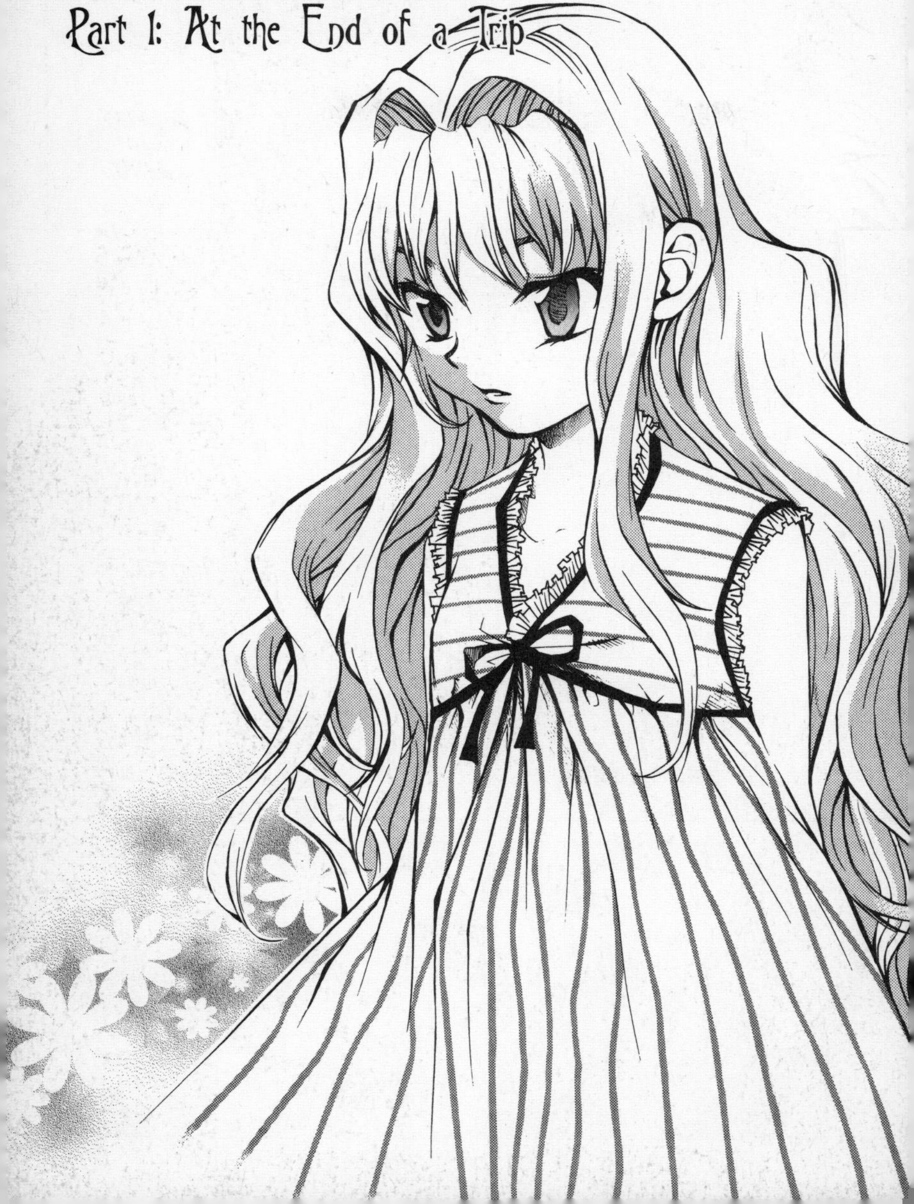

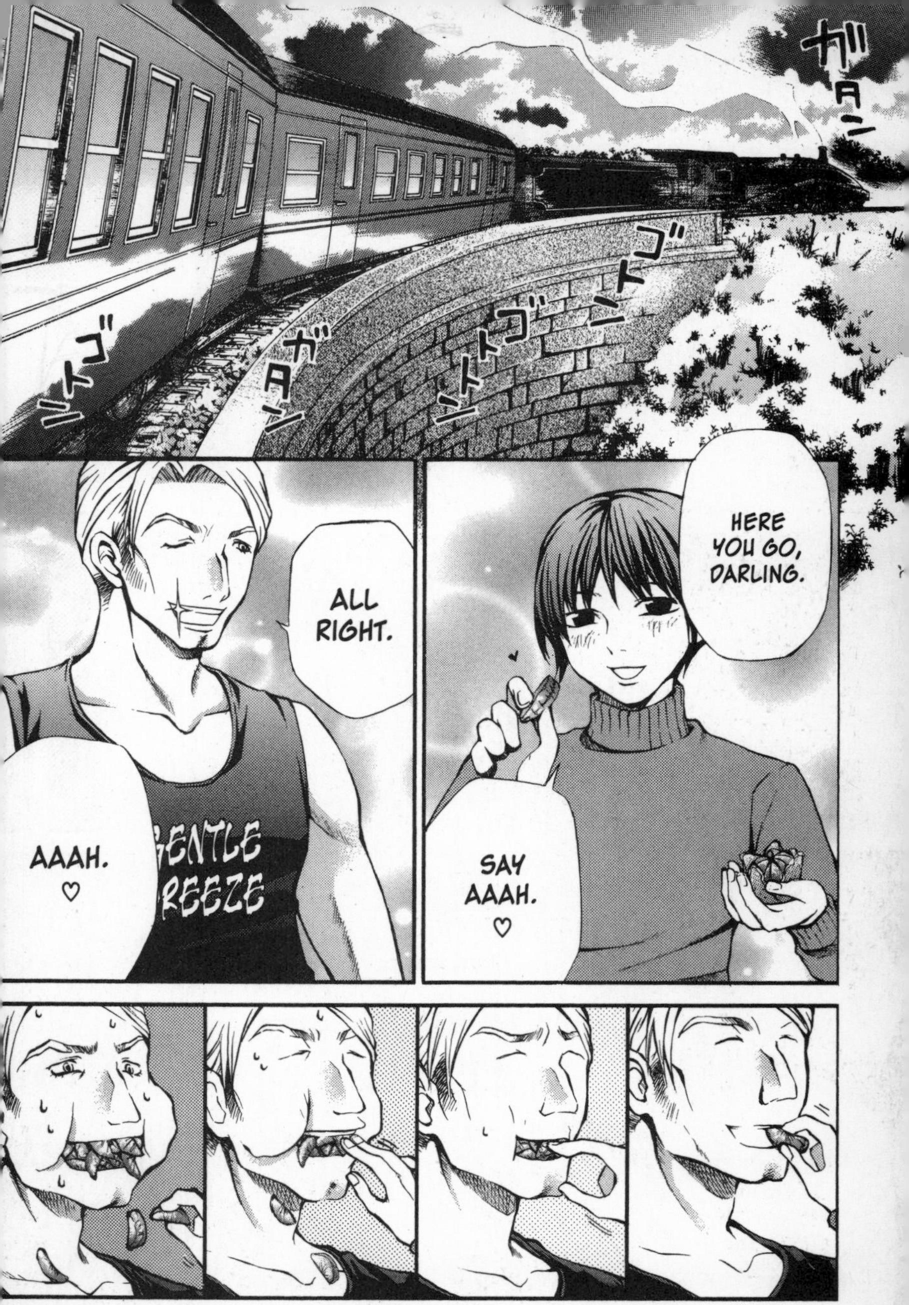

ガタン
ゴトン
ゴトン
ガタン
ゴトン
HERE YOU GO, DARLING.
SAY AAAH. ♡
ALL RIGHT.
AAAH. ♡

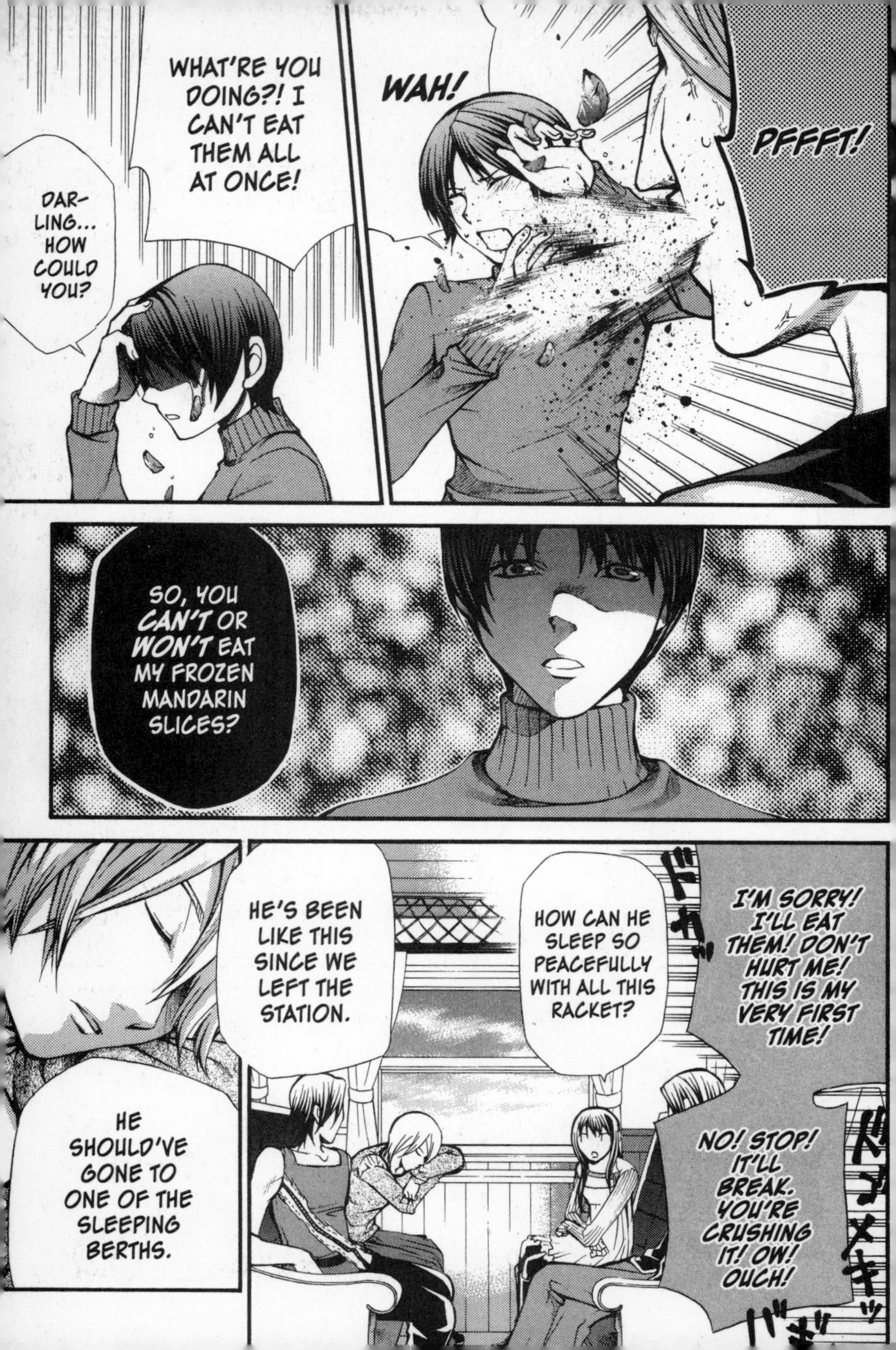
PFFFT!
WAH!
WHAT'RE YOU DOING?! I CAN'T EAT THEM ALL AT ONCE!
DAR-LING... HOW COULD YOU?
SO, YOU *CAN'T* OR *WON'T* EAT MY FROZEN MANDARIN SLICES?
I'M SORRY! I'LL EAT THEM! DON'T HURT ME! THIS IS MY VERY FIRST TIME!
HOW CAN HE SLEEP SO PEACEFULLY WITH ALL THIS RACKET?
HE'S BEEN LIKE THIS SINCE WE LEFT THE STATION.
NO! STOP! IT'LL BREAK. YOU'RE CRUSHING IT! OW! OUCH!
HE SHOULD'VE GONE TO ONE OF THE SLEEPING BERTHS.

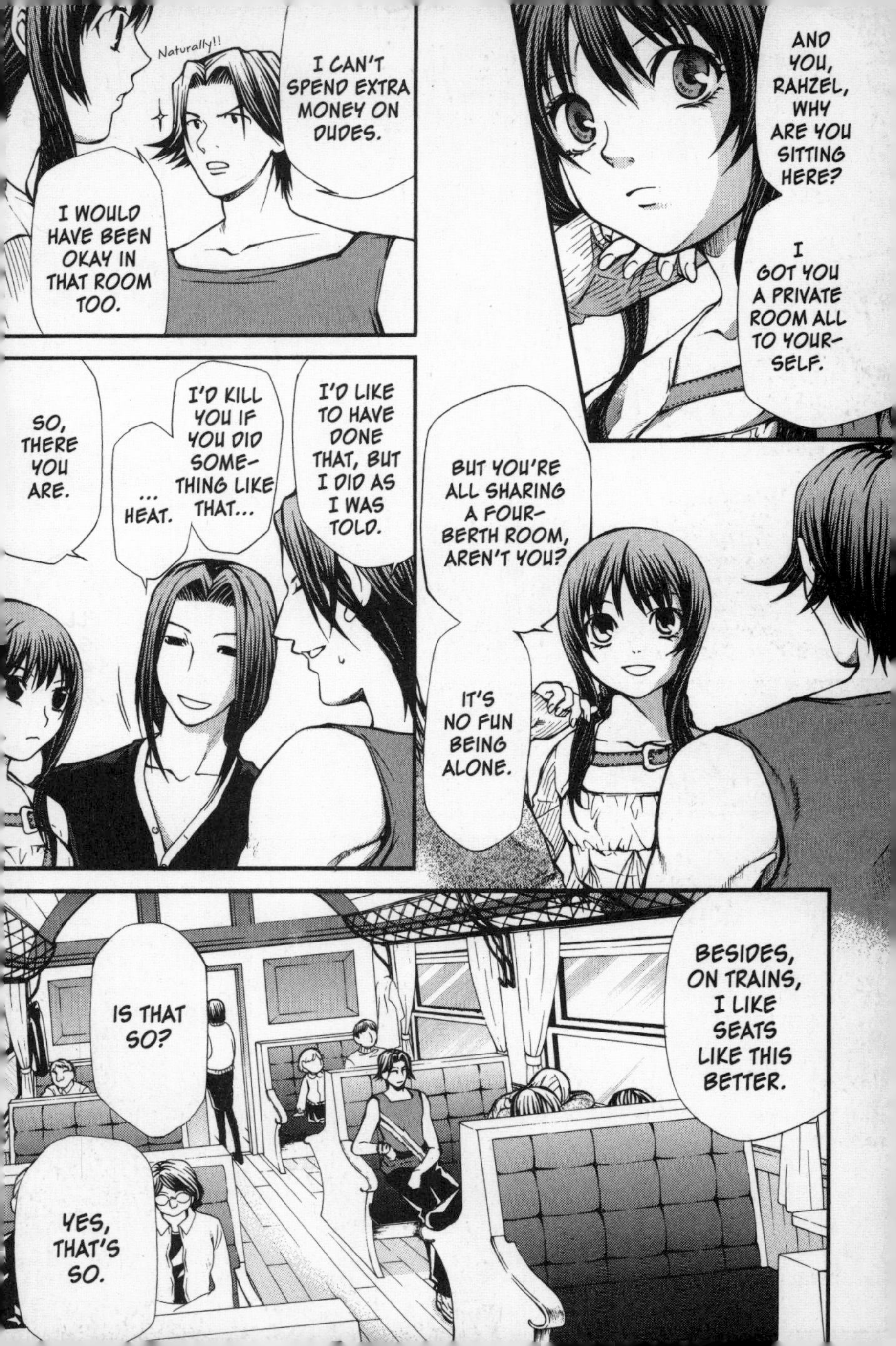

AND YOU, RAHZEL, WHY ARE YOU SITTING HERE?
I GOT YOU A PRIVATE ROOM ALL TO YOURSELF.
I CAN'T SPEND EXTRA MONEY ON DUDES.
Naturally!!
I WOULD HAVE BEEN OKAY IN THAT ROOM TOO.
BUT YOU'RE ALL SHARING A FOUR-BERTH ROOM, AREN'T YOU?
IT'S NO FUN BEING ALONE.
I'D LIKE TO HAVE DONE THAT, BUT I DID AS I WAS TOLD.
I'D KILL YOU IF YOU DID SOMETHING LIKE THAT...
... HEAT.
SO, THERE YOU ARE.
BESIDES, ON TRAINS, I LIKE SEATS LIKE THIS BETTER.
IS THAT SO?
YES, THAT'S SO.

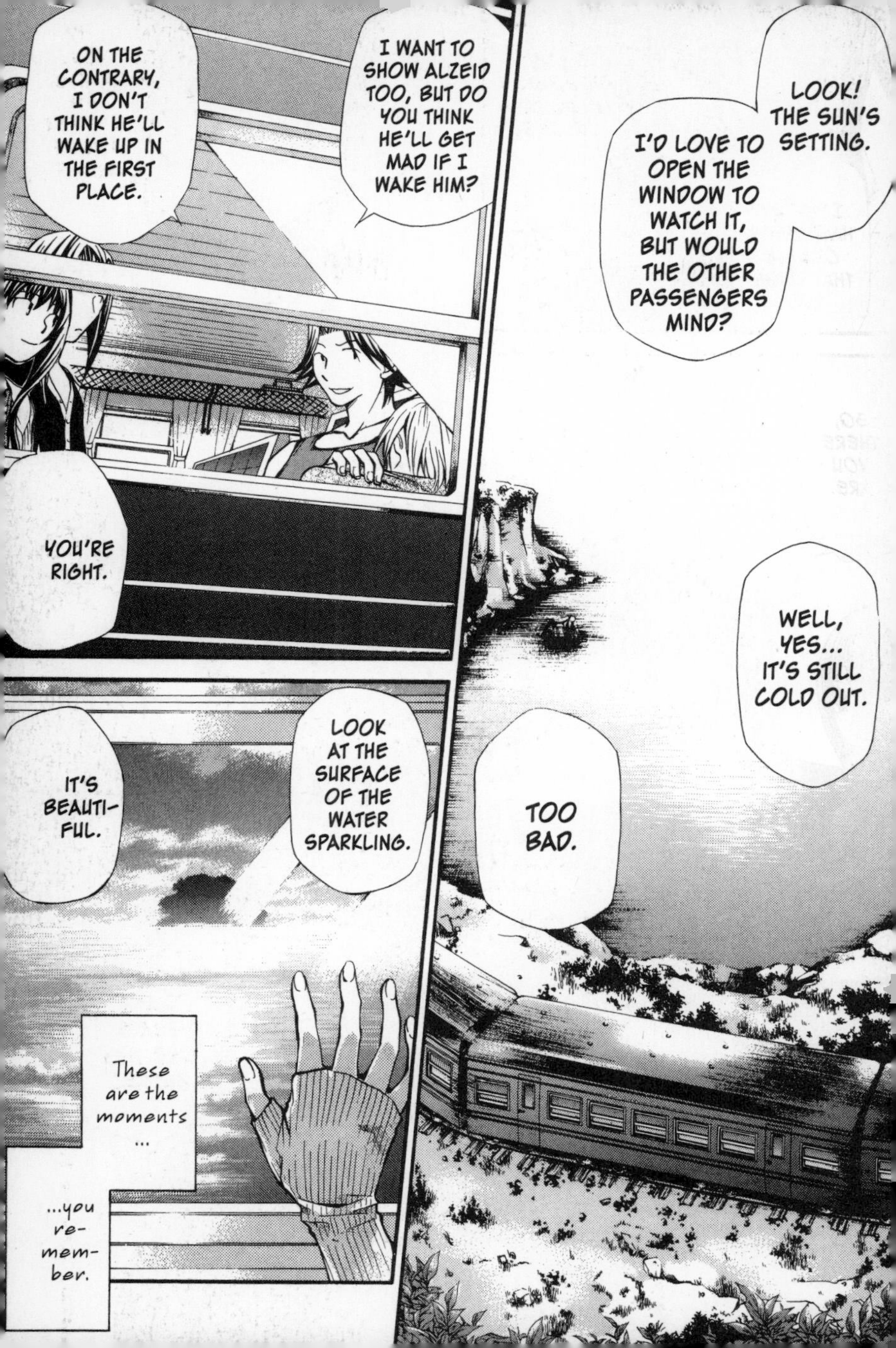
LOOK! THE SUN'S SETTING.
I'D LOVE TO OPEN THE WINDOW TO WATCH IT, BUT WOULD THE OTHER PASSENGERS MIND?
WELL, YES... IT'S STILL COLD OUT.
TOO BAD.
I WANT TO SHOW ALZEID TOO, BUT DO YOU THINK HE'LL GET MAD IF I WAKE HIM?
ON THE CONTRARY, I DON'T THINK HE'LL WAKE UP IN THE FIRST PLACE.
YOU'RE RIGHT.
LOOK AT THE SURFACE OF THE WATER SPARKLING.
IT'S BEAUTI-FUL.
These are the moments ...
...you re-mem-ber.

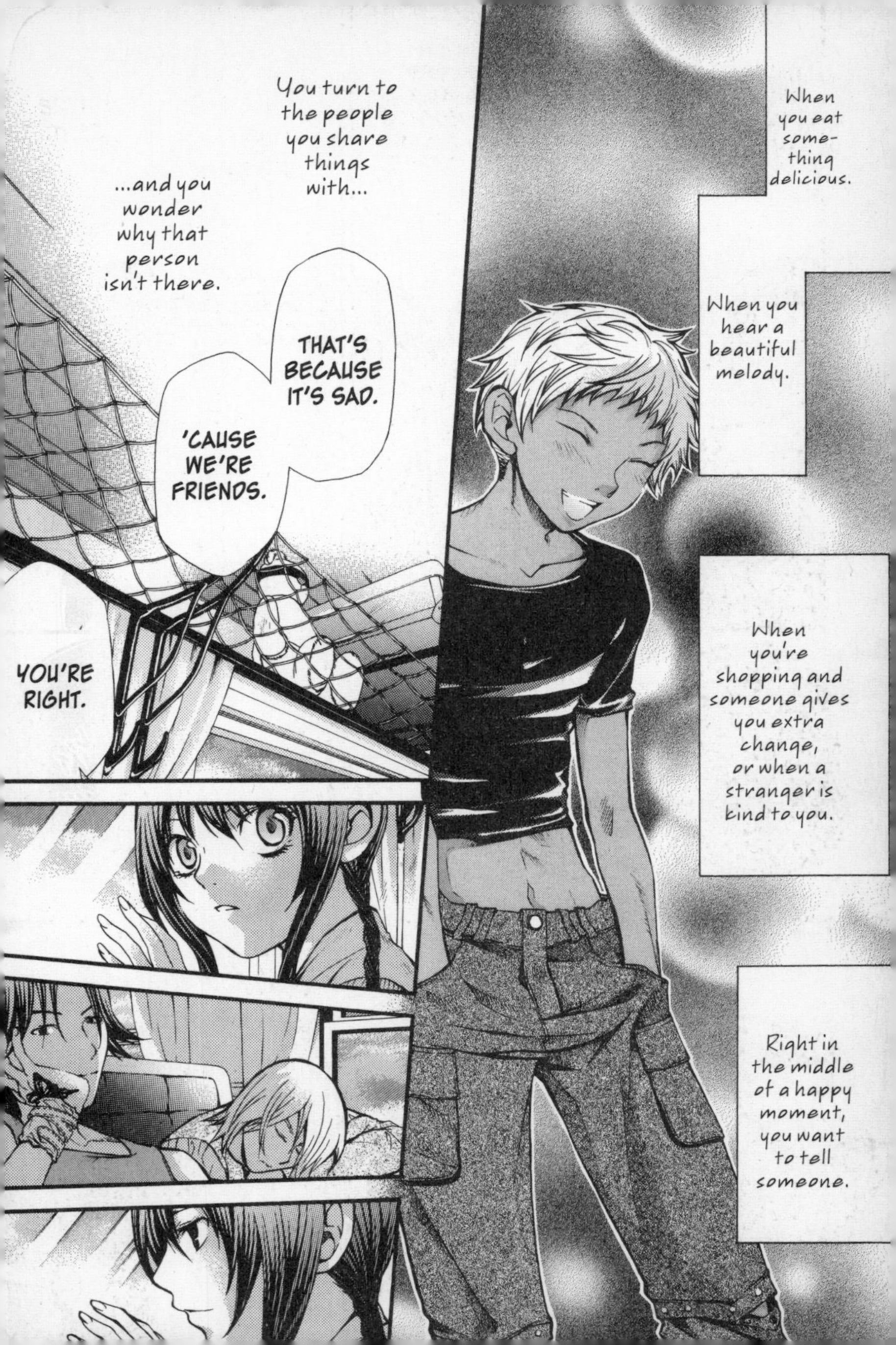
When you eat something delicious.
When you hear a beautiful melody.
When you're shopping and someone gives you extra change, or when a stranger is kind to you.
Right in the middle of a happy moment, you want to tell someone.
You turn to the people you share things with...
...and you wonder why that person isn't there.
THAT'S BECAUSE IT'S SAD.
'CAUSE WE'RE FRIENDS.
YOU'RE RIGHT.

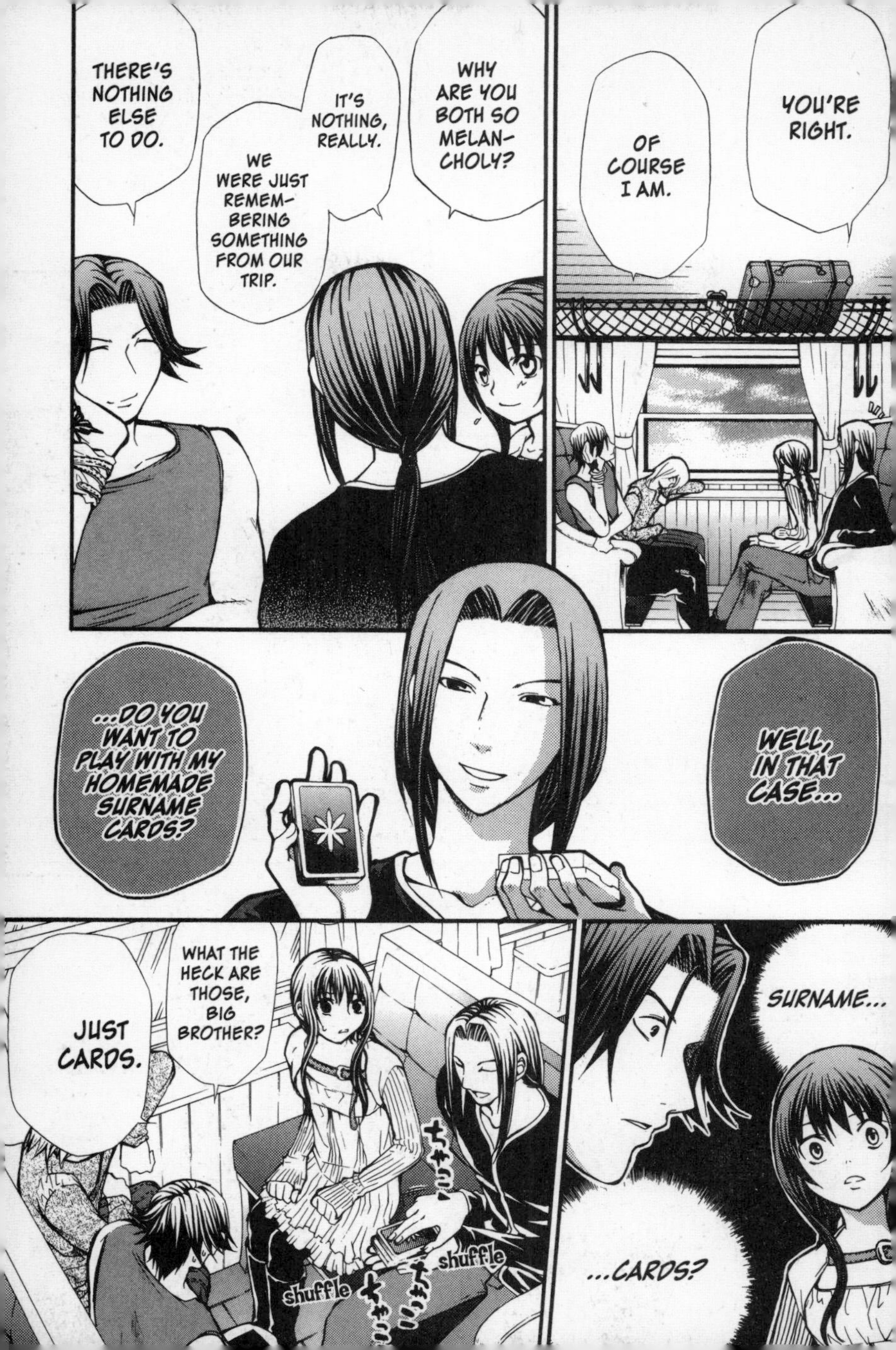
YOU'RE RIGHT.
OF COURSE I AM.
WHY ARE YOU BOTH SO MELAN-CHOLY?
IT'S NOTHING, REALLY.
WE WERE JUST REMEM-BERING SOMETHING FROM OUR TRIP.
THERE'S NOTHING ELSE TO DO.
WELL, IN THAT CASE...
...DO YOU WANT TO PLAY WITH MY HOMEMADE SURNAME CARDS?
SURNAME...
...CARDS?
WHAT THE HECK ARE THOSE, BIG BROTHER?
JUST CARDS.
shuffle
shuffle

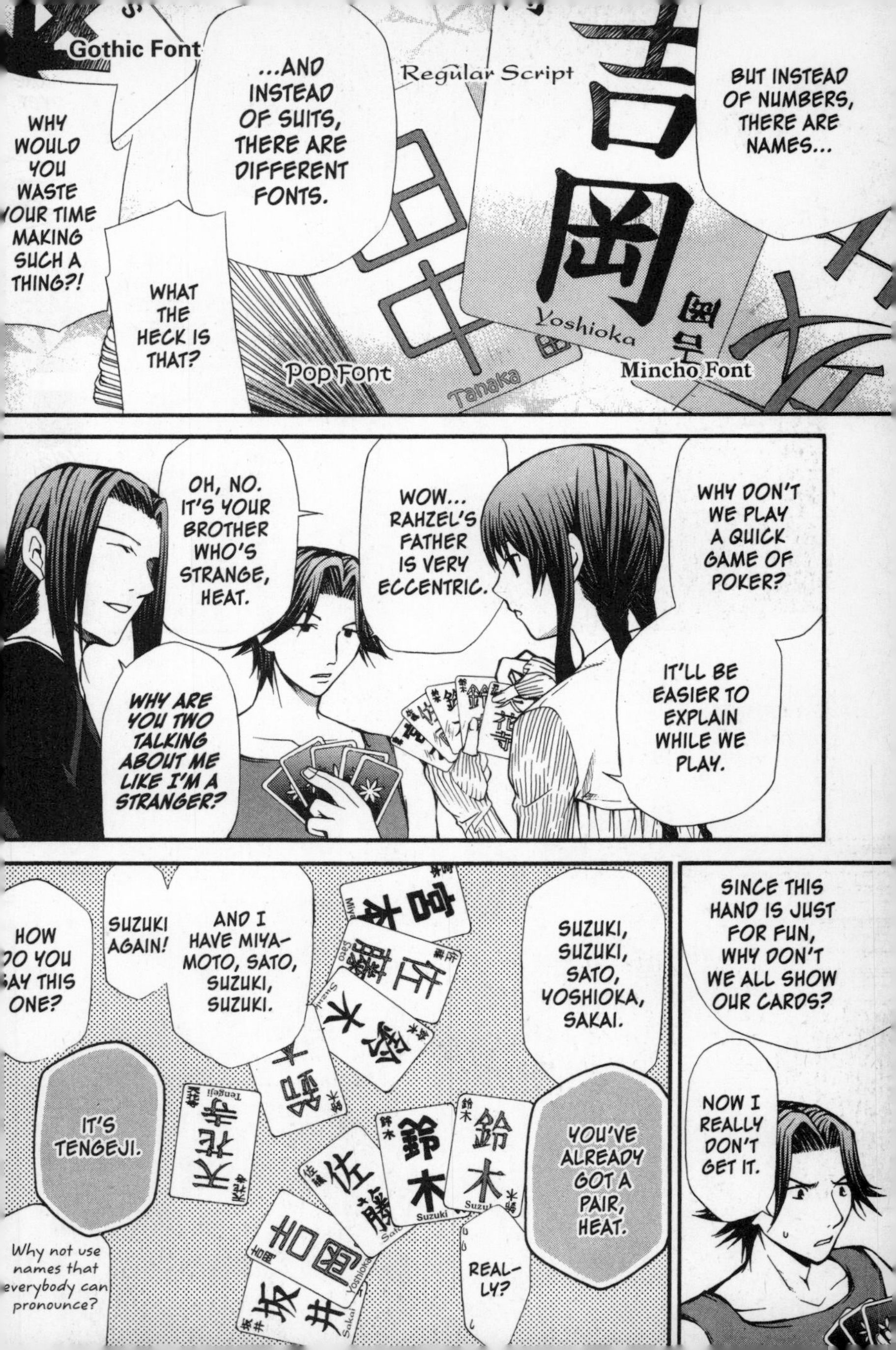

BUT INSTEAD OF NUMBERS, THERE ARE NAMES...
Regular Script
Mincho Font
Yoshioka
...AND INSTEAD OF SUITS, THERE ARE DIFFERENT FONTS.
Pop Font
Tanaka
WHAT THE HECK IS THAT?
Gothic Font
WHY WOULD YOU WASTE OUR TIME MAKING SUCH A THING?!
WHY DON'T WE PLAY A QUICK GAME OF POKER?
IT'LL BE EASIER TO EXPLAIN WHILE WE PLAY.
WOW... RAHZEL'S FATHER IS VERY ECCENTRIC.
OH, NO. IT'S YOUR BROTHER WHO'S STRANGE, HEAT.
WHY ARE YOU TWO TALKING ABOUT ME LIKE I'M A STRANGER?
SINCE THIS HAND IS JUST FOR FUN, WHY DON'T WE ALL SHOW OUR CARDS?
NOW I REALLY DON'T GET IT.
SUZUKI, SUZUKI, SATO, YOSHIOKA, SAKAI.
YOU'VE ALREADY GOT A PAIR, HEAT.
REAL-LY?
AND I HAVE MIYA-MOTO, SATO, SUZUKI, SUZUKI.
SUZUKI AGAIN!
HOW O YOU AY THIS ONE?
IT'S TENGEJI.
Why not use names that everybody can pronounce?

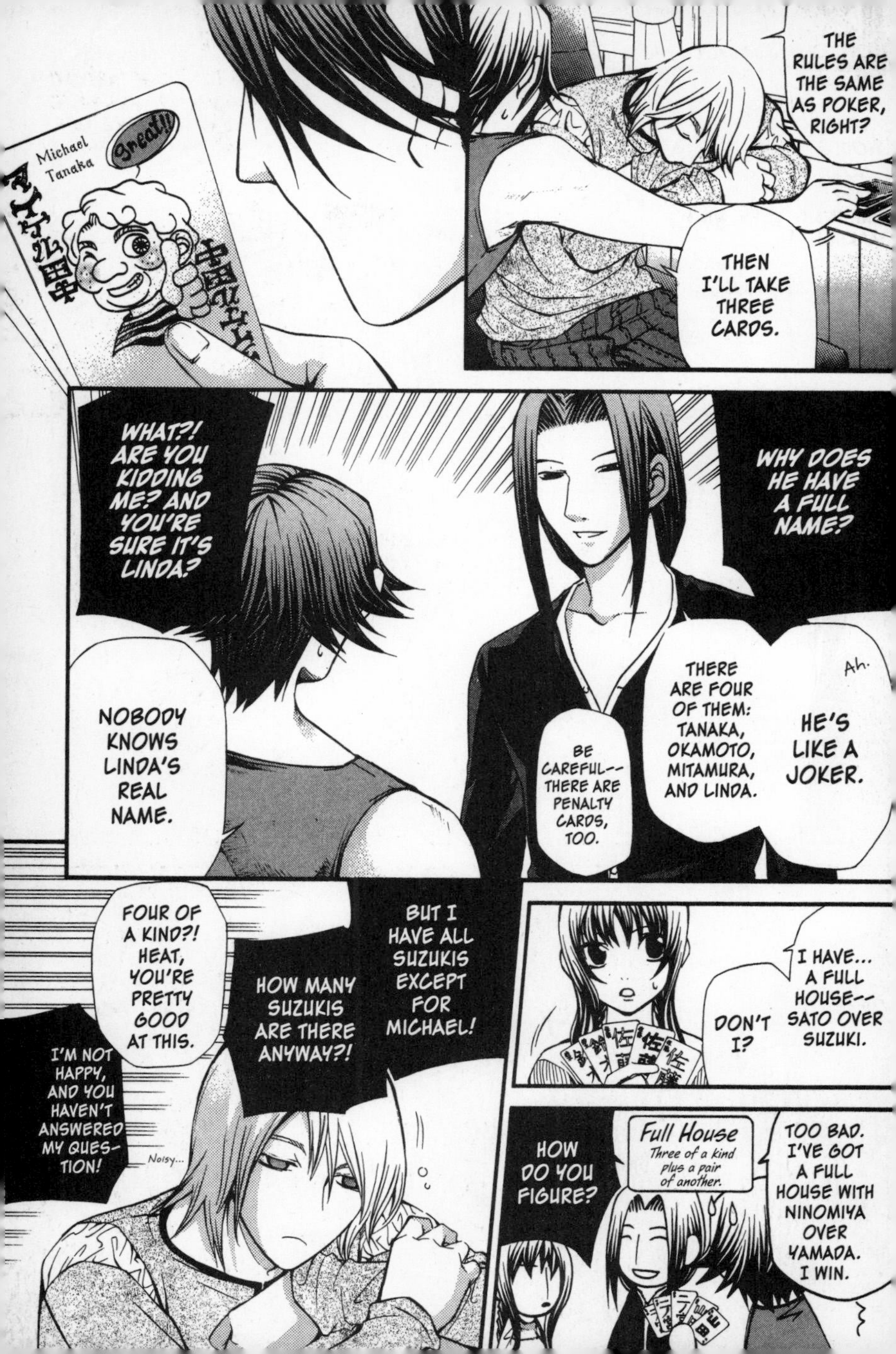

THE RULES ARE THE SAME AS POKER, RIGHT?
THEN I'LL TAKE THREE CARDS.
Michael Tanaka
Great!!
WHY DOES HE HAVE A FULL NAME?
Ah.
HE'S LIKE A JOKER.
THERE ARE FOUR OF THEM: TANAKA, OKAMOTO, MITAMURA, AND LINDA.
BE CAREFUL--THERE ARE PENALTY CARDS, TOO.
WHAT?! ARE YOU KIDDING ME? AND YOU'RE SURE IT'S LINDA?
NOBODY KNOWS LINDA'S REAL NAME.
I HAVE... A FULL HOUSE--SATO OVER SUZUKI.
DON'T I?
TOO BAD. I'VE GOT A FULL HOUSE WITH NINOMIYA OVER YAMADA. I WIN.
Full House
Three of a kind plus a pair of another.
HOW DO YOU FIGURE?
BUT I HAVE ALL SUZUKIS EXCEPT FOR MICHAEL!
HOW MANY SUZUKIS ARE THERE ANYWAY?!
FOUR OF A KIND?! HEAT, YOU'RE PRETTY GOOD AT THIS.
I'M NOT HAPPY, AND YOU HAVEN'T ANSWERED MY QUESTION!
Noisy...

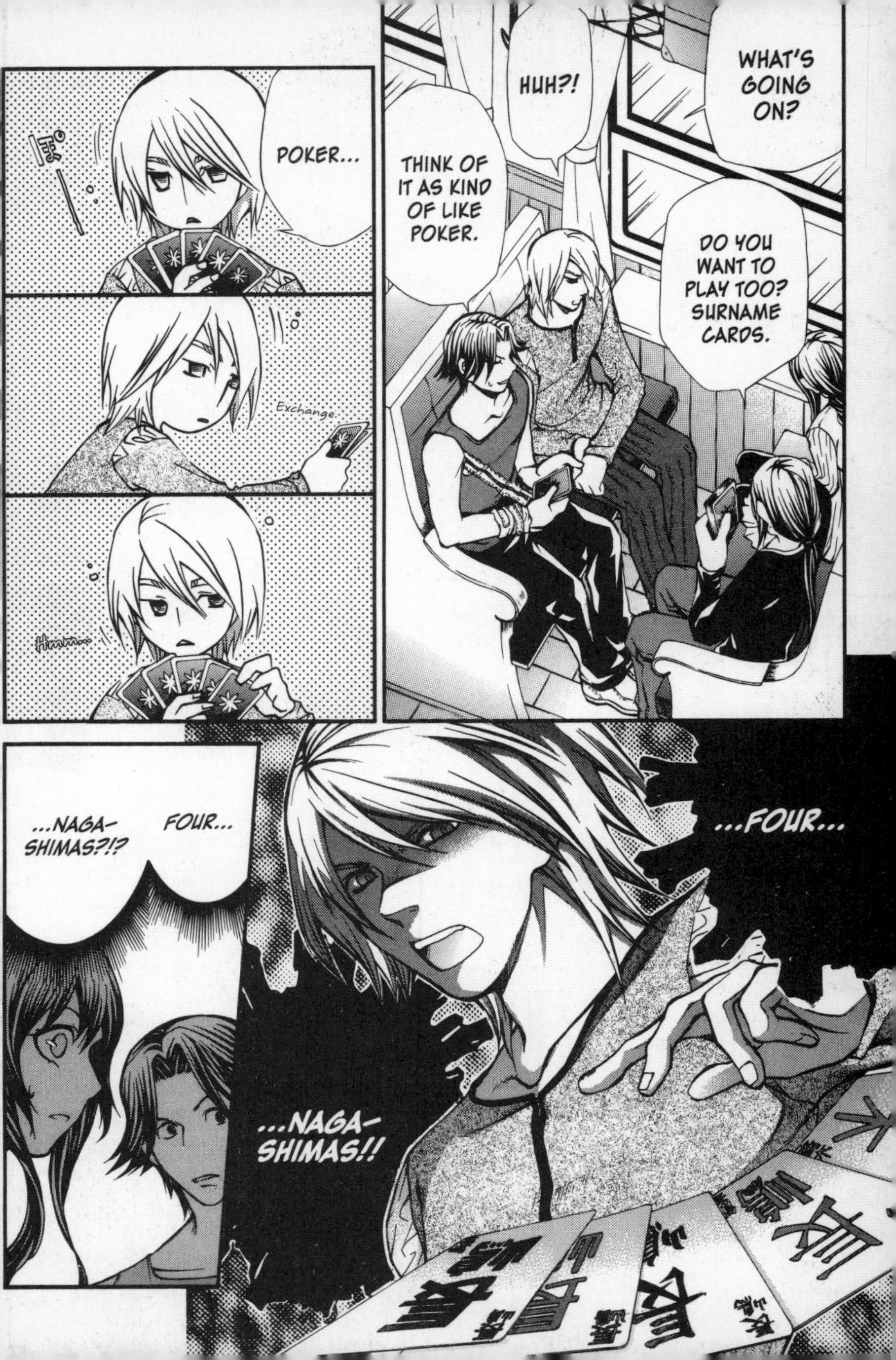
WHAT'S GOING ON?
HUH?!
DO YOU WANT TO PLAY TOO? SURNAME CARDS.
THINK OF IT AS KIND OF LIKE POKER.
POKER...
ぽ
Exchange
Hmm...
...FOUR...
...NAGA-SHIMAS!!
FOUR...
...NAGA-SHIMAS?!?

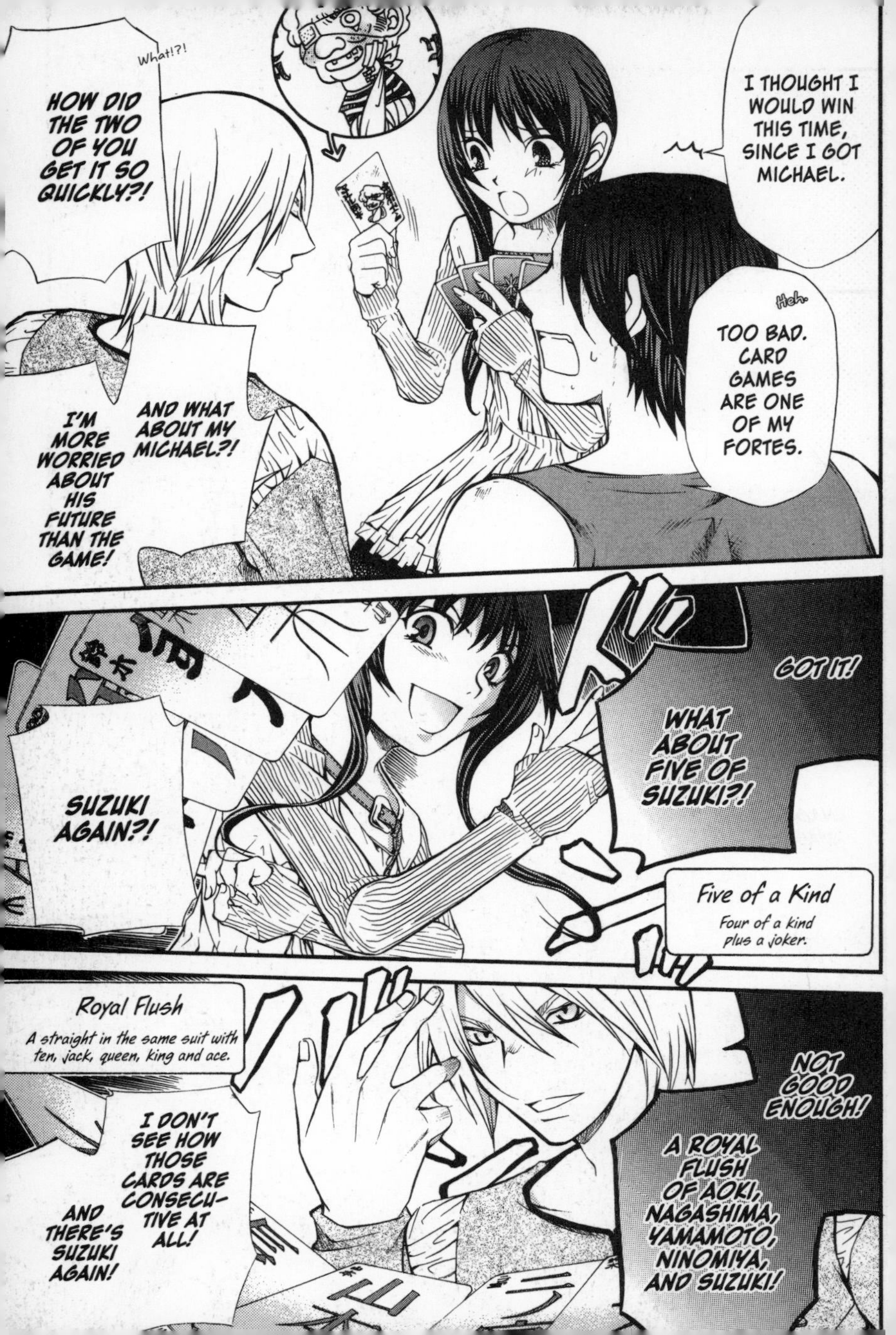
I THOUGHT I WOULD WIN THIS TIME, SINCE I GOT MICHAEL.
Heh.
TOO BAD. CARD GAMES ARE ONE OF MY FORTES.
What!?!
HOW DID THE TWO OF YOU GET IT SO QUICKLY?!
AND WHAT ABOUT MY MICHAEL?!
I'M MORE WORRIED ABOUT HIS FUTURE THAN THE GAME!
GOT IT!
WHAT ABOUT FIVE OF SUZUKI?!
Five of a Kind
Four of a kind plus a joker.
SUZUKI AGAIN?!
NOT GOOD ENOUGH!
A ROYAL FLUSH OF AOKI, NAGASHIMA, YAMAMOTO, NINOMIYA, AND SUZUKI!
Royal Flush
A straight in the same suit with ten, jack, queen, king and ace.
I DON'T SEE HOW THOSE CARDS ARE CONSECU-TIVE AT ALL!
AND THERE'S SUZUKI AGAIN!

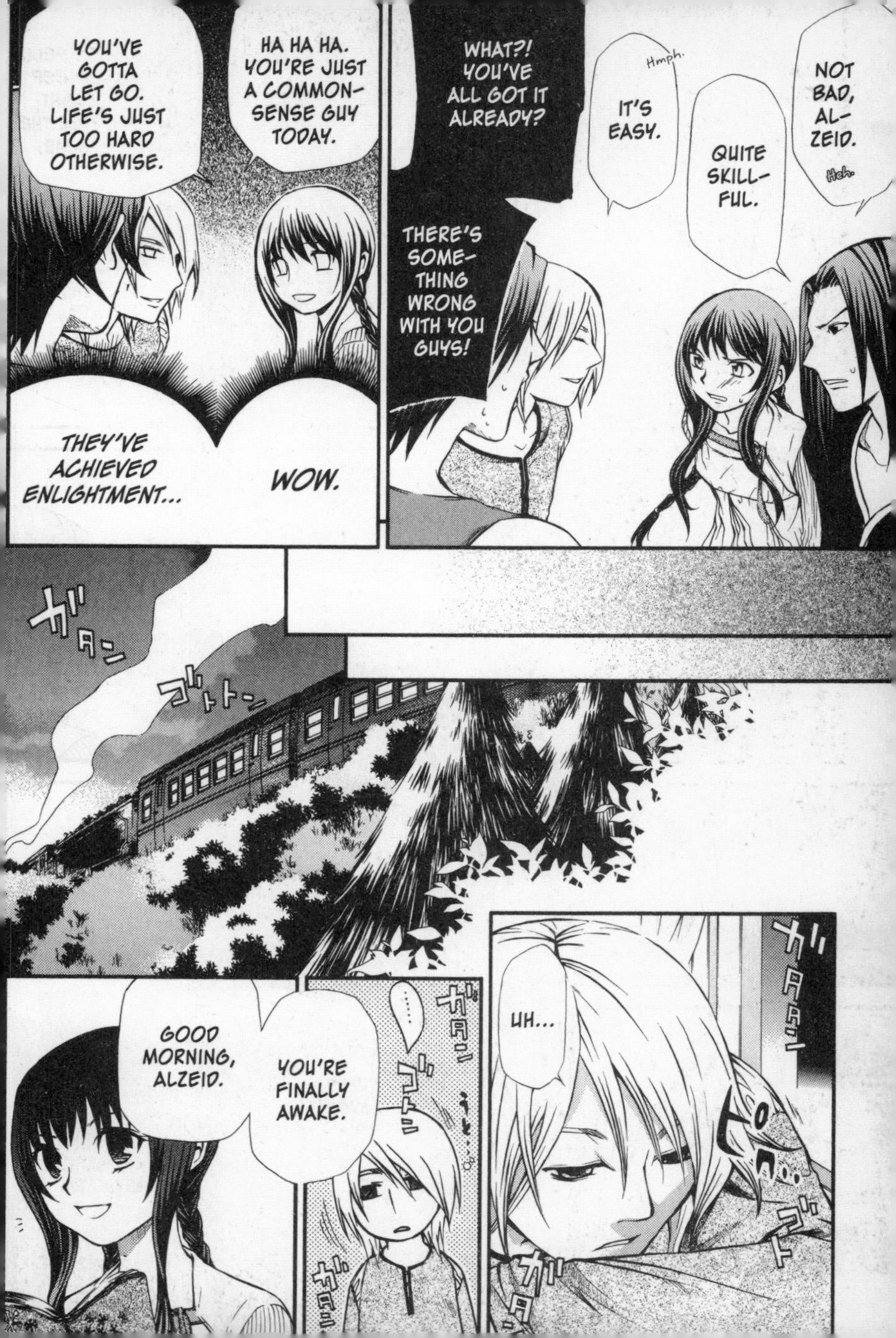
NOT BAD, AL-ZEID.
Heh.
QUITE SKILL-FUL.
IT'S EASY.
Hmph.
WHAT?! YOU'VE ALL GOT IT ALREADY?
THERE'S SOME-THING WRONG WITH YOU GUYS!
HA HA HA. YOU'RE JUST A COMMON-SENSE GUY TODAY.
YOU'VE GOTTA LET GO. LIFE'S JUST TOO HARD OTHERWISE.
WOW.
THEY'VE ACHIEVED ENLIGHTMENT...
UH...
......
GOOD MORNING, ALZEID.
YOU'RE FINALLY AWAKE.

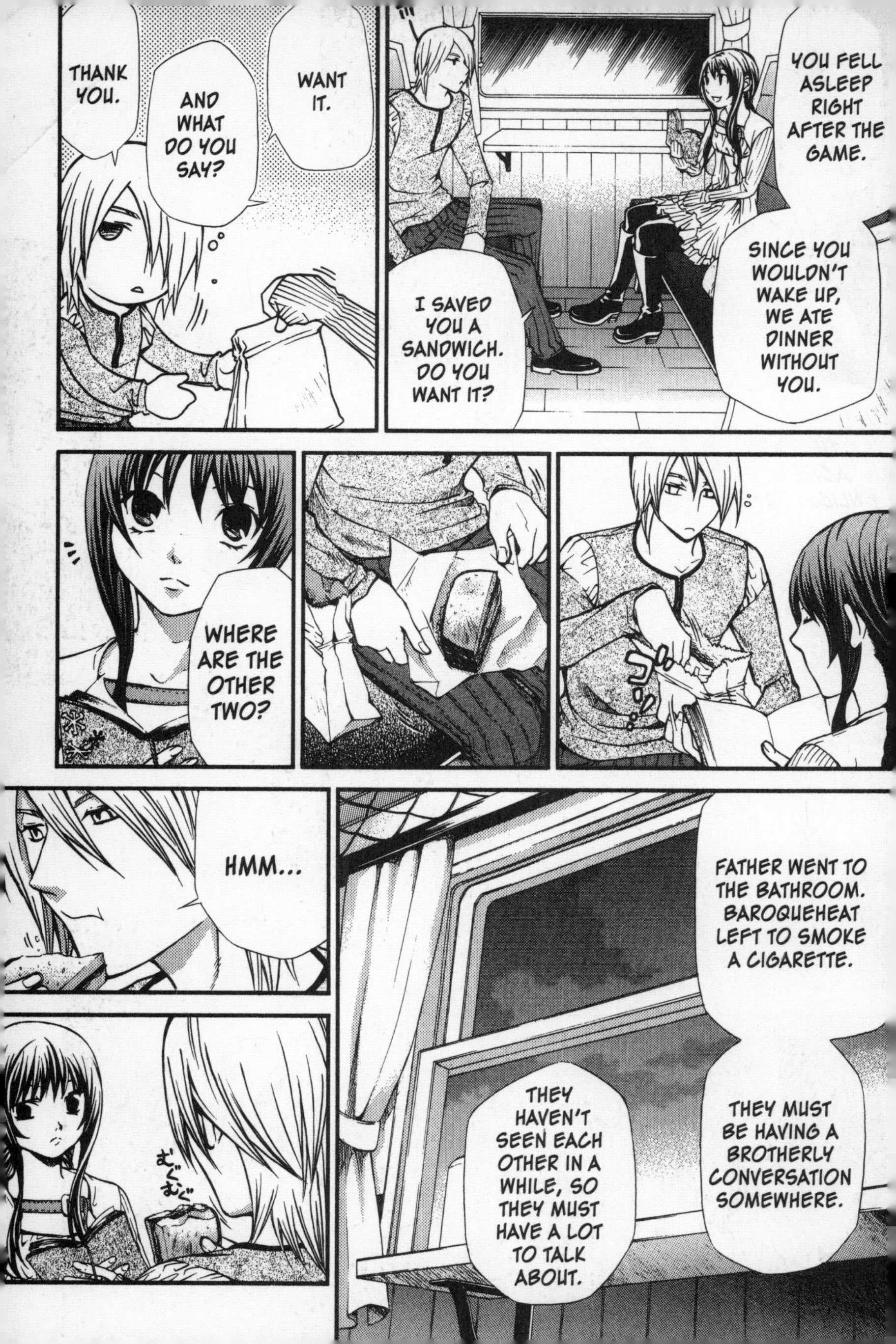

YOU FELL ASLEEP RIGHT AFTER THE GAME.
SINCE YOU WOULDN'T WAKE UP, WE ATE DINNER WITHOUT YOU.
I SAVED YOU A SANDWICH. DO YOU WANT IT?
WANT IT.
AND WHAT DO YOU SAY?
THANK YOU.
WHERE ARE THE OTHER TWO?
FATHER WENT TO THE BATHROOM. BAROQUEHEAT LEFT TO SMOKE A CIGARETTE.
THEY MUST BE HAVING A BROTHERLY CONVERSATION SOMEWHERE.
THEY HAVEN'T SEEN EACH OTHER IN A WHILE, SO THEY MUST HAVE A LOT TO TALK ABOUT.
HMM...
むぐむぐ

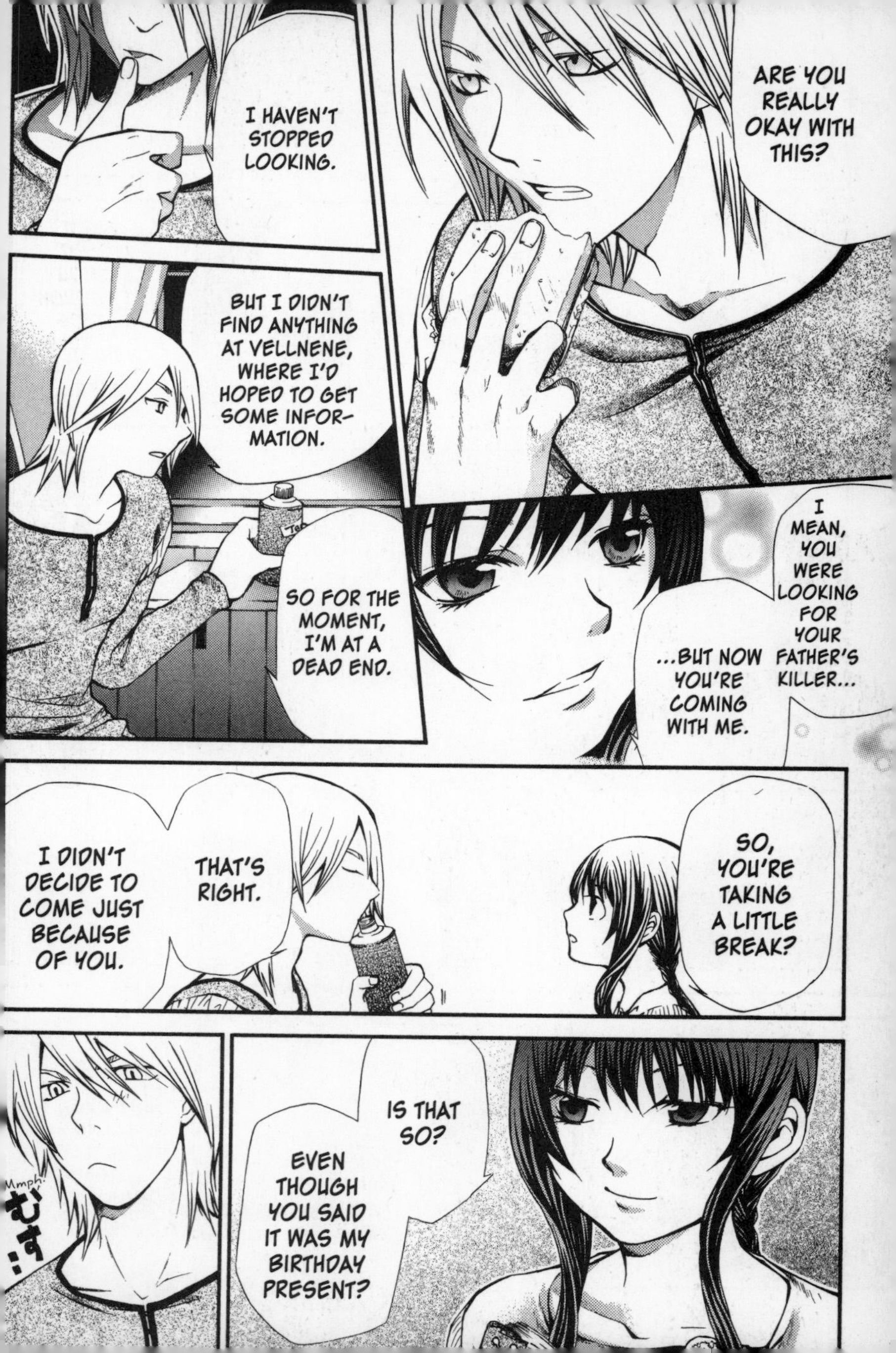
ARE YOU REALLY OKAY WITH THIS?
I MEAN, YOU WERE LOOKING FOR YOUR FATHER'S KILLER...
...BUT NOW YOU'RE COMING WITH ME.
I HAVEN'T STOPPED LOOKING.
BUT I DIDN'T FIND ANYTHING AT VELLNENE, WHERE I'D HOPED TO GET SOME INFOR-MATION.
SO FOR THE MOMENT, I'M AT A DEAD END.
SO, YOU'RE TAKING A LITTLE BREAK?
THAT'S RIGHT.
I DIDN'T DECIDE TO COME JUST BECAUSE OF YOU.
IS THAT SO?
EVEN THOUGH YOU SAID IT WAS MY BIRTHDAY PRESENT?
Mmph.
むす

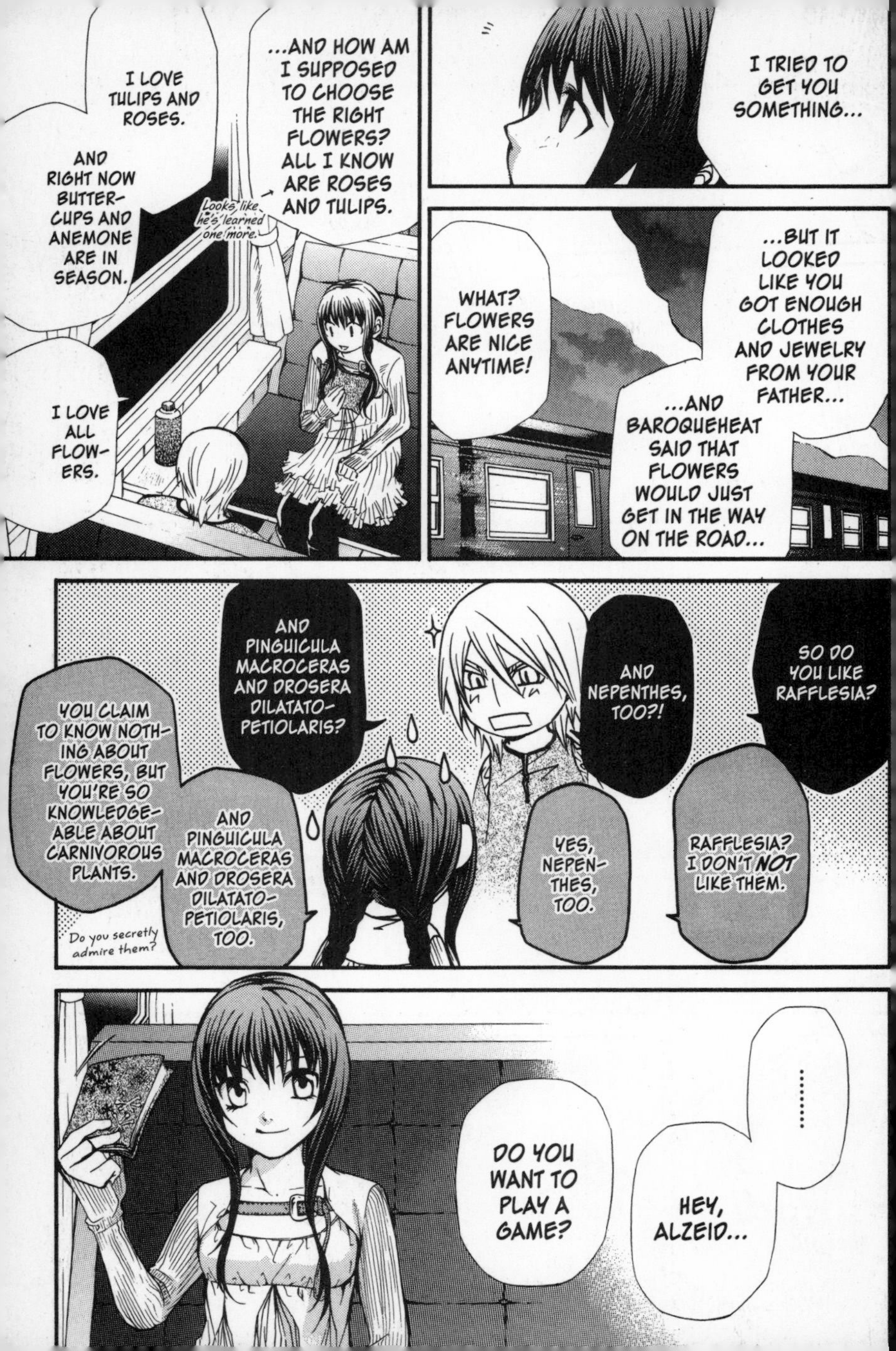
I TRIED TO GET YOU SOMETHING...
...BUT IT LOOKED LIKE YOU GOT ENOUGH CLOTHES AND JEWELRY FROM YOUR FATHER...
...AND BAROQUEHEAT SAID THAT FLOWERS WOULD JUST GET IN THE WAY ON THE ROAD...
WHAT? FLOWERS ARE NICE ANYTIME!
...AND HOW AM I SUPPOSED TO CHOOSE THE RIGHT FLOWERS? ALL I KNOW ARE ROSES AND TULIPS.
Looks like he's learned one more.
I LOVE TULIPS AND ROSES.
AND RIGHT NOW BUTTER-CUPS AND ANEMONE ARE IN SEASON.
I LOVE ALL FLOW-ERS.
SO DO YOU LIKE RAFFLESIA?
RAFFLESIA? I DON'T *NOT* LIKE THEM.
AND NEPENTHES, TOO?!
YES, NEPEN-THES, TOO.
AND PINGUICULA MACROCERAS AND DROSERA DILATATO-PETIOLARIS?
AND PINGUICULA MACROCERAS AND DROSERA DILATATO-PETIOLARIS, TOO.
YOU CLAIM TO KNOW NOTH-ING ABOUT FLOWERS, BUT YOU'RE SO KNOWLEDGE-ABLE ABOUT CARNIVOROUS PLANTS.
Do you secretly admire them?
......
HEY, ALZEID...
DO YOU WANT TO PLAY A GAME?

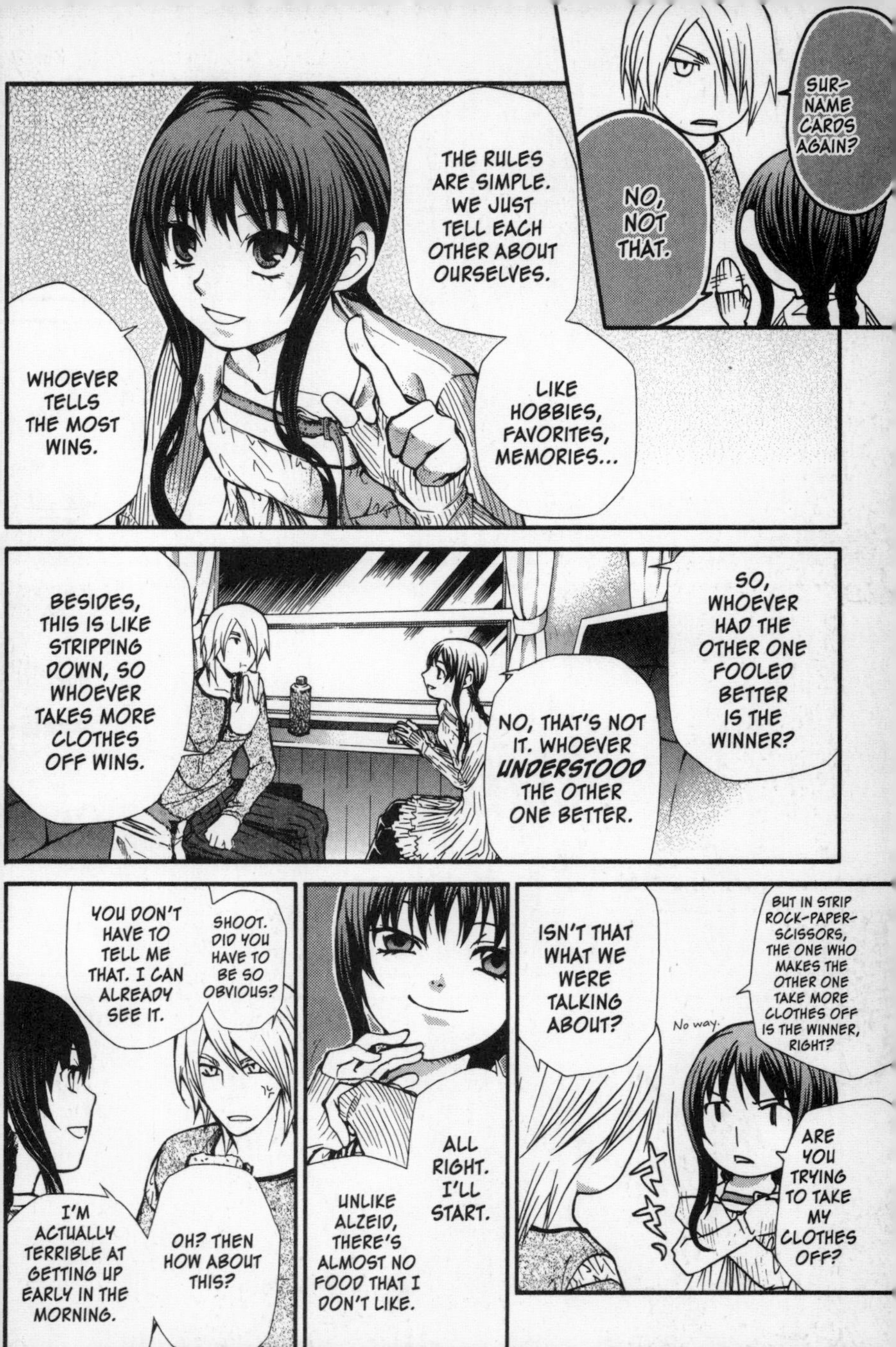
SUR-NAME CARDS AGAIN?
NO, NOT THAT.
THE RULES ARE SIMPLE. WE JUST TELL EACH OTHER ABOUT OURSELVES.
LIKE HOBBIES, FAVORITES, MEMORIES...
WHOEVER TELLS THE MOST WINS.
SO, WHOEVER HAD THE OTHER ONE FOOLED BETTER IS THE WINNER?
NO, THAT'S NOT IT. WHOEVER UNDERSTOOD THE OTHER ONE BETTER.
BESIDES, THIS IS LIKE STRIPPING DOWN, SO WHOEVER TAKES MORE CLOTHES OFF WINS.
BUT IN STRIP ROCK-PAPER-SCISSORS, THE ONE WHO MAKES THE OTHER ONE TAKE MORE CLOTHES OFF IS THE WINNER, RIGHT?
ISN'T THAT WHAT WE WERE TALKING ABOUT?
No way.
ARE YOU TRYING TO TAKE MY CLOTHES OFF?
ALL RIGHT. I'LL START.
UNLIKE ALZEID, THERE'S ALMOST NO FOOD THAT I DON'T LIKE.
SHOOT. DID YOU HAVE TO BE SO OBVIOUS?
YOU DON'T HAVE TO TELL ME THAT. I CAN ALREADY SEE IT.
OH? THEN HOW ABOUT THIS?
I'M ACTUALLY TERRIBLE AT GETTING UP EARLY IN THE MORNING.

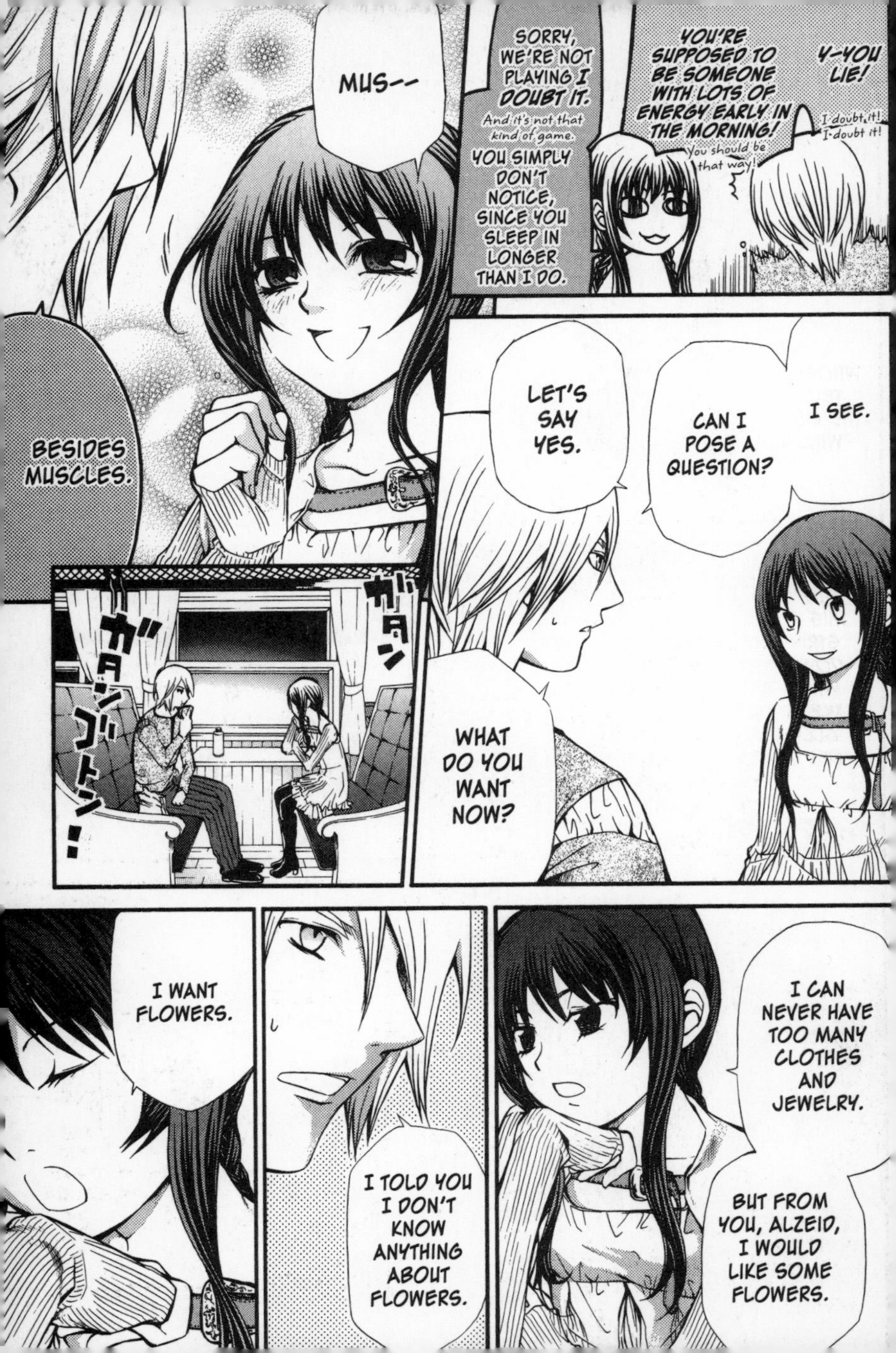
Y-YOU LIE!
YOU'RE SUPPOSED TO BE SOMEONE WITH LOTS OF ENERGY EARLY IN THE MORNING!
I doubt it! I doubt it!
You should be that way!
SORRY, WE'RE NOT PLAYING I DOUBT IT.
And it's not that kind of game.
YOU SIMPLY DON'T NOTICE, SINCE YOU SLEEP IN LONGER THAN I DO.
MUS--
BESIDES MUSCLES.
I SEE.
CAN I POSE A QUESTION?
LET'S SAY YES.
WHAT DO YOU WANT NOW?
ガタン
ガタンゴトン!!
I CAN NEVER HAVE TOO MANY CLOTHES AND JEWELRY.
BUT FROM YOU, ALZEID, I WOULD LIKE SOME FLOWERS.
I TOLD YOU I DON'T KNOW ANYTHING ABOUT FLOWERS.
I WANT FLOWERS.

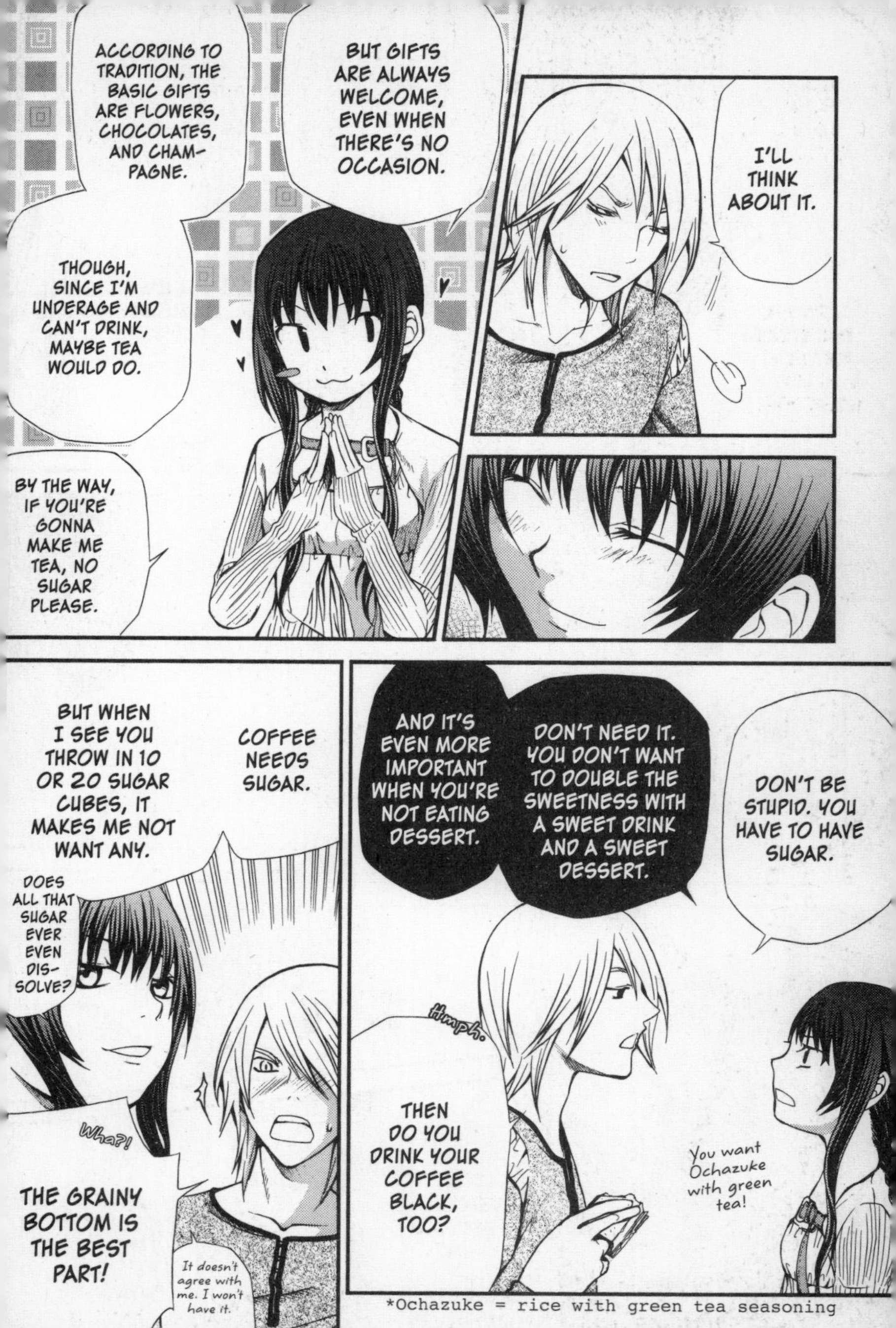
I'LL THINK ABOUT IT.
ACCORDING TO TRADITION, THE BASIC GIFTS ARE FLOWERS, CHOCOLATES, AND CHAMPAGNE.
BUT GIFTS ARE ALWAYS WELCOME, EVEN WHEN THERE'S NO OCCASION.
THOUGH, SINCE I'M UNDERAGE AND CAN'T DRINK, MAYBE TEA WOULD DO.
BY THE WAY, IF YOU'RE GONNA MAKE ME TEA, NO SUGAR PLEASE.
DON'T BE STUPID. YOU HAVE TO HAVE SUGAR.
DON'T NEED IT. YOU DON'T WANT TO DOUBLE THE SWEETNESS WITH A SWEET DRINK AND A SWEET DESSERT.
AND IT'S EVEN MORE IMPORTANT WHEN YOU'RE NOT EATING DESSERT.
Hmph.
THEN DO YOU DRINK YOUR COFFEE BLACK, TOO?
You want Ochazuke with green tea!
COFFEE NEEDS SUGAR.
BUT WHEN I SEE YOU THROW IN 10 OR 20 SUGAR CUBES, IT MAKES ME NOT WANT ANY.
DOES ALL THAT SUGAR EVER EVEN DISSOLVE?
Wha?!
THE GRAINY BOTTOM IS THE BEST PART!
It doesn't agree with me. I won't have it.

*Ochazuke = rice with green tea seasoning

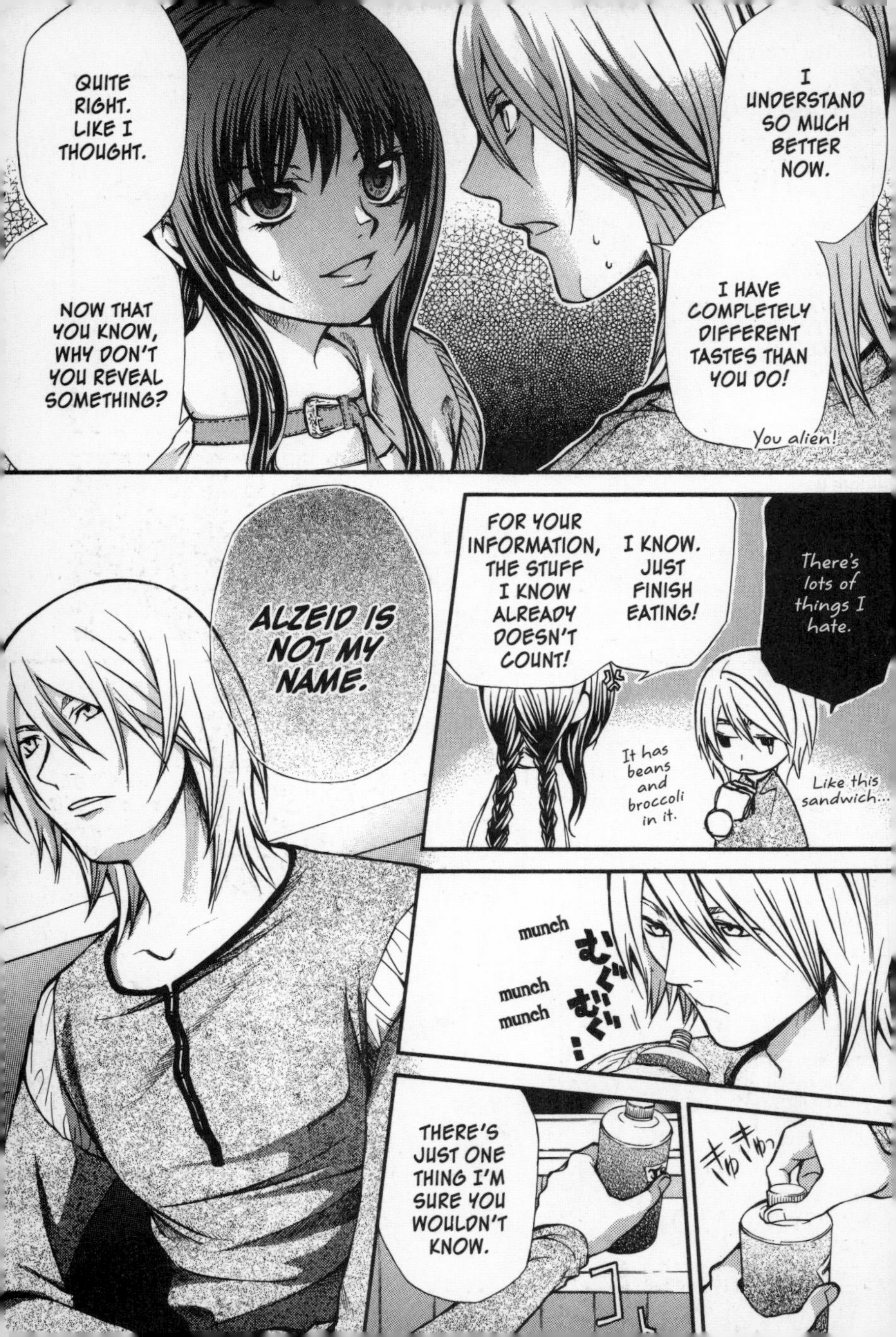
I UNDERSTAND SO MUCH BETTER NOW.
I HAVE COMPLETELY DIFFERENT TASTES THAN YOU DO!
You alien!
QUITE RIGHT. LIKE I THOUGHT.
NOW THAT YOU KNOW, WHY DON'T YOU REVEAL SOMETHING?
There's lots of things I hate.
I KNOW. JUST FINISH EATING!
FOR YOUR INFORMATION, THE STUFF I KNOW ALREADY DOESN'T COUNT!
Like this sandwich...
It has beans and broccoli in it.
munch
munch munch
むぐむぐ
きゅきゅっ
THERE'S JUST ONE THING I'M SURE YOU WOULDN'T KNOW.
ALZEID IS NOT MY NAME.

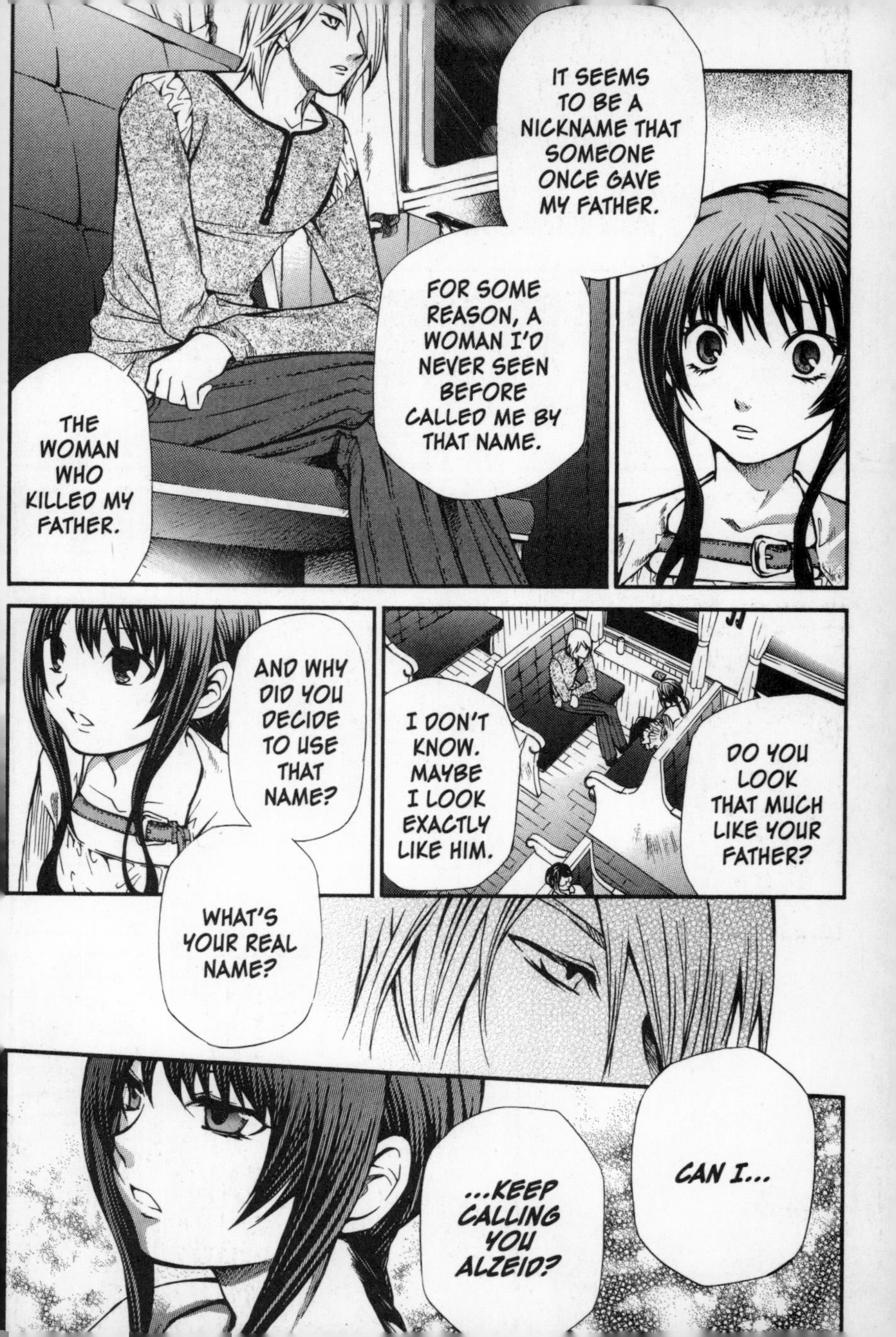
IT SEEMS TO BE A NICKNAME THAT SOMEONE ONCE GAVE MY FATHER.
FOR SOME REASON, A WOMAN I'D NEVER SEEN BEFORE CALLED ME BY THAT NAME.
THE WOMAN WHO KILLED MY FATHER.
DO YOU LOOK THAT MUCH LIKE YOUR FATHER?
I DON'T KNOW. MAYBE I LOOK EXACTLY LIKE HIM.
AND WHY DID YOU DECIDE TO USE THAT NAME?
WHAT'S YOUR REAL NAME?
CAN I...
...KEEP CALLING YOU ALZEID?

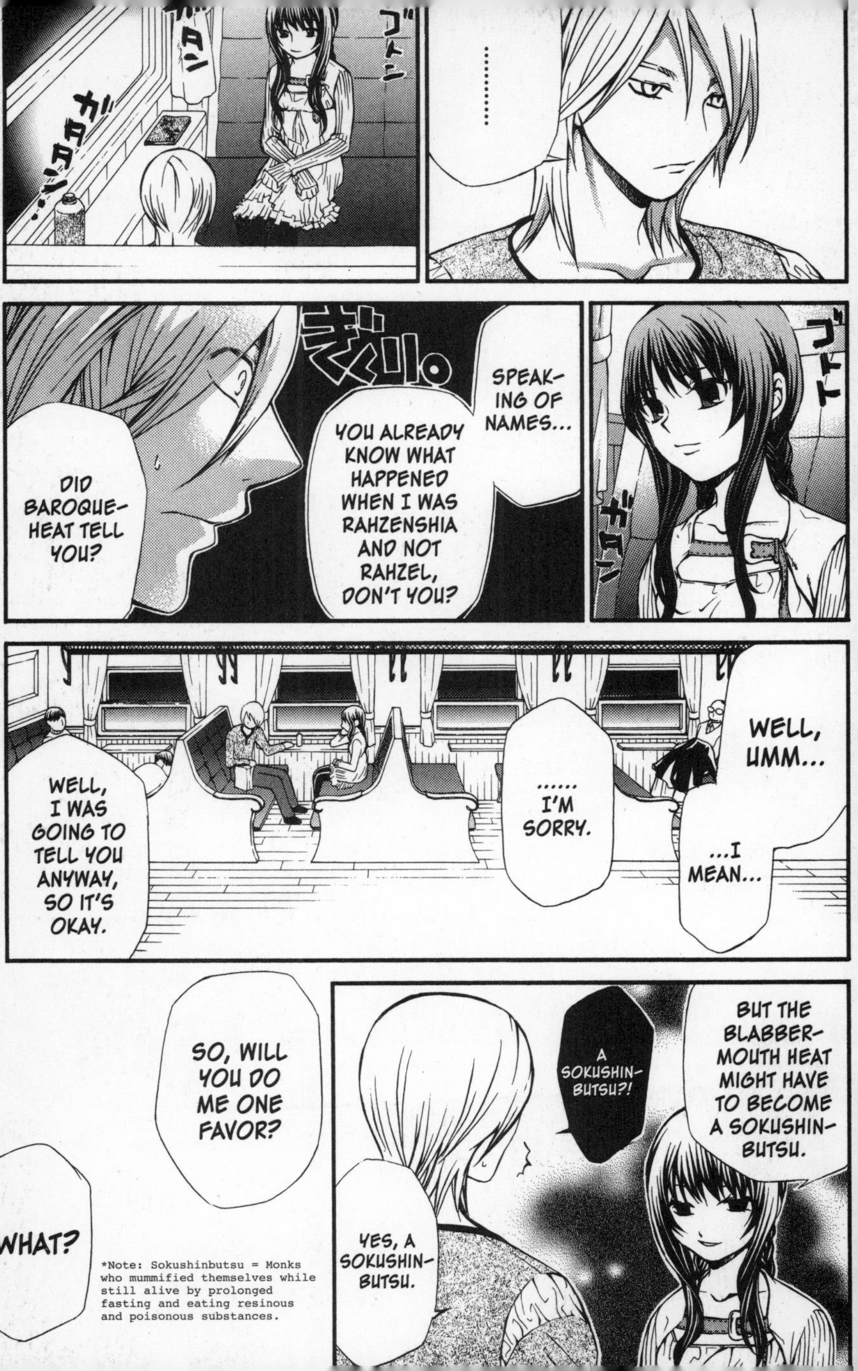
......
ゴトン
ガタン
ガタタン…
ゴトト
ガタン
SPEAK-ING OF NAMES...
YOU ALREADY KNOW WHAT HAPPENED WHEN I WAS RAHZENSHIA AND NOT RAHZEL, DON'T YOU?
DID BAROQUE-HEAT TELL YOU?
WELL, UMM...
...I MEAN...
......I'M SORRY.
WELL, I WAS GOING TO TELL YOU ANYWAY, SO IT'S OKAY.
BUT THE BLABBER-MOUTH HEAT MIGHT HAVE TO BECOME A SOKUSHIN-BUTSU.
A SOKUSHIN-BUTSU?!
YES, A SOKUSHIN-BUTSU.
SO, WILL YOU DO ME ONE FAVOR?
WHAT?

*Note: Sokushinbutsu = Monks who mummified themselves while still alive by prolonged fasting and eating resinous and poisonous substances.

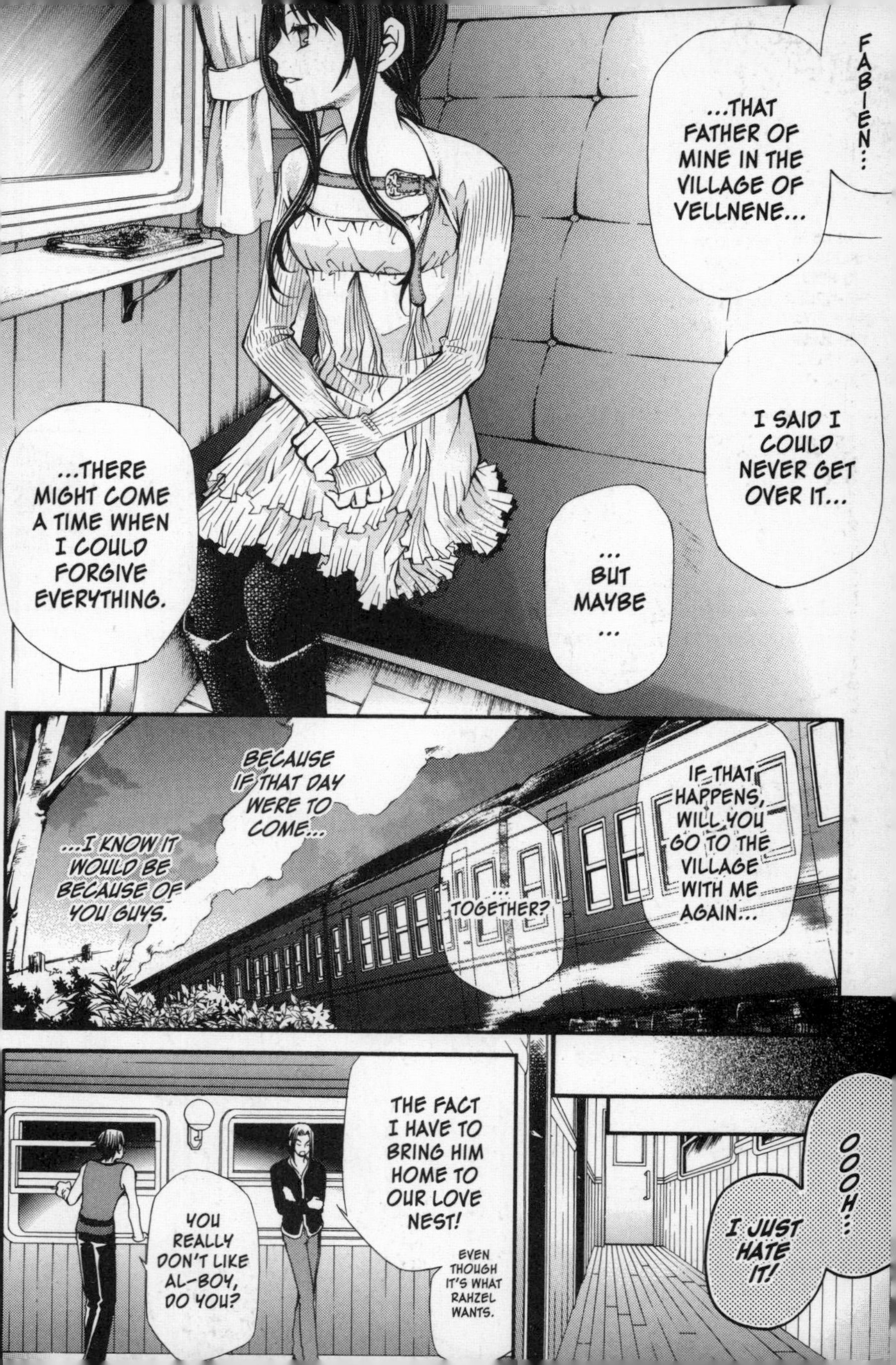
FABIEN...
...THAT FATHER OF MINE IN THE VILLAGE OF VELLNENE...
I SAID I COULD NEVER GET OVER IT...
...BUT MAYBE...
...THERE MIGHT COME A TIME WHEN I COULD FORGIVE EVERYTHING.
IF THAT HAPPENS, WILL YOU GO TO THE VILLAGE WITH ME AGAIN...
...TOGETHER?
BECAUSE IF THAT DAY WERE TO COME...
...I KNOW IT WOULD BE BECAUSE OF YOU GUYS.
OOOH...
I JUST HATE IT!
THE FACT I HAVE TO BRING HIM HOME TO OUR LOVE NEST!
EVEN THOUGH IT'S WHAT RAHZEL WANTS.
YOU REALLY DON'T LIKE AL-BOY, DO YOU?

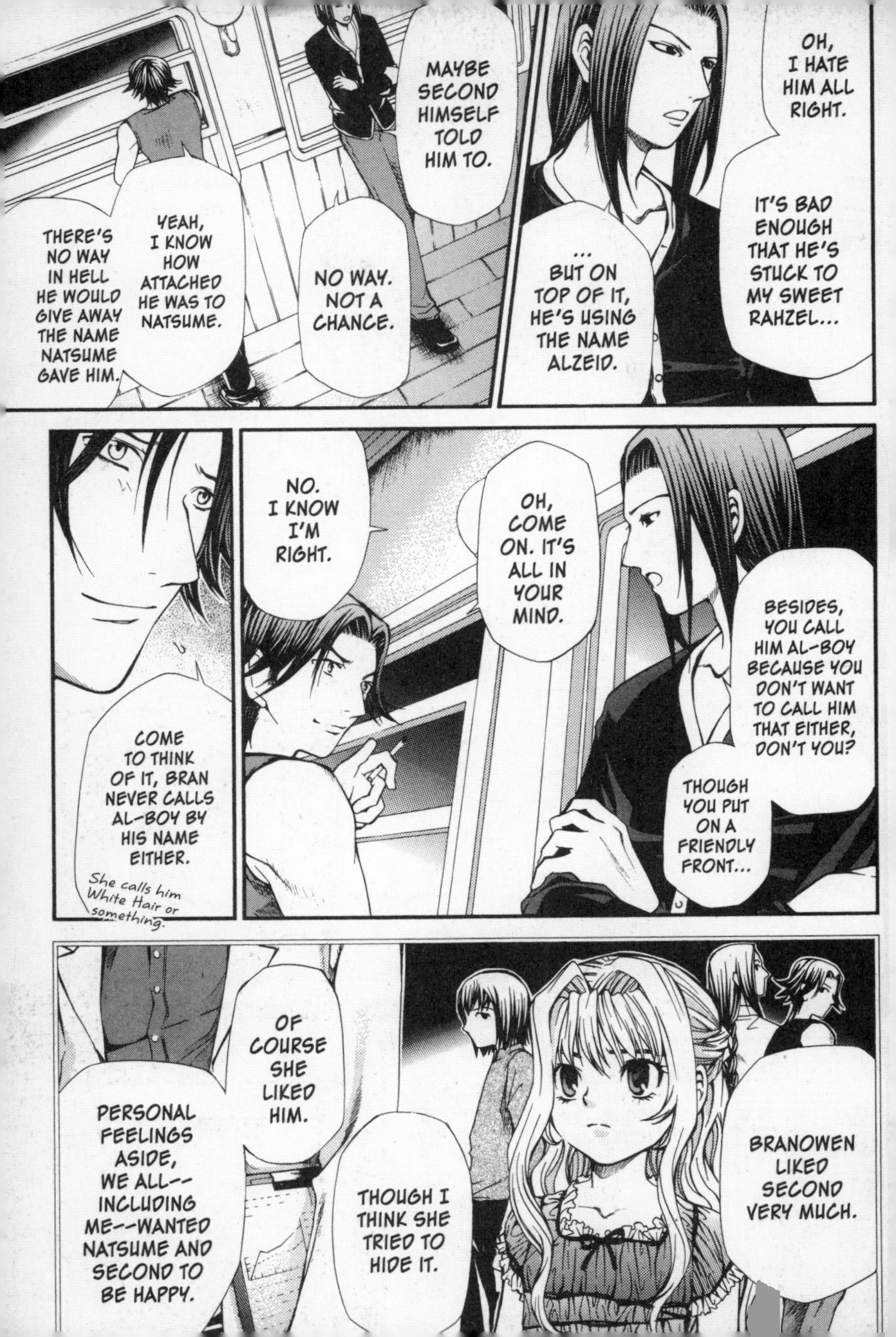
OH, I HATE HIM ALL RIGHT.
IT'S BAD ENOUGH THAT HE'S STUCK TO MY SWEET RAHZEL...
... BUT ON TOP OF IT, HE'S USING THE NAME ALZEID.
MAYBE SECOND HIMSELF TOLD HIM TO.
NO WAY. NOT A CHANCE.
YEAH, I KNOW HOW ATTACHED HE WAS TO NATSUME.
THERE'S NO WAY IN HELL HE WOULD GIVE AWAY THE NAME NATSUME GAVE HIM.
OH, COME ON. IT'S ALL IN YOUR MIND.
NO. I KNOW I'M RIGHT.
BESIDES, YOU CALL HIM AL-BOY BECAUSE YOU DON'T WANT TO CALL HIM THAT EITHER, DON'T YOU?
THOUGH YOU PUT ON A FRIENDLY FRONT...
COME TO THINK OF IT, BRAN NEVER CALLS AL-BOY BY HIS NAME EITHER.
She calls him White Hair or something.
BRANOWEN LIKED SECOND VERY MUCH.
OF COURSE SHE LIKED HIM.
THOUGH I THINK SHE TRIED TO HIDE IT.
PERSONAL FEELINGS ASIDE, WE ALL--INCLUDING ME--WANTED NATSUME AND SECOND TO BE HAPPY.

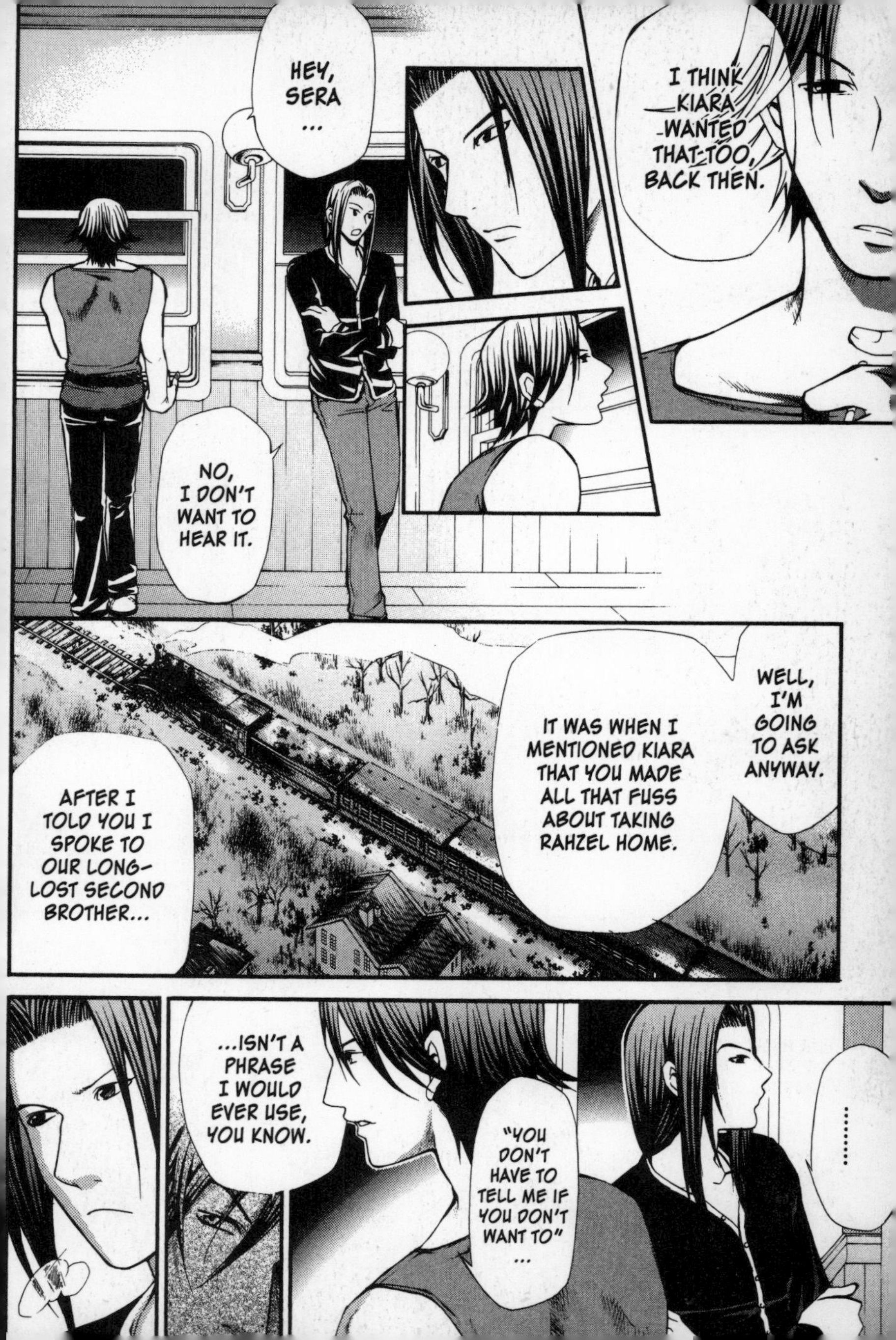
I THINK KIARA WANTED THAT TOO, BACK THEN.
HEY, SERA ...
NO, I DON'T WANT TO HEAR IT.
WELL, I'M GOING TO ASK ANYWAY.
IT WAS WHEN I MENTIONED KIARA THAT YOU MADE ALL THAT FUSS ABOUT TAKING RAHZEL HOME.
AFTER I TOLD YOU I SPOKE TO OUR LONG-LOST SECOND BROTHER...
......
"YOU DON'T HAVE TO TELL ME IF YOU DON'T WANT TO" ...
...ISN'T A PHRASE I WOULD EVER USE, YOU KNOW.

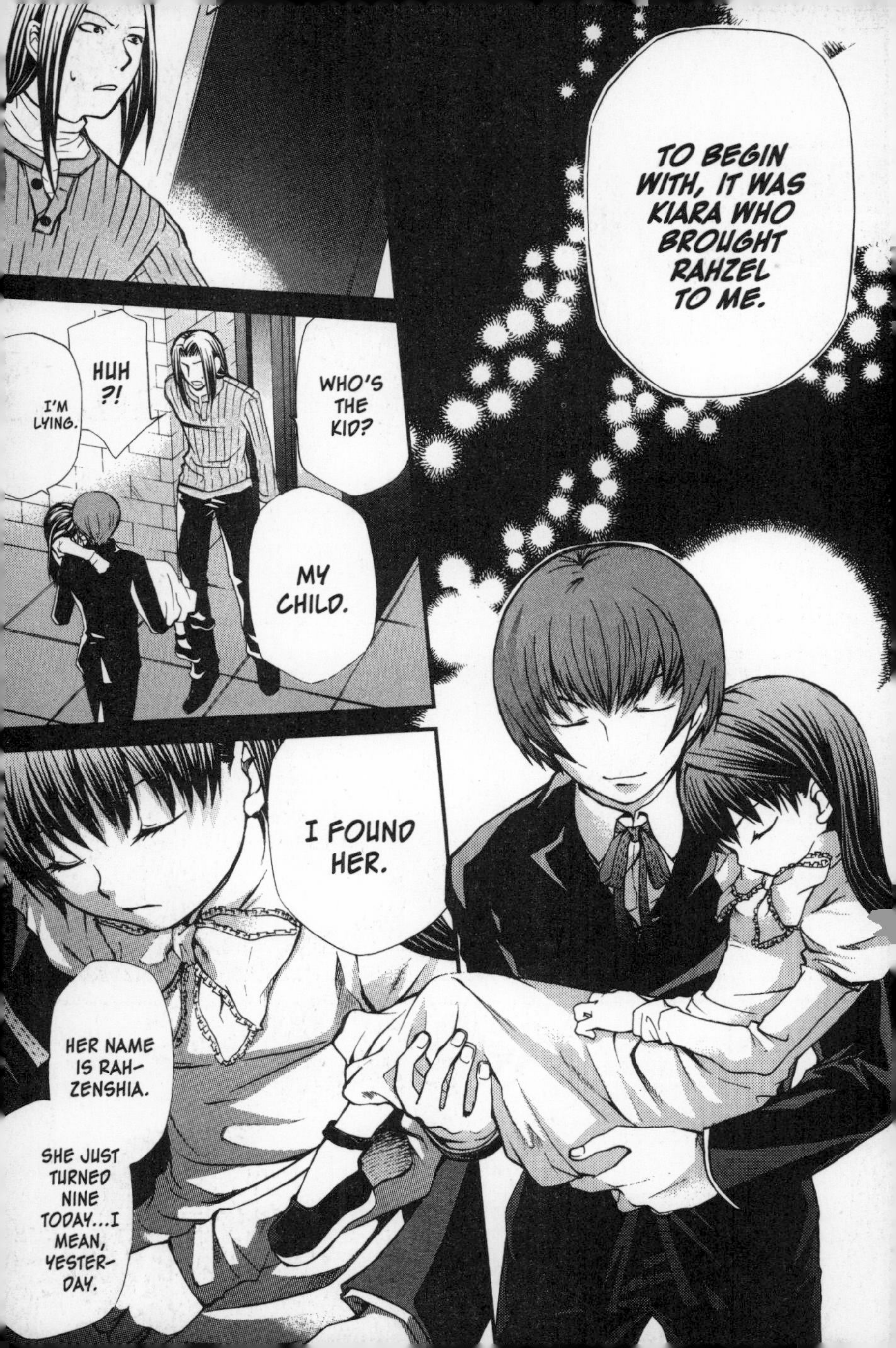

TO BEGIN WITH, IT WAS KIARA WHO BROUGHT RAHZEL TO ME.
WHO'S THE KID?
MY CHILD.
HUH ?!
I'M LYING.
I FOUND HER.
HER NAME IS RAH-ZENSHIA.
SHE JUST TURNED NINE TODAY...I MEAN, YESTER-DAY.

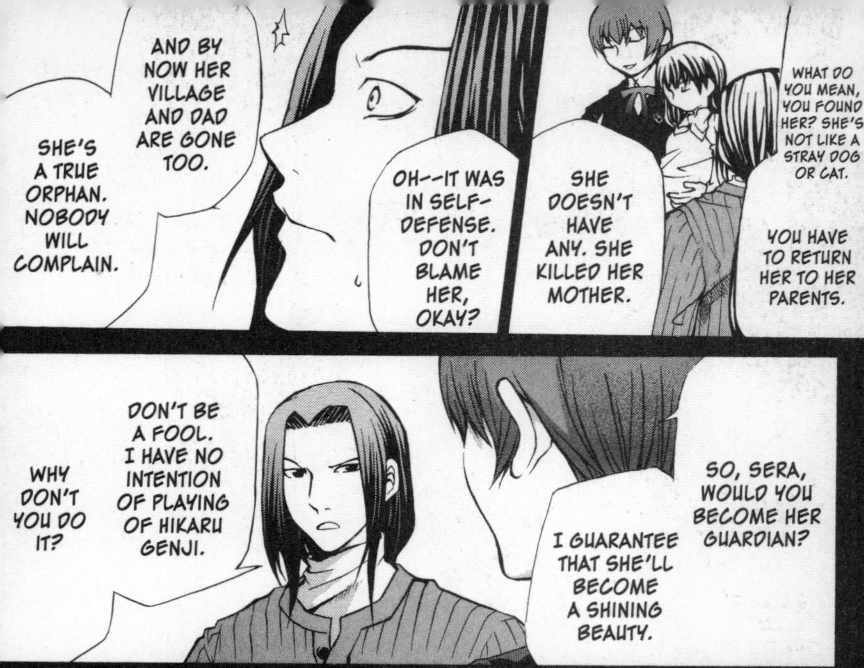
WHAT DO YOU MEAN, YOU FOUND HER? SHE'S NOT LIKE A STRAY DOG OR CAT.
YOU HAVE TO RETURN HER TO HER PARENTS.
SHE DOESN'T HAVE ANY. SHE KILLED HER MOTHER.
OH--IT WAS IN SELF-DEFENSE. DON'T BLAME HER, OKAY?
AND BY NOW HER VILLAGE AND DAD ARE GONE TOO.
SHE'S A TRUE ORPHAN. NOBODY WILL COMPLAIN.
SO, SERA, WOULD YOU BECOME HER GUARDIAN?
I GUARANTEE THAT SHE'LL BECOME A SHINING BEAUTY.
DON'T BE A FOOL. I HAVE NO INTENTION OF PLAYING OF HIKARU GENJI.
WHY DON'T YOU DO IT?

Note: Hikaru Genji = The hero of the *Tale of Genji* who brings up Murasaki no Ue to become his ideal wife.

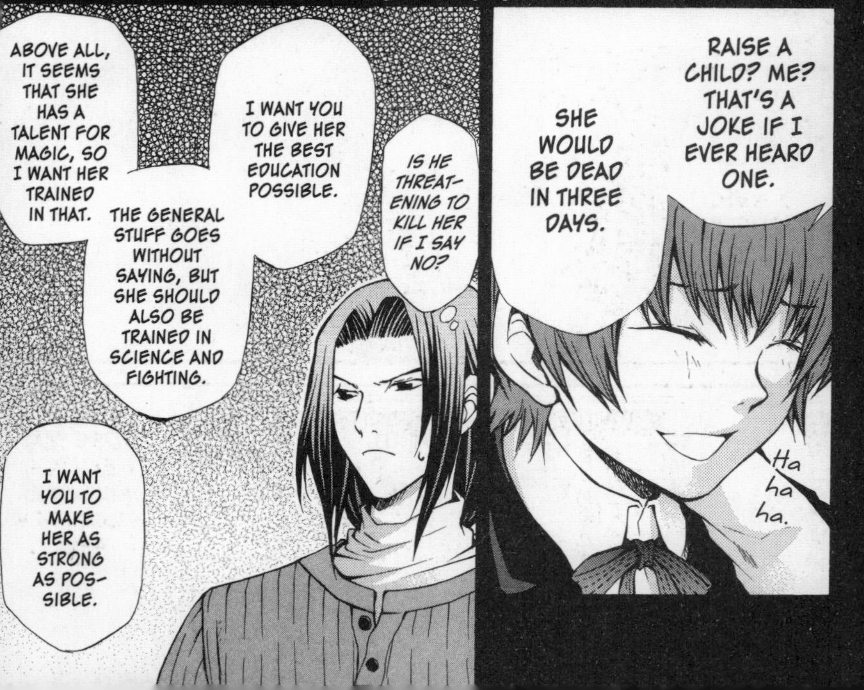
RAISE A CHILD? ME? THAT'S A JOKE IF I EVER HEARD ONE.
SHE WOULD BE DEAD IN THREE DAYS.
Ha ha ha.
I WANT YOU TO GIVE HER THE BEST EDUCATION POSSIBLE.
ABOVE ALL, IT SEEMS THAT SHE HAS A TALENT FOR MAGIC, SO I WANT HER TRAINED IN THAT.
THE GENERAL STUFF GOES WITHOUT SAYING, BUT SHE SHOULD ALSO BE TRAINED IN SCIENCE AND FIGHTING.
IS HE THREAT-ENING TO KILL HER IF I SAY NO?
I WANT YOU TO MAKE HER AS STRONG AS POS-SIBLE.

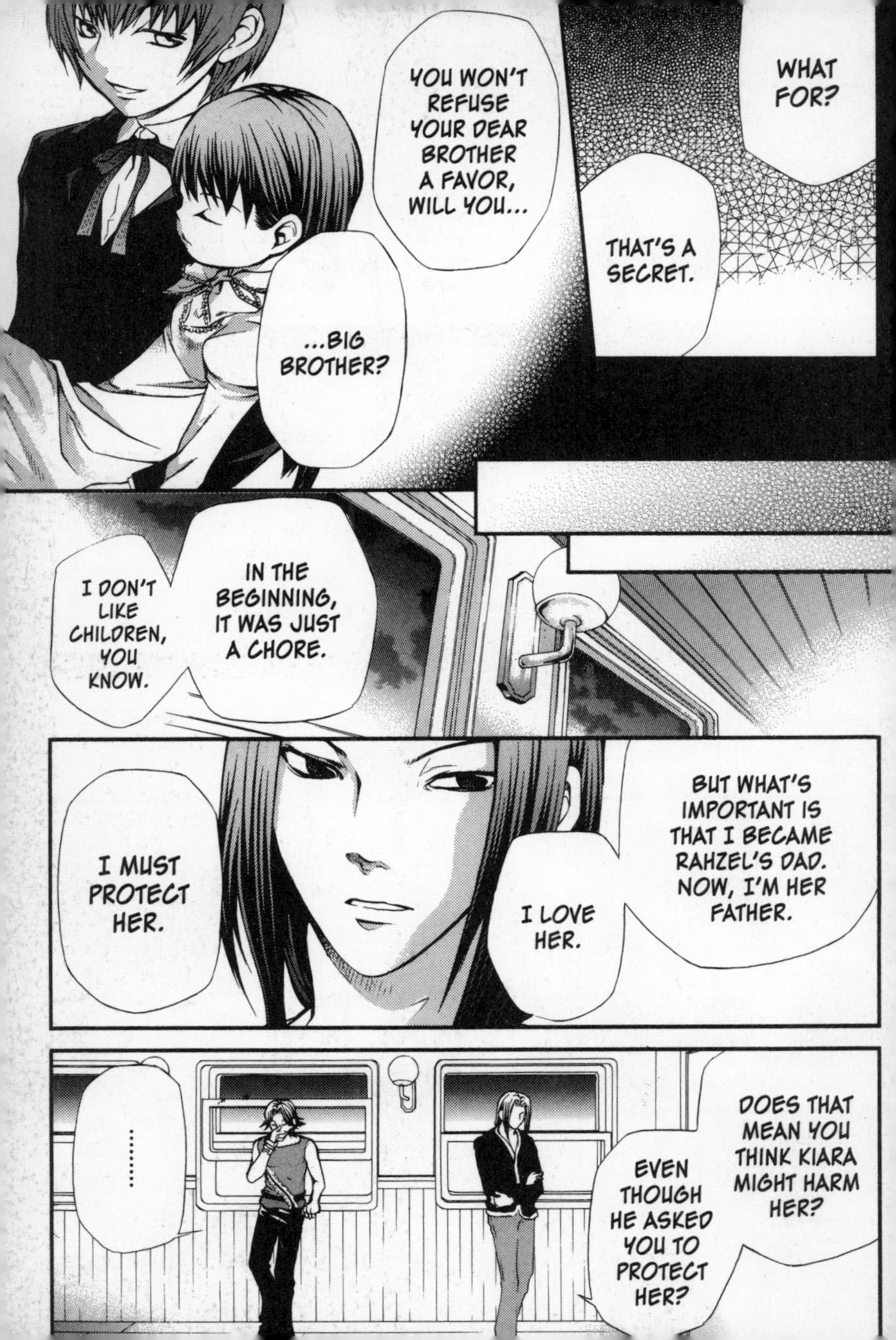
WHAT FOR?
THAT'S A SECRET.
YOU WON'T REFUSE YOUR DEAR BROTHER A FAVOR, WILL YOU...
...BIG BROTHER?
IN THE BEGINNING, IT WAS JUST A CHORE.
I DON'T LIKE CHILDREN, YOU KNOW.
BUT WHAT'S IMPORTANT IS THAT I BECAME RAHZEL'S DAD. NOW, I'M HER FATHER.
I LOVE HER.
I MUST PROTECT HER.
DOES THAT MEAN YOU THINK KIARA MIGHT HARM HER?
EVEN THOUGH HE ASKED YOU TO PROTECT HER?
....

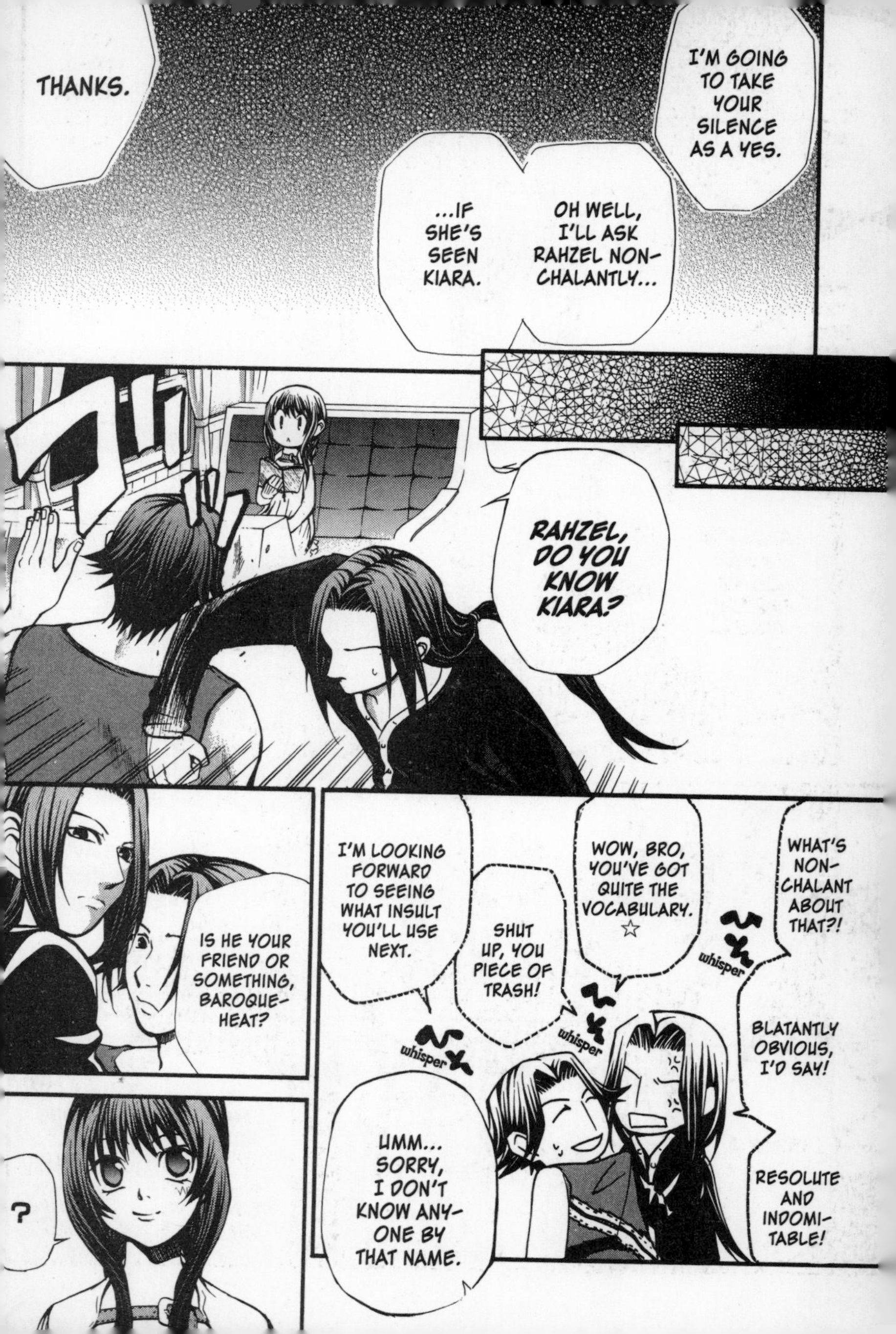
I'M GOING TO TAKE YOUR SILENCE AS A YES.
THANKS.
OH WELL, I'LL ASK RAHZEL NON-CHALANTLY...
...IF SHE'S SEEN KIARA.
RAHZEL, DO YOU KNOW KIARA?
WHAT'S NON-CHALANT ABOUT THAT?!
BLATANTLY OBVIOUS, I'D SAY!
RESOLUTE AND INDOMI-TABLE!
whisper
WOW, BRO, YOU'VE GOT QUITE THE VOCABULARY. ☆
whisper
SHUT UP, YOU PIECE OF TRASH!
I'M LOOKING FORWARD TO SEEING WHAT INSULT YOU'LL USE NEXT.
whisper
UMM... SORRY, I DON'T KNOW ANY-ONE BY THAT NAME.
IS HE YOUR FRIEND OR SOMETHING, BAROQUE-HEAT?
?

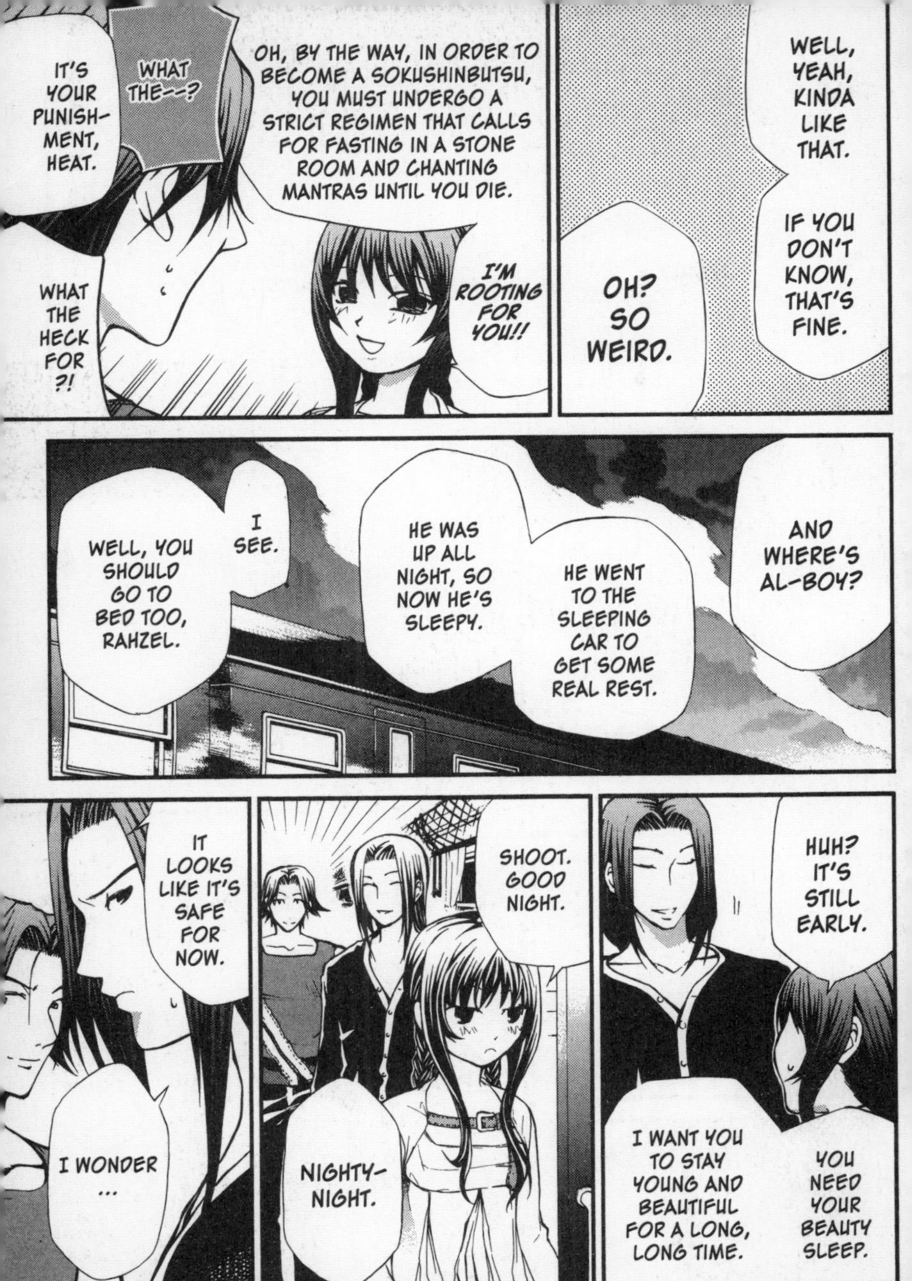
WELL, YEAH, KINDA LIKE THAT.
IF YOU DON'T KNOW, THAT'S FINE.
OH? SO WEIRD.
OH, BY THE WAY, IN ORDER TO BECOME A SOKUSHINBUTSU, YOU MUST UNDERGO A STRICT REGIMEN THAT CALLS FOR FASTING IN A STONE ROOM AND CHANTING MANTRAS UNTIL YOU DIE.
WHAT THE--?
IT'S YOUR PUNISHMENT, HEAT.
I'M ROOTING FOR YOU!!
WHAT THE HECK FOR ?!
AND WHERE'S AL-BOY?
HE WENT TO THE SLEEPING CAR TO GET SOME REAL REST.
HE WAS UP ALL NIGHT, SO NOW HE'S SLEEPY.
I SEE.
WELL, YOU SHOULD GO TO BED TOO, RAHZEL.
HUH? IT'S STILL EARLY.
YOU NEED YOUR BEAUTY SLEEP.
I WANT YOU TO STAY YOUNG AND BEAUTIFUL FOR A LONG, LONG TIME.
SHOOT. GOOD NIGHT.
NIGHTY-NIGHT.
IT LOOKS LIKE IT'S SAFE FOR NOW.
I WONDER ...

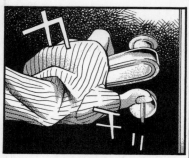

...UNFORTU-
NATELY, I
TAUGHT HER
HOW TO
LIE, TOO.

OH
DEAR...

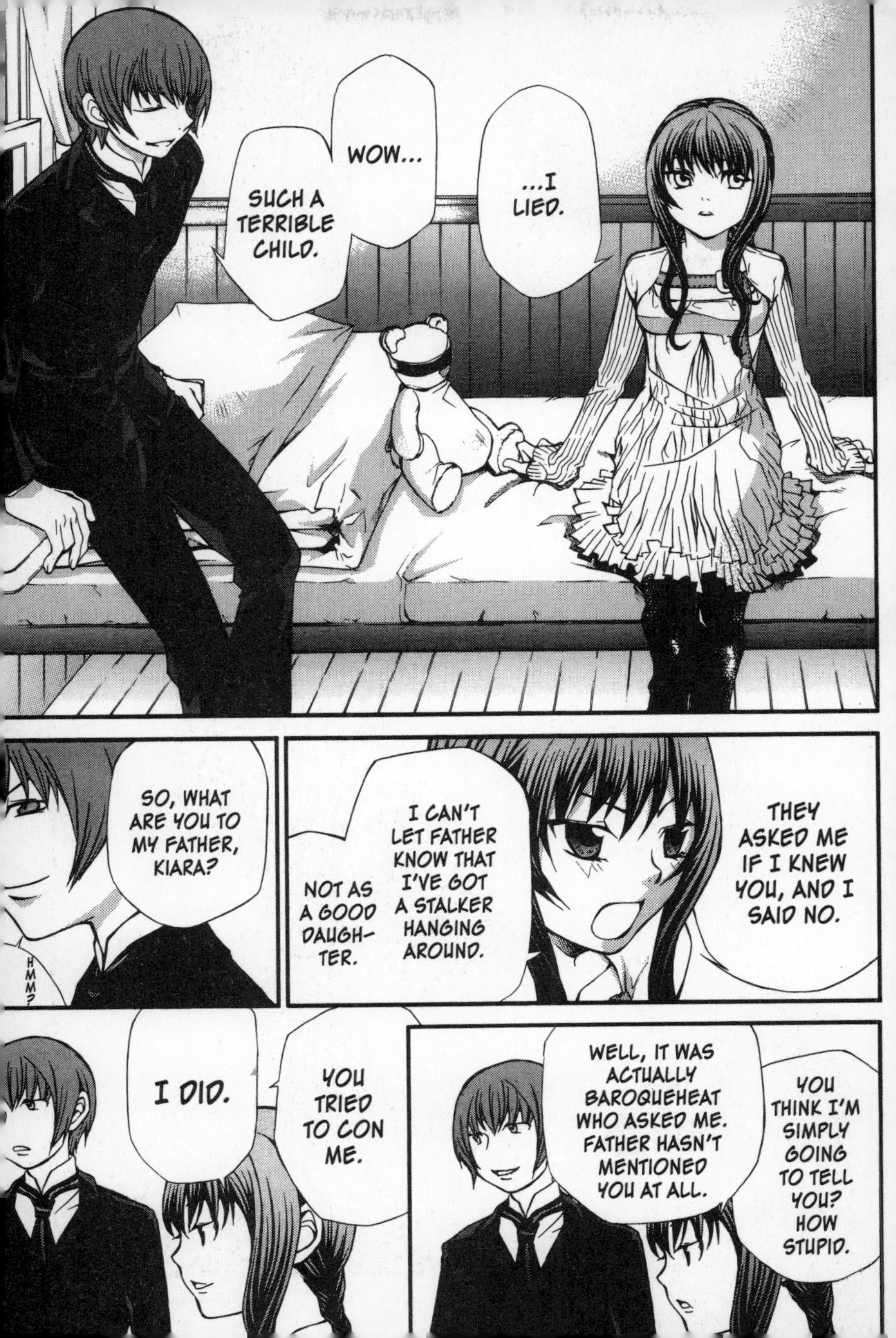
...I LIED.
WOW...
SUCH A TERRIBLE CHILD.
THEY ASKED ME IF I KNEW YOU, AND I SAID NO.
I CAN'T LET FATHER KNOW THAT I'VE GOT A STALKER HANGING AROUND.
NOT AS A GOOD DAUGH-TER.
SO, WHAT ARE YOU TO MY FATHER, KIARA?
HMM?
YOU THINK I'M SIMPLY GOING TO TELL YOU? HOW STUPID.
WELL, IT WAS ACTUALLY BAROQUEHEAT WHO ASKED ME. FATHER HASN'T MENTIONED YOU AT ALL.
YOU TRIED TO CON ME.
I DID.

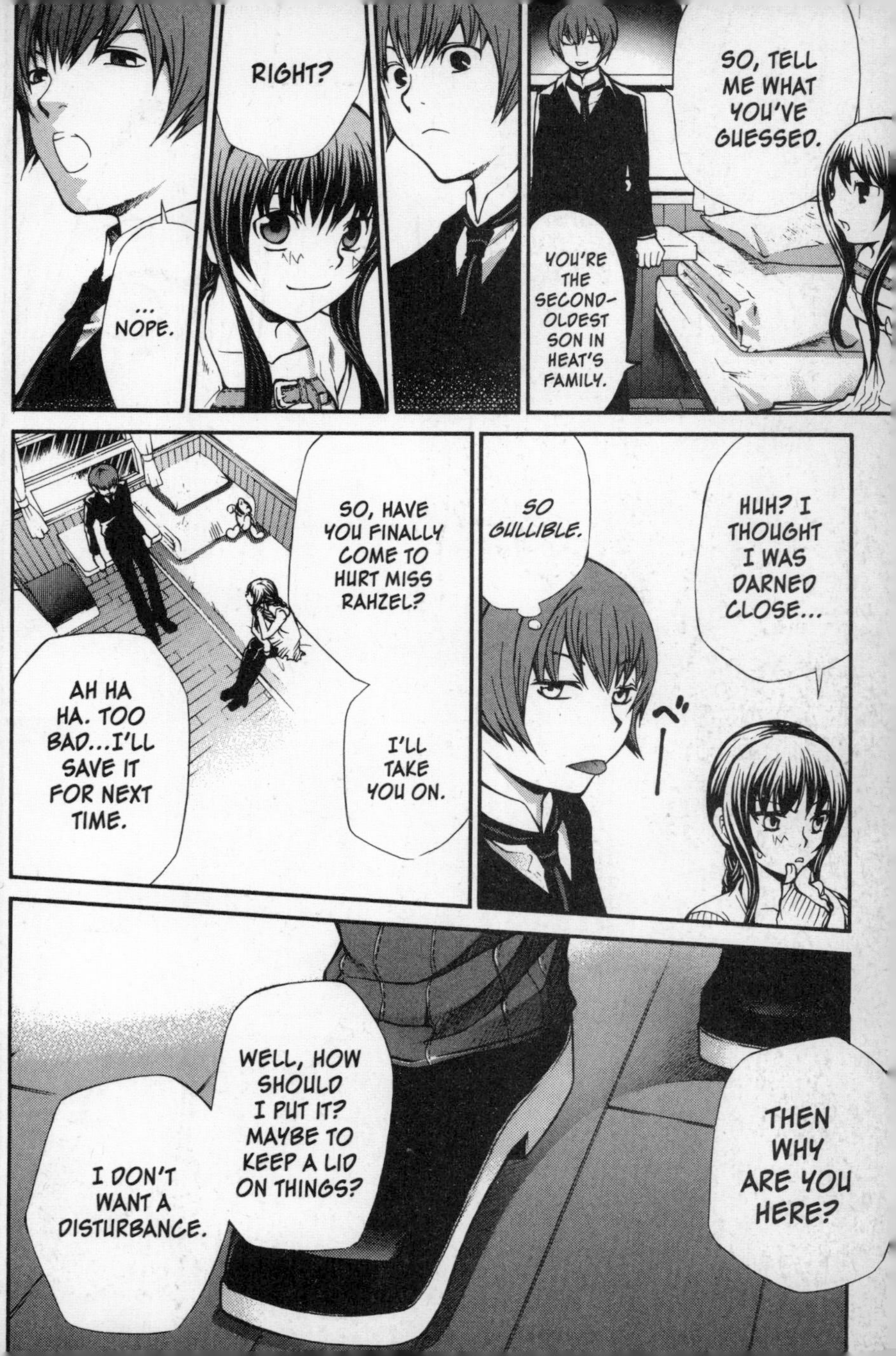
SO, TELL ME WHAT YOU'VE GUESSED.
YOU'RE THE SECOND-OLDEST SON IN HEAT'S FAMILY.
RIGHT?
... NOPE.
HUH? I THOUGHT I WAS DARNED CLOSE...
SO GULLIBLE.
べ
SO, HAVE YOU FINALLY COME TO HURT MISS RAHZEL?
I'LL TAKE YOU ON.
AH HA HA. TOO BAD...I'LL SAVE IT FOR NEXT TIME.
THEN WHY ARE YOU HERE?
WELL, HOW SHOULD I PUT IT? MAYBE TO KEEP A LID ON THINGS?
I DON'T WANT A DISTURBANCE.

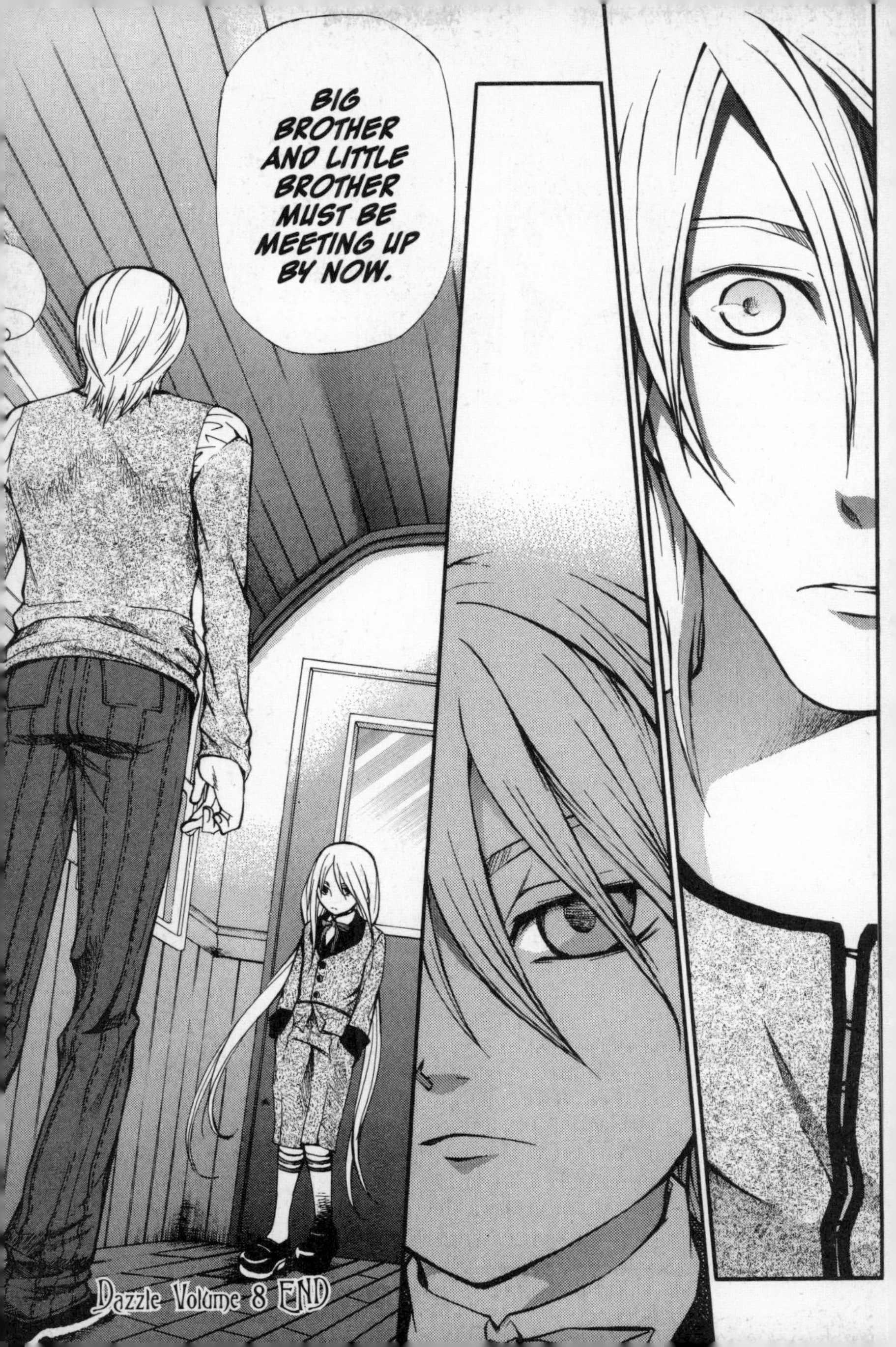
BIG BROTHER AND LITTLE BROTHER MUST BE MEETING UP BY NOW.
Dazzle Volume 8 END

Chapter 55: My Home, My Family

In Dazzle, a series full of characters who are as spacey as the cosmos, Saivah-kun is the one who is refreshingly inquisitive and full of comebacks. I'm filled with the desire to have him show up whenever possible, so he can more easily get involved with other characters.

However, I chose him for this episode's color front page, not out of personal preference, but because Pie-san, one of my assistants, "wanted to see Saivah in an apron in color." A manga artist who even sucks up to the assistants. That's Minari Endoh.

Chapter 56: People We Meet in a Mysterious Town

I really love Miss Kynlenn, so I want to draw her even more. Her curls are a hassle to draw though, so maybe not.

I love Shogetsu, but he's also hard to draw. When these characters appear, on one hand it's heaven, but on the other it's hell.

Chapter 57: And So a Girl Meets Her Fate

The relationship between Kiara and Rahzel is so criminal that it's kinda nice. I've reconfirmed my taste in characters.

I think Kiara was Rahzel's first love, but maybe it's better that her memory is buried.

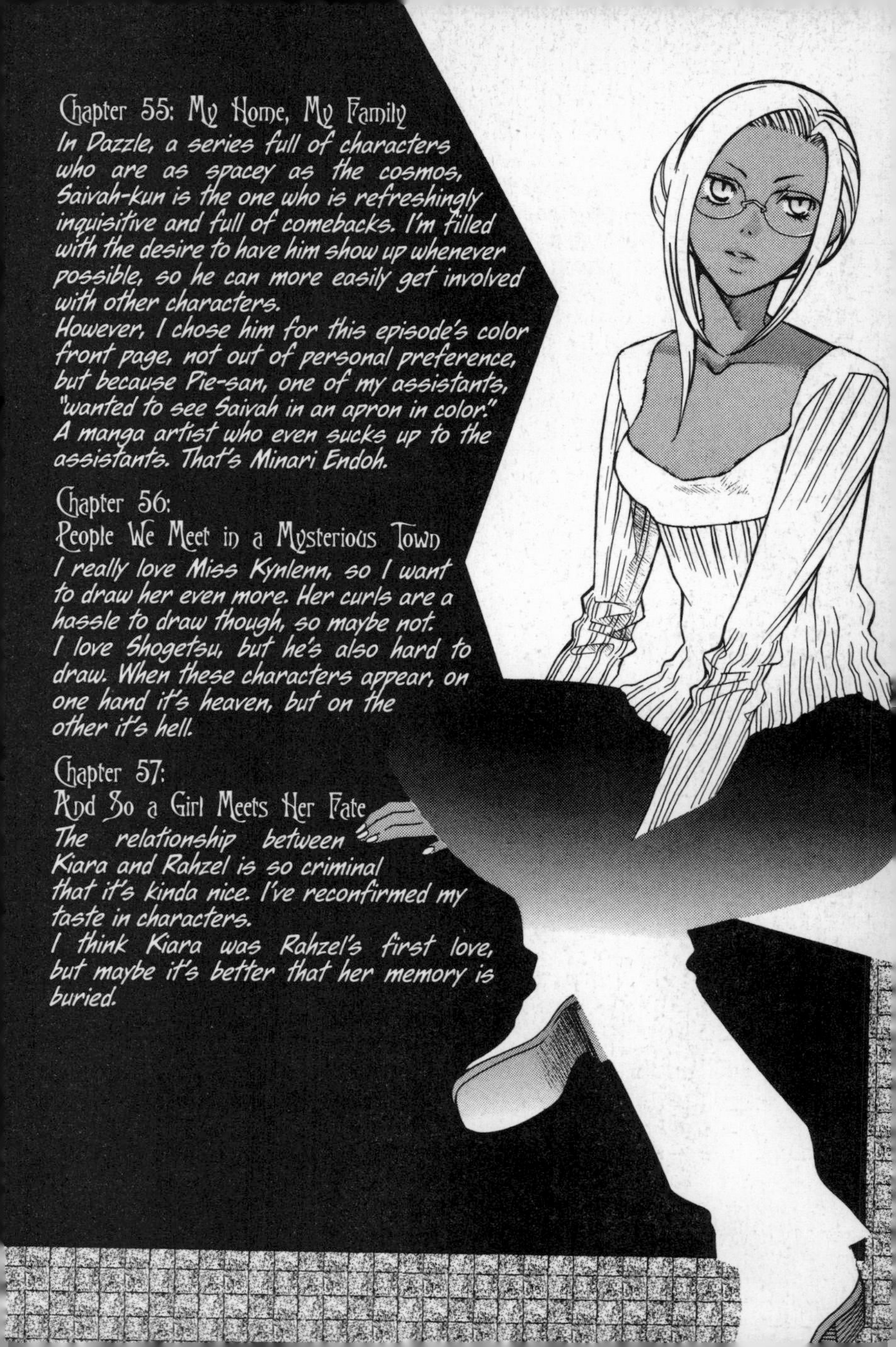

Chapter 58: March 21st

The reason that there are no birthdays listed in the bios in volumes one to three is simply because I forgot.

Baroqueheat's birthday is August 6, and Alzeid's is November...when was it? I can't find my notes, so I can't remember. The other day, Bobko-san, one of my assistants, was looking for a pair of scissors, but instead of asking me where they were, even though we were in my room, she asked someone else. She said it was because she couldn't count on me finding anything in my room. Well, because my workroom is chaos.

Chapter 59: Reunion and a Premonition of Parting

He finally showed his face, but a friend was disappointed that he wasn't "as beautiful as I thought." I was genuinely saddened. Ha! A beauty?! I just can't draw them. Not me! Like Alzeid! I've never thought he was good-looking. He's just a mean-looking sad case of a lad.

I thought Dee was the only good-looking guy when I was drawing him. Too bad he won't be making any more appearances.

Chapter 60: I Spit on the Meeting of a Lifetime

I don't like the phrase "once in a lifetime." It just seems cheap, and makes me sad.

I didn't use any particular perfume as a model for the one that Heat gave as a gift, but there really is one that uses sake as the top note. If you're interested, look into it.

Chapter 61: At the End of a Trip

I wanted to add Surname Cards as a prize this time, but I gave up because I thought no one would really want them after all. I'd recommend playing the memory game where you match two cards. The possibility of getting a match is quite high, especially Suzukis. On the other hand, I'd stay away from Old Maid. You'll match so many cards that your hand will probably be gone before you even start the game.

Thanks for waiting. That's volume eight. Thanks for buying the book once again. I hope to have volume nine out before the year is over.

Minari Endo
遠藤海成

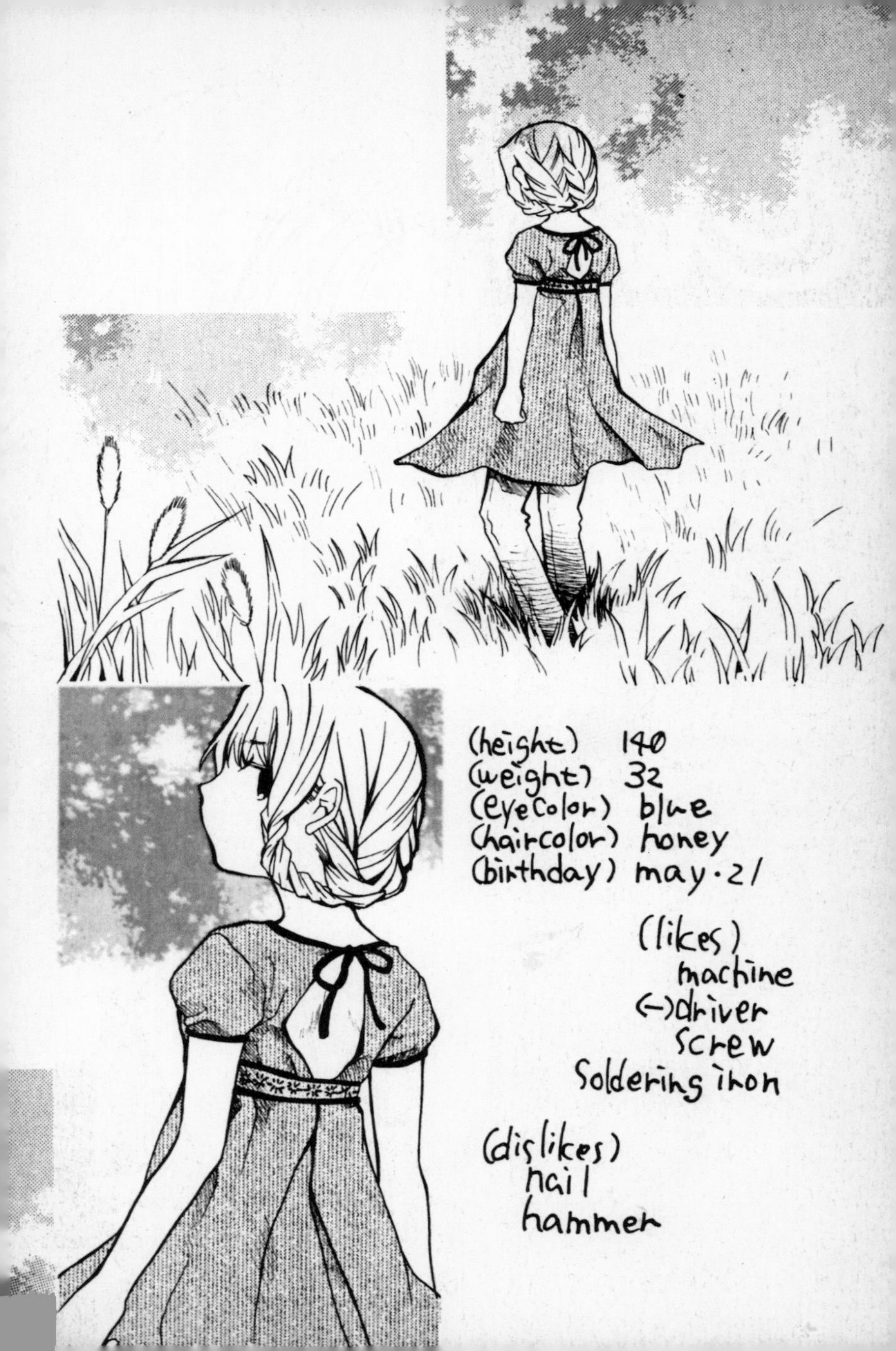
(height) 140
(weight) 32
(eyecolor) blue
(haircolor) honey
(birthday) may・21
(likes)
machine
(-)driver
screw
Soldering iron
(dislikes)
nail
hammer

Bran Owen

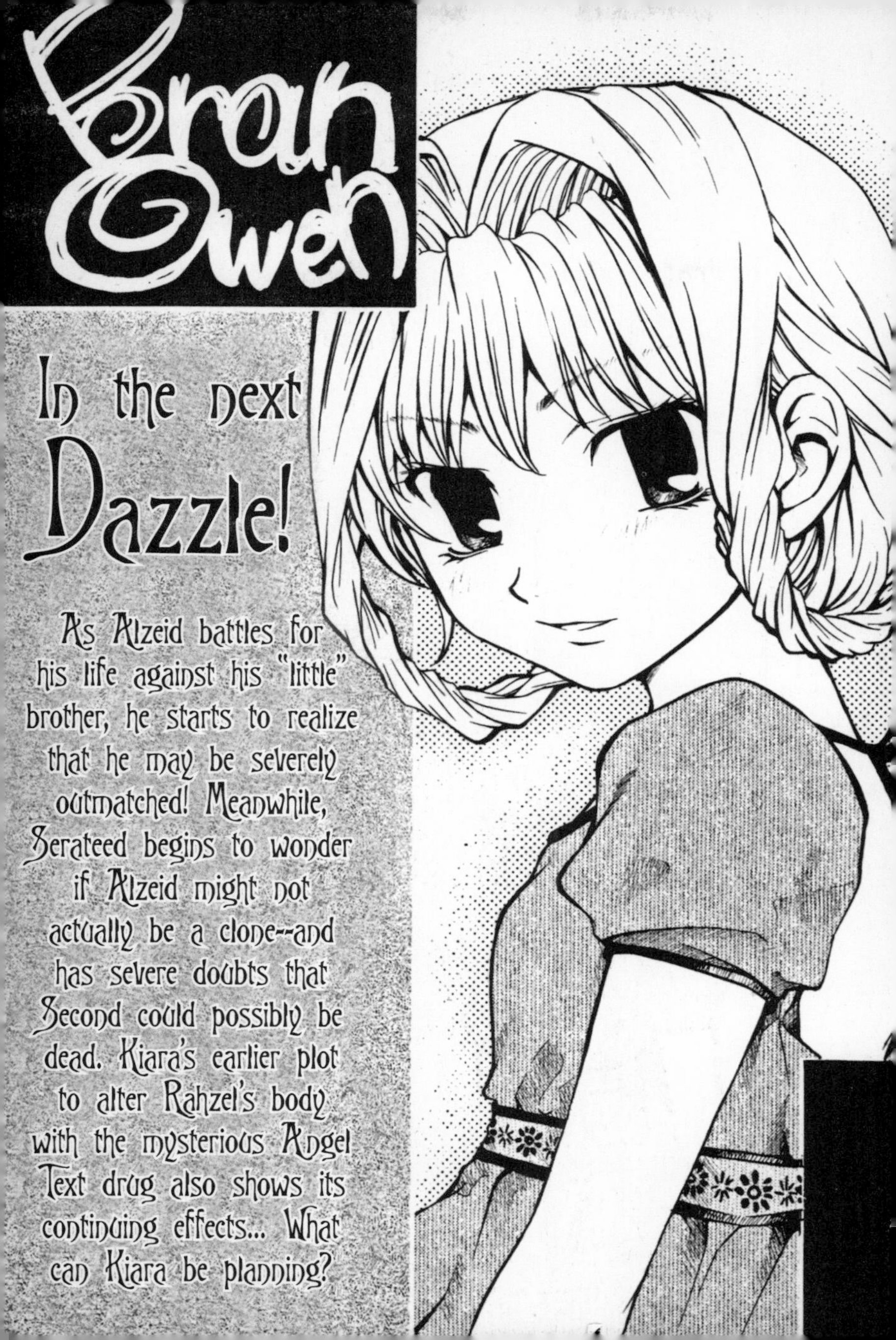

In the next Dazzle!

As Alzeid battles for his life against his "little" brother, he starts to realize that he may be severely outmatched! Meanwhile, Serateed begins to wonder if Alzeid might not actually be a clone--and has severe doubts that Second could possibly be dead. Kiara's earlier plot to alter Rahzel's body with the mysterious Angel Text drug also shows its continuing effects... What can Kiara be planning?

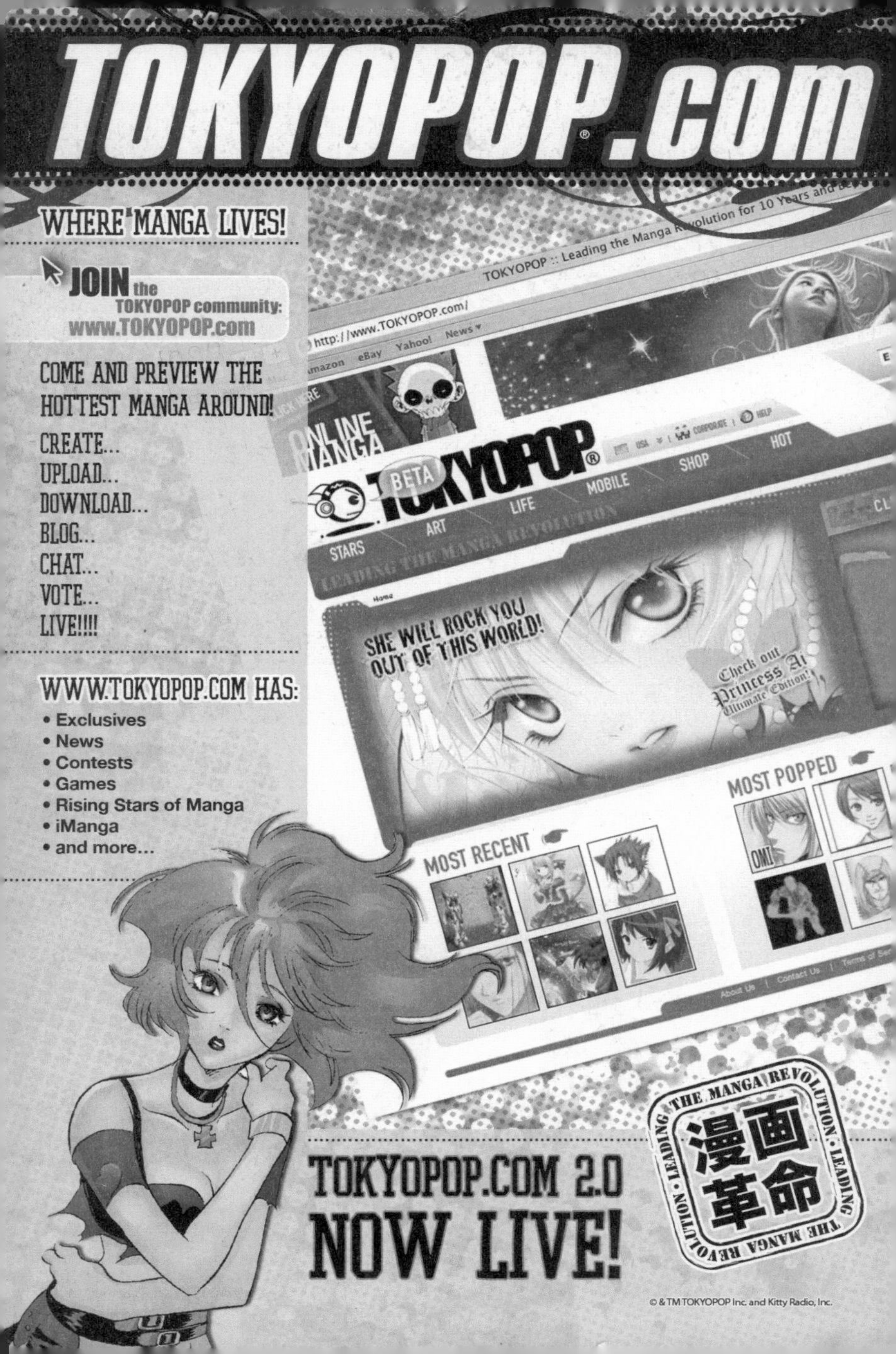
TOKYOPOP®.com
WHERE MANGA LIVES!
JOIN the TOKYOPOP community: www.TOKYOPOP.com
COME AND PREVIEW THE HOTTEST MANGA AROUND!
CREATE...
UPLOAD...
DOWNLOAD...
BLOG...
CHAT...
VOTE...
LIVE!!!!
WWW.TOKYOPOP.COM HAS:
• Exclusives
• News
• Contests
• Games
• Rising Stars of Manga
• iManga
• and more...
TOKYOPOP :: Leading the Manga Revolution for 10 Years and Beyond
http://www.TOKYOPOP.com/
ONLINE MANGA
TOKYOPOP®
STARS
ART
LIFE
MOBILE
SHOP
HOT
LEADING THE MANGA REVOLUTION
SHE WILL ROCK YOU OUT OF THIS WORLD!
Check out Princess Ai Ultimate Edition!
MOST POPPED
MOST RECENT
TOKYOPOP.COM 2.0 NOW LIVE!
LEADING THE MANGA REVOLUTION
漫画革命
© & TM TOKYOPOP Inc. and Kitty Radio, Inc.

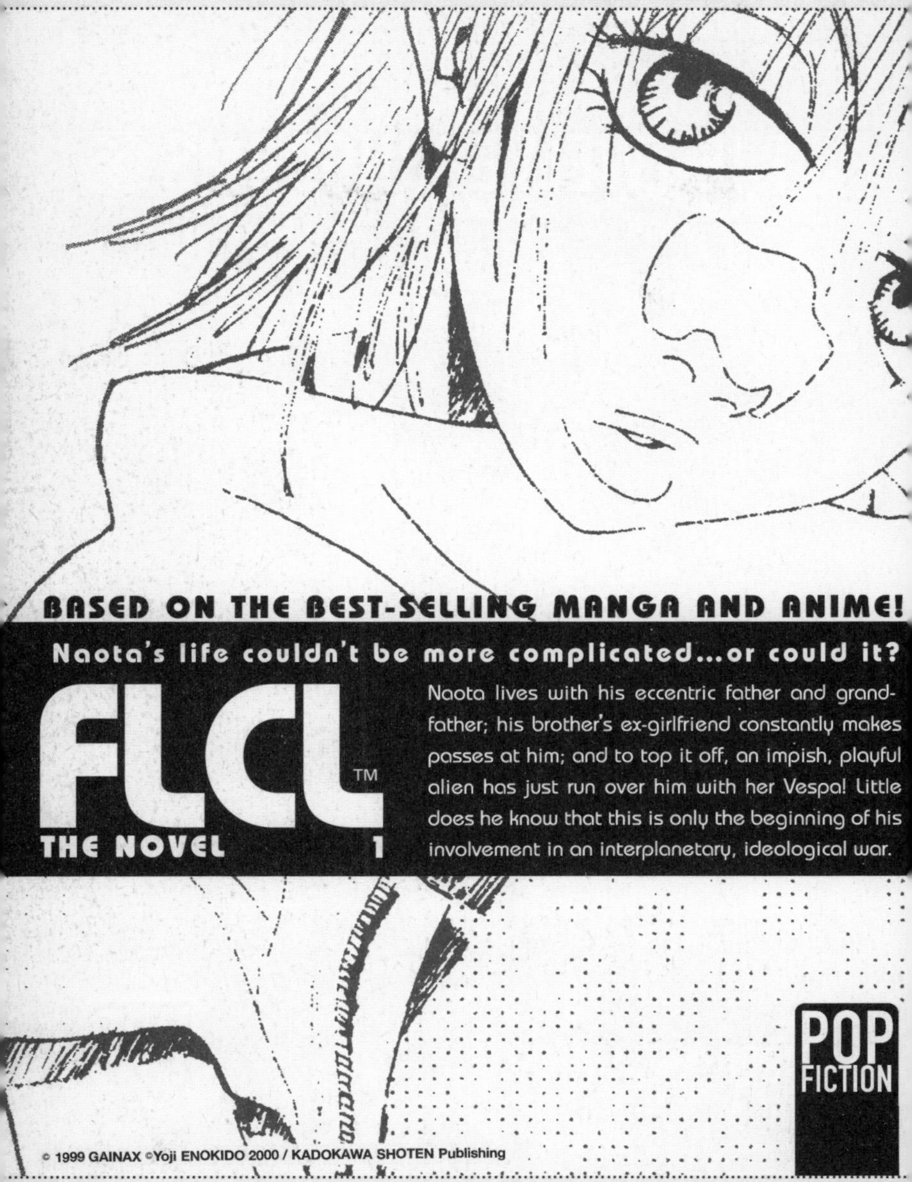
BASED ON THE BEST-SELLING MANGA AND ANIME!
Naota's life couldn't be more complicated...or could it?
FLCL™
THE NOVEL 1
Naota lives with his eccentric father and grandfather; his brother's ex-girlfriend constantly makes passes at him; and to top it off, an impish, playful alien has just run over him with her Vespa! Little does he know that this is only the beginning of his involvement in an interplanetary, ideological war.
POP FICTION
© 1999 GAINAX ©Yoji ENOKIDO 2000 / KADOKAWA SHOTEN Publishing

Fruits Basket™

By Natsuki Takaya

Volume 19

Can Tohru free Kyo of his curse?

Tohru is conflicted as she realizes she might love Kyo more than she loves her mom. Then Shigure shows up to let her know that all the members of the Zodiac look down on Kyo. If she wants to save Kyo, she'll have to break his curse first!

Winner of the American Anime Award for Best Manga!

The #1 selling shojo manga in America!

ROMANCE

T
TEEN
AGE 13+

© 1998 Natsuki Takaya / HAKUSENSHA, Inc.

FOR MORE INFORMATION VISIT: WWW.TOKYOPOP.COM

GAKUEN ALICE VOLUME TWO

Mikan is officially accepted into the mysterious Alice
Academy, but things aren't exactly going smoothly...

Mikan is off to a rough start! Natsume
still bullies her, her class ranking
couldn't be lower, some of the
teachers are outright hostile and
she has been forbidden to
contact anyone outside of the
school. Will she be able to
find others like her at the
Academy, or will she be
betrayed by the only
people she still trusts?

The hit series
from Japan
CONTINUES!

FANTASY

T
TEEN
AGE 13+

+ANIMA™ 7

The extraordinary adventures of the +Anima continue...

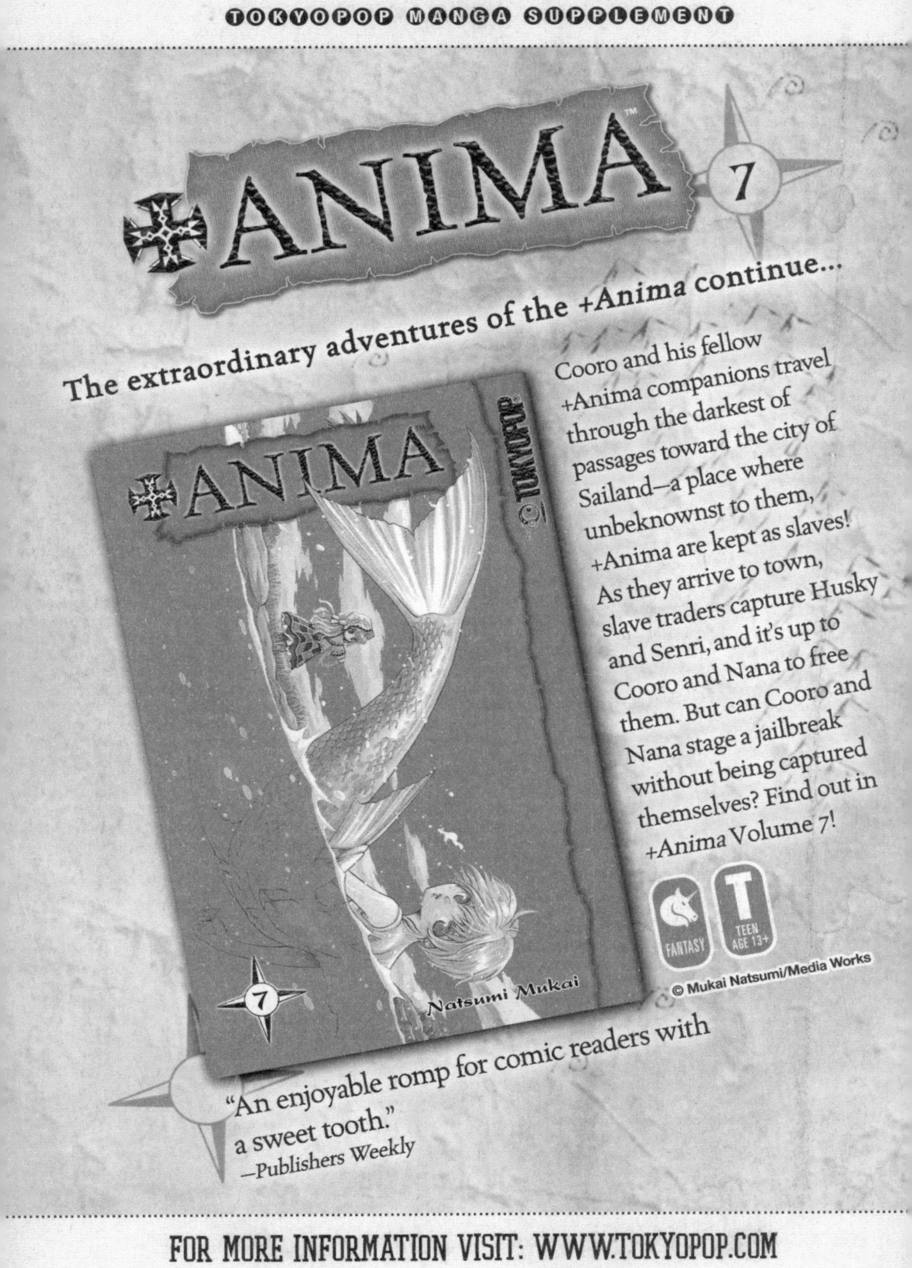
+ANIMA™
TOKYOPOP
7
Natsumi Mukai

Cooro and his fellow +Anima companions travel through the darkest of passages toward the city of Sailand—a place where unbeknownst to them, +Anima are kept as slaves! As they arrive to town, slave traders capture Husky and Senri, and it's up to Cooro and Nana to free them. But can Cooro and Nana stage a jailbreak without being captured themselves? Find out in +Anima Volume 7!

FANTASY

T TEEN AGE 13+

"An enjoyable romp for comic readers with a sweet tooth."
—Publishers Weekly

FOR MORE INFORMATION VISIT: WWW.TOKYOPOP.COM

STOP!

This is the back of the book.
You wouldn't want to spoil a great ending!

This book is printed "manga-style," in the authentic Japanese right-to-left format. Since none of the artwork has been flipped or altered, readers get to experience the story just as the creator intended. You've been asking for it, so TOKYOPOP® delivered: authentic, hot-off-the-press, and far more fun!

DIRECTIONS

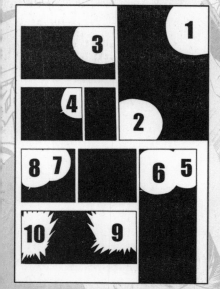

If this is your first time reading manga-style, here's a quick guide to help you understand how it works.

It's easy… just start in the top right panel and follow the numbers. Have fun, and look for more 100% authentic manga from TOKYOPOP®!